HADD[…] SHIRE.

NORTH SEA

Bass
Tantallan Cas.
Scarr
Sea Cliff
N. Berwick Ho.
Ravensheugh Craig
Peffer B.
Whitekirk
Whitberry Hd.
WHITEKIRK
Newbyth
Binning Wood
Tynningham Ho.
Smeaton
Prestonkirk
Tyne W.
Belhaven B.
Castle
Belhaven
DUNBAR
56°
Linton
Fantassie
Beltonford
W. Barns
Lochend
Broxmouth
Nineware
DUNBAR
Belton Place
Broxburn
KIRK
Hailes Cas
Biel
Bowerhouses
Barnyhill
E. Barns
STENTON
Spott K.
PARISH
Pinkerton
Spott
Skateraw
Whittingham K.
Stenton K.
Thorntonloch
Presmennan
Innerwick K.
Thurston
SPOTT
Whittingham Ho.
Thornton
Dod Hill
INNERWICK
Branxton
Rammer Law
To Berwick
Cocklaw Hill
Dunglass
Nunraw
OLDHAMSTOCKS
Part of DUNBAR
Watch Law
Oldhamstock
Dean B.
West W.
East B.
Monynut Edge
Eye W.
Mors Law
Black Law
Part of SPOTT
Part of STENTON
Monynut W.
Whare B.
Kingside Edge
Bothwell Hill
Peat Law
Mayshiel
Kelly
Priestlaw Ho.
Whiteadder W.
Phillip B.
Collar Law
Priestlaw Hill
Faseny B.
Kilmade B.
Cranshaws K.
Abbey St. Bathans
Kilpallet Rig
Whiteadder W.
BERWICKSHIRE
To Dunse
To Dunse
Longformacus

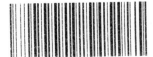

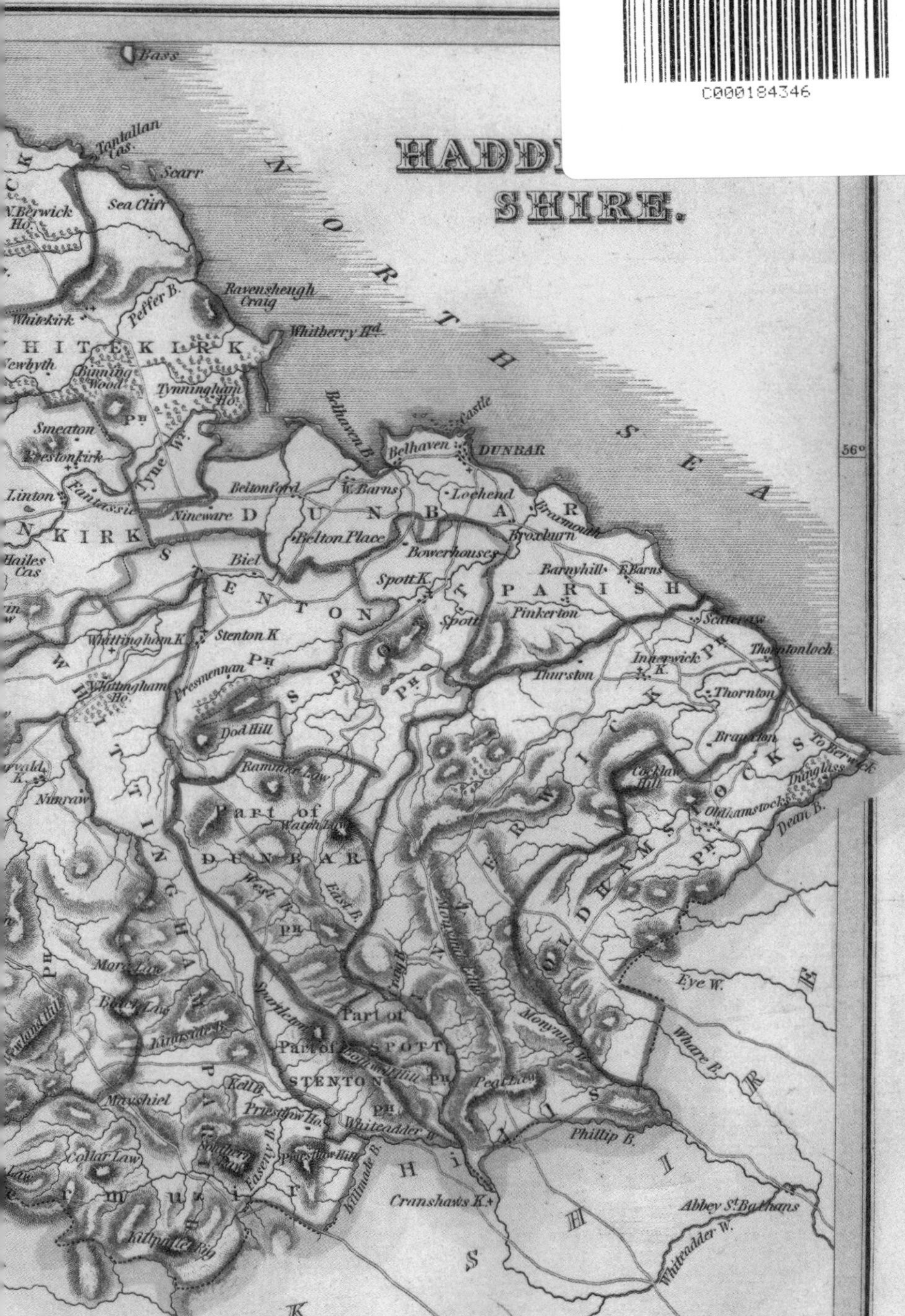

Engd. on steel by W.H.Lizars.

Library Of The Ghost Woodland

This Too Shall Pass

This Too Shall Pass

Reflections on East Lothian

Roddy Martine

BIRLINN

First published in 2009 by
Birlinn Limited
West Newington House
10 Newington Road
Edinburgh
EH9 1QS

www.birlinn.co.uk

ISBN: 978 1 84158 605 2

British Library Cataloguing-in-Publication Data
A catalogue record for this book is available from the British Library

Designed and typeset by Iolaire Typesetting, Newtonmore
Printed and bound by MPG Books Ltd, Bodmin

The endpapers show the county of Haddingtonshire from Blackwood's Atlas of Scotland (1838). Reproduced by permission of the Trustees of the National Library of Scotland.

In memory of

Lady Marioth Hay

(1918–2006)

Contents

List of Illustrations

Third plate section

Fourth plate section

Acknowledgements

The author would like to thank the following for their support and invaluable help in compiling this book:

Bill Anderson, Sheila Asante, Archie Baird, Richard Blake, Michael Brander, Ludovic Broun-Lindsay, Alastair Brown, John and Sarah Brownlie, Hugh Buchanan, Stephen Bunyan, John Burns Snr, Alison Campbell Kinghorn, Stewart Chalmers, Keith Chalmers-Watson, Alex Dale, Robert and Michelle Dale, Peter and Andrea de Pree, Lady Hugh Douglas-Hamilton, Bridget Ellwood, Elizabeth Fenton Barnes, John Fergie, Virginia Fitzwilliams, Martin A. Forrest, John and Denise Gray, the Duke of Hamilton and late Elizabeth, Duchess of Hamilton, Paul Harris, Catherine Home, George and Anna Hope, Sir Malcolm Innes of Edingight, Pauline Jaffray, Simon Kesley, Malcolm and Avril Kirk, Barry and Sarah Laird, Finlay Lockie, Angus McGregor, Ella MacGregor, Ian and Irene Martine, Patricia Martine, Viscount Maitland, Lady Militza Maitland, Aidan Matthew, Elaine Meeks, Ian Middlemass, Tom Middlemass, Sir Garth Morrison, Arthur Neil, Dave Neillans, William Nimmo, Sir Francis Ogilvy, Louise Ramsay, David Richardson, Sheila Richardson, Elizabeth Roads, Patricia Stephen, Sya Simpson, Simon and Jane Stodart, John Taylor, David Thompson, Johnny Watson, Annabel Younger.

And Norma Buckingham, who was in the process of compiling a biography of Dr James S. Richardson when she died in October 2007.

My thanks in particular to Victoria Fletcher, Hugh and Sarah Dodd, and a very special thank you to Sheila Millar and Craig Statham of East Lothian Council Library and Museum Services; Hugh Andrew, Andrew Simmons, Patricia Marshall and the team at Birlinn; and, of course, my agent, John Beaton.

Introduction

> So, perhaps his eye shall be opened to behold the series of the generations, and he shall weigh with surprise his momentous and nugatory gift of life.
>
> *Catriona*, dedication to Charles Baxter, WS
> – Robert Louis Stevenson

I used to dread those excursions to East Lothian. To be fair, it cannot have been easy for him either, my father, expected to entertain a thirteen year-old when he himself was over sixty. But he did his best.

After an absence of forty years, most of them passed in South-East Asia, he had chosen to live in Scotland's capital, not Haddington, the town of his birth, or anywhere else in East Lothian, for that matter. To his mind, that would have been too retrograde a step.

In Haddington, he would always be the doctor's son, even after having been away for so long. Not that being the second son of William Robert Martine MD was anything to be ashamed of. Three generations of a medical dynasty had come and gone, all based in Haddington, and my grandfather was greatly respected; they had, indeed, presided over the births of large numbers of the county. During his lifetime, his name was highly revered – as was that of his predecessor, also Dr William, who had, in 1847, become a favourite student of Sir James Young Simpson at Edinburgh University when that great man discovered chloroform.

But that was not the point. Four decades earlier, my father had escaped from the limitations of a small-town birthright in the belief that anything was possible. With Haddington far behind him, he had married my mother and they had made their home on the far side of the world. For a golden interval, they basked in the twilight of the British Empire before the Second World War blew that world to pieces. Even then, grateful to have survived where others had not, they had picked up the pieces of their lives in South-East Asia and begun again. When they eventually retired home with my sisters and me in 1950, it was to a very different Britain from the one they had left behind them. But Scotland, in many ways, remained the same.

My father's career could not have been more different from that of the serried ranks of remote ancestors who had toiled the rich red soil of East Lothian and serviced its needs in the market town of Haddington. For them, as with so many of Scotland's rural populace, the fracturing of our family began with the catastrophic farming blight of the 1860s, when droves of east-coast tenant farmers moved away from the soil they had cherished for generations.

Inevitably, this impacted upon the market towns. As the twentieth century dawned, a restlessness entered the blood. With the Martines, it led to Great Uncle Patrick emigrating to the USA, where he became a cowpuncher in Texas. Having survived the Kaiser's war, Uncle Will, heir apparent to the family's Haddington medical practice, took up public health posts in Croydon and Birmingham. Uncle Dave became a banker and settled in Edinburgh.

In 1936, my grandfather retired, closed down the family medical practice, sold the family home and moved to Edinburgh. After 800 years, it was the end of the line for the Martines of East Lothian and Haddington.

Yet somehow . . . somehow, those territorial ties refuse to let go. To this day, when asked where my family comes from, my response is East Lothian, even though I have never lived there. I was born in Sarawak on the island of Borneo, in South-East Asia, and have lived for most of my life in Edinburgh. So why should I feel compelled to turn to the past for my identity?

Of course, there is a choice. I could opt to ignore my predecessors or, as the grim reaper approaches, make peace with them, as my father did through the copious family notes which he compiled and sentimentally entitled *Long Ago People*. In writing this book, I suppose that, to some extent, I am taking up where he left off. Certainly it would not have been possible had he not already prepared the groundwork. On top of which, there was also a precedent. More than a century ago, John Martine, my first cousin thrice removed, published a series of arcane books with such challenging titles as *Reminiscences of the County of Haddington* (volumes one and two) and *Reminiscences of the Royal Burgh of Haddington and Old East Lothian Agriculturists*. He even produced a slimmer volume entitled *Reminiscences of the Port and Town of Leith* but that has no relevance in this context.

Classics of the genre, the Haddington books chronicled in detail East Lothian's domestic past – the families, characters, events and anecdotes which have moulded that rich but overlooked county since the beginning of time. For me, such influences were coupled with the knowledge that there were two Martine provosts of Haddington in our family tree – John in 1781 and his eldest son, also John, in 1807, 1813 and 1815. Moreover, in 1781, Great-great-great-grandfather John also took on the not-insignificant task of being Haddingtonshire's County Post Master, an appointment continued by his youngest son Peter, my direct ancestor, and which possibly explains the obsession successive members of my family have had with stamp collecting.

Over an identifiable span of six hundred years, and presumably before, the Martines reliably married into the families of the county – farmers and tacksmen, clerics, merchants, tanners, bakers, brewers, bankers and the burgesses of Haddington, Tranent and North Berwick, being tantalisingly described in George F. Black's *The Surnames of Scotland* as 'a once great East Lothian family'. Justified or not, that has to be a challenge to live up to, as surely is the family motto – *Hinc Fortior et Clarior* which translates as 'Hence Stronger and More Illustrious'.

For the remaining twenty-four years of his life, my father made it his mission to track those ancestors down, visiting their last resting places, inspecting their headstones and taking notes so as to somehow connect with them. Often I accompanied him, and occasionally we would drive to 7 Tantallon Terrace, North Berwick, to collect his elderly friend Dr James Richardson. Even my father considered Dr Jimmy, as we called him, old, so you can imagine how I viewed him. He was a great bear of a man, invariably dressed in a worn three-piece tweed suit which reeked of pipe tobacco. If the truth be known, I was totally in awe of him. Yet it is to Dr Jimmy that I owe my greatest debt. A retired Chief Inspector of Ancient Monuments in Scotland, he would set off with us in the front passenger seat of my father's Humber Hawk to explore the castles of the coastline, from Winton and Saltoun inland, to the picturesque ruins of Tantallon, Fast and Dunbar.

And it was on one such visit to Hailes Castle, north-east of Haddington, that Dr Jimmy came and stood beside me. I was staring moodily out of a window wishing that I was somewhere more exciting, anywhere but where I was, when he said to me, 'Look hard at that view and try to imagine who once stood where you are standing now, gazing at those same fields over that same stretch of river, under that same expanse of sky. Four hundred years ago, on such a day, Mary, Queen of Scots stood where you are standing now and she looked at that same view. She was twenty-five years old and had been brought here by her lover, the Earl of Bothwell, the man blamed for the murder of her husband, Lord Darnley. She knew that her half-brother and a contingent of her Scottish nobles were out looking for her and she was on her way back to Edinburgh to face them. Bothwell was not only her abductor but also her protector. Ten days later she became his wife. We'll never know if she married him willingly. She must have known how it would end. When she looked out of this window at that view, she must have felt terribly alone.'

I had never before seriously considered the passing of time in such a way.

'Just stand there and think about Mary Stuart,' said the old man with a chuckle as he wandered off.

I recall hearing the creaking sounds of some large black crows circling over a clump of trees on the horizon and noticing the diagonal furrows of a recent plough. It was then that it dawned on me that distant history can be every bit as real as the present, if we allow it to be – often more so because we know the outcome. With a thousand or more years to contemplate, it made me feel very small and insignificant, sheltered as I was within those weathered stone walls.

In later years, I mentioned this experience to Nigel Tranter, the historian and novelist, who lived at Aberlady. He told me that he too found inspiration under such circumstances, being physically close to where great events had taken place in the past. It was that which excited him; the exploration of landscapes which allowed him to conjure up those long-ago emotions. It brought his narrative to life. Scotland is unequalled for such adventures. The ghosts are everywhere, all about us, crying out for attention.

I soon found myself sharing my father's fascination with our ancestors and the passage of centuries – albeit that it took a long time for me to admit to it. If his churchyard and document discoveries were accurate, then, in the spring of 1567, James Martyne, Portioner and Bailie of Haddington, Patrick (whose surname often appears as Martine), Burgess of Haddington, and their brother Robert (another variant spelling of their surname for him was Martene), farming Mainshill of Morham, were, all three, living less than two miles from Hailes Castle.

Too young to have been recruited for the Scots army at the Battle of Flodden, where several of their kin were among the 12,000 dead, they had, for the previous two decades, been preoccupied with recovering from the Siege of Haddington, when not one dwelling house had been left intact from the ferocious barrage of cannon imposed by fellow Scots and French mercenaries. As if that episode had not been traumatic enough for all concerned, the Black Plague was continuing its relentless path of carnage. The Martines were lucky to have survived thus far, although both Robert and his wife Christian would ultimately succumb within two days of each other in the winter of 1580.

In the countryside, news travels like a tornado. In a Scotland undergoing the birth pains of the Reformation, word of the Queen's scandalous elopement to Dunbar caused outrage; added to which, her visit to Hailes on 5 May 1567, with the man blamed for the murder of her second husband, would undoubtedly have set my ancestral tongues a-wagging.

So one wonders what they must have thought about it. Six months later Patrick's name appears on a petition served on behalf of the 'Commonite and inhabitants' of Haddington in wholehearted endorsement of the Earl of Moray, Queen Mary's half-brother, becoming Regent of Scotland.

CHAPTER ONE

The Land of Plenty

IT HAS BEEN CALLED 'the Surrey of Scotland', principally because it provides some of the more affluent commuter dormitories for Scotland's burgeoning capital. But it was ever thus, was East Lothian, framing the country residences of Scotland's ruling elite and serving their needs.

East Lothian has it all – fertile arable fields on the coastal plain and the mixed livestock and agrarian farmland of the inland River Tyne Valley. There are thick coverings of mixed woodland, the sheep-filled slopes and grouse moors of the Lammermuirs and picturesque coastal and inland towns interspersed with buildings of unique historic interest. Romans, Vikings and the Saxon English, they all came this way intent on conquest but, finding it impossible to impose authority over an evolving Lowland Scotland, melted back from whence they came.

In his three Haddingtonshire books, published in 1883, 1890 and 1894, the last after his death, my relative John Martine provided detailed insights into the parochial passage of East Lothian life from the Middle Ages to the late Victorian era. In so doing, his books bear intimate witness to the sweeping advances which took place over the eighteenth and nineteenth centuries.[1]

The age of the motor car, let alone the advent of the A1 or an Edinburgh City Bypass, would then have been beyond his comprehension. Local journeys were made by coach and horse or on foot. And who could have foreseen the impact the railways would have in 1846? Returning to her birthplace in 1849 and staying at the George Hotel, Jane Welsh Carlyle wrote to her husband, the essayist Thomas Carlyle, 'It was the same street, the same houses, but so silent – dead petrified. What could have come to the place to strike it so dead? I have been answered – the railway has come to it and ruined it.'[2]

As a branch rail line, the freight traffic which had previously passed through the centre of Haddington by coach was diverted elsewhere. Rail travellers north and south now journeyed on the direct east-coast line between Edinburgh and Dunbar, ignoring Haddington. It was a mixed blessing. With Haddington bypassed and, therefore, preserved, North Berwick and Dunbar prospered.

Yet, across time, the long, low tranquillity of the coastal scenery between Musselburgh in the north and Dunbar in the south remains intact – the same sea views unspoiled. Jane would still recognise many of the topographical landmarks with the same pockets of population, although how she would respond to today's juggernauts, hurtling to and from East Lothian's border with Berwickshire, is anyone's guess.

To commence my personal voyage of discovery, I set off to explore first the Parish of Morham, to the east of Haddington. It was here that the writer John Martine and his provost father lived over a century and a half ago in a pretty Georgian farmhouse known as Morham Bank and where, four hundred years earlier, my first identifiable direct ancestors, Robert Martine and his wife Christian Johnestoun, occupied the farmhouse of Mainshill.[3]

From the village of Garvald, in a dip of the Lammermuir Hills, the small stream of the Morhamburn collects its headwaters and flows six miles north to enter the South Tyne. In a secluded hollow, below the main street of today's Morham village, I found a pretty manse house, today the home of Patrick Gammell, Deputy Chairman of the Lamp of Lothian Trust, and his wife Sally, a talented artist. Nearby stands a picturesque church with well-tended burial ground, encircled by a wall.

However, Morham Church, dating as it does from 1724, was far too modern for what I had in mind. Even the discovery that its predecessor was built in 1685 was not what I had hoped for. Given the timeline, the chances of my finding gravestones relating to my family were minimal – a view endorsed by a note left by my father to suggest that, in the sixteenth century, those not contaminated by the plague and cremated would, in all probability, have been buried in the much older Baro churchyard. The problem was that Baro Church, its roof having fallen in, was itself abandoned in 1743 and its formal churchyard has long since vanished – or almost vanished, for today it lies beneath a field on Baro Farm. Until his death in 2005, Simon Younger, whom I knew well, owned the land here. The Youngers arrived at Baro in 1937, after which it was farmed first by Simon's father Hugh, then Simon's brother Gavin, before it passed on to Simon and now his son James.

On a Sunday evening in July 2007, I was taken to inspect the site of the old graveyard by Dave Neillans, Baro's farm manager. Dave has been at Baro since 1995 but, in the tradition of East Lothian farms, did not have far to travel. He was brought up at Whittingehame and his mother's family, the Laings, were the last tenants at Nunraw before it became a monastery. A century earlier, John Martine makes regular mention of Robert Neillans, the cooper in Garvald, of whom Dave is a descendant.

With waist-high thistles and battalions of vicious nettles smothering the churchyard, it was hard to make out the fine old Garvald freestone tombstones, although those we did come across were notably impressive, with skulls and crossbones and heraldic symbols.

'Come back in the winter and you'll be able to see them better,' advised Dave.

Disappointed but stoical, what held my attention was the panoramic view across the fields towards the coastline. What more idyllic spot could there possibly be for a final resting place? Alas, the names of those privileged few to whom these memorials belong are now irretrievably lost. Even the exact location of where the church once stood is uncertain. Only an old stone wall can be seen which might simply have been just a boundary enclosure.

Also beyond recognition are the remains of Morham Castle, a small Pele Tower which, along with the original village situated a few hundred yards south of Morham Church, belonged to the Hepburns of Hailes. Nevertheless, there is still a farmhouse called Mainshill, a Victorian villa with steadings which have been transformed to create eighteen houses – a pattern that has emerged throughout the county. Today, Mainshill is farmed by the Drysdale family who, although they have been there since 1884, are still in the third generation. Longevity is a side benefit of agricultural life.

Of course, in the time of my ancestors such habitations as existed would have been fabricated in wood and thatch although, during some renovation work in recent years, an ancient wall of stone was exposed. Experts suggest that this might have belonged to a tower of sorts but, it having been photographed, permission was given to clear it away. That is what we do with the past when it gets in the way of the present. What is certain, however, is that the outlook towards North Berwick Law and east to Traprain Law remains unchanged. With the flatness of the land, the vista is of seemingly endless open fields and a big sky. What a view to wake up to every morning.

Having said that, how the Martines came to be tenants of Mainshill in the late sixteenth century remains a mystery to me but, from their joint will of 1580, it emerges that Robert and Christian Martine had six sons and a daughter. The antecedents of the occupants of the adjacent Northrig (sometimes spelt Northrigg) Farm are rather easier to pin down as, on 24 October 1497, a William Sinclare de Northrig appears as the first witness to a charter signed at Samuelston, three miles south of Haddington.[4] Under the circumstances, this suggests that he must have been related by marriage to his Hepburn landlords.

The lands of Morham, which included Northrig, were granted in the twelfth century to the Hepburns, a family from Northumbria, by Cospatrick, Earl of Dunbar, and, around 1533, Patrick Hepburn, 3rd Earl of Bothwell, married an Agnes Sinclair. They later divorced but, as part of her separation settlement, Agnes was given a charter for the lands of Morham, where she spent the remaining years of her life residing in the tower house. There are those who might envy her.

When she died in 1572, the 'lands and barony of Morham with the mill of Morham, the lands of Mainshill, Pleuchfield, the Briar Meadow, and the feu mails of the Northrig and all other mails, ferms, profits and duties in the Constabulary of Haddington, sheriffdom of Edinburgh' were inherited by her son, James Hepburn, 4th Earl of Bothwell.

With everything that we know about Bothwell and his capricious relationship with Queen Mary, Agnes Sinclair remains a shadowy figure. However, she was very much alive in the days of his notoriety and he was often at Morham Tower, if not at Hailes Castle. Although Agnes predeceased him, it must have been hard for her when he was forced to flee abroad, and she never saw him again.

In comparison to the Hepburns and Sinclairs, next to nothing is known about Robert and Christian Martine – only that they died almost simultaneously of the Black Plague on 21 and 24 December 1580. According to some local historians, however, some years prior to the Martines' tenancy, the farm of Mainshill had been occupied by the family of the Reformer John Knox.[5] This seems entirely plausible since the surname of Knox's maternal grandparents was Sinclair and, despite the almost conclusive proof that his parents latterly occupied a house in the Giffordgate at Haddington, there are those firmly of the opinion that Mainshill was where his mother chose to give birth to one if not both of her two sons.

Until relatively recently, there remained in a field a rocky outcrop known as 'the Knox Stones', reputed to be the remains of the cottage occupied by Knox's parents. Might this have been the site of the original Mainshill farmhouse? Again, no proof exists to substantiate any of this speculation, only that several Knoxes of a later period are buried in Morham churchyard. If anything, this merely confuses the issue.

In the practice of medieval feudalism, inheritance was rigidly biased towards the firstborn male, with power and patronage directly equated to the ownership of land. In sixteenth-century Scotland, with a total population of less than 300,000, younger sons and daughters continually moved up and down the social scale, dependent upon their abilities and such prospects as became available to them. Thus it became perfectly normal for a wealthy nobleman to have large numbers of his relatives among his tacksmen and for his children and grandchildren, sharing his surname, to be allocated 'livings' upon his estates. That was the way the system worked.

Land was allocated by the Crown, with rentals from the tenantry to fund the lifestyles of the feudal superior, while younger brothers and sisters were on their own – hence the importance attached to marriage settlements and dowries. Military service and the Church were the principal options available to young men wishing to improve their situations but no such opportunities were available to women, who were treated very much as second-class citizens. Thus, for example, we do not even know the Christian name of John Knox's mother. All that is confirmed is that her maiden name was 'Sinclare' and that she was, in the opinion of her son, 'an educated woman'.[6]

To Mary, Queen of Scots, the Reformer revealed that his family had been dependents of the Hepburns of Hailes. In a conversation with the 4th Earl of Bothwell himself, he gave the following account of his ancestors: 'My Lord, (says he), my great grandfather, gudeschir, and father, have served your Lordship's predecessors, and some of them have died under their standards; and this is a part of the obligation of our Scottish kindness.'[7] Knox is never known to have spoken ill of Bothwell, either father or son, and possibly, if the tradition of clan loyalty is valid, this stems from his being related to them through his maternal Sinclair blood.

The Sinclairs were well known throughout East Lothian (see Chapter 15) and one of his mother's sisters was beyond doubt Marion Sinclair from Northrig, the wife of George Ker, the feu holder at Samuelston.[8] In times of danger, especially when travelling, Knox often used the pseudonym of John Sinclair.

There will be more about John Knox in Chapter 4 but my specific interest in his family at this juncture concerns Robert Martine's fifth son, William, who married an Issobel Sinclair and took up the tack of Colstoun Mill in the neighbouring Parish of Bolton. Since Issobel was from Morham and was born at Northrig, she was certainly a relative and in all probability a great-niece of Knox's mother, the lady about whom virtually nothing is known.

Shortly after his return to Scotland in 1961, my father renewed his acquaintance with Lady Broun-Lindsay, owner of the Colstoun Estate, and there began a friendship centred on the East Lothian Antiquarian and Field Naturalists' Society, of which she was then president. Born in 1893, Edith Broun-Lindsay was a bright, highly intelligent woman who had inherited Colstoun from her mother, Susan Baird, it having been passed on to her by her great-aunt. When Edith married Major Sir George Lindsay in 1921, he assumed the additional surname of Broun.

Edith Broun-Lindsay was as knowledgeable and absorbed by her family's East Lothian antecedents as was my father by his. A member of East Lothian Council, she successfully campaigned to stop the quarrying of Traprain Law and, through public protest, managed to prevent the felling of the extensive woodland surrounding Yester Castle, which had been bought by Dr James Lumsden of Quarryford Farm. She also played a prominent part in the rescue of Haddington House (see Chapter 7).

As early as the twelfth century, during the reign of Alexander I, a Walterus de Broun was to be found at Colstoun and, on 13 May 1128, a Sir David le Brun was present for the laying of the foundation stone of Holyrood Abbey. In 1548, George Bruin was granted a charter for Colstoun from Mary, Queen of Scots, which included a barony court, the sole centre for rural justice in those days. The antiquity of the Broun dynasty at Colstoun is therefore beyond dispute, but what is in some ways remarkable is that Ludovic Broun-Lindsay, Lady Edith's grandson, still manages the estate and serves on East Lothian Council.

And it was through Ludovic's sister, Christian, that the Australian Scottish Heritage Council came to invite me to be their guest for Sydney Scottish Heritage Week 2002, an experience I am unlikely to forget. Founded in 1981, this unlikely Antipodean tartan event celebrates the contributions made by Australian Scots towards the formation of modern Australia. In 2002, the council's Vice President was Malcolm Broun, a leading Sydney divorce lawyer, and a senior figure in the society's hierarchy was Sir William Broun, 15th Baronet of Colstoun, a fourth generation Australian.

Perhaps I need to explain further. This branch of the Broun Family descends directly from the first Broun Baronet of Colstoun, who had a remainder to his male heirs forever. Thus, after the deaths of the 2nd and 5th baronets, neither having sons, the title passed to cousins whose descendants emigrated to live in New South Wales and are recognised as Hereditary Chiefs of the Name of Broun. With Sir William Broun's death in 2007, the baronetcy has now passed to his nephew, Sir Wayne Broun, a film producer and distributor based in Sydney.

Before her tragically early death in 2002, Christian greatly assisted me in my research into the legend of the Colstoun Pear for my book *Supernatural Scotland*. I make no apology for repeating here what she told me then.

Following her grandmother Edith's version of the story, around the year 1270, Sir David Broun, Laird of Colstoun, married Marion, daughter of Hugo Gifford who, for his exploits in the Black Arts, was known as the Wizard of Yester. As the bridal party proceeded towards the church at Bothans for the ceremony, Gifford stopped under a pear tree to pick a fruit. Handing this to his daughter, he told her that he could not afford a dowry but that so long as the pear was kept safe, so long would flourish the owners of Colstoun.

It comes as no surprise to learn, therefore, that the pear was thereafter lovingly preserved and the Brouns' link with Yester was further enhanced during the late fifteenth century when George Broun of Colstoun married Jean, daughter of the 2nd Lord Hay.[9] In 1692, however, Sir George Broun, 2nd Baronet of Colstoun, married Lady Elizabeth Mackenzie, daughter of the 1st Earl of Cromarty, and there are two variations as to what happened next.

The first is that Lady Elizabeth was pregnant and asked to see the pear, whereupon she promptly bit into it. The second is that she dreamt that the pear had been harmed and asked to see it. On it being brought to her in good condition, she took a bite out of it. Whichever version holds true, the repercussions were significant. Sir George, a gambler, incurred devastating debts. To save the day, his younger brother Robert, who was married to an heiress, sold his wife's inheritance and bought Colstoun from his brother.

But the curse of the pear was not to be ignored. Robert Broun was a member of the Scottish Parliament and, on 31 May 1703, was returning home from a late sitting accompanied by his wife, two sons and two daughters. The Colstoun Water was in full spate and, when the coach driver missed the ford, the laird and his two sons were thrown into the water and drowned. His wife and two daughters were only saved by the air trapped in their crinolines, which turned them into floating boats.

Thus was sealed the fate of the Brouns of Colstoun. Between Robert Broun and his descendant through the female line, the 1st Marquis of Dalhousie, and between the Marquis and Colin Broun-Lindsay, Ludovic's father, there were no direct male heirs. Having been entailed during the lifetime of Robert Broun, Colstoun was to pass almost exclusively through the female line, with each heiress taking the additional surname of Broun.

I have a vague memory of my father and me being shown the pear by Edith Broun-Lindsay and thinking that it resembled a shrivelled-up walnut. When I mentioned this to Christian, I was told that I was extremely privileged, since it was always kept under lock and key and was not supposed be shown to anyone outside the immediate family. I remember wondering why her grandmother might have let us see the pear but then, when I first met Beatrice Broun-Lindsay, mother of Ludovic and Christian, she said to me, 'You used to live in our mill!'

Not knowing what she meant, I replied, 'No, I don't think so.'

'Oh yes, you did,' she continued. '1700.'

How fleeting is the passage of centuries. Perhaps that was the reason my father and I were allowed to see the pear. At the time of the Brouns' coach disaster in 1703, the Martines had been settled at Colstoun Mill for three generations. Not only were William and Issobel Martine to be found at the Old Myln in 1600 but their daughter Margaret had married George Hamilton, the farmer at Sandersdean; George Martine, a cousin, was installed on Easterhaugh and on Castlehaugh and James Martine, another cousin who was married to Margaret Hay from Duncanslaw on Yester, was at Seggieshaugh and Nethermyln, all of them on the Colstoun Estate.

Talk about an incestuous community. Barbara, another of William and Issobel's daughters was married to James Begbie, the farmer at Westfield, on the adjacent estate of Liddington (otherwise known as Lethington) and, at Garvald Grange in the next-door parish, was William's sister Isobel with her husband Thomas Wood, while Margaret, another sister, was married to a Peter Gullen of Eistbarnes, near Haddington. Only their brother Archibald appears to have stayed behind at Morham.[10]

William and Issobel's only surviving son, Thomas, was born at Over Myln in 1602. In 1626, he married Margaret Home, daughter of the Reverend James Home (see Chapter 29) and a niece of Andro Home, the farmer at Busheheids on Colstoun. Thomas and Margaret also lived at the Old Myln for the greater part of their lives and, when he died in 1665, he was buried in Bolton Kirkyard. His grave is marked by a small square stone engraved with the initials T. M. The tack of Over Myln then passed to his son, also Thomas, who married first Margaret Smyth, a farmer's daughter from Woodhead of Newhall, a farm lying east of the present-day Gifford Golf Course, but then part of the Yester Estate.

The second Thomas Martine and his wife Margaret had six children. Their son David took over Sandersdean, their daughter Margaret married Thomas Wilson of East Monkrigg, now long disappeared, and their daughter Euphan married William Hunter of Colstoun East Mains. Margaret, it appears, must have died before 1687, because that year Thomas married as his second wife Anna Carson, from whose descendants my immediate family originates.

Born on the farm of Sandersdean in the following century was Sir Peter Laurie, a future chairman of the Union Bank and, in 1832, Lord Mayor of London. Noted for his outspoken opinions, he once observed in an after-dinner speech, 'See before you the examples of myself, the chief magistrate of this great empire, and the Chief Justice of England sitting at my right hand; both now in the highest offices of the state, and both sprung from the very dregs of the people!'[11] Had they still been alive, I am sure that his parents would have been thrilled to hear themselves so described.[12]

According to the lease of 1697, the property of Over Myln comprised the houses and lands of Seggiehaugh and Gouk's Hill, plus one quarter of the laird's Hained Muir (reserved land). Seggiehaugh was described as the meadowland along the water and Gouk's Hill as the fields on the heights above the houses. In 1830, my great-great-grandfather Peter wrote that, in addition to harvesting his own crops and milling them alongside those of other tenant farmers, Thomas Martine had a brewery which was considered at the time to be the largest in East Lothian. 'The maltings were in Haddington, where the Reverend Joseph Young's Church [East United Secession Chapel in Back Street] at present stands.'[13]

Edith Broun-Lindsay, who died in 1981, told my father that there had once been a dam on part of the Gifford Water above Old Myln, and that this was marked on the estate map as Tam's Linn, a tribute to one or other of the two Thomases. When I went to have a look at the spot in 2007 with Sheila Millar of the East Lothian Local History Centre, I was happy to discover that this stretch of water is still known by that name. Peter Martine himself revisited Over Myln in 1830, only a few years after the original mill wheel had been in existence, and mentions that the then tenant was using the lade to convey water to a new wheel to drive his threshing mill. Today, only the wall of this mill survives.

On that visit, he also observed that a new habitation was in the process of being built. Almost certainly this is what exists today, there being evidence of a much older building to its rear. In either case, the situation is idyllic. At the end of a long, irregularly surfaced woodland drive, the house sits on a leafy rise overlooking the Gifford Water and is occupied by Andrew Draper, a furniture designer who relishes the peace and tranquillity of this hidden-away fold of the Colstoun Estate. He has been there nineteen years and never wants to leave.

'It's a timeless place,' he observed. 'The outside world doesn't intrude.'

That is certainly true. Over the 130 years that my ancestors lived here, they must, at times, have felt not only distanced but entirely protected from the momentous changes taking place all around them. It was a century that began with their ruling monarch, James VI, becoming King of England and during which anti-Episcopal and Anti-Catholic riots brought violence to the streets of Edinburgh; a century when a Civil War divided England and culminated in the execution of their anointed King, Charles I; and, in 1650, less than thirty miles away, a Scots army at Dunbar was wiped out with 3,000 dead and 10,000 captured by Oliver Cromwell, the self-styled Lord Protector.

Thirty-five years later, the Duke of Monmouth, the illegitimate son of the reinstated Charles II, was executed for leading a rebellion against his uncle, James VII and II. In 1689, the first Jacobite Rising shocked the Highlands and culminated with the Battle of Killiecrankie. Two decades later, Haddingtonshire's Member of Parliament, the patriot Andrew Fletcher of Saltoun, stood up in bitter opposition to the proposed political union between Scotland and England.

Singularly remote from the world that surrounded their south-east corner of Scotland, the small feudal colony of Martines at Colstoun simply kept their heads down and got on with their everyday lives.

But in 1714, the tack of Over Myln expired and Thomas and Anna moved swiftly to the neighbouring Liddington or Lethington Estate, where they took over the lease of Westfield from Thomas's widowed aunt, Barbara Begbie. No explanation exists as to why they should have so promptly abandoned the spot where their immediate family had prospered for three generations, but it may have had something to do with the arrival of a new bailie on the Colstoun Estate. He was James Douglas, by all accounts a self-important individual with whom most of the tenants eventually fell out.[14]

More likely, however, their departure was prompted because Thomas's eldest son by his first marriage, yet another Thomas, had made a new life for himself at Gifford (see Chapter 10) and showed no interest in farming. This, coupled with the situation of Thomas's widowed aunt and the conditions of her tenancy, was a good enough reason for them to move on.

Barbara Begbie's husband, James, belonged to an old and much respected East Lothian farming family, long associated with Lethington in so much as one of the five farms belonging to the estate (Acredales, Westfield, Begbie and Upper and Lower Bolton) carried their name. These Begbies at one time or another farmed Northfield, Barney Mains, Gifford Vale in Yester Parish and as far away as North Belton, by Dunbar. It was an altogether interdependent community. At various intervals, Begbie Farm was occupied by members of the Ainslie Family, who were also widely represented throughout the county – at Merryhatton, part of the Huntington Estate; Peaston and Dodridge, in the Parish of Ormiston; and Elvingston and Trabroun at Gladsmuir.

With all of these neighbouring families intermarrying, a picture of mid-millennium feudal rural life soon emerges – one that was mirrored throughout countryside communities the length and breadth of the land. Unfortunately, the Martines' move to Westfield from Old Myln was to be the beginning of a particularly tragic chapter in our family's story.

Thomas, by then, was seventy-three years old. Eight years later, at the age of eighty-one, he fell from his horse while jumping a style in Haddington churchyard and broke his leg. The shock killed him. In the churchyard at Bolton, where he is buried, stands a big 'thruckstane' – a large horizontal stone tablet also called a throughstone – carrying an inscription in his memory and the initials of his second wife, who survived him by fourteen years.

As has been explained, Thomas's eldest son by his first marriage had moved to Gladsmuir, where he had become preoccupied with the building of Gifford Village (see Chapter 10). So it was their second son John who took over the farm at Westfield. In 1722, John married Margaret Ainslie, whose brother farmed The Abbey, then the home farm of the old Cistercian nunnery, downstream from Haddington. Two sons and two daughters were born but then, most distressingly, Margaret died in the tenth year of their marriage.

Three years passed and, on the night of 17 March 1736, at six o'clock in the evening, John was riding home from Haddington and, while crossing a field on Acredales, was thrown from his horse into an old abandoned coal pit. It had been raining heavily and he drowned, leaving four orphaned children under the age of ten.

John Martine's death shocked the tight-knit agricultural community, the majority of whom were in some way or another related to him, but the immediate concern was the welfare of his children and a group of seven 'tutors', was hurriedly appointed: their uncles David Fairley and John and Robert Ainslie and close family friends Robert Dagger, William Youll, James Forrest and John Cadell.

Fortunately, the estate of the deceased was considerable for that of a small tenant farmer and, when finally wound up in 1744, realised £7,100. John had left no will and the children were obviously too young to manage their own affairs; on top of which the lease on Westfield required to be sorted out and money on loan bonds recovered. In those days, the only way to earn income from capital was to lend, and the sum of 2,000 merks had been advanced by John Martine to each of two neighbouring landowners, Henry Fletcher of Saltoun and the 6th Earl of Haddington.[15] This money needed to be recovered, but it took twelve years to do so.

Out of adversity rises spirit and, with the exception of young Thomas, who never fully recovered from losing both parents and died three years later, the deceased farmer's children fared as best they could under the circumstances. Some household accounts of the period make for a melancholy read:

Small things to Thomas when seek 4s 11p
A spelling book to Agnes 1s 3p
A pair of shous to Peg 1s 4p
Ell to the men that brough hoom the corps 4s 4p
A pair stoken to John 1s 8p
Wool Reid suiping the Loum 1s 5p
Mendin the school window 0s 2p
Fish to the Children and Herin to the hous 1s 6p

Of the surviving Martine children, Margaret married Andrew Hunter, a brewer, and they had eight children. In 1772, Agnes married Patrick McClarran, a merchant who, in 1783, was elected Provost of Haddington. John Martine himself became Provost in 1781 and his son-in-law, Alexander Maitland, followed suit in 1797, while John, his eldest son, held the post in 1807, 1813 and 1817.

CHAPTER TWO

Lennox's Love to Blantyre

IT WAS DURING A CASUAL conversation with my enigmatic publisher Hugh Andrew at the Open Arms in Dirleton that the seeds for this book were sown. Hugh is the founder of the Edinburgh-based publishing house of Birlinn, today one of Scotland's largest independent publishers, and, up until then, I had had no idea that a full century and a half after my own ancestor's fateful demise on Acredales, on the outskirts of Haddington, his family had farmed there for three generations. Although he himself was born and brought up in the west of Scotland, Hugh, not unlike myself, acknowledges that his roots are inescapably entwined with Haddington and East Lothian.

Acredales, the 250 acres situated between the entrance gates of the Lennoxlove Estate, formerly Lethington, and the wooded banks of the River Tyne, has now been occupied by the Andrew family since 1874. That was the year in which its then owner, Lord Blantyre, offered the lease to Hugh's great-grandfather, also Hugh, the son of his tenants at Allands, a farm at Inchinnan, west of Paisley, a site that is currently occupied by Glasgow Airport. This Hugh Andrew died in 1896 and was succeeded by his son, yet another Hugh, known in the family as Hugo. It was Hugo and his widowed mother Margaret who bought the land from Sir David Baird in 1919.

Also brought up on the farm and schooled at Knox Academy was Hugo's younger brother James, who departed Haddington to join his maternal uncle in a family veterinary practice based in Paisley. Following his death in 1962, this was taken over by James's son Hubert, father of the present Hugh, and it continues to this day.

Having himself left school at the age of fourteen, Hugo Andrew soon became a familiar figure in Haddington, riding his horse into the town on market days. 'He was a founder member of the British Friesian Society and, being an accomplished horseman, on one occasion won at Hamilton Park Races riding his horse "Lady Polwarth",' recalled his nephew John Taylor, who succeeded him at Acredales.

Although there was never any shortage of lady friends, Hugo remained a lifelong bachelor but, shortly before his death, much to his amusement, he received a visit from the child of one of his early liaisons. It came as a complete revelation to him but cheered him enormously. John also remembers him as a snappy dresser, with a good sense of humour. 'He always wore a bow tie and carried a cane, except at funerals,' he said.

John Taylor, the son of Hugo's sister Madge, spent his school holidays from 1941 working on the farm at Acredales and then took over at the age of eighteen when his uncle died in 1948. He eventually bought over the shares held by his remaining uncle and aunt and he and his wife Trish have been there ever since.

On a wall of the graveyard of St Mary's Church less than a mile from the gates of Acredales, are plaques commemorating the passing generations of the Andrew family since 1896, the most recently being Hubert, the present Hugh's father, in 2005. 'Well, it's curious,' said Hugh. 'If I were asked where my heart lay, because of family holidays, I would probably say Argyll but Haddington and this long family line is a point of still and calm in a world whirling ever faster. It is where my father came back to at the end of his life and it is probably where I will end up as the last of our line of the family.'

Final resting places command that sense of attachment. When called upon to propose the Immortal Memory at a Burns Supper, I like to reveal that I have something in common with the bard, which is that several of my Martine ancestors share the same graveyard at Bolton Church as his mother Agnes, sister Anabella, brother Gilbert, and his nephews and nieces. In 1804, Gilbert Burns, his wife Jean and their eight children moved from Morham West Mains, which he had managed for the Dunlop family since 1800, to become factor of the 11th Lord Blantyre's Lennoxlove Estate. A further three children were born to them and, until Gilbert's death in 1827, aged sixty-seven, the Burns family lived in an old house called Grant's Braes which overlooked the banks of the River Tyne. Anabella, his sister, lived on there until 1832.

Gravestones can reveal as much about life as they do about death: Isabella Burns died aged seven; Agnes aged fifteen; Janet aged eighteen; Jean aged twenty; and John aged twenty-five. How painful these losses must have been for their parents, let alone for the senior Agnes, whose golden boy Robert had himself died in 1796. That was twenty-four years before her own death at Grant's Braes at the noble age of eighty-eight.

A church was erected at Bolton in the first half of the thirteenth century and, until the Reformation 300 years later, came under the authority of the Canons of Holyrood. Although the present church at Bolton dates from only 1809, the graveyard contains burials from long before that.

'Liddington' or 'Lethington' was the ancient name for the Lennoxlove Estate which lies to the north-west of Bolton and was yet another of the properties once owned by the Giffords and Hays of Yester. From 1338, it was held in feu by the Maitland family of Thirlestane, a landholding on the far side of the Lammermuirs.

In the sixteenth century, Richard Maitland of Thirlestane was a poet of some distinction and rose in legal circles to become a Lord of Session. He was the father of William Maitland, 'secretary' to Mary, Queen of Scots, and at some stage he had acquired the lease of Lethington from his nephew James, a tenant of the Hays of Yester. In the next generation, William's son John, the 1st Lord Maitland, succeeded his father as Secretary of State and served as Lord Chancellor of Scotland from 1586 to 1595. In 1591, however, the 6th Lord Yester died with no male heir and without entailing the family estates to his brother. The 7th Lord Yester therefore approached the Lord Chancellor for his help and Maitland, a canny individual, agreed to affix the seal in arrears but only on the condition that Lethington was made over to him in perpetuity.[1]

Heredity counted for a lot in those days. Lord Chancellor Maitland's son, having become President of the Council after his father's death, was made 1st Earl of Lauderdale by James VI in 1616. According to the Latin inscription over the main entrance to the tower at Lethington, it was he who embellished the original fourteenth-century stronghold and enlarged the windows. Up until then, Lethington had been just another of those defensive rectangular keeps, the ruins of which are to be found strategically spaced out all over the Scottish landscape. But there were a large number of small Maitlands to accommodate. The 1st Earl's wife, Lady Isabel Seton, gave birth to fifteen children before her untimely death at the age of forty-four.

By then, the Maitland dynasty had become a force to be reckoned with and its members were determined to be recognised as such. This was especially true of the 1st Earl's eldest son and heir, John, 2nd Earl and 1st and only Duke of Lauderdale, who became Charles II's Secretary of State for Scotland.

Unpredictable and widely disliked, the Duke of Lauderdale dominated Scottish politics for over twenty years. His contemporary, Bishop Gilbert Burnet, wrote of him:

> In his person, he made but an ill appearance. His stature was large, his hair red, his tongue too big for his mouth, and his whole manner rough and very unfit for a court . . . His learning was considerable, for he not only understood Latin, in which he was a master, but Greek and Hebrew; had read a great deal

> of divinity, almost all historians, both ancient and modern; and having besides an extraordinary memory, was furnished with a copious but very unpolished way of expression. The sense of religion that a long imprisonment has impressed upon his mind was soon erased by a course of luxury and sensuality, which ran him into great expense and which he stuck at nothing to support . . . he was the coldest friend and most violent enemy that ever was known.

In stark contrast to his prolific father, the Duke fathered only one daughter who, in 1666, married the 2nd Marquis of Tweeddale, son of their East Lothian neighbour, but there appears to have been little affection between father and daughter. After the death of his first wife Anne in 1671, Lauderdale rapidly married the wealthy Countess of Dysart and the Duke and his second Duchess largely based themselves at Ham House, her London home at Richmond, or at Thirlestane Castle, where they entertained lavishly. For visits to Edinburgh they increasingly made use of Brunstane House, near Portobello, rebuilt for the Duke in 1639 and modernised by the architect Sir William Bruce in 1672.

With no male heir on his death ten years later, the Lauderdale dukedom became dormant although the earldom and Thirlestane estates devolved upon his brother Charles, from whom the senior Maitland line continued. Lethington, however, was bequeathed to his stepson, Lord Huntingtower, who had no interest in holding on to a Maitland property in Scotland and sold it to Alexander Stuart, 5th Lord Blantyre.

The one important East Lothian possession which therefore remained in the Maitland family was the Lauderdale Aisle in St Mary's Church, Haddington, where, in 1682, the Duke was interred amid great pomp and circumstance. Over 2,000 horsemen accompanied his funeral procession.[2] His wife and daughter, however, did not attend.

'La Belle Stuart', as Frances Stuart, Duchess of Richmond and Lennox, became known in her youth, was the granddaughter of the 1st Lord Blantyre. At the age of fourteen she was appointed a Maid of Honour to Queen Catherine, wife of Charles II. As fate would have it, she soon caught the eye of the libertine King, who proposed that she model for the figure of Britannia, which still features on our national coinage. However, despite rumours to the contrary, the teenage Frances resisted his more amorous advances and, in 1667, eloped with his twenty-seven year-old cousin Charles Stewart, 3rd Duke of Richmond and 6th Duke of Lennox. King Charles was incensed and banished his errant relative to Denmark as British Ambassador, obliging him to leave his bride behind in England. Five years into his exile, Lennox died in a drowning accident at Elsinore.

La Belle Stuart was devastated and, when she herself died in 1700, she bequeathed the sum of £50,000 to her nephew with the instructions that he buy a house for himself and name it 'Lennox's Love to Blantyre'. The purchase of Lethington was completed in 1702 but, with the passing of time, the name was shortened to Lennoxlove.

The Lennoxlove Estate thereafter remained with the Stuarts of Blantyre for almost two centuries until the marriage of Ellen Stuart, second daughter and co-heiress of the 12th Lord, to Sir David Baird, 3rd Baronet of Newbyth, a hero of both the Crimean War and the Indian Mutiny. It was he who, in 1912, commissioned the architect Sir Robert Lorimer to refurbish Lennoxlove's interiors but such improvements came at a cost. In 1919, his son the 4th Baronet, while retaining Westfield, sold the Acredales farm. Four years later, Begbie was sold to its tenant, John Steven.

Until 1853, the farmhouse of Bolton, a stone's throw from the Gifford Water which trickles through the little glen below the village, was tenanted by Alexander Wyllie from Hatton Mains at Ratho, on the outskirts of Edinburgh. From 1872, Wyllie also farmed Under and Upper Bolton, in total some 700 acres on the Lennoxlove Estate. He and his wife Janet Turner had five sons. James, the eldest, went on to farm at Innerwick and, underlining yet again the incestuous nature of rural East Lothian, James was the father of my uncle David Martine's wife Janet (see Chapter 29).

While Upper and Lower Bolton and Begbie were later bought back into the Lennoxlove fold by Hamilton & Kinneil Estates, Acredales remains with the Andrew family in the person of John Taylor.

In 1941, the somewhat depleted Lenoxlove Estate was inherited by Sir David Baird's nephew, the fifth Sir David, who passed it on to his younger brother Robert who, by then, was domiciled in the Bahamas. It soon became obvious that he was unlikely to return and, in 1946, the estate was purchased by the 14th Duke of Hamilton and 11th Duke of Brandon, his family having two decades earlier abandoned the mammoth Hamilton Palace in South Lanarkshire.[3]

The eldest of four brothers who, by the outbreak of World War II, had all become squadron leaders in the Royal Air Force, the 14th Duke had inherited his titles from his father in 1940. Earlier, he had been a Scottish Amateur Middleweight Boxing Champion, had represented East Renfrewshire in parliament from 1930 and, in 1933, been the chief pilot of a cockpit biplane which he had flown over Mount Everest. This adventurous Duke thus became the epitome of a *Boy's Own* hero – or so at least thought Albrecht Haushofer, a close friend of the German Chancellor Adolf Hitler and Rudolf Hess, Hitler's deputy. In September 1940, just about the same time as the German Luftwaffe launched their bombing campaign on London, Haushofer wrote to the Duke proposing that they meet in Portugal to discuss a 'German–English' agreement. In the event, the letter was intercepted by MI5 who suggested that the Duke act as a double agent.

Then an even more extraordinary occurrence took place. On 10 May 1941, Rudolf Hess himself parachuted from a plane above Renfrewshire on to a farm at Eaglesham in the hope that the Duke of Hamilton, then living not so far away at Dungavel, might introduce him to George VI. Hess not only sought an audience with the King but sincerely believed that he would be able to convince him to sack the British Prime Minister, Winston Churchill.

Hess's mission rapidly became a farce, with Adolf Hitler hurriedly distancing himself from his now former deputy. Hess, in the meantime, was incarcerated in the Tower of London and, when hostilities came to an end in 1945, was sent to Nuremberg for trial. Found guilty of crimes against peace, he spent the remaining years of his life under maximum-security conditions in Spandau Prison in West Berlin.

The 14th Duke of Hamilton meanwhile continued his responsibilities for air defence in Scotland, taking on the command of the Air Training Corps. When the war ended, he and the Duchess began house-hunting. Their third son, Lord Hugh, was born in North Berwick in 1946 and, with the duke's duties as Hereditary Keeper of the Palace of Holyroodhouse in Edinburgh to fulfil, the Lennoxlove Estate was seen as an entirely suitable place to house a family and the remains of the Hamilton Palace collection.

Set in 460 acres of parkland and gardens, Lennoxlove House was first opened to the public in the 1970s. With the interiors redecorated by the London-based designers Colefax & Fowler and the rooms filled with many of the treasures of Hamilton Palace, including the Death Mask of Mary, Queen of Scots, it rapidly proved a popular visitor attraction. In 2007, following the sale of the Gavin Hamilton portrait of Elizabeth Gunning, wife of the 6th Duke, to the Scottish National Portrait Gallery, a further £3 million was spent on refurbishment and the luxurious upgrade of residential features took place to accommodate corporate and commercial lets.

During the 1990s, I regularly visited the whitewashed farmhouse of Westfield adjacent to Lennoxlove, when it was the home of the 15th Duke's brother, Lord Patrick Douglas-Hamilton, a talented photographer who was working with me on our book, *Scotland: the Land and the Whisky*. In retrospect, I find it inexplicable that at the time I was entirely unaware that this was exactly the spot, if not in the same building, where my Martine ancestors had lived 300 years earlier and where so much misfortune had befallen them.

It took this voyage into their lives for me to make that discovery and perhaps it illustrates just how carelessly we treat the past – that is, until the moment arrives when we find ourselves becoming part of that past.

CHAPTER THREE

Canons, Fire and Plague

THE YEAR WAS 1794 and, towards the end of the summer, there took place an escapade involving a spirited group of Haddington youths, comprising John and William Haldane, Peter Martine and his cousin Benjie Hunter, John David, known as 'Lettie', and Henry Davidson, afterwards sheriff-clerk of the county. Having hired a boat at Prestonpans, the teenage boys unanimously elected George Neill, a future bailie of the town, bookseller and printer, to be their 'commodore'. They then set off to row across the estuary of the Firth of Forth to land at the Fife coastal town of Kirkcaldy.

Intent on nothing more than harmless mischief, the boys dispatched the town drummer to announce that, at three o'clock that afternoon, a renowned diver and swimmer would exhibit his prowess with 'high and lofty vaulting from a boat in the harbour'.[1] A large crowd of spectators soon assembled which, when the performance failed to take place, became increasingly agitated. Realising that they had been hoaxed, the locals threw stones at the Haddington crew who, for self-preservation, rapidly cast off. They were hotly pursued by a group of Kirkcaldy youths in another boat but eventually managed to out-row them. Having spent the entire night at sea in a fog, the six Haddington boys landed safely at Prestonpans in the early dawn, 'sair worn out and forfeuchin'.[2]

I introduce this anecdote simply to illustrate just how closely connected the Kingdom of Fife was by sea to the East Lothian coast in an age when people travelled inland either on foot or on horseback but, when journeying north or south, went by water. All of the coastal villages, from Leith to Musselburgh, and Aberlady to North Berwick and Dunbar, had ports. It can therefore be assumed that it was the ease of this very same maritime access which, six centuries earlier, encouraged the Priory of Augustinian Canons in St Andrews to locate a great parish church dedicated to St Mary the Virgin in Haddington. It was this decision which also inspired Ada de Warenne, the widowed Countess of Huntingdon and mother of two future Scottish kings,

Malcolm IV and William the Lion, to take up residence in the town and to endow a Cistercian nunnery and a chapel dedicated to St Martine de Tours. I deliberately use the spelling of St Martine with an 'e' because, with the majority of the population illiterate, that is the way the name was commonly spelled by the scribes and notaries throughout mainland Europe in the Middle Ages – the 'Sancte Martine' which Sir Walter Scott uses in his novel *Quentin Durward*.

I warm to the idea of having a saint in the family but there is, of course, not even the remotest connection by blood to Martin of Tours. In the Middle Ages, it was common practice to adopt surnames from places or professional associations. Before reading too much into this, it should be appreciated that the surname Martin, with its Martini/Martinez/Martineau variations, is among the most common worldwide. My father's take on the subject was principally that, in our particular case, there might be circumstantial evidence but nothing conclusive to suggest a French origin – that Martine was spelled phonetically, according to the old dialect of Haddingtonshire, where the family must have resided for at least 800 years, and it was similar, for example, to the retention of the surname Broun over the more usual Brown. It is also highly plausible that the surname of Martin – or Martine as it was regularly spelled in surviving documents – was either given to or taken by somebody associated with the church.

St Martin(e) de Tours was born in the year 316, the son of a tribune of the Imperial Horse Guard serving in the Roman province of Pannonia (an area which includes Hungary). As far as we know, he never set foot in the British Isles but it has to be remembered that St Margaret of Scotland, the grandmother of the husband of Ada de Warenne, under whose patronage this Cistercian church of St Martin's in Haddington was built, was born in Hungary and was a niece of the Holy Roman Emperor.[3] Whether this had anything to do with the naming of St Martin's Church can only now be speculation but St Martin certainly emerged as a popular idol in medieval Scotland.[4]

In the eyes of medieval men and women, the building of a place of worship was synonymous with creating heaven on earth. Once St Andrews had been established as the epicentre of Roman Christianity in Scotland, its various religious orders rapidly preoccupied themselves with extending their influence under the patronage of the Crown: the Benedictines at Dunfermline; the Cistercians (the 'White Monks') at Melrose and Newbattle; and the Tironensians similarly at Kelso and Selkirk.

The first stone-built Glasgow Cathedral, erected on the site of a previous church fabricated of wood, was dedicated in the presence of David I in 1128. By then, the Augustinians – or the 'Black Canons' as they were known – were already entrenched at Jedburgh and Holyrood. When, in 1139, King David gifted the lands of Haddington in the valley of the River Tyne to his daughter-in-law Ada de Warenne, he also granted permission for the building of St Mary's, the 'Ecclesia Parochialis' or 'Hie Kirk' of Haddington.

In keeping with the times, the religious fervour of Ada, Countess of Huntingdon, soon proved to be as profound as that of St Margaret of Scotland and when, after the Earl of Huntingdon's death in 1152, she founded a Cistercian nunnery, Haddington was transformed into a thriving Christian community. Within its town walls sprang up a Franciscan friary, a Greyfriars monastery and seven local chapels – St Martin's, St Ann's, St Catherine's, St John's (which was associated with the Knights Templar), St Ninian's, St Laurence's (under the patronage of the nunnery) and another on the western extremity within the barony of Penston.[5]

Of the chapels, only the nave of the ruined red sandstone St Martin's remains, surrounded by grass and walled in on the edge of the Nungate. It is the oldest surviving edifice in the town, but its significance, so far as I am concerned, is personal in that the lands upon which it was built were gifted by Countess Ada to Alexander St Martine, Sheriff of Haddington, who was also Sheriff to Hugo Gifford of Yester, and who then proceeded to endow the nunnery with them.[6] He already held the 'land which Arkil held by the boundaries between Haddingtoun and Athelstanefurd' by a charter from David I,[7] and 'Ada Comitissa, Mater Regis Scotorum' (Mother of the King of Scots) later conveyed on him the lands of Baro, Duncanlaw and Banglaw.[8]

Towards the end of his life, Alexander St Martine granted a peat-moss called Crumuber-struther to the Monks of Newbattle[9] and, after his death, his daughter Ada, who was presumably named after the Queen Mother, granted half a merk annually to the Abbey of Holyrood from the rent of her mill at Athelstaneford.[10]

So far, that is all that I have been able to discover about either Alexander or Ada, except that the former originated from the hamlet of St Martin, beside Bellencombre in Upper Normandy, and that he was related to the de Warenne Family and, therefore, to Countess Ada whose Anglo-Norman credentials provided an unsurpassed network of influence throughout Western Europe.[11] The youngest daughter of the volatile 2nd Earl de Warenne and Surrey, her paternal grandmother was Gundrada, daughter of William the Conqueror, and her maternal great-great-grandfather was Henry I of France.

In 1139, she married Henry, 3rd Earl of Huntingdon, son of David I of Scotland and a nephew of Henry I of England. Henry of Huntingdon died in 1152, aged thirty-eight, which meant that when his father died the following year, the throne of Scotland passed to their eldest son, who became Malcolm IV at the age of eleven.

And it was in the Royal Palace in Haddington that Malcolm and his brother, the future William the Lion, grew to maturity, surrounded by the bastions of Mother Church. The Palace, according to the early fourteenth-century chronicler John of Fordun, stood at the west end of the High Street, on Court Street, and occupied the site of today's County Buildings which date from 1833. In 1198, this was the birthplace of Alexander II, son of William the Lion and Ermengarde de Beaumont, the natural granddaughter of Henry I of England. At this stage in its history, Haddington ranked as the fourth largest town in Scotland and was second only to St Andrews in ecumenical significance. In the centuries that followed, it would pay a heavy price for such a distinction.

One of the most frustrating aspects of ancestral research in Scotland is that, in company with the entire National Archive of Scotland which was carried off by Edward I's army in 1296 and lost at sea, the subsequent records of the monastic establishments of Haddington, between the thirteenth and fifteenth centuries, were deliberately and efficiently obliterated by a relentless stream of invaders. The oldest book in the record chamber of the burgh extends no further back than 1426.[12]

Even the origin of the name of Haddington itself is in doubt. One suggestion is that it was the hamlet of Haden, an eleventh-century Saxon settler, hence 'Haden's tun'.[13] In his *History of Haddington,* published in 1844, James Miller prefers a monastic association. *Hading* in the Anglo-Saxon world signified 'a place of ordination', while *tun* indicated 'a dwelling place or location'. Another proposal is that it was the residence of Countess Ada – hence 'Ada-ing-tun'.[14]

As for Alexander and Ada St Martine, there is no mention of them to be found after 1150, which suggests that the former had died and the latter had married. However, around 1189, a 'Martin' appears in Haddington as chancellor to William the Lion[15] and, in the early years of the following century, the name of Magistro Alexandro do St Martino occurs frequently in clerical charters connected with St Andrews.[16] Three hundred years later, a family of de Martyne emerges at Carden in Fife, ancestors of both a Thomas Martine whose family, in the reign of James I, became pre-eminent among the citizens of St Andrews,[17] and George Martine, who served as Secretary to Archbishop Sharp before his assassination in 1679.[18]

Normal practice when tracing early Scots ancestry is to consult the Ragman Roll of 1296, which lists anyone considered to be anybody in a population of between 500,000 and 1,000,000. The English King, Edward I, was determined to appoint himself overlord of Scotland and, if you were not prepared to render homage to him, there were likely to be serious consequences. Under the circumstance, the majority signed up and, although at the time it must have seemed a national humiliation, it ironically provided one of the earliest records of who was who in late thirteenth-century Scotland. Unfortunately, the best my search could come up with was a Wautier fitz Martin, 'del burk de edeneburgh'.[19] Well, that certainly put me in my place.

Heraldry is a magical art form. After a casual enquiry at the Court of the Lord Lyon in Edinburgh concerning the family crest featured on my father's signet ring Elizabeth Roads, the Lyon Clerk, confirmed that the heraldic devices employed by all of the Martin/Martine families I had been pursuing showed the same medieval origin. Which makes me wonder even more about Alexander St Martine and his beginnings in Bellencombre. For the best part of his lifetime, Haddingtonshire, with its market centre of Haddington and seaport of Dunbar, enjoyed an interlude of unequalled peace and prosperity but with the restless ambition of human nature, particularly given the greed of the volatile Anglo-Normans south of the Border, it could never have lasted. Over the three centuries that followed, wave after wave of English incursion into Scotland was to batter, burn and systematically raze to the ground everything that lay in its path. It is a miracle that anyone, let alone any of my ancestors, lived to survive the cyclical holocausts which so cruelly enveloped them.

The first assault came in 1216 when, in reprisal for the Haddington-born Alexander II's support of a group of rebellious English barons, England's King John turned the town's wooden buildings with their thatched roofs into a bonfire. In the next generation, John's son, Henry III, repeated the carnage, on the same night burning Roxburgh and Lanark, in the south of Scotland, and Stirling, Perth, Forfar and Montrose in the north. In 1296, Edward I rampaged over the Border to force the Scots to pay him homage as overlord and, in 1314, his son Edward II marched his soldiers straight through East Lothian on his way to Bannockburn. His defeat brought little comfort to those who had already encountered his men on their path of destruction. In February 1356, the English marauders were back under Edward III to cause havoc on Market Day, a calendar event which became known as the 'Burnt Candlemas', when 'every public record shrivelled beneath the torch of the invader'.[20] Twenty-nine years later, there was a repeat performance and, in 1385, Edward's successor, Richard II, utterly destroyed both the parish church and the friary, 'the singular solace of the pious in that part of the country'.[21] In defiance, the citizens of Haddington raised an even more imposing house of prayer formed in the shape of a cross. Being 206 feet long and 62 feet wide, St Mary's became the largest parish church in Scotland. But, yet again, it was only a matter of time before the enemy returned.

Sir Henry Percy, known as Harry Hotspur, invaded on behalf of Henry IV in 1400 and, with forays in between, they came again in 1482, this time under the Duke of Gloucester, later Richard III. The greatest amount of carnage, however, took place sixty-two years later in the period known as The Rough Wooing, when the flames engulfing Edinburgh and the Abbey of Holyrood continued for three days.

Then came the unthinkable. While the infant Mary, Queen of Scots was in the process of being despatched to France to marry the Dauphin Francis, Haddington was seized and occupied by the English and, for almost eighteen months, came under siege from a Scottish–French alliance. This bizarre confrontation, where English soldiers were quartered alongside townsfolk, culminated in a stalemate but not before almost every building within the town was reduced to rubble. In a final act of spite against the Scots, who had used St Mary's as their headquarters, the English commander, Henry Manners, 2nd Earl of Rutland, carried off the church's three bells.[22] But by this stage, both the parish church and the town were in such a state of collapse that hardly anyone noticed.

With such a relentless record of disruption, it never ceases to amaze me that anything, let alone anyone, was left standing before the dawn of the seventeenth century. But then, medieval Haddingtonians were a stoic breed who were particularly adept at side-stepping the politics of the day, as is instanced by the Forrests of Gimmersmills.

During the Siege, Sir James Wilford, the English commandant, makes reference to 'two Scotsmen burgesses of this town, who have served very honestly during the siege, and have suffered great losses. One of them is George Forresse, brother to Davy Forresse, the other, John Rickenton, is his cousin German . . .' It has also come to light that the same Davy Forrest was deeply involved in intelligence to and from English statesmen such as the Duke of Somerset, Sir Ralph Sadler and Sir William Cecil.[23]

Now it does not surprise me in the slightest that the Forrests should have so readily co-operated with the English, because ostensibly this was not Haddington's war. In this instance, the English had invaded Scotland in a legitimate attempt to prevent the betrothal of the six-year-old Queen Mary to the heir to the French throne, a union seen by a growing number of Protestant Scots, which included the majority of Haddington's citizens, as an overt Catholic alliance.

And against this background was emerging a series of increasingly bitter confrontations between the Queen Mother, Mary de Guise, and Scotland's Protestant Lords of Congregation. It was also no coincidence that the aforementioned David Forrest was a childhood friend of John Knox and had been with him a year earlier throughout the siege of St Andrews Castle.

I also find myself smiling when I read that an invoice was submitted by one John Forrest on 9 December 1554, six years after the end of the siege, for the rebuilding of mills and cleaning the dams 'after the departure of the Englishmen out of the said burgh'. At least somebody in the family was sharp enough to capitalise on the situation but, then again, it may have been at the suggestion of his Uncle Davy, who that same year was appointed General of the Mint and Auditor of the Exchequer.

Three years before the siege, John's other uncle, George Forrest, a member of the Council Court also appears in the Haddington Council records:

> Which day George Forrest announced that an Act had previously been passed by the Provost, Bailies and Council, in which it was stated that all manner of persons who were still unclean or suspected of having the plague, should leave the town within eighteen hours, under penalty of death and confiscation of goods.

From this it becomes abundantly clear that in the second half of the sixteenth century, the townsfolk of Haddington, not to mention those who lived in the surrounding countryside, had rather more than the English occupation to think about.

CHAPTER FOUR

Town of the Goat

TWO EARLY HADDINGTON residents were James and Patrick Martine. Both were born around the year 1500 and, in records of 1566, James is listed as the owner of 'Land within the Town and a Burgess therof'.[1] As his name does not feature in the record of land-holders in 1567, it can only be presumed that by that time he had died. What occupation he followed is unfortunately unknown but Haddington was by then a prosperous community, exporting all manner of commodities, in particular wool, fleeces and hides, through its port of Aberlady on the estuary of the River Forth.

Of Patrick, there is rather more information. A minute of the Town Council, dated 22 October 1545, reads as follows:

> The quhulk day ye Provost, baillies, Counsall and Comunite of yis Burgh, has all with ane voice and consent geven and granted till Patric Martyne ye Office of ye common handbell of yis Burgh, for all ye days of his lif, for his gude service done to ye toun in tyme of ye pest.[2]

He is subsequently referred to on various occasions as the Town Official or 'Sarjeand'. In an entry in 1557, a payment was made to him as follows: 'To Patrick Martine twa days in Edbro, speking with John Young anents the furth ganging of ye Toun of Edinburgh to ye Army – in expense of 8 shillings.'[3]

That he was associated with the pre-Reformation church of St Mary's is shown by an entry in Haddington Burgh Court Book, Vol. 3/67v, dated 14 October 1556. 'Sir Thomas Mauchline appointed Patrick Martine Procurator for Three Kings of Culane, in name of alterage and chaplain thereof.'[4] This Catholic chapel or 'sacellum', one of twenty or more instigated by the nobility and town trades, was situated in the north-west section of St Mary's in honour of the 'undivided Trinity, of the glorious Virgin Mary, of the Most-Sanctified Three Kings who are buried in Cologne'.

With the parish church being the focal point of the community, such endowments were critical to the popular rituals of the time. The shoemakers, for example, adopted St Crispian; the bakers, St Aubert; the smiths, St Eloi (Blaise); and the tailors, St Anne, the Mother of the Virgin. Other altars that we know of in St Mary's include those in honour of St Peter, St Salvator (the Holy Blood), St Andrew, St Michael the Archangel, St John the Baptist, St John the Evangelist, St Katherine the Virgin, St Michael, St Nicholas, St James the Apostle, St Severus, St Bartholemew, St Crispin, St Thomas and St Towbert.[5]

Life expectancy was short. Belief in an afterlife was the norm and such altars served as a direct line to God's call centre. Masses, specified by parishioners, were celebrated at one or other of these altars throughout the year and the wealthier the individual, the more elaborate the ceremony. For example, the widow of one local burgess left instructions for seven priests, the parish clerk of the choir and two chaplains to hold Masses annually for her husband, her dead son and herself at the altar of St Katherine the Virgin.[6]

The altar of the Three Kings of Cologne was endowed and presented on 20 October 1522 by David Forrest, Burgess of Haddington, with the grant of sasine to the Reverend George Sidsarf.[7] Thirty-four years later, Patrick Martine's duties as Procurator would have included responsibility for its maintenance and the collection of subscriptions. Later that same century, the Provost, Bailies and Council of the Burgh of Haddington decreed that 'all the annuals of the Chaplainries and Altarages within the Burgh should be collected and applied to a Master of the school or a reader for teaching of bairns and exhorter in the Kirk and that there be a qualified man gotten with advice of the Council and the town.'[8] Not a bad stipend for a dominie, all things considered.

So who exactly were the Forrest family mentioned in the previous chapter and who continued their association with this altar of the Three Kings until long after the Reformation had swept such practices away? And what, if anything, was the significance of the Three Kings of Cologne? In a masterly dissertation, 'The Forrests of Haddington and the Reformation', Martin A. Forrest, in 2002, confirmed that the first recorded David Forrest, father of four sons – William, George, David and Alexander – was evidently a wealthy man.[9] There is some evidence that David was engaged in the wool trade and also brewing. There are later accounts of the Forrests in Haddington being involved in weapon-making and carting but, however their wealth was acquired, there is no doubt that, by this time, a large proportion of their income simply came from rentals of properties the family owned.[10]

Of David's four sons, William was also a burgess of Haddington,[11] owning properties in Market Place, Smiddy Row and Tentercroft, to the north of the town. George is mentioned in 1543 as a sheriff of Edinburgh in the Constabulary of Haddington, and is described as a wine *cunnar*, meaning 'taster', who presumably was responsible for buying wine for the town. Alexander, who was seemingly a close confidant of the Regent Arran, became Secretary to the Bishop of St Andrews and, from 1526 to 1561, was Provost of St Mary's in the Fields or Kirk o' Field, a collegiate church situated next to the Palace of Holyroodhouse. The site is probably best known as being close to the spot where Lord Darnley, the husband of Mary, Queen of Scots, was unceremoniously murdered on 10 February 1567.

The younger David Forrest is described by John Knox as a man of judgement at the royal court who had helped promote the Earl of Arran as Governor and Regent of Scotland and who, as one of his most trusted counsellors, warned the Regent against surrounding himself with relatives and so-called friends. David shared Knox's Protestant leanings and provided shelter to the Reformer George Wishart in Haddington and to Knox in Edinburgh. Through his influence with Arran, he was appointed General of the Mint in 1554 and, in 1560, was nominated to sit at the first General Assembly of the Church of Scotland. Although he continued to refuse to take up the ministry, he was a contributor to the *First Book of Discipline*, *the Confession of Faith* and *the Book of Common Order*.[12]

Between 1552 and 1557, the Reverend Alexander Forrest obtained a nineteen-year lease on the flourmills known as Gimmersmills from the prioress of the Cistercian nunnery of St Mary, otherwise known as the Abbey. Later, when such religious seminaries were abolished, full ownership of the mill and surrounding land in the Nungate was taken over by the Reverend Alexander's nephew John. This remained in the possession of his descendants under charter from the Crown until the death of Dr George Forrest in 1795, when they passed into the hands of George's nephew, Dr Alexander Maitland, husband of Margaret Martine. Forrests served as Provosts of Haddington in 1555, 1564, 1710, 1714, 1720 and 1736 and, in 1797, Alexander Maitland himself became Provost.[13] There is nothing like keeping it in the family.

When the Gimmersmills in Whittingehame Drive was acquired by Montgomerie & Company Limited in 1897, a number of papers were discovered in an ancient charter chest. This Gimmersmills Charter Chest is now stored in Edinburgh's Register House and among the papers is a Power of Attorney granted by Archibald Forrest, a Lieutenant in the 105th Company, and dated 1759. He is credited with having gifted to the town the land at the Sands, opposite Lady Kitty's Garden, for use as a recreation ground. Today, it forms the town's bowling green. The site of Gimmersmills is currently occupied by Pure Malt Products.

The iconography of the Three Kings of Cologne represents the Three Wise Men of the Bible – Balthasar, King of Saba, Gaspar, King of Tarsus, and Melchior, King of Araby – who visited Bethlehem after the birth of Jesus. Their bodies are said to have been found and reburied in north Italy but later they were transferred to Cologne Cathedral where, by 1225, they had been interred in a basilica-shaped gold tomb encrusted with enamel and studded with precious stones. Symbolic of pilgrimage, the Three Kings soon became a popular motif for worshippers in pre-Reformation Europe. But all of that came to an abrupt end in 1560 with the abolition under Scots Law of the Latin Mass and papal authority.[14]

There was nothing that the Haddington-born John Knox, leader of Scotland's Reformation movement and founder of the Church of Scotland, despised more than idolatry. In the entire history of Scotland, no more controversial or complex a figure exists than John Knox, who was born, in the lack of any conclusive evidence to the contrary, around 1515, in the Giffordgate of Nungate, on the far side of the river from St Mary's. We can only conjecture on the influences of his indoctrination as a priest at St Mary's that led to his subsequent loathing of everything associated with the Church of Rome.

In the early sixteenth century, the Giffordgate of Nungate comprised a tract of land on the east side of the River Tyne. This extended southward from the ford at Haddington to the Sandyford Burn, which flowed at the foot of the rise leading up to Slateford and Myreside, where it marched with the lands of Yester. All of this territory belonged to the Gifford and Hay Families of Yester. It comprised not only the area known as Nungate, but also the village known as Giffordgate, on the far side of the river from Haddington, and the whole of Lethington Estate. The village to the south which is today known as Gifford, it should be explained, was not created until 1680.[15]

In 1785, the Reverend George Barclay, who had become minister of St Mary's in 1766, observed, 'The house in the Giffordgate, in which Knox was born, still remains; it has but a mean appearance: and, together with two or three acres of land adjoining, belonged for centuries to a family of the name of Knox, until they were purchased, about ten or twelve years ago, by the present Earl of Wemyss.'[16]

In 1830, Peter Martine, who was born in 1775, wrote, 'Now there is not one stone of the house as the park where it stood was bought by Wm. Aitchison, a baker, and he removed every stone of the house and it cannot be found except by the people who had seen it before it was taken down.'[17]

On the instigation of the Scottish essayist Thomas Carlyle, a commemorative stone was laid and a sapling was planted in 1881 to mark the spot where the house allegedly stood.[18] To reconcile the debate as to whether or not Knox was actually born here or, as some still insist, in the village of Gifford itself, an oak from the Yester Estate was donated by the 10th Marquis of Tweeddale. It now spreads its branches wide over a circular enclosure, with modern houses to the side and behind.

Thomas Carlyle died a few weeks before the planting ceremony took place but had long been fascinated by the Reformer, encouraged by the knowledge that Jane, his wife, was descended from the marriage of Knox's youngest daughter Elizabeth to Jane's forebear, the Reverend John Welsh of Ayr. Jane was not alone in claiming the connection. Dr John Witherspoon, born in Gifford in 1772 and the only clergyman to sign the American Declaration of Independence, was Knox's great-great-grandson through the same line.[19]

However, a plethora of debate still surrounds Knox's early life – a period about which he himself chose to reveal virtually nothing. It is almost as if he had determined to cover his tracks. Perhaps, as a 'man of base estate and condition' he considered his birth and parentage of no consequence, although he must have known that this in itself would arouse curiosity.[20]

Writing in 1811, Dr Thomas M'Crie, the Church historian, gives the year of the Reformer's birth as 1505, an error which has been much repeated since and which also features on the Giffordgate memorial stone. Subsequent research, notably in 1905 by Dr Hay Fleming, confirms that Knox must have been born considerably later, in all likelihood between 1513 and 1515. Does this really matter? Well, it does insofar as it has been claimed by some writers that Knox's Sinclair mother died young and that his father, William Knox, re-married and died in the service of the Earl of Bothwell, fighting for James IV against the English at the Battle of Flodden in 1513. Victorians were prone to fantasy and, in the light of Hay Fleming's research, such details simply do not stack up. On the evidence that Knox was in his mid fifties when he suffered his first stroke in 1568, and that he was in his late fifties when he died in 1572, it is safe to assume that he was born in either 1514 or the following year, so his father could not have died at Flodden.

The key to Knox's early credentials, however, is that, for the time in which he lived, he was highly literate. This at least indicates that his parents, or whoever was responsible for his upbringing, had the means to support him and his brother William, who later became a successful merchant in Preston. So we first find the two boys enrolled at the Grammar School of Haddington and it was here, 'musing in the shades of its monkish cloisters, and poring over his favourite St Jerome and St Augustine, that he imbibed those free ideas of church government which afterwards astonished the world'.[21] Afterwards, at St Andrews, he studied divinity under John Major (or Mair), yet another potent East Lothian-born revisionist (see Chapter 27).

Even after the passing of four centuries, the shadow of Knox still looms massively over the Scottish psyche. In the multicultural, multi-faith society of the third millennium, I think it perfectly justifiable to wonder why.

For a start, with his wide-ranging proposals outlined in the *First Book of Discipline*, this man was directly responsible for the infant Church of Scotland's acceptance of Calvinism rather than Lutheranism. Although Knox's fundamentalism finds few admirers nowadays, he was certainly the key figure in the early stages of the Scottish Reformation and certainly deserves to be remembered for far more than the misogynist abuse he is accused of ladling out in the text of his *First Blast of the Trumpet against the Monstrous Regiment of Women*.

As for his relationship with the town of his birth, it is hard to assess the size of his following during his lifetime but it must have been substantial. Remember that, by the time he achieved real prominence, it was barely twenty years since Haddington had been garrisoned by the English and bombarded by French mercenaries and fellow Scots soldiers. Knox had been absent from the town for a decade but his contacts were everywhere. As has been noted, one friendship in particular was important and that was with David Forrest. Forrest's family had endowed the altar of the Three Kings of Cologne at St Mary's but following the siege, in company with almost the entirety of Lowland Scotland, turned Protestant. Tellingly, Knox received a generous pension from St Mary's.[22]

In revolutionary terms, there are undoubtedly similarities between John Knox and a modern middle-eastern Ayatollah – both sharing many of the same prejudices and convictions. A dogmatist endowed with genius, he brooked no opposition but, given the censorship of the Catholic Church and the brutal fate meted out to so many of his contemporaries, not least the stalwart George Wishart (see Chapter 14), his courage under assault was certainly admirable. Through the enforcement of strict moral guidelines, Scotland was, within the span of his lifetime, transformed from a Papist to a Protestant nation. This was not achieved by Knox alone, but it was his uncompromising commitment to the scriptures that played the central role in the transition. His platform of moral ascendancy has not been matched to this day.

And if it was a stern and unforgiving wisdom, in its wake came that indomitable sense of duty and personal sacrifice which we find embodied in the missionary zeal of the Victorians. For better or for worse, we Scots have moved on to live in a very different world with very different ideological values from those espoused by Knox, but his fundamental beliefs – ethical conduct and an aspiration towards educational excellence – remain. His legacy to Scotland should never be underestimated.

And all of this emanated from a modest Haddington suburb. Aware of this, Thomas Carlyle, Provost John Brook, a local merchant, James More of Monkrigg and others, including my great-grandfather, contributed in 1878 towards the building of a secondary school to be called The Knox Institute where, high up on the tower wall, was positioned a statue of the Reformer by the Victorian sculptor Sir Joseph Boehm. My grandfather Robert was among its first pupils and my father and uncles were also enrolled there in their early years. Generations to follow learned their first lessons in this austere institution until a major overhaul took place in 2005. The old Knox Institute building has since become a private retirement housing development.

Although still designated the market town of East Lothian, Haddington no longer ranks among the major towns of Scotland but, in some ways, this has been to its advantage. It has remained unspoiled. Its remarkable shape, resembling a crossbow, survives intact and many of its more spectacular buildings dating from the eighteenth and nineteenth centuries have withstood the test of time. Despite the ravages inflicted upon it in the first half of the second millennium and the intrusion of charity shops and a supermarket, it still combines a striking sense of its own dignity and physical beauty.

A few years ago, I was invited to a one-night performance in the Town Hall of the novelist Alanna Knight's play based on a local investigation conducted by her fictitious Victorian detective, Inspector Faro. As a member of the audience, I was transported back in time to the 1880s when my great-grandparents were actually living in the house next door to where the crime supposedly took place. It was a memorably surreal experience.

In an age obsessed with climate change, it would be inappropriate not to mention that other great Haddington saboteur – flood water. The havoc floods have wrought to the town ranks alongside the damage caused by the English invasions and the plague. Nobody knows for sure how many times the River Tyne has overflowed its banks but the earliest record dates from 1358, when the Nungate was swept away with considerable loss of life. Although there must have been many incidents in between, subsequent reports of further disasters start in 1421, when townsfolk entered St Mary's Kirk in a big boat, and lead on to the 4th October 1775, when the river rose 8 feet 9 inches, submerging half the town.

Great-great-grandfather Peter Martine used to say that nobody could ever mistake his age since he was born in the week of this particular flood. And, during the time of his birth, his future wife's uncle, Robert Forrest, had to spend a night up a pear tree in his garden. Not only was the Lauderdale Aisle in St Mary's penetrated but the wooden Chinese Bridge in the Haugh was swept away and its remains were later found on the sands at Tyninghame. In 1846, the waters yet again reached the Custom Stone and, in the autumn of 1891, on the Upper Mill Dam, a field of wheat belonging to Hugh Andrew of Acredales, with the produce of three acres, was completely carried away.

In the twentieth century, the flooding was back in 1931 and again in 1956 and 1984, leading to the conclusion that such incursions were operating on a twenty-five-year cycle. Only after ten bridges on the main-line railway line had been destroyed was a map of the flood plain finally drawn up and it became County planning policy to refuse permission for new buildings within it. Landowners alongside the riverbank were made responsible for clearing the debris of fallen trees and, in 1997, the Flood Prevention and Land Drainage Act made it mandatory for Scottish local authorities to monitor water levels at all times.

Haddington's town symbol of a goat was adopted as early as 1296 and, like many others, I was appalled when Haddington became a Burgh Council and it disappeared off the town's coat of arms in 1975. I was equally gratified when it was reinstated in 1979 as the coat of arms for the Royal Burgh of Haddington and District Community Council. Somehow the character of a goat – stubborn and resilient – seems to suit Haddington.[23]

But that still does not solve the puzzle of why it was chosen. Most Scottish towns, Galashiels with its 'soor plooms' and Glasgow with its St Mungo associations – the fish that never swam and the bird that never flew – have explanations for their emblems but Haddington does not. John Martine devotes a chapter to the subject in *Reminiscences of the Royal Burgh of Haddington* but reaches no conclusions. 'Perhaps their domestic habits, and the fact of their supplying food for man by their milk and flesh, and raiment by their skins and hair, suggested the idea . . .' is the best he could come up with, before going on to bemoan that in his day less than a dozen could be rounded up in the neighbourhood. Presumably they had all been skinned and eaten.

Towards the end of the 1950s, the population of Haddington stood where it had been for 100 years, in the region of 5,500. However, that was set to change. On the west coast of Scotland, a post-war decline accompanied by significant levels of unemployment, brought a critical housing shortage to the circumference of Glasgow, leading to the creation of new towns such as East Kilbride and Cumbernauld. As this took place, the Artillery Park Housing estate on the former site of Amisfield was developed at a cost of £304,500 and Glasgow families with a cross-section of skills were encouraged to move into the area to significantly increase Haddington's population.[24] A new era had begun.

For most of the twentieth century, the politics of East Lothian, with a consistently high turnout of voters, remained entertainingly unpredictable. In the 1922 general election, it was a tight three-way marginal with Labour, the Liberals and the Conservatives all within 9.65 per cent of each other.

In the 1923 general election, Berwickshire and Haddingtonshire, as the constituency was then called, was won by Labour's Robert Spence with a majority of sixty-eight. In 1931, it passed to the Conservatives.

After John J. Robertson, who held the newly formed Berwickshire and East Lothian constituency for Labour from 1945 until 1951, the parliamentary seat was kept for fifteen years by Sir William Anstruther-Gray of the Scottish Conservative and Unionist Party. It then fell to Labour's John Mackintosh for four years and was briefly returned to Michael Ancram of the Scottish Conservatives in 1974. Ancram held it until the second election of that same year when Mackintosh was re-elected, reflecting the fickle mood swings of the era.[25] In 1978, John Mackintosh was succeeded by John Home-Robertson who, with the re-introduction of the Scottish Parliament in 1999, was also elected a member of the devolved assembly, from which he stood down in 2007.

As editor of *Business Scotland* magazine in the late 1970s, I regularly encountered the late Professor John P. Mackintosh MP, an astute and likeable man. I last saw him in 1977, a year before his untimely death, when I drove him home from a conference in Glasgow. Some years later, in my capacity as editor of *Scottish Field*, I met his successor on a visit to Paxton, the Home-Robertsons' stately home in Berwickshire. To my mind – and I do not mean this in any uncomplimentary sense – both men were unlikely socialists in the old-fashioned understanding of the word. Politicians in the village that is Scotland can be mercifully unpredictable. At the general election of 2001, Home-Robertson was succeeded at Westminster by New Labour's Anne Picking and, in May 2007, Iain Gray, a former teacher and Scottish Justice Minister, was elected as the constituency's member for the Scottish Parliament.

Boundaries and personalities change but the volatile mainstream politics of East Lothian were epitomised by that great turn-of-the-century Liberal turned Labour statesman Richard Burdon Haldane who, towards the end of his career, was created Viscount Haldane of Cloan. Having in 1885 won the Haddington seat, which for the first time incorporated the burghs of Haddington, North Berwick and Dunbar, Haldane went on to hold it for over a quarter of a century. As Secretary of State for War, he reorganised the British Army, then served as Lord Chancellor of England in the governments of both H. H. Asquith and Ramsay MacDonald. Moreover, his East Lothian connections were beyond reproach. A century earlier, his grandfather, the evangelist preacher James Haldane, had built a chapel in Haddington's West Port. In 1815 he followed this up with the Baptist Chapel in Hardgate, thereby suggesting that the zeal to reform, though it might skip a generation or two, can be a hereditary compulsion.

The Haldanes built a house in Court Street which they called Haldane Cottage. This in time passed through the female line to the Cockburn family of Sandybed who, in 1868, altered their surname to Haldane so as to inherit the Gleneagles Estate in Perthshire. In 1881, Haldane Cottage was bought by my great-grandfather Dr William Martine, who built on an extension and renamed the property Weston, considering this to be more in keeping with its location in the West Port of the town. After that, the Martine family occupied Weston for fifty-five years until my grandfather's retirement, when it was sold to the East Lothian County Constabulary and Fire Brigade. The medical practice in the surgery adjoining the house continued until 1985, when it moved to a purpose-built medical centre in Newton Port. The extensive orchard to the rear of the house was, to begin with, run as a nursery garden but has since been transformed into a small housing development. Only the street façade of Weston remains unchanged, with a blue lamp inserted into the old wrought iron fitting above the front door.[26]

CHAPTER FIVE

Bibles, Books and Postage Stamps

THE FOUR ORPHANED children of John and Margaret Martine moved into Haddington from Westfield of Lethington in 1736 and there are now over twenty-five of their descendants to be found commemorated on memorial stones in St Mary's churchyard.

It must have been a traumatic transition for them. Thomas, the eldest, never recovered from the loss of his parents and, having entered the home of John Cadell, a close family friend, on 2 February, died there two months later. John Cadell was the brother of William Cadell who, in the absence of a will, was appointed Thomas Martine's executor. In the century that followed, their Cadell descendants were to become iron masters and coal owners, developing the salt and vitriol (sulphuric acid) works at Cockenzie (see Chapter 17).

Meanwhile, the three surviving Martine children were boarded with relatives, and John was indentured to William Kirkwood, a cabinet maker for five years, subject to the conditions that 'should John shall happen to commit the sins of fornication, or adultery, as God forbids, during the said space, he obliges himself to serve his said Master, two years after the expiry'.[1] In addition, he was also expressly forbidden to drink excessively or to play cards or dice or other unlawful games at unreasonable times – quite a load of restrictions for a teenager to be burdened with in any generation.

Yet, having completed his apprenticeship four years earlier, he must surely have witnessed Colonel Gardiner's Government Dragoons lined up in Haddington's High Street on the eve of the Battle of Prestonpans in 1745. Indeed, several of his contemporaries and friends volunteered as Government Scouts but John had the sense to keep his distance. For, despite the hold of the Hanoverian-supporting Protestant Kirk on the hearts and minds of its congregation, Jacobite sentiment ran rife throughout the Lothians. Only three days earlier, in Edinburgh, John's kinsman, Alexander Martine, Islay Herald at the Court of the Lord Lyon, had accompanied Robert Chalmers of Portleithen, Ross Herald, to read out Prince Charles's

Proclamation of Regency before a cheering crowd at the Mercat Cross, an action for which they were both later dismissed.[2]

These were unsettled and uncertain times in Scotland but, contrary to expectations, John did well not as a cabinetmaker but as a successful tanner. Quite why he should have taken up this particular trade is unknown but tanning was soon to become a booming industry in Haddington and would make him comfortably well off.

Once a week, the folk of the surrounding countryside would arrive in town to purchase leather goods and items of clothing, exchanging them for poultry, eggs, grain and fruit. John, an astute businessman, prospered. Around 1765, aged over forty, he married Isabella Carfrae, daughter of Patrick Carfrae of West Garleton, and they had two sons and four daughters, the first and third of the girls dying young.

In 1781, when aged almost sixty, he was elected Provost of Haddington and, the following year, he took on the added responsibility of County Post Master with an annual salary of £25. In addition to owning a tenement of houses and a yard in the Nungate, the family now occupied a property which had previously been owned by the Halyburtons of Eaglescairnie. This was directly opposite Haddington House on the Sidegate.

Within ten years of each other, the eldest son, yet another John, and the youngest, Peter, married two sisters, Alison and Janet Forrest, daughters of a prosperous farmer at Gullane. Margaret Martine, the eldest surviving daughter, married Dr Alexander Maitland from a branch of the Lauderdale Family, a great grandson of the builder of Haddington House. Agnes, the youngest daughter, married her cousin William Hunter, a baker, brewer and banker who, for many years, campaigned for the abolition of slavery and survived to see his fondest wishes in this respect realised.[3]

John Martine senior died in 1812 aged eighty-seven, having lived long enough to witness his eldest son John follow him as Provost for the first time in 1807. By then, the tannery business had expanded to include a tenement and yard in the Nungate and the family were modestly affluent. This third John Martine's contribution to Haddington was especially notable in regard to the rescue and restoration of what then remained of St Mary's Church but, in retrospect, it was soon apparent that it was at the expense of his other interests.

During the Reformation, the Protestant mob had ransacked places of worship throughout Scotland, failing to differentiate 'between these places of idolatorie, and many parish kirks where God's word should have been preached'. As a result, the eastern part of St Mary's remained un-roofed, the quire had been destroyed, the arches that canopied its storied windows were broken and its altars demolished, and every item associated with the image of a saint was mutilated.

St Mary's Parish Church was therefore reduced to half of its former size and, with no opportunity to expand outwards, it was decided to wall off the east end and create galleries for extra seating. These were known as lofts and, to begin with, were allocated to various families. Local landowners had their lairds' lofts and, before long, the local magistrates decided that they would like one too, rapidly followed by the nine Trades Incorporations – Baxters, Hammermen, Masons, Wrights, Fleshers, Cordiners, Skinners, Tailors and Weavers. Each balcony front was decorated with an appropriate motif to identify its occupants.

In such a relatively small community, trade associations strongly influenced the social fabric of the town and pretensions ran high. There was much jostling for rank and position and, as a conciliatory gesture, the town magistrates introduced the practice of inviting the Convenor of the Deacons of Trades to join them in their pew on Sundays. That was until 1809, when a much disliked coppersmith and tinsmith called George Harley was elected to the post and the magistrates issued instructions that, under no circumstances, would his company be welcome. On this being conveyed to the Trades, however, it was seen as an affront and Mr Harley was encouraged to take his seat regardless. Anticipating this, the magistrates directed that, should he attempt to do so, the Town Officer was to exclude him by force. Harley nonetheless remained resolute and, when he found his entry barred, clambered over the public pews in front. It comes as no surprise therefore to learn that this caused a great uproar just as the Reverend Dr Robert Lorimer was preparing to address the congregation.

Inevitably, such unseemly behaviour gave rise to much disapprobation as well as hilarity. In a ribald response, notices commemorating the event were posted on church doors and on buildings throughout the town.

HADDINGTONSHIRE KIRK THEATRE

This is to give notice to the inhabitants of Haddington and vicinity that, on Sunday next, the twelfth current, there will be repeated in the Haddington Kirk Theatre, the celebrated tragedy which was enacted there last Sunday, on which occasion the characters will be supported by the following gentlemen:

Harlequin Jumper Mr Ha[r]ly
Boxall Mr Ma[r]tine
Judge Fair Mr De[a]ns
Ganint [Old Scots meaning 'suitable'] Helper Mr Do[nald]son[4]

But, in the first decade of the nineteenth century, something other than parochial one-upmanship was taking place. Church attendance had risen dramatically and increasingly there was not enough space to accommodate the number of worshippers turning up for Sunday services. Matters rapidly came to a head and, following a complaint to the Presbytery, it was even suggested that St Mary's be demolished to make way for a new and larger parish church.

On 16 October 1806, a group of the Church heritors, comprising Lord Hepburn, Alexander Houston of Clerkington and Robert Stewart of Alderston, met with Provost John Martine, Bailie James Deans and George Banks, Dean of Guild, to discuss the situation.[5] The heritors, needless to say, were anxious to know how much this was all going to cost them and, before anything could get started, demanded confirmation as to how the expenditure was to be divided up between them and the town. Furthermore, the number of seats required had to be agreed.

There followed a protracted wrangle during which time the heritors attempted to stall the situation and the nine incorporated trades bodies decided to lay claim to their rights. Nothing ever changes, does it?

Following his first term as Provost, John Martine became Dean of Guild and, showing infinite patience and shrewd diplomacy, set about brokering an agreement between the various factions. The Town Council, representing the community, agreed to meet half the costs on the understanding that the landward heritors were relieved of all claims. As a gesture, the 3rd Earl of Hopetoun, his family by then established in Hopetoun House at South Queensferry, conceded his patron's seat in the gallery to the town magistrates.

Although the ruined east end of the existing church remained untouched, work on the habitable portion began in 1810 under the supervision of Archibald Elliot, the architect of St Paul's Episcopal Church in Edinburgh. Old seating was removed, the interior arches were cut up and raised to make room for new galleries and the floors were re-laid.[6] By 1813, the year in which John Martine was once again elected Provost, the medieval Parish Church of St Mary's was back in business.

Hanging on a wall in my parents' home for the duration of my childhood was a cartoon of a trio led by a thin man wearing a tricorn hat and gripping a pibroch. I always wondered who he was and I now know that he was James Livingstone, the Haddington Piper, a former soldier who had fought under the Duke of Cumberland at the Battle of Fontenoy in present-day Belgium on 11 May 1745. That was two months before Prince Charles Edward Stuart set off from France to rally his Jacobite supporters in Scotland. In the conflict that followed, Livingstone no doubt supported the government and afterwards retired on a pension to Haddington.

Haddington had its town piper as far back as 1542 and a drummer by 1572, when the town treasurer was instructed to buy a *swasche*, a 'drum'. The purpose of this was to awaken the townsfolk at four in the morning and encourage them to go to their beds at eight in the evening.[7] The practice continues. In 1831, the architect James Gillespie Graham was commissioned to replace Haddington's Town House steeple, and to this day a bell is sounded at 7 a.m. and 10 p.m.

Another of the second Provost John Martine's principal interests was the town library which, for many years, was housed in a room in the Haddington Burgh School in Court Street. Possibly because it was where pupils were taught to read and write, this school was known as the 'English School'. It was the practice of the magistrates of the Burgh to meet in this room every Sunday before progressing to St Mary's wearing their chains of office, escorted by the town officers with shouldered halberds and dressed in the town's livery. Provost John's son, the writer, in 1883 describes their attire as follows:

> The coats and surtouts were of the old fashioned cut, with single collar and broad lapels, well trimmed with black braid, and mounted with large black buttons; long waistcoat, short-kneed trousers, black leggings and cockades on their hats. The cloth was of a coarse darkish grey colour, which was long manufactured in the town and called Gilmerton grey.

In the year 1717, a valuable collection of books, largely works of divinity, had been donated to the town by the Haddington-born Reverend John Gray, minister of Aberlady, and this became the nucleus of one of the oldest libraries in Scotland. Accompanying the gift was 3,000 merks Scots, the interest from which was to be devoted to charitable purposes. Of this sum, 25 merks Scots was set aside to support the library and, in 1807, the Town Council voted a further allowance of £2 10 shillings annually for the same purpose, allowing several additions to the collection to be made. John Martine devotes a chapter of his reminiscences to Haddington's library and the great significance attached to John Gray's generosity. He also exposes the guilt of those who failed to return books and who were, in the majority, clergymen.

In 1880, Gray's books were transferred to a former church in Newton Port. This building, built on the site of a malt store, had previously belonged to the East United Presbyterian Church which merged with the Free Church in 1852 and became known as the Knox Church. Robert Baillie was the last trustee of the congregation. He was a shepherd at Coates, a farm partly between Haddington and Garvald, and, in 1880, he sold the old church building to Haddington Council for £120. As the twentieth century progressed, concern over the preservation of the Gray bequest increased and, in 1961, the collection was loaned to the National Library of Scotland. As from

2010, however, a purpose-built Gray's Library, incorporating the headquarters of the Local History Centre and Archives and a long-overdue Haddington Museum, is to open in Lodge Street, at the end of Court Street, an exciting development of which Provost John Martine would most certainly have approved.

The position of Post Master in late Hanoverian and Victorian Britain was an important one. Prior to the introduction of Royal Mail coaches in 1786, letters and packages were carried on horseback, using a relay of mounts, and the schedule was erratic. All of this changed with the Turnpike Acts of the mid eighteenth century and the building of the Great North Road from London, which fortuitously passed straight through Haddington's town centre.

In 1812, John Martine Senior was succeeded as Post Master by his youngest son Peter. The Post Office was then located in the Sidegate but, in 1818, Peter moved it to the 'Custom Stone' and, later, to a purpose-built property in the High Street, in close proximity to where the coaches stopped at the George Inn.

In 1827, he purchased a house in the Back Street (now Market Street) for £170 and in this house his family were born. His next-door neighbour, incidentally, was Samuel Smiles, a former paper maker turned general merchant and shopkeeper, who is probably best remembered as the father of the celebrated author of *Self-Help*. Smiles Senior, however, was far from being an ideal neighbour and there were several altercations over 'easements'.[8]

Postage rates in the early nineteenth century were as follows:

a single letter from Edinburgh 5½d
a double letter from Edinburgh 10½d
a single letter from London 1s 1½d
a double letter from London 2s 2½d

The letters were charged at a universal rate no matter where they were going and it was their departure point that determined how much you paid. Letters which had been prepaid were marked in red and unpaid ones in black.[9]

For the most part, they were delivered by James 'Letter a Penny' Anderson, who was succeeded by his daughter Kirstie and a Mrs Bell, who carried the letters in her white apron. Their wages were one halfpenny for delivering each letter in the town area and one penny for delivery out of town. In 1844, the London and Edinburgh Mails arrived and departed at midnight. The Haddington and Dunbar postbags were forwarded by the same stagecoaches.[10]

Mail coaches during this period stopped in the High Street at the George Inn (later George Hotel) to change horses and allow refreshments for the passengers.[11] Many years later, the historian and author J. H. Jamieson, then Rector's Clerk at Edinburgh Academy, informed my father that his grandmother, when a very young girl, had been employed by Peter Martine to carry the mail daily to and from Haddington and Gosford House and for this long walk she was paid the handsome sum of twopence, with a cup of tea.

Peter Martine latterly acquired the property Maryville in Station Road, where he died at the age of ninety in 1865. Alas, by then a serious family rift had come about between him and his brother, Provost John. Writing on the subject a century later, my father observed, 'With so many living in each other's pockets, so to speak, such schisms within a family were not uncommon, and the split in this case appears to have been a complete one.'

Further enlightenment is found in notes attached to Peter's will of 1865:

> If any money that is due to me is ever got back from either my late brother's widow, or from any of his family, it must be equally divided between my three [surviving] sons – the amount due to me is entered in a book, but no interest is charged on the account. It was for money lent to my brother and nephew, besides the thousands I had lent to my brother without interest to enable him to carry on his business [tanning]. Otherwise he would be bankrupt long before he gave up business, and I have been rewarded like a great villain by them.[12]

Ten years before his death, a greater tragedy had struck. Peter's eldest son, yet another John, had succeeded his father as Post Master. On 15 October 1855:

> . . . having just mounted his horse for the purpose of going to the county, the animal suddenly ran off and, getting unmanageable, galloped furiously to the bottom of a hill, where, failing to make a turn, it dashed its rider with terrible violence against a stone wall . . . Amiable manners, first rate business habits, and the highest respectability, had procured for Mr Martine the esteem of the whole community who greatly mourn his loss and deeply sympathise with the afflicted family.[13]

The Martines do not appear to have had much luck with their horses.

Through his wife's family, the Forrests, the second Provost John inherited Morham Bank, a quiet and substantial Georgian house three miles south of

Haddington, and here John died in 1849. At this juncture, the ongoing repetition of family Christian names becomes even more complex to understand because, in 1811, he had also christened his second son John. For some years, this John Martine ran a brewing business in Sidegate, which he operated until 1863, when he moved to Portobello to run a grain-commissioning agency. In 1864, he married Jane Thompson from Gateside, near Newcastle, and, when his mother died two years later, he succeeded to the property of Morham Bank. A victim of the changing nature of agriculture, he soon rented out the house and farm and retired to live in Edinburgh.

However, this move was to be the beginning of an entirely new vocation that was to make him famous. Returning to visit his native town on Corn Exchange days, John came into contact with the brothers David and James Croall, then busy building up the circulation of their weekly newspaper, the *Haddingtonshire Courier*, which they had founded in 1859. Recognising the retired farmer as a useful source of local information, they entertained him lavishly and out of this came regular articles for their periodical. These were eventually compiled into book form, the final volume of which was published three years after his death in 1894.

Peter Martine's fourth son, William, first cousin to the writer John Martine and my great-grandfather, was born in 1828 and it was he who founded the family's medical practice in Haddington. A man of considerable scholastic and professional attainment, he was educated at the local burgh school before proceeding to Edinburgh University where, in 1846, he graduated in medicine before he was twenty-one years of age. After twelve months working as a junior doctor in Fife, where he met his future wife Jessie Dun, he secured an appointment with the Edinburgh Maternity Hospital and worked under his old college chief, Sir James Young Simpson. During his subsequent professional connection with Haddington, he experienced the outbreak of cholera, a disease in which he specialised, and, for nineteen years, he was Surgeon Major to the Haddingtonshire Militia. In 1894, he was co-opted as Medical Officer to the then Western District Fever Hospital, which later became known as Herdmanflat Hospital. Records that he left behind him showed that he had attended 2,450 births.

On a civic and more commercial level, however, he was one of the founders of the Haddington Gas Works Company. In its day, this old gas works, managed by James Robb and a Mr Blair, provided a first-class lighting service in the town, taking over as it did from oil lamps. In time, it too was taken over by the South of Scotland Electricity Board and, as technology raced ahead, was gradually closed down.

But the rigours of visiting up-country patients involved long hours and being out in all weathers and eventually this took its toll on William, who died of heart trouble in 1895 at the age of sixty-nine. His son William Robert, having graduated from Edinburgh University and secured an appointment as a House Surgeon at the Royal Infirmary, immediately returned to Haddington to take over his father's practice. He was aged only twenty-four and the arrival of a young unmarried doctor caused a degree of concern among his father's more established patients. Summoned before Mrs Fletcher of Saltoun, for example, he was informed that, with a number of adolescent daughters to consider, it was out of the question that a bachelor of his years should attend on them. Fortunately, her views were in the minority and the practice flourished.

Like the majority of Victorian country practitioners, my grandfather's rounds were made by horse and trap. Not surprisingly, when the motor car first appeared, he was among the first to appreciate its potential. Of course, not everyone agreed with him. On 8 July 1904, the *Haddingtonshire Courier* carried details of a lawsuit between Charles Russell, farmer at Westfield on Lennoxlove, and the Western Committee of the Community Council. Whilst driving in his cart to Haddington, Mr Russell's horse had been startled by a motor tricycle belonging to Dr Martine and, swerving to the side of the road where there was an open ditch, the driver was overturned into it. The damages of £12 which Mr Russell sought were not, however, from my grandfather but from the Community Council, whom he held responsible for the inadequate fencing of the road. Fortunately nobody was harmed on this occasion but the incident must have aroused uncomfortable echoes of our ancestor's untimely end on the same stretch of farmland two centuries earlier.

The first motor car in Haddington belonged to another physician, Dr Robert Howden of Maitlandfield. My father described it as 'an extraordinary vehicle with tiller steering, carriage wheels and numbered SS1'.[14] Grandfather Martine, so as not to be upstaged, bought a Clement-Talbot, numbered SS8. It was powered by a battery with an entrance door to the back and a mass of brassware in front. In 1908, he replaced this with a two-seater Renault 8HP, plated SS28, the twenty-eighth car to be registered in Haddington. However, he never enjoyed driving himself and retained John Black, a former cavalry soldier who had served in the Boer War as batman to Prince Francis of Teck, as his driver.

One of my father's earliest memories was of a night bell ringing somewhere downstairs in the house followed by a brief mumble through a window and, moments later, hearing the clip-clop of horses setting off on a trip into the countryside to deal with some remote casualty, with John Black in charge. In those days people expected, and usually received, medical attention at any hour of the day or night. It was therefore John Black who saw my grandfather through the transition from horse to motor car. However, being a Reservist, he was called up for military service in 1914. A year later he was killed in France serving with the ASC (Motor Transport).

In addition to the demands of being a family doctor, my grandfather succeeded his father as the Superintendent of the County Fever Hospital and was appointed Parish Medical Officer for Morham, Athelstaneford, Garvald and Gifford. Being also Surgeon Lieutenant to the 7th Volunteer Battalion of the Royal Scots, he was rarely idle.

Photographs of family life at Weston show croquet on the lawn, tennis matches and the comings and goings of friends and relatives. As they grew older, my father and his brothers were sent to schools in Edinburgh – with Uncle Will going to Fettes College and my father and Uncle Dave attending Edinburgh Academy – and where they lodged, during the week, with their maternal grandmother in Great King Street. Of her it was said that 'all were welcome in her house except those who spoke ill of Mr Gladstone'.[15]

Also growing up in Haddington, but two years older than my father, was William Gillies, the painter of Lowland Scotland landscapes. He was born in Haddington in 1898, the son of John Gillies, owner of a tobacconist shop in the High Street and whose family later moved to a newly built house, Westlea, at Meadow Park on the fringe of the town.

William Gillies's early aptitude for art was actively supported by his parents and, in particular, by his uncle, William Ryle Smith, who taught art at a school in Broughty Ferry. From an early age, Gillies accompanied his uncle on sketching expeditions. Encouraged by Miss Fordyce, the art teacher at the Knox Institute, of which he was to become dux, his work was soon brought to the attention of R. A. Dakers, who, in addition to being editor of the *Haddingtonshire Courier*, regularly exhibited his own paintings at the Royal Scottish Academy. Dakers, recognising a rising young talent, allowed him to make use of his studio.

William Gillies enrolled at Edinburgh College of Art in 1916, but the following year was called up to join the 10th Battalion, Scottish Rifles at Arras. Before being discharged in 1919 he was wounded twice and gassed. On returning to Edinburgh, however, he was awarded a travelling scholarship to London. His future looked promising until, a year later, when his father died. Fortunately, a close bond existed between him and his eldest sister, Emma, who took over the family business, and she continued to support him in his studies. In 1922, he gained his diploma and, with contemporaries such as William Crozier and William MacTaggart, a future President of the RSA, formed the 1922 Group.

Although for many years he made his home in the Midlothian village of Temple, Gillies retained a deep affection for his birthplace. Writing of his childhood, he reminisced:

The shops were the greatest interest. First, my own father's, the tobacconist's at 5 High Street, with Cunningham, the clothier, and Nisbet the fishmonger on either side. Close by was the high class dressmakers, owned by the three Misses Frier. Miss Thomson's china shop, Leslie the chemist's, Hutchison the bookseller, and Barrie's and Ramsay's boot-maker shops, Hardie the harness-maker, Spiers the barber, and McNeill's and Wilson's, long-established family grocers.

There was a magnificent mahogany counter in Wilson's, which was fed and polished with linseed oil every week. I hope it's still there! Mention of the mahogany counter brings up that treasure house of antiques, Leslie and Leslie (Ronnie will be the owner today), a marvellous shop.

What a host of characters the mere recital of names conjures up, and I must not forget Brown & Murray's, the ironmonger, that huge shop that could supply anything you could ask for, or the pie shop in Kilpair Street, wonderful tuppeny pies!

What a busy place Haddington was on a Friday when the farmers from miles around came to the market in their gigs. I remember it was my job to place the weekly tobacco parcels in those gigs at the various yards of the hotels – like 'the George', where the horses were stalled for the day.

Talking of farmers, quite a few may still recall the dashing, sporty figure of Hugh Andrew of Acredales, riding into town daily on his well-groomed horse. He was a great hero of mine. For years I used to fill in the shape of the spots on his calves in the book of outlines of cattle, when he registered them.[16]

In 1946, William Gillies was appointed Head of Drawing and Painting at Edinburgh College of Art and, in 1960, he was made Principal. By then he was rapidly being acclaimed as one of the leading Scottish artists of his generation.

In a letter to a friend, his sister Janet recalled:

> When I look back to our childhood days, I feel so thankful that we were all born in Haddington and the grand East Lothian farms all around us. We spent our young days rambling among the farms and country lanes. He [William] used to sketch so well and got such enjoyment out of life.[17]

Despite my father's reluctance to return to live again in Haddington, I am certain that he shared her sentiment.

CHAPTER SIX

Antiquarian Notes

On a nostalgic visit to Weston with Dr Jimmy Richardson in 1974, my father became uncharacteristically agitated over the fate of an ancient tombstone that had once been a feature of his grandfather's orchard wall. This stone commemorated Sir James Stanfield MP of Newmilns and, like Sir James himself, it had enjoyed a chequered history.[1]

Sir James, a Yorkshire man, had started up a cloth-making business under the patronage of Oliver Cromwell during the Commonwealth period in the seventeenth century. However, in 1687 his body was found floating in a stretch of river near his mill. Now Sir James's son, Philip, was a profligate young man with a taste for alcohol. Violent arguments were known to take place regularly between father and son but, on the November morning when Philip roused the household to report that his father was dead, it was assumed that Sir James had committed suicide and his body was taken without further ado for interment in Morham Kirkyard.

Then the rumours started and, before long, they had reached Edinburgh. Sir James was an influential man and the Lord Advocate wasted no time in despatching two surgeons to conduct an autopsy. These men arrived at Morham late in the evening and the exhumation of Sir James's corpse took place after dark by the light of lanterns. It must have been a gruesome spectacle and, irrespective of what the surgeons actually discovered, an incident occurred which sealed the fate of Philip.

As the corpse was being replaced in its coffin, wounds in Sir James's neck began to bleed. This, in the superstitious climate of seventeenth century Scotland, was regarded as clear evidence of murder and, in this instance, can claim to be the last recorded incident where an accused was convicted by 'touch'. The wretched Philip, being the obvious suspect, was immediately sent for trial, found guilty of patricide and taken to the Mercat Cross in Edinburgh where his tongue was cut out and he was burnt on the scaffold. His right hand was then cut off and affixed to the East Port of Haddington. His body was, thereafter, carried to the Gallowlee between Leith and Edinburgh, where it was 'hanged up in chains'. They were certainly thorough in those days.

Following the post-mortem, Sir James's remains were reburied in the west side of St Mary's Churchyard and a large and ornate tombstone was erected against a wall. Two hundred years later, when the church renovations of 1891 were taking place, it was decided to demolish this wall and the weathered tombstone, by then broken into two pieces, was jettisoned. My great-grandfather, on coming across the pieces, had asked if he could have them and they were later built into the garden wall at Weston. On discovering that they were no longer there in 1974, it was natural for my father to wonder what had become of them.

There followed an embarrassed silence on the part of East Lothian Constabulary until it emerged that when the property had been divided up between the police, the fire station and Weston Nurseries, the then Chief Constable of East Lothian, William Merrilees, later Chief Constable of Edinburgh and Peebles, had much admired the stones and taken them to his Edinburgh garden. A high-profile and colourful character, the Chief Constable was the last person anyone would ever have accused of absconding with a gravestone.

Needless to say, the matter was followed up, and the two halves returned to Haddington by an apologetic Willie Merrilees. For three decades thereafter, they were fixed to a wall in the hallway of the town library in Newton Port but in 2007, following complaints that they frightened schoolchildren, they were removed for safekeeping to the Haddington Museum collection.

Sir James's Cloth Manufactory stood at Newmilns, half a mile north-east of Haddington, on land which then belonged to the Cistercian nunnery, and remarkably it continued to function until 1713, when it closed down and the site, including half the barony of Morham, was sold to Colonel Francis Charteris. Incorporating Abbey Mill, the grain mill of the monastery of Haddington, Colonel Charteris renamed his estate Amisfield, after a property which his family already owned in Dumfries.

Gambler, loan shark and womaniser, money was no object to Francis Charteris, who was immortalised in the artist William Hogarth's paintings *The Rake's Progress* and *The Harlot's Progress*. Before purchasing the Newmilns estate, he had served in the British Army as a Cornet of Dragoons under the Duke of Marlborough but, having cheated at cards and ruthlessly relieved several fellow officers of considerable sums of cash, he was tried by court martial in Brussels and discharged.

In 1730, Charteris was once again brought to trial, this time accused of raping a servant girl, a crime for which he was sentenced to death and then pardoned by George II. Somewhat subdued, he retreated to Scotland where he died two years later. But further humiliation was to follow. Stirred up by the pamphleteers of his time, some might say the equivalent of our tabloid press, his funeral procession on its way to Greyfriars Kirkyard in Edinburgh, was attacked by the mob and dead cats were thrown into his grave.[2]

However, all was not lost. Colonel Charteris had married Helen, the daughter of Sir Alexander Swinton, a Court of Session Judge who held the courtesy title of Lord Mersington. In 1720, their only daughter Janet married James, 5th Earl of Wemyss, and it was to their youngest son, Francis Wemyss, that the Colonel's East Lothian estates passed on his death. Given his grandfather's widespread notoriety, it seems a little confrontational that he should have wanted to adopt the Charteris surname but then, at the same time, the Wemyss surname was not exactly in favour either.

On the eve of the Battle of Prestonpans, Francis married Lady Frances Gordon, daughter of the 2nd Duke of Gordon, and the bridal party, progressing from Prestonhall to Amisfield, mischievously caused great alarm among the government troops quartered nearby who assumed them to be the approaching Jacobite army. It was well known that the deceased Duke of Gordon had supported the Old Pretender in 1715 and also that Lord Elcho, Francis's elder brother, was aide-de-camp to Prince Charles Edward Stuart, so there was just cause to be suspicious.

Elcho's baptism in battle came the following day at Prestonpans and, whilst Francis Charteris remained neutral, it did begin to look as if the elder brother had backed the winning side. As the Jacobite army surged south, their numbers swelled. Then somebody decided to turn back from Derby.

With the Jacobite rout at Culloden Moor in the following spring, Elcho fled to France with a price on his head. His lands were confiscated under the Act of Attainder but he defiantly continued to make use of his titles, as did his brother Francis when his turn came to inherit them. With a more than substantial legacy to play with, Francis, the future de jure 7th Earl of Wemyss, in 1756, commissioned the English architect Isaac Ware to commence the building of Amisfield House using the site of his grandfather's less ambitious residence, which he pulled down.

According to the architectural historian Ian Gow, this Francis Charteris 'was to develop into the greatest patron of architects in eighteenth-century Scotland, constantly testing new talent and always in search of fresh ideas'.[3] For yet more improvements to Amisfield, he commissioned the young architect John Henderson in 1784 but, having that same year purchased the Gosford Estate, he became increasingly preoccupied with building his second grand house and made Amisfield over to his eldest son, Lord Elcho, whom John Martine describes as 'a public spirited nobleman who did much good to the burgh and county of Haddington'.[4] Following Elcho's death, his son, another Francis, having inherited Gosford from his grandfather, succeeded his cousin, William Douglas, in 1810, to the earldom of March, a title previously held by the ducal Queensberry Family. With the March earldom came Neidpath Castle and estates in Peeblesshire and, by 1826, he had succeeded in having the Wemyss attainder reversed in favour of his son, who thereafter became the 8th Earl of Wemyss and 4th Earl of March.

With at least two significant houses, a Border keep and the acquisition of the elegant manor of Stanway in Gloucestershire through the 8th Earl's marriage into the English Tracy family in 1817, the Wemyss and March dynasty triumphed. From the nineteenth century onwards, they vacillated between one or the other of their homes, latterly making increasing use of Stanway and Gosford (see Chapter 19).

During the First World War, Amisfield became a prisoner-of-war camp and by the early 1920s had been abandoned, as its red freestone fabric had deteriorated beyond recovery. In 1928, it was sold to Richard Baillie & Sons of Pencaitland and demolished. Some of the stone was used to create the Vert Memorial Hospital, a gift to Haddington from John Vert of Oregon, an American property tycoon who had been born there in 1852. The remaining stone was used in the building of the clubhouse at Longniddry Golf Club and for Preston Lodge High School.

Something that you very soon become aware of in East Lothian is the intense interest shared by local people in the common history that surrounds them. Not only is this well evidenced by the continual flow of enquiries received by the Local History Centre under Sheila Millar and Craig Statham, but it is also to be seen in the local support given to such organisations as the East Lothian Antiquarian and Field Naturalists' Society. Founded in May 1924 by a group of local gentry, the ownership designations of the committee alone reflect the changes that have since taken place: Major Arthur Baird of Lennoxlove; Lieutenant-Colonel Patrick Hamilton-Grant of Biel; Sir Archibald Buchan Hepburn of Smeaton; and Sir J. Dobbie of Edinburgh. The former British Prime Minister, the Earl of Balfour, while living at Whittingehame, was the society's first, and to date, only Honorary President, with Major Baird as the first President and Lord Balfour's sister Alice as Vice-President. Colonel Hamilton-Grant became President in 1934 and was followed by the Reverend Marshall Lang in 1937. Gilbert Ogilvy of Winton took over in 1944. Then came Colonel Chichester de Windt Crookshank of Johnstounburn in 1948 and Lady Broun-Lindsay of Colstoun in 1949. Sir David Ogilvy Bt of Inverquharity, living at Winton succeeded her in 1979. Professor Rosalind Mitchison succeeded him in 1990 and was followed by Stephen Bunyan, the current President, in 2000. The 12th Earl of Wemyss was a Vice-President until his death, together with Sir Hew Hamilton Dalrymple.

Bt. Lord Wemyss, having held that office since 1949, was made an Honorary Life Member in May 2004, the sixtieth anniversary of the Society.

Since its beginning, the society has set out to pioneer not only the study of antiquities, archaeology and the local and natural history of East Lothian but, in addition, the collection and publication of relevant documentary evidence. Influenced over the years by its council and office bearers, who have included many distinguished figures such as George Murray, Dr Jimmy Richardson, Norman Cartwright, Professor Rosalind Mitcheson and Stephen Bunyan, the 'Transactions of the Society' continue to provide a treasure trove of academic papers.

And, in regard to this, it was my father's involvement with the antiquarians from the 1960s up until his death in 1984 which introduced me to many of the places I was to get to know well later in life – that and fishing, of course. To this day, I can vividly remember glimpsing the derelict mansion house of Clerkington behind trees on the far side of the River Tyne from Grant's Braes. Part of the original house was swept away in the flood of 1775 but it still had forty-three rooms, enough to accommodate Prince Arthur of Connaught on his visit in 1876. Latterly, it was bought by the Ford family and during the Second World War was occupied by the No. 405 Searchlight Company of the 4th/5th Battalion, The Queen's Royal Scots.

When I first saw Clerkington, it had recently been boarded up and sold by the racing driver John Ludovic Ford to Captain Tony Stevenson, then living at Seton House at Longniddry. It was a sad day when it was pulled down for land development.

The melancholic ghosts of great houses in fiction spring to mind – Thornfield Hall in *Jane Eyre*, Brideshead in *Brideshead Revisited*, Manderley in *Rebecca*, the House of Shaws in *Kidnapped* – all such places have their secrets. Clerkington House was once occupied by a branch of the Cockburns of Ormiston and, afterwards, by Robert Alexander Houston, Governor of Grenada. The Houston family's fortune at their Belmont home in Grenada was derived from slave ownership. It was, therefore, curious to find them domiciled in Haddington, where a particularly militant anti-slavery movement existed. It was led by William Hunter, who so tenaciously petitioned the Westminster Parliament on behalf of the Haddington Missionary Society.[5] With such associations, perhaps that was when the fate of Clerkington House was sealed. Yet, whenever I cast a fly, I still see those shuttered windows in my mind's eye. Alas, it serves no purpose being sentimental about the irretrievable and it would have needed a considerable fortune to save Clerkington.

On the other hand, Stevenson House, another fine property located over the Nungate Bridge, still stands in all its splendour. In 1624 John, the younger son of Matthew Sinclair of Longformacus, having amassed a fortune as a merchant in Edinburgh and, indeed, achieving the distinction of being elected Lord Provost of that city, purchased the estate and bought himself a Nova Scotia baronetcy into the bargain. Among his descendants were Sir Robert Sinclair, who represented Haddingtonshire in Parliament, and Sir John Gordon Sinclair, Admiral Lord Nelson's Ensign on HMS *Victory* at the Battle of Trafalgar.

Sir John entertained lavishly at Stevenson House and, following the withdrawal of the ladies after dinner, the port would be circulated with the dining room door locked from the inside. The key was then thrown out of the window with the instruction that it was not to be retrieved until the following morning.

Admiral Sir John died in 1863 and although his son, Sir Robert, married twice, there were no children. Following the death of his second wife in 1931, the three-storey mansion house was sold to William Brown Dunlop who, some years before Captain Tony Stevenson, had taken the lease on Seton House at Longniddry.

Dunlop died in 1946 and thereafter Stevenson House, which had been built around a square open courtyard with Georgian and Victorian 'improvements', was restored by his son John and daughter-in-law Betty. To accommodate John's two sisters, Jean Ronaldson and Isobel Dunlop, Mary Tindall, the architect wife of the county planner Frank Tindall, was employed to convert the laundry wing and coach house. It therefore became something of a family compound and, in 1958, was incorporated as the Brown Dunlop Country Houses Trust.

Over the years of their occupancy, the Dunlops hosted a series of memorable Christmas concerts given by the Saltire Singers and presided over by the conductor Hans Oppenheim. So far as I am concerned though, I shall always associate Stevenson House with a pug dog called Hernia – a pug bitch to be precise.

Hernia was the cherished pet and companion of Christian Orr Ewing, a scion of the well-known Stirlingshire family of that name but himself a citizen of Edinburgh and today a sometime gardener at Hamilton House in Prestonpans. In her colourful life, Hernia was to feature in such diverse media as the *Spectator*, *Harpers & Queen* magazine and even on Channel4's *Breakfast Television*. As devoted to her owner as he was to her, she barely ever left his side although she once experienced the indignity of being kidnapped for ransom by somebody Christian had met in a pub . . . or at least that was the story that went about at the time.

In 1996, at the age of thirteen, Hernia died and Orr Ewing was distraught until it was suggested by his friend Alistair Dunlop that she deserved an appropriate send-off from her many admirers. On a late summer morning in June, therefore, the earthly remains of Hernia Orr Ewing were committed to the ground and a tree planted in her name on the edge of a field on the Stevenson Estate. Forty mourners attended the ceremony while the rites were performed by a robed priest. Today, an urn on a pedestal marks the spot.

In 2000, Stevenson House was sold to Ray and Anita Green. I sometimes wonder if they are aware of the canine celebrity who lies in their field.

By 2006, my rediscovery of Haddington had centred on Kesley's Bookshop in Market Street. It began when Simon Kesley invited me to speak at the launch of a book of East Lothian photographs by Liz Hanson which also included an essay by Alistair Moffat, whom I had first met when he was director of the Edinburgh Festival Fringe. Today, Alistair writes prolifically on Scottish history and administers the Borders Book Festival in Melrose so he needed no introduction, but I was flattered to oblige. Simon and Susan Kesley deserve their success. Their bookshop combines a remarkably diverse selection of reading with a coffee shop and has become a Mecca for the local community.

By the time I had lunched with Councillor Ludovic Broun-Lindsay in the Poldrate and with Sheila Millar from the Haddington Library at the Peter Potter Gallery in the former Haddington Fire Station on the Sands, I was becoming seriously engaged with what twenty-first-century Haddington has to offer. I wonder what my father would think about that?

Established in 1976 by Peter Potter and Tom Criddle, the Peter Potter Gallery is run by a charitable trust and offers a lively programme of exhibitions, evening talks and concerts. When the weather obliges during the summer months, it is possible to lunch and dine out of doors at the Waterside Restaurant and Bistro, originally the Weir House, on the banks of the River Tyne. At the time of writing, the George Hotel, where I used to accompany my father to the Crow's Nest Bar, named after its one-time owner Provost Crow, awaits a complete refurbishment.

For an overview of the past century in Haddington, there is no better source than George Angus who, over his lifetime, has amassed a collection of 25,000 colour photographs, 6,000 of which feature Haddington and its immediate environs. His contribution to the Haddington archive is two volumes entitled *Haddington, Old and New*, a deeply nostalgic record of the changing face of the town he loves. He plans a third volume.

George was born and brought up at Alderston Lodge, about 20 feet outside the town boundary. One of his earliest memories, he told me, is of a playground collision with a boy called MacAlpine at Knox Academy, over seventy-five years ago, and being rushed to the doctor by the janitor Mr Murdoch, who was known as 'Whistler' because he 'siffled' a lot. He was taken to Dr Robarts[6] but protested, 'This is not my doctor!' So he went to see

Dr Martine, who stitched him up and gave him sixpence for being a good boy.

George's grandfather (also George) was born in Caithness, where *his* father was managing an estate. However, the family returned to Edinburgh for his education and, although he was scheduled to become a teacher, he took a post with the Inland Revenue. His first 'posting' was to their office in Haddington and there he developed a love of the town which lasted all of his life.

In later years, when he worked in the Edinburgh office, he used to arrange for his family to spend the summers in Haddington while he commuted. His youngest son, Alexander, was born in Edinburgh but educated in the Royal Burgh and spent most of his life there. 'Eck', as he preferred to be known, was rejected by the Royal Flying Corps and had to be satisfied with the Argyll and Sutherland Highlanders but, while serving with them, he was wounded and gassed in the First World War. Following the fashion of many Scottish families, he called his eldest son George, and this George had no difficulty in joining the Royal Air Force train in Canada as a navigator.

After the Second World War, George's final posting was to Kabrit, in the Suez Canal Zone. He used an old box camera and initially he had been shocked by the poor standard of the local developing and printing so was pleased when the young army officer he shared a room with showed him how to process his own films. Photography became his principal hobby and, in 1952, he switched to 35mm in order to use colour film.

Following five years' study at Edinburgh College of Art, George became an architect and worked for three years with Alexander Esmé Gordon and Stanley Ross-Smith, but his heart was always in aviation. Much to everyone's surprise, when he applied to rejoin the RAF again, his application was accepted and he returned for seventeen years as a navigator. When he retired for good from the RAF in 1973 he went back to architecture again and worked for a time with David Brown in Haddington. When regionalisation came along, he was offered a post with the County Architects Department, where he worked for fifteen years, before taking retirement from the Local Authority in 1989. Recently he has resigned from reading the talking newspaper for the blind and from riding shotgun on the Lunch Club bus, a local authority initiative to provide meals for pensioners.

Among George's collection are two photographs taken on Saturday, 3 December 1949 of his aunt, Helen Tinline, standing on the platform of Haddington station on the last day of scheduled passenger services. A railway historian reckons that George's photos are the *only* record of that fateful day. A recent view of the same location shows part of a row of small factory units and little trace of the old station remains. More recently, George has been lending sets of his 'Old and New' slides of Haddington to the Community Council so that they can feature them, complete with George's captions, on their website.

CHAPTER SEVEN

The Lamp of Lothian

IN THE IMMEDIATE aftermath of the Second World War, local authorities throughout Britain appeared to be determined to complete the work of the German Blitz. In a frenzy of architectural vandalism, it was almost as if anything that showed even the slightest resonance with the past was deliberately targeted for demolition.

Fortunately, a rearguard conservation movement soon emerged and, to this end, Haddington was immensely well served by its Town Clerk, John McVie, a solicitor, who began his tenure of office by persuading the Council not to demolish the Town House simply to ease the growing traffic bottleneck between Court Street and Market Street and the High Street. Instead, this fine municipal building, designed by William Adam in 1742 and housing the Town Council, the Sheriff Court and Town Jail, was restored with a complete refurbishment of interiors to honour Queen Elizabeth II's coronation in 1953.

And this, in turn, led to a general sprucing up of Haddington's town centre which, in 1967, happily coincided with the formation of the Lamp of Lothian Collegiate Trust, a charity set up to engage in the life of the local community. The concept originated from concerns expressed in the parishes of Bolton and Saltoun as to how to keep small rural communities viable. The idea of a 'whole community', with an ecumenical base and linking town and country, emanated from the 14th Duke and Duchess of Hamilton and soon involved a very wide spectrum of people and interests. The arts, for instance, proved a major catalyst, led by the actor Tom Fleming.

The first Lamp of Lothian trustees were the Duchess of Hamilton, the 12th Earl of Wemyss, Lady Broun-Lindsay, Mrs A. H. Greenlees and, by virtue of their offices, John Rattray, Chairman of East Lothian County Council and John Wood, Provost of Haddington.

As early as 1942, the East Lothian Antiquarian and Field Naturalists' Society had been discussing the possibility of rescuing Haddington House, an imposing mansion house in the Sidegate. This had been built c. 1650, at which time the front door was located at the foot of a turret stair to the rear of the building. However, a new entrance was later opened up on to the street and on the lintel above were carved the misleading date 1680 and the initials AM and KC, those of Alexander Maitland and his wife, Katherine Cunningham.[1] As a young man, Alexander Maitland was Chancellor and Factor to his relative, the 2nd Earl and 1st Duke of Lauderdale and, in July 1673, became a Burgess of Haddington.

An offshoot of the Maitlands of Schivas in Aberdeenshire, Alexander therefore belonged to an earlier branch of the Maitlands of Lauderdale. Both his father and grandfather before him were employed as servitors to the 1st Earl of Lauderdale, his grandfather Richard also becoming a Burgess of Haddington and his father Robert, Deputy Governor of the Bass.[2] 'It was normal practice to employ your relatives because you knew that you could count on them,' explained the 18th Earl of Lauderdale. 'Alexander, his father and grandfather were among quite a large number of Maitlands who benefited considerably from their being related by blood to the Lord Chancellor and the Duke.'

Alexander and Katherine had eight daughters and two sons and my interest was aroused because they were the great-grandparents of yet another Alexander Maitland (of Gimmersmills) who, around 1792, married as his first wife Margaret, sister of the second Provost John Martine. In 1797, this Alexander Maitland too became Provost of Haddington.

During the eighteenth and nineteenth centuries, the Sidegate of Haddington must have given the impression of being something of a Maitland compound. Maitlandfield, almost directly opposite St Mary's, was built as Bearford House in 1654 and, having been briefly occupied by Captain Roger Legge, General Monck's Commander in Haddington, it was bought by Francis Charteris, de jure 7th Earl of Wemyss. However, in the following century it was purchased and renamed Maitlandfield by Lieutenant Thomas Maitland of Pogbie, whose grandfather James was the brother of the builder of Haddington House.[3]

Maitlandfield stayed under Maitland ownership until it was sold in the 1840s to the Howden Family, who had accumulated a fortune as goldsmiths in Edinburgh. Thomas Howden served as Provost of Haddington in 1877 and his son Robert, a ship's doctor, and his grandson Thomas continued to live there into the twentieth century. During the Second World War, it was handed over to the Ministry of Food for offices and, in 1952, the British Transport Commission had taken it over to enable the widening of the Mill Wynd. In 1999 the house was purchased by the De Freitas family, who today run it as a luxury hotel.

Haddington House similarly remained a Maitland family home until the early nineteenth century, when it was acquired by James Wilkie, known as

'Old Justice Wilkie', the first agent of the Bank of Scotland in the town. From him it passed to his daughters, the Misses Wilkie, 'whose names for their affability and kindness of heart will long be remembered by all who knew them'.[4]

In 1948, Mr Purves, the then owner, offered to sell Haddington House for £1,500 and the Earl of Wemyss generously purchased the house on behalf of the East Lothian Antiquarians, proposing that it be endowed to the National Trust for Scotland. The only problem was that the society had no surplus funds for either an endowment or restoration and, besides, there was a sitting tenant, Harry Faunt, a retired fruiterer, whom it proved impossible to dislodge. When the property did eventually become vacant on his death in 1966, it was in such a state of decay that demolition seemed to be the only option. That was when the Duchess Elizabeth and the Hamilton and Kinneil Estates stepped in to purchase it for the princely sum of £4,700 on behalf of the recently formed Lamp of Lothian Collegiate Trust.

Both determined and eloquently persuasive, Duchess Elizabeth, who died in September 2008, was never one to sidestep a challenge. The daughter of a duke (Northumberland), married to a duke, and closely related by blood and through marriage to five other dukedoms (Argyll, Richmond and Gordon, Portland and Sutherland), she, if anyone, knew how to use social influence when it came to fund-raising for a good cause. Spurred on by a £1,000 bequest, she recruited both the Carnegie Trust UK and the Scottish Development Department and, two years later, restoration work on Haddington House commenced. The project architect was W. Schomberg Scott, well known for his work with the National Trust for Scotland and who, during the 1950s, had restored his own seventeenth-century home, Northfield House at Prestonpans (see Chapter 18).

In the meantime, the orchard garden of Haddington House, known as St Mary's Pleasance, had been sold to David Reid, son of Admiral Sir Peter Reid of Membland, who had obtained planning permission to build sheltered housing. This greatly concerned the Duke of Hamilton, who felt that the garden should remain with Haddington House as a whole and be kept for the benefit of the community. He therefore bought the four-acre orchard along with the planning permission himself, to prevent it from being developed.

With the Duke as Chairman, and Stewart Chalmers, the factor at Lennoxlove, as its first Secretary, the Haddington Garden Trust was formed. This was largely made possible through the Stanley Smith Garden Trust and, latterly, East Lothian District Council, which supplied a salaried gardener. Under the joint supervision of the Edinburgh-born botanist Sir George Taylor, a former director of London's Kew Gardens who lived at Belhaven, and Sir David Lowe, living at Gladsmuir, a pleached laburnum colonnade walk was introduced to lead from the house to the churchyard. A wildflower garden and a sunken garden were planted with fragrant seventeenth-century herbs. In 2006 it became part of a renewal project chaired by Dr David A. H. Rae, Director of Horticulture of the Royal Botanic Garden, Edinburgh.

In addition to becoming the headquarters of the Lamp of Lothian Collegiate Trust, Haddington House made a room available for the East Lothian Antiquarian and Field Naturalists' Society in which to keep their records. More importantly, it provided accommodation for exhibitions and concerts and housed community volunteers and university aspirants. For a couple of decades it therefore offered a much needed focal point for the town but, in 1994, the Trust transferred its headquarters to the Poldrate Mill and Haddington House was leased as office accommodation to East Lothian Council. Since 2008, the building has been occupied by the chartered surveyors and land agents Smiths Gore.

It was in a small house behind the Poldrate Mill that Sir Alistair Grant, a future Chairman and Chief Executive of the £2-billion Argyll Group and of Scottish & Newcastle Brewers, was brought up until the age of nine, when his family moved to Yorkshire. A gentle, scholarly man who loved horses and books, Alistair's financial skills were recognised early on by Argyll's founder, James Gulliver, whom he helped steer through the controversial Guinness/Distillers Company take-over battle of 1986.

Before taking up the post of Governor of the Bank of Scotland, he and his wife Judy had made the library wing at Tyninghame House their home (see Chapter 28). Alistair was proud of his East Lothian roots, and in 1997 succeeded Duchess Elizabeth as Chairman of the Lamp of Lothian Collegiate Trust. His early death in 2001 at the age of sixty-three robbed Scotland of one of its most astute public figures.

Milling operations at the Poldrate Mill had ceased in the mid 1960s and the buildings, being no longer in use, were becoming derelict. At that time, the St Mary's Church Youth Fellowship were in search of suitable premises and approached the Duchess with the suggestion that the mill cottages might be suitable and available. She immediately approached the owner of the buildings, Courtenay Morrison, grain merchant and farmer at West Fenton, who sold them to the Lamp of Lothian Trust in May 1967 for the sum of £2,000, the price that he had paid for them a decade earlier.

Soon afterwards, a fund-raising concert in the mill was organised by Tom Fleming and, commencing with the mill cottages, restoration work to convert the buildings was soon begun. Today's complex now incorporates the mill, granary, malt house, mill cottages and the Bridge Youth Centre, with all its many activities for all ages, including the motorcycle and music project. The Poldrate Arts and Crafts Centre houses activities which include painting, sculpture, wood-carving, pottery, weaving and stained glass. After a successful National Lottery Fund application in 2001, the provision on the site was augmented in 2001 by the addition of the Alistair Grant Building, and following the death of Duchess Elizabeth in 2008, the entire complex was re-named the Elizabeth Hamilton Building.

But the loss of Haddington House was not an entirely happy outcome for the East Lothian Antiquarian and Field Naturalists' Society. Edith Broun-Lindsay and others, including my father, had always considered it an ideal setting for a permanent town museum. North Berwick and Dunbar had such facilities so why not East Lothian's very own market town? The answer was simple – lack of funding.

Fortunately, the concept survives and proves that all things are possible given the will of individuals. With support from the National Lottery Fund and East Lothian Council, the society's museum items will soon see the light of day in an East Lothian Museum incorporated into the Edinburgh-based architect Gray, Marshall & Associates design for a library and museum centre in Lodge Street.

Historic Haddington has been lucky in its champions. By 1966, John McVie had already begun negotiations to reinstate the partially ruined St Mary's Parish Church. Now this was an undertaking on an entirely different scale from the work involved at Haddington House or the Poldrate.

John McVie's daughter Fiona Sheldon has recently retired from McVies WS, the family law firm in Haddington, and is proud of her father's achievement. 'My father was a modest man but he was passionate in his enthusiasm for the people of Haddington and their heritage, in particular for the restoration of St Mary's Parish Church,' she told me. 'When he died in 2006, his funeral service was a joyful celebration of thanks held in his beloved and now restored St Mary's, complete with peel of bells. He is buried in the old churchyard.'

Almost a century earlier, the Reverend Dr Robert Nimmo Smith, Minister of St Mary's, had overseen a programme of alterations to the nave, followed by various internal improvements such as the lowering of the floor and introduction of two galleries and a new organ. But it was well known that he would have liked to have seen the entire church restored. This opportunity presented itself fifty years after his death when his youngest daughter Hilda approached the then Minister, the Reverend James Thomson, with an offer to endow a church hall in memory of her father. As Convenor of the Restoration Committee, John McVie realised that her gesture provided him with the ideal opportunity to propose a complete restoration.

In his memoirs, Frank Tindall, the County Planning Officer for East Lothian between 1950 and 1975, writes that he was ambivalent about the plan, rather liking 'this romantic ruined church in the great bend of the River

Tyne with the large copper beech tree at its east end'.[5] Such thinking was typical of the time.

Planning officers and conservationists in Scotland have often shown a disconcerting tendency to ignore piles of old rubble lying around the countryside whereas continental European authorities have moved mountains to reinstate them to their former glories. To give Tindall his credit, however, he was to oversee the benign restoration of many an East Lothian gem and he was certainly not alone in believing that St Mary's should be left as it was.

Any number of bureaucratic arguments were raised but John McVie persevered with his dream to see the entire church made whole again and astutely enlisted the advice of Wilson Paterson, a retired Edinburgh-based architect who had been involved in the previous work on St Mary's thirty years earlier. Not unreasonably, the prospect of having to find large amounts of money alarmed several of the elders who were concerned that the church's Christian Stewardship Campaign might suffer. Then, after a number of setbacks, the Lamp of Lothian Collegiate Trust and Duchess Elizabeth stepped into the breach, rallying support from such diverse quarters as the 6th Marquis of Bute, the Research for Truth Foundation and the violinist Yehudi Menuhin and his pianist sister Hephzibah. Miraculously, the necessary money was found.

Work on the repair and opening up of the east end of St Mary's commenced under the supervision of architects Ian G. Lindsay & Partners and structural engineers Harley Haddow and, on 17 March 1972, Hilda Nimmo Smith, watched by the Parish Minister, the Reverend James Riach, Provost Fraser Spowage, John McVie and the Duchess and her family, removed the first stone from the barrier wall separating the west end. With the vaulting of the east end re-created in fibreglass, St Mary's was returned to its original shape and size. For a sensitive account of the entire project, I recommend Rosalind K. Marshall's *Ruin and Restoration: St Mary's Church, Haddington*, published by East Lothian Council Library Service.

It should be underlined, of course, that it was not St Mary's Parish Church that was long ago known as 'Lucerna Laudoniae', 'The Lamp of Lothian', but the thirteenth-century Franciscan friary, destroyed in the Burnt Candlemas of 1356. Much admired for its physical beauty, this ancient friary was situated between Haddington's Hardgate and the River Tyne. Standing where the Scottish Episcopalian Church now rises, it took its name from the enlightenment preached by its friars, coupled with the warm glow of candlelight seen through its windows.[6] When its ruins were finally demolished in 1572, a quantity of its stones were removed to floor St Mary's nave and with the dazzling white light which today streams through the clear glass windows of the choir, St Mary's is today a worthy claimant to the title.

In 1968, Patrick Maitland, a successful journalist and one-time Member of

Parliament for Lanark, inherited the earldom of Lauderdale from his brother but, to some extent, it was a mixed windfall. By then, the once extensive family estates had been dispersed through cousin marriages and, apart from a seat in the House of Lords, virtually all that remained of his personal ancestral prestige in Scotland was the Lauderdale Aisle located on the north side of the ruined east end of St Mary's Parish Church in Haddington.

On a visit to St Mary's with his son in 1945, Robert Waterston, of the well-known Edinburgh stationery company, gave the following account of what they found:

> We were fortunate enough to be permitted to go right below ground into the bowels of the earth, down a steep ladder to the damp, dripping crypt to view, by the flickering light of a candle, the serried rows of oak coffins, each the same, fitted with large brass handling rings, the majority being in fair condition, but the older ones pretty well in pieces. Under them all lapped the muddy waters of the River Tyne which, when in spate, rises up to the planks supporting these coffins to make them float – at least so we were told! A ghoulish sight!!! Horrid! It was a relief to get back to the fresh air of the living and to have time to admire the magnificent marble renaissance monument standing above the crypt of the North wall of the revestry showing the four recumbent figures of Lord Thirlestane, the Chancellor, and of John, the first Earl of Lauderdale with their respective wives, the whole adorned with heraldic emblems in colours of related families, which, one may say, takes in practically the whole of our old Scottish nobility, including Flemings, Douglases, Cranstons, Setons, Crawfords, Drummonds and all the rest.[7]

Twenty-two years on, it should be noted, little had changed.

Prior to inheriting his earldom, the 17th Earl of Lauderdale, a devout Christian, was already a trustee of the Anglican shrine dedicated to the Virgin Mary at Walsingham in Norfolk, where Father Hope-Patten, who had been instrumental in this restoration, had repeatedly suggested that he use his influence to reinstate the Shrine of Our Lady of Haddington. The St Mary's restoration project of 1966 thus provided him with the ideal opportunity not only to reinstate his desperately neglected ancestral burial vault but also to make it the focus for an annual interdenominational pilgrimage.

In 1978, therefore, the Lauderdale Aisle was reconsecrated and dedicated to the Virgin Mary, the Christ Child and the Three Kings by Alistair Haggart, Episcopal Bishop of Edinburgh. By this association, the chapel was directly reconnected to the pre-Reformation altar endowed by the Forrests of Gimmersmills, whose direct descendant was, of course, Alexander Maitland of Gimmersmills.

The Three Kings are principally associated with pilgrimage and, in recognition of this, an anonymous Welsh woodcarver who was living in Norfolk at the time was commissioned to carve a set of appropriate decorative figures. These highly painted images are positioned directly facing the bold memorials to Lord Lauderdale's ancestors. But Patrick Lauderdale, who died in December 2008, was also aware of another pre-Reformation shrine that had been dedicated to Our Lady of Haddington at Whitekirk, a distance of approximately five miles from St Mary's. For generations, this had been a sacred destination for pilgrims and, in May 1971, he launched the first annual Whitekirk and Haddington Pilgrimage of the twentieth century. There were thirty participants. By 2007, the numbers had swollen to 3,000.

Commencing at ten o'clock in the morning with a communion at Whitekirk, the physically fit are encouraged to hike the distance while the less energetic take motor transport to Haddington where a mass is celebrated in St Mary's at noon. In the afternoon, an ecumenical blessing of the sick and disabled takes place, followed, in alternate years, by either a Eucharist according to the Episcopalian tradition or a Church of Scotland service of Communion. The consecration is usually performed by an Anglican bishop. Many of those who attend are already conscious that, before the Reformation, Haddington was second only to St Andrews as a religious community. If nothing else, the spiritual triumph that is the Pilgrimage proves that the town still has a significant contemporary role to play in the pursuit of faith.

But not only that – Haddington's European links too remain strong. In 1965, the town was twinned with Aubigny-sur-Nère in France which is situated 100 miles south of Paris and, once again, history is the talisman. In 1419, during the Hundred Years War, when England controlled more than half of France, the future King Charles VII of France, hemmed in by the English at Bourges, invoked the Auld Alliance between Scotland and France. A large Scots army under Sir John Stuart was sent by James I to assist him and, over the following months, the Scots made a significant contribution towards vanquishing the enemy back from whence they came. In 1423, Sir John was given Aubigny and its surrounding lands as a reward.

During the seventeenth century, this Seigneurie of Aubigny passed to Louise de Kérouaille, who became one of several mistresses of Britain's Charles II. After her death, it was inherited by their illegitimate son who, when their kinsman, Charles Stuart, was drowned in Denmark (see Chapter 2), was created 4th Duke of Richmond and Lennox. The town of Aubigny finally reverted into French ownership after the French Revolution of 1812. Its twinning with Haddington today serves as a lasting remnant of the bonds that continue to exist between the two countries.

CHAPTER EIGHT

Foothills and Tragedy

ON THE OPPOSITE SIDE of the road from the gates of Lennoxlove are the lodge gates of Monkrigg, where the Augustinian brothers of old worked their rigs of land and gave the fields names such as Upper and Lower Purgatory. In the seventeenth century, this estate was acquired for £8,000 by the Reverend George Home, Minister of Greenlaw and Laird of Gunsgreen at Eyemouth. He later sold it for £18,000 to Fletcher of Saltoun's trustees, who then sold it on for £12,500 to Captain Keith. It was Captain Keith who in 1832 commissioned William Burn to design the present house for £5,000, and then sold it to George More for £16,000. After that it was inherited by George More's cousin James and later bought by a Mr Laurie for £22,000.

Paltry by present standards, such sums provide an interesting reflection on the steady escalation of property values over two centuries, a phenomenon shrewdly harnessed in the latter half of the twentieth by Monkrigg's current owner, James Manclark, a much respected and eminently successful property developer. In 1947, Monkrigg was given to his mother Elma Manclark as a gift from her father Sir William Thomson, who paid £17,600 for it. At the time, the house had four public rooms, a billiard room, eight bedrooms, four dressing rooms and three bathrooms. There were also offices, fruit and vegetable gardens and 200 acres of cultivated arable land. Elma then embarked upon a major refurbishment to make the house more comfortable for her young family.

Sir William was one of a remarkable breed of twentieth-century Scottish entrepreneurs. Having begun his business career by owning one horse bus, he eventually controlled every bus company in Scotland. Added to this, he built aircraft and tank landing equipment and founded the first hire-purchase company in Britain, which later became known as Lloyds & Scottish.

When his grandson James returned from working in the City of London to take over the Monkrigg farms during the 1960s, taxation rates had reached a premium. Aware of the crippling implications for landowners, James astutely sold the estate but retained the tenancy while using the capital for property development. When his lease ran out, he bought Monkrigg back.

Meanwhile, his fearlessness in winning a powerboat speed racing championship soon earned him a spot on the British luge team in the 1968 Grenoble Olympics and on the bobsleigh team in the 1972 games in Sapporo. Since then he has ridden in hunter trials and point-to-points, launched a hot air balloon attempt to circumnavigate the world and is credited with the invention of elephant polo. At Monkrigg, James and his wife, Patricia, keep a string of polo ponies which participate in contests throughout Britain. Elephant polo, however, takes place in Nepal, Thailand and Sri Lanka on rather larger beasts – an unconventional idea which has captured the imagination and attracted sponsorship from international companies such as Chivas Regal and Coca-Cola.

From Monkrigg, the road takes a turn towards Gifford village, flanking Colstoun until it passes Beech Hill House which, in 1876, was sold by Sir George Yule, formerly of the Bengal Civil Service (for more on the Yule family, see Chapter 24). From him this fine mansion house passed to the Houston family, then in 1922 to Colonel de Pree. During the Second World War, it was witness to two traumatic flying incidents over the Lammermuirs and Peter and Andrea de Pree, who today occupy Beech Hill House, have kindly permitted me to make use of an account of what took place written by Peter's grandmother. She entitled her essay 'The Battle of Beech Hill'.

> On the morning of Saturday 18th October 1939, I was eating my breakfast as usual in my hut when Tito and Hugh came to say there was 'one of these air warnings'. Hughie had 24 hours leave, so he and Tito went off to shoot at Whitburgh. About half an hour after they had gone – in the distance behind me – towards the Firth of Forth, I heard shooting and the now familiar sound, low, deep, almost guttural of a Hun Heinkel Machine. At about 10.20am I watched a fight to the death. A huge Hun, flying low followed by three Spitfires, appeared with shattering noise round the corner of the house from the garden side. A fourth Spitfire swirled towards the Heinkel.
>
> The noise was deafening – all firing at once. One darting below and pouring shrapnel with withering accuracy into the tummy of the German plane. Down the 'Clarty' they went – bullets rattling against the doomed foreigner. She shuddered and at last, slowly, with nose down, sank from my view behind our little field on the west side of the front field.
>
> Phoebe rushed out. 'Oh, Mummy, did you see that?'
>
> I think we would have both liked to have taken part in the fight. I watched

the Spitfires like large elegant birds, circling round and round, anxious to see that their prey was really there, never to rise again. The German plane fell behind Newton Hall, on Longnewton Hill, and after lunch Phoebe, Enid and I drove there to see it. We drove to Kidlaw Reservoir, then walked up a steep, heathery hill – about 10 minutes' easy going. There, with its propeller in the peat lay the German Mammoth riddled with bullets. The navigator was uninjured and he pulled the other three men out of the plane. The mechanic and wireless operator were found to be dead. The pilot was very seriously injured but is expected to recover. When the Policeman from Gifford appeared, the navigator rushed up to him and asked him if he was Scotch. On getting a reply in the affirmative, the German then informed the constable that he could speak English, and said, 'I surrender as a prisoner-of-war.' It was evident from the German's demeanour that he expected something dreadful would happen to him. On being told that he would be well cared for, his relief was very noticeable.

All the front glass, like talc, had been blown off in bits and the right hand side of the tail was shattered in pieces. There were two incendiary bombs found in the plane which in all probability would have been used to demolish the machine if the navigator had had time to do so. The Gifford folks were too quickly on the scene to allow this. Three cameras, three riddled thermos flasks, one black leather case, several black metal containers full of ammunition, packets of 'Milch' biscuits, and blankets were all found on the plane. The biscuits were like dog biscuits and so hard that they would have taken a dog some time to demolish.

Our Air Force was soon there measuring and taking notes. By the following day every detail of the plane had been photographed.

We were so quickly on the spot that the crowd was very small. Next day there were over 600 cars and queues of people going round the barrier of thick cord. We went down the hill again leaving the dark winged thing on the lonely hillside with its large white outlined cross and evil Swastika painted on its tail.

Almost exactly five years later, Beech Hill was to be the scene of yet another flying incident – this time a truly dreadful tragedy. On the night of 22 October 1944, a Mosquito of No. 132 Operation Training Unit based at East Fortune was on a training flight when one of its fuel tanks exploded and the aircraft crashed into the house, killing six people. The aircraft's two crewmen, Ruth de Pree, her brother Lieutenant-Colonel John Haig, the de Prees' grandson, David Pitcairn, and his nurse, Daisy Spears, all died in the accident, although seven other family members and household staff who were in the house at the time mercifully escaped.

The Mosquito had hit a tree and was diverted off course to demolish a wall in the garden. One of the engines and part of a wing fell into the kitchen garden while the other engine was found in a nearby field. When the aircraft wreckage hit Beech Hill House, the west wing was totally wrecked and the fire continued to smoulder until the following day. This was deemed to be the worst accident involving a flying aircraft from East Fortune during the Second World War and was particularly felt locally because of the personalities involved.

North-west of Gifford is the mansion house of Eaglescairnie, which is described by John Martine as a pretty place surrounded with fine old trees. Until 1747 it was owned by the Haliburtons of Dirleton until Margaret, daughter and heiress of Thomas Haliburton, married Patrick Lindsay. Their oldest daughter married Alexander, 10th Lord Blantyre, and the estate was made over to their eldest son, General Sir Patrick Stuart. In more recent years it was acquired by Major Robin Salvesen, a scion of the Leith-based Salvesen shipping family, who, in 2006, was appointed Vice Lord-Lieutenant of East Lothian. Eaglescairnie Mains, owned by Michael and Barbara Williams, was in October 1992 launched as the Lothians' Farming and Wildlife Advisory Group (FWAG) Demonstration Farm. Since then, its mission statement has been to combine wildlife and landscape conservation with profitable agriculture and, in 2001, Michael was awarded the MBE for pioneering eco-friendly agriculture.

The Cistercian Convent of Nunraw (or Nun's Row) in the Parish of Garvald was founded by the Countess of Huntingdon between 1152 and 1153 and dedicated to Saint Bernard of Clairvaux, the French abbot who created the order and who had been an influential advocate of the Second Crusade. With the constant ebb and flow of English invasion over the years that followed, no convent records survive from that time. However, we do know that the nuns of 'Nunhopis formerly Yesterhopis' were self-sufficient, having the kirk and 120 acres of land adjacent, a toft with a garden and eleven acres at Popple and a strip of land in Stoneypath.[1]

A great deal was expected of the nuns in those days, defying the image of unworldly spinsters. During the Siege of Haddington, for example, the Lords of Council instructed the prioress to defend 'the place and fortalice of Nunraw, also known as Whitecastle' against the English and to take no prisoners.[2] Both a religious sanctuary and a fortress, it was at Nunraw that the Scottish Parliament in 1548 endorsed the betrothal of the six-year-old Mary, Queen of Scots to the Dauphin of France.

The last three prioresses were members of the Hepburn family of Hailes Castle and when the last of them, Prioress Elizabeth, died in 1563, Nunraw was taken over by Patrick Hepburn, with the substantial mansion shown in

Timothy Pont's 1610 map of East Lothian passing to Hepburn's successors. It was over this period that the painted ceiling was installed, each panel featuring images of birds, animals, allegorical figures and the title and armorial bearings of medieval monarchs. From the monogram P. C. H. it can be assumed that the work dates from the occupancy of Patrick Hepburn and his wife Helen Cockburn in the late sixteenth century.

In 1747, the estate was purchased by James Dalrymple, youngest son of Sir Hew Dalrymple of North Berwick, Lord President of the Court of Session. Thirty-three years later it was sold to James Hay, whose family had already acquired the next-door Linplum Estate.

Then, around 1880, Nunraw was acquired by Lieutenant-Colonel Walter Wingate Gray of the Lothian and Berwickshire Imperial Yeomanry. Soldier, churchman, agriculturist, landowner and sportsman, among his other pre-occupations Gray was Vice President of the East Lothian Ice Rink Club. On his death in 1931, Nunraw was sold to Marcus Spurway, the husband of Margaret Baird, whose father Sir David Baird, 4th Baronet, had, in 1900, succeeded to the Blantyre estates, which included Lennoxlove.

In 1945, it emerged that Dom Camillus Claffey, Lord Abbot of Mount St Joseph Abbey in Ireland was searching for a suitable site for an abbey in Scotland and, with the help of the Archbishop of St Andrews and Edinburgh, Nunraw was acquired for that purpose. Thus the first Cistercian religious house to be created in Scotland since the Reformation was founded on a property which, four centuries earlier, had already been a Cistercian convent.

On my most recent visit in the summer of 2007, I was taken on a tour of the cloisters that had been built by the monks on their arrival there in 1946. Father Stephen, a kindly, soft-spoken man attired in black and white robes, was my guide. 'We've had quite a few recruits recently,' he told me optimistically, 'mostly young men over fifty. Some of them stay; others find the isolation too hard.'

That being the case, the numbers are admittedly in decline but a constant stream of visitors nonetheless ensures that the abbey fulfils its purpose. There is an all-embracing sense of tranquillity and spiritual calm about the place. At the red stone Nunraw Visitor Centre, which is the former Nunraw House, I was introduced to Dom Raymon, the abbot, who, having been at work on the farm, was wearing a tracksuit, and together we enjoyed a pot of tea and a chat with Brother Patrick.

I then went for a stroll in the scrupulously maintained gardens, screened from intrusion by broadleaf woodland and monkey puzzle trees. In a dip above the gorge of the Papana Water there is a statue of Our Lady, in recognition of the disastrous flood of 1356. As the waters of this tributary of the River Tyne threatened to immerse the abbey on the Feast of Our Lady's

Nativity, a pious nun defiantly threatened to throw Our Lady from a window should the waters not retreat. Miraculously, they did.[3] Having seen the depth of the gorge, my only observation is that it must indeed have been a flood of massive proportions.

In a hedged enclosure to the side of the abbey building is the cemetery where the monks themselves are interred when their time comes. Here I paused for thought beside a stone bench carrying a memorial plaque upon which are carved the names of Christian, Luc, Christophe, Michel, Bruno, Célestin and Paul. These were the seven French Cistercian Trappist monks who, on 21 May 1996, were abducted from the Monastery of Our Lady of Atlas in Algeria and decapitated by the terrorist Armed Islamic Group (GIA). Even on such a tranquil July day, in such a peaceful place, the cruel realities of the distant world cannot be entirely ignored.

The Barony of Linplum, which adjoins that of Nunraw, was purchased in the early seventeenth century by Lady Yester, mother of the 1st Earl of Tweeddale, for her second son, Sir William Hay. From him descend the Hays of Duns Castle in Berwickshire. As for the farm of Linplum, its most famous occupant was Adam Bogue, who transformed the thick clay soil with large quantities of dung and lime and later acquired the adjacent farm of Baro. In partnership with Francis Walker, farmer at Whitelaw, he in addition took on Snawdon in the Lammermuirs, the highest arable land in the county, and that too was transformed. The uncle of George Hope at Fenton Barns (see Chapter 21), he initiated the county's first sheep show and, in later years, bred several champion racehorses.

In 1881, the Linplum Estate was sold for £35,000 to Robert Edgar, a wealthy seed merchant from George IV Bridge in Edinburgh.[4] It was he who commissioned architects Shiells and Thomson to build the 'strongly modelled baronial house with a dominating central drum tower'.[5] The property then passed from Edgar's descendants, the Harding Edgar family, to the Shaw-Stewarts. Today, it is the home of Edinburgh-based investment banker Douglas McDougall and his wife Margaret.

With the popularity of Scottish wilderness destinations such as Rannoch Moor and Loch Lomond, it strikes me as astonishing that the bleak majesty of the Lammermuirs is so often bypassed. From the summit of the B8355 from Gifford, a view of the entire coastal plain of the Firth of Forth, stretching from Cockenzie to North Berwick Law, emerges in all its splendour; to the south, as the south-eastern hills of East Lothian spill onto the north-eastern approaches of Berwickshire, there unravels a landscape which John Martine, writing in 1883, a trifle over indulgent, compares to Afghanistan and Zululand.[6] He also observed:

> In the month of July when the bell heather is in full and splendid bloom on the hill sides and tops, a day's ramble among the Lammermuirs will, to a lover of wild and beautiful natural scenery, afford much delight; and when he comes to view the camps of Brookside, if he is of a contemplative mind, he will wonder how the old inhabitants of this land could live in their hill-forts, clothed in skins of wild beasts, and depending for their daily food on the chase and slaughter of wild animals and birds, while resisting the attacks of their enemies with slings, bows and arrows, and flint-headed javelins.[7]

In recent conversations with David Thompson, Chairman of the St Andrews Society of East Lothian, I was to discover that his maternal second cousin, Hilda Shirreff, who died in 1962, was the last of the Darling family of Millknowe and Priestlaw. Both are at the heart of the Lammermuirs, although the former is now totally submerged under water.[8] The Darlings arrived in the neighbourhood around 1770 and, like my own Carfrae ancestors, were tenants of the Tweeddale estates for over 200 years. And such was the hospitality that travellers and fishermen received from them, that Priestlaw became known as 'the Hotel of the Lammermuirs'. On one occasion, an angler, having stayed overnight, actually asked for his bill, much to the astonishment of his host and hostess.[9]

Of the surrounding panorama, the following account is given by A. G. Bradley after a visit in 1929:

> It lay in the very heart of the wild, and the sheep upon a thousand hills appertained to it. Its boundaries marched with our more limited ones. How far they extended to north and south over heathery hills and boggy, stream-furrowed glens, I do not know.[10]

This was very much my first impression when I took part in Combined Cadet Force exercises here in the early 1960s.

David Thompson first visited Priestlaw himself after the farm had been sold to James Sharp in 1963, when the house was vacant but the cottages were still occupied by John and Mary Jaffray and Mrs Elliot, whose families had lived in them for two generations or more. In prospect at this time was the creation of the Whiteadder Reservoir. At this stage, nobody could be certain what would become of the surrounding land until it was announced that only Millknowe and the little Kingside School were to be demolished, with the valley flooded to a level of some 40 feet below the original proposal. Priestlaw was saved.[11]

In 1965 work started on the great dam that would change the scenery forever. Today the reservoir is populated by shoals of brown and rainbow trout and it has become a haven for fishermen. Coinciding with this, Priestlaw was sold to the Straker-Smith family from Cornhill, who made use of it as a holiday home. In the long hot summer of 1990, when water levels throughout the country dropped, rumours abounded that the volume in Whiteadder Reservoir would have to be increased. Then the rains came and the threat disappeared.

In the late 1990s, the estate of Mayshiel, to the east of Priestlaw, was bought by Fred and Dulcie Packard, who proceeded to build a striking, ginger-harled, chateau-style mansion house. With business interest, in Brazil and being a grandson of the film mogul J. Arthur Rank, Fred Packard is Chairman of the Rank Foundation and has since bought most of the land surrounding Cranshaws and now Priestlaw itself.

David Thompson nevertheless retains a strong affinity with the Whiteadder Valley of his ancestors. 'There is still the bleat of the lamb, the cry of the curlew and the laughter of children to be heard,' he says. 'Cherish it well as we have done. It is the land of our past, of our future. It is our children's heritage until the very end of time.'

CHAPTER NINE

Old East Lothian Agriculturists

I TAKE THE CHAPTER TITLE 'Old East Lothian Agriculturists' from John Martine's *Reminiscences of the Royal Burgh of Haddington*, published in 1883, in which he pays tribute to the members of the Society of Improvers of Knowledge of Agriculture. This revolutionary body, founded in 1723 by John Cockburn of Ormiston, put Scotland at the forefront of European agronomics during the eighteenth century. By following its lead in recommending drainage and crop experimentation, astonishing advances took place in agricultural practices throughout Britain.

At the time of the Union between Scotland and England, all of East Lothian's landed estates were divided into small farms, with few of them exceeding 150 acres. By 1778, there were still only ten holdings consisting of more than 300 acres. By 1810, the average size had increased significantly to 500 acres but the number of farmers had dropped by a quarter.[1]

Traditional land ownership was coming under increased scrutiny, with the relationship between landlord and tenant being openly challenged. In 1793, George Rennie of Phantassie, Robert Brown of Markle and John Shirreff of Captainhead, near Drem, were selected by the British Board of Agricultural and Internal Improvement to undertake a survey of the West Riding of Yorkshire. Their findings give an unexpected insight into the social structure of the age:

> Agriculture is a living science which is progressively improving, consequently what may be esteemed a good course of cropping at one time, may from experience and observation, be afterwards found defective and erroneous. To us it would seem as incongruous to tie a man's legs together and then tell him to run, as to suppose that improvements are to be made by a farmer without the security of a lease. The great charm which sets industry everywhere in motion is the acquisition of property and the security of it when acquired. When tenants hold by a precarious tenure, and are removable at the will of the proprietor, or after a short period, then undoubtedly their labour

will be spiritless and languid, as they have no inducement to enter upon improvements when they have no certainty of enjoying the immediate benefit.[2]

This was especially apposite in the case of my great-great-great-uncle Peter Forrest who, at the age of forty, signed a lease for the 336 Scotch acre farm of Northrig at Morham. His landlord was Francis Charteris, de jure 7th Earl of Wemyss, brother of the attainted 6th Earl who had died in 1787.

Peter rapidly set about repairing the neglect of his predecessors:

> [H]aving thoroughly limed and highly manured the farm, which he entered into in bad order, during the first five or six years of his lease of nineteen years, he reclaimed and made arable the Haggs Muir, fifty to sixty acres in extent which was in a state of nature when he entered covered with whins and heather and unenclosed.[3]

In regard to cropping and management, Northrig was held under unrestricted lease and so Forrest decided to sow between 100 and 120 acres with wheat which, at the time, was selling at Napoleonic war prices of 90s–100s per quarter. Charteris soon got word of this and, being of an autocratic nature, raised an action against his tenant to restrict the sowing of wheat on more than a fourth of the farm. When the matter came before the Sheriff of Haddington, Forrest was adamant – when the season and condition of his land so warranted it, he was entitled to sow as much wheat as he chose to.

Legally, the case was cut and dried but Charteris, infuriated that his tenant was making such a large profit, was not above exercising feudal pressure. Sheriff Burnet, nervous of defying the most influential landowner in the county, remitted the case to 'two gentlemen of landed property, and to three farmers, for consideration'.[4] In the event, Peter Forrest was fully vindicated and the landlord was called upon to meet the legal expenses.

Not prepared to let the matter rest, Charteris next turned to the Court of Session and the case was passed to Dr Coventry, Professor of Agriculture at Edinburgh University, who, 'to the astonishment of all practical and sensible men, decided in favour of the landlord'.[5] The judgement caused consternation throughout East Lothian's farming community, the consensus being that Peter Forrest had been very harshly treated. It was also widely circulated that Dr Coventry had been inappropriately influenced, thus proving that noblesse oblige can, on occasion, be a contradiction in terms.

On the termination of his lease in 1812, Peter Forrest, described as 'a very stout, tall and stalwart man, and fine specimen of the East Lothian farmer', retired to live in the old Port House at the East Gate of Haddington until he died at the age of eighty-three in 1836.[6] He is interred in the Forrest Aisle at the Church of St Andrew, Gullane, where a weathered plaque on the wall commemorates his life.

One positive outcome of this unhappy dispute, however, was that, in the relentless passage of time, landlord/tenant restrictions in regard to cropping were dropped. But that brought little comfort to Peter Forrest.

Over the nineteenth century, Northrig changed hands several times and expanded to 413 acres. Until 1847, these were tenanted by James Lauder, whose epitaph in Morham Kirkyard tells us that he was charitable to the poor, a wise councillor, a dutiful son and an affectionate husband – 'As his life was lovely, so his end was peace.' From his tombstone, Northrig can just be glimpsed in the distance over the churchyard wall.

Lauder was succeeded on the farm by Thomas Turner. From 1904 until 1910 the farmhouse was let to Thomas Anderson, an astronomer, who had moved out of Edinburgh when the introduction of electricity made it impossible for him to study the night sky. Until 1914 the farm was leased to Sydney MacDonald but, when he enlisted to fight in the Great War, John Middlemass (see Chapter 23) acquired the lease for his son Finlay.[7] Then in 1915 Finlay himself signed up, so John was called upon to manage the farm until his son's return in 1919. Finlay's grandson, Ian Middlemass, has a sepia photograph of the returning hero standing at the side of the house where there are signs of a privet hedge having just been planted. This hedge now stands tall and proud.

When Northrig was put up for sale by Wemyss Estates in 1946 it was bought by Finlay, who continued to farm it until his death in 1968. It then passed to his sons – John, who died in 2006, Finlay, who died in 1989, and Jim, who died in 1979 – and Jim's twin sister Nancy, who died in 2001. A fourth son, Bertie – who was Finlay's twin brother – decided not to remain in the family partnership. Bertie was the last of that generation, dying in 2006. Today, Northrig is farmed by Jim's son, Ian, who was made a partner in the business upon his father's death, when he was eighteen.

On a brisk, sunny day in February 2008, Ian took me to inspect the Haggs Muir, the section of the farm which Peter Forrest had so successfully drained all those years ago. 'At some later stage it was planted with trees,' he told me, 'but after the Second World War they were cleared by my father. The result is that the field of the Haggs Muir looks exactly as it must have looked after Peter Forrest turned it over for planting in 1795.'

Today, roughly one third of the land is reserved for barley, winter and spring, a third for beet crops and the final third for wheat. 'Which is what Peter Forrest's battle was all about,' says Ian with a satisfied smile.

Yet another milestone East Lothian controversy between landlord and tenant was to occur over a half a century after the Northrig episode and, this time, it concerned the Hope Family of Fenton Barns, not to be confused in any way with the Hopes of Hopetoun or Luffness (see Chapter 24). These Hopes were of Dutch origin, descended from a soldier who had arrived in England with William of Orange and who afterwards settled in Edinburgh.[8] In 1773, his great-grandson, Robert Hope, became tenant of Ferrygate on the coastline of the Dirleton Estate opposite Fidra. He remained there until 1796, when he took on the leases of Fenton and Fenton Barns, approximately 670 acres in total.

At this stage, the soil was in such a poor state – a mix of stiff, retentive clay and moorish sand – that the Dirleton Estate, owned by Mrs Ferguson (see Chapter 25), allowed him to have it rent-free until he could turn it around. This he and his son, another Robert, proceeded to achieve by introducing tile-drainage, subsoiling and heavy manuring and, in time, producing new varieties of cereals. In the process, they also gave lessons on farming practice to the sons of British and European landowners.

A friend of both Robert Brown of Markle (see Chapter 23) and the Liberal politician and agricultural reformer Sir John Sinclair of Ulbster, the younger Robert Hope became a regular contributor to the *Farmer's Magazine*. In 1841 he was author of a treatise 'Observations on the County of Haddington' which provoked fierce debate when published in the *Statistical Account of Scotland, Haddington County*.

His son George was, if anything, even more confrontational and, by regularly writing in support of tenants' rights for the *Scotsman* newspaper, it was inevitable that he would come up against Robert Christopher Dundas Nisbet Hamilton, who had married Mary Ferguson's daughter. Nisbet Hamilton was 'banker' of the Tory Party in Scotland and was incensed by Hope's membership of the Anti-Corn Law League, not to mention his standing as the tenant-farmers' candidate against the up-until-then unchallenged Lord Elcho in the Haddington election of 1865. When the lease on Fenton Barns expired, therefore, he churlishly refused to renew it. Presumably, Hope must have seen this coming as his landlord had earlier ejected William Sadler, the tenant at Ferrygate, under similar circumstances.[9]

The writer A. G. Bradley, who had visited Fenton Barns as an agricultural student the year before Hope's eviction, later observed of Robert Nisbet Hamilton that '[h]is Toryism was of a type which proved too much even for the faith of his fellow-Tories, and what that signified in the Scotland of the 'seventies cannot be expressed in modern terms'.[10]

In a memoir of her father published in 1881, Charlotte Hope provides a further insight into the relationship between landlord and tenant:

> [Nisbet-Hamilton] also endeavoured to prevent people from crossing the Dirleton common (land which my father rented from him). Seeing someone driving there he despatched one of his underlings to shut and lock a certain gate, so as to prevent the vehicle from passing through, but the messenger failed to accomplish this, the vehicle having passed before he arrived at the gate. It so happened that the person whom Mr Hamilton had attempted to shut into the common was Prince Napoleon who, after having inspected Fenton Barns, had gone to examine my father's farm at Dirleton; Mr Hamilton, on learning that the trespasser was a live Prince, sent after him to the station in hot haste to beg him to return.[11]

By not renewing the Fenton Barns tenancy, Nisbet-Hamilton unleashed a torrent of political protest throughout Scotland and England which, to his astonishment, created a major shift in future landlord/tenant legislation. But that brought little comfort to George Hope. Nothing if not stoical, he relinquished the tenancy that his family had held for seventy-eight years and purchased the 480-acre estate of Borelands in Peeblesshire. However, the scandal that surrounded the injustice done to him made him famous. On passing Fenton Barns on a train several years later, a fellow passenger, unaware of his identity, informed him that this was the farm from which Mr Hope had been evicted by his landlord![12]

In the latter half of the nineteenth century, the fortunes of Britain's farming communities fluctuated dramatically. Prices soared and tumbled without warning and the deluge of cereals from North America proved devastating for many of the old-established tenants of East Lothian land. With poor returns and high rentals, a large number of them simply gave up the struggle and, in doing so, cleared the way for a new wave of smallholders, mostly from Ayrshire and Lanarkshire in the west of Scotland. 'There is an old saying in farming circles,' says Tom Middlemass, who farms Markle Mains at East Linton and is a second cousin of Ian Middlemass at Northrigg, ' "Go east to a farm and west for a wife!" When you look at the statistics and analyse them, this certainly holds true.' Tom Middlemass, whose family has farmed Markle Mains for five generations (see Chapter 23) has looked up the 1896 Valuation Roll for East Lothian and discovered that only five or six farmers are still on the same land as their forebears – not that many when you consider that there are still around 250 farms in the county. However, there is one long-established farming family which has staunchly persisted in bucking the trend and that is the Dales of Auldhame and Scoughall.[13]

An extract from the 1872 Memoriam to John Robert Dale of Auldhame gives some indication of the esteem in which his particular dynasty was held:

> Mr Dale had farmed Auldhame for the best part of two leases, having been its tenant for nearly forty years. He had almost an hereditary claim to the occupancy of the land, his uncle, Mr Robert Dale, late of Liberton Windmill Farm, having at one time been tenant of West Barns and was no unworthy representative of the tenant farmers of East Lothian. Men of large experience have said that, thirty years ago, Mr Dale was in many respects one of the most skilful and advanced agriculturists of his day, his farm being a model of tidiness and good management.[14]

His parents being in India where his father worked for the East India Company, John Robert Dale was brought up by his uncle and aunt at Liberton West Mains, which today is the site of the Edinburgh campus of the Scottish Agricultural College. In 1834, he took out the lease of Auldhame, which was followed in 1848 by that of the adjoining farm of Scoughall for his son Thomas.

The years between 1880 and 1900 saw the price of grain falling by a half. To add to the problems of Britain's hard-pressed agricultural communities, although refrigeration transport was in its infancy, it was beginning to enable the import of mass-produced inexpensive lamb from New Zealand. To make matters worse, there were soaring rent increases. In 1881, Thomas had renegotiated a nineteen-year lease and was forced to increase his payments in line with the incoming tenant of the neighbouring farm of Whitekirk. This individual had come from Glasgow and, two or three years into his tenancy, became bankrupt. In the meantime, Thomas Dale held on with resilience. It was a lesson the family would never forget.

Eleven years later, he took over the lease of Lochhouses, a farm on the Tyninghame Estate which, up until then, he had been taking care of for a Miss Mitchell. In a gesture tantamount to feudal bribery, his landlord, the 11th Earl of Haddington, had presented Thomas's daughter Connie with a new pony to encourage her father to continue the arrangement. But Thomas persevered. In 1900, his eldest son Jack returned from college, followed soon afterwards by his youngest son Tommy. Both Jack and Tommy enlisted in the Lothian & Border Horse Yeomanry but, in 1913, Jack resigned his commission to help his father on the farm. With the outbreak of war, Tommy was mobilised and sent to Salonica. When he returned in 1919, he found not only that his father had died two years earlier but also that his brother was married. His sister-in-law was Mary Paterson, the daughter of Professor Paterson, who had been the acting minister at Whitekirk while the Reverend Edward Rankin was away at the battlefront. Only months later, Tommy was killed in a motorbike accident.

Jack Dale continued his father's good work. With the help of William

Purvis, his farm manager, he bought the Seacliff Estate at North Berwick when it came on the market in 1920 and, given the difficult decade that followed the stockmarket crash of 1929, he managed to do remarkably well. 'I would rather go bust by employing too many people rather than too few', he said at the time. His philosophy paid off. After World War Two, he took his sons Tommy and Willie Dale into partnership and, when a year or so had passed, handed over all of his agricultural assets to them for two ten shilling stamps. He died at Auldhame in 1968.

It is a remarkable story of fortitude and continuity. John Robert Dale's great-great-great-grandson Douglas still farms Auldhame and Scoughall, while his cousin Robert farms Lochhouses and Robert's brother Alex, Hedderwick Hill, by Dunbar. At Seacliff, Jack Dale Junior has become involved in the fishing/seafood business and his son Tom runs a green waste recycling company. In 1945, Jack Dale's daughter Anne married George Gray of Smeaton Hepburn at East Linton. Strengthening the link, George's sister Gladys was married to Tommy Dale. Today, George and Anne Gray's son John farms East Fenton (see Chapter 21) and, in 2005, with his brother Quentin and cousins Robert and Alex Dale, purchased the farms of Lawhead and Tyninghame Links, along with Binning Wood.

On revisiting East Lothian in the early years of the last century, A. G. Bradley noted that nearly all of the old names he had known as an agricultural student in the 1870s had long gone.

> The high standard of farming had carried on, but for many years at what a price no one will ever know. And then new men had come in, a rather different class, or perhaps a more varied one. Hard-working grieves who had saved money, merchants' sons with capital ready to risk for a Lothian farmer's life, which had always in the past, like English gentleman farming, a glamour for the cities and even a touch of social attraction.[15]

This was not necessarily a bad thing – in fact, far from it. Several of the newcomers did remarkably well. As a number of the old East Lothian estates were sold and split up, tenants were given the option to buy their own farms. From then on, the ownership of land became less about social prestige than market economics. When tractors and electric powered machines replaced working horses after the Second World War, a corresponding decline in the agricultural labour force took place. Although agricultural productivity actually increased, the bulk of the rural population who for generations had been employed on the land migrated towards towns for employment. Farmhouses and cottages fell vacant, only to be increasingly snapped up by wealthy urban commuters in search of a taste of country life.

After 1945, there were only seven East Lothian dairy farms. Sheep farming crept onto the Lammermuirs. By the turn of the twentieth century, the introduction of oilseed rape was transforming the central landscape into sheets of canary yellow. With pastures increasingly being handed over to contractors and wholesalers, an alternative vision of land tenure began to emerge. Tom Middlemass explains:

> Up until around 1960, the majority of East Lothian farms were mixed, and most of them were involved in a wide spread of enterprises. My father was no exception. He grew wheat, barley, oats, hay, silage, turnips, rotational grass, cabbages, potatoes, sugar beet, mangolds, kale. He kept cows, pigs, feeding cattle, sheep and hens and horses to do the work. Today, the only enterprise from that extensive list is wheat, as well as winter oilseed rape and spring beans, which can all be sown by the same seeder and harvested by combine harvester.
>
> In the old days, we all kept sheep and cattle. Some farms had a ewe flock and others bought sheep at the market and fattened them on rape and turnips. Now, sheep are mostly relegated to the hill foots, from Innerwick along to Humbie, and a shepherd up there most probably looks after twice as many of them as before and has a four-wheeled motorbike to help him do the rounds!
>
> As for cattle, suckled calves were bought at St Boswells or big Irish cattle from the 'Linton Fair', which was held every autumn. Wartime was a particularly busy time because of the demand for food and, although those who lived on the farm were subject to the same stringent rationing, they did much better than those in the large towns and cities, even if it meant that rabbit was on the menu rather a lot.
>
> On the cropping side, turnips were grown on every farm, sown in drills using a two row seeder. Singling and hoeing was done by hand, as was shawing and loading turnips on a frosty morning with wet gloves – something I remember as though it were yesterday!

During the 1950s, he would bolt his school dinner at East Linton School and rush to the sale ring for a glimpse of those larger than life characters – the Irishmen who always wore glazed raincoats and cut hats and always held a 'Capstan' in their nicotine-stained hands. As well as the seasonal livestock sales, there were the weekly fat stock sales which alternated between the sale rings of East Linton and Haddington. These were held on a Monday when fat cattle, sheep and pigs were sold to local butchers or their agents. Tom continues:

> It used to be that every town also had its own slaughterhouse but now everything has been centralised. The nearest fat stock auction mart is at St

Boswells and the nearest abattoirs are at either Galashiels or Wishaw so, really, is that any better? The animals have to endure much longer journeys to get there and the farmers no longer have a weekly excuse to go to the local market, which was a very social occasion.

With land prices having increased dramatically, prospective buyers are now coming from Europe and elsewhere and there is no guarantee that those farms which have survived as single units for over two hundred and fifty years will, in future, remain intact. Whereas it used to be that our market place was virtually on our doorstep, we now live in a worldwide arena preoccupied with watching the level of global stocks of grain and the futures prices on the Stock Exchange. It's a far cry from taking your sample to the Corn Exchange in Haddington on a Friday!

It used to be that the prime work of a farmer was to produce food but now we are expected to manage the countryside as well, with grants to plant more trees and hedges under various schemes such as Rural Stewardship and Land Management Contracts.

Mac Henderson, who celebrated his one hundred and first birthday in May 2008, was in a unique position to appraise the fluctuating fortunes of the farming community, being able to look back over an astonishing century of agricultural change with complete recall. 'It was all mines around Ormiston and Tranent where I went to school before going to Edinburgh Academy at the age of ten,' he reflected when we talked at his daughter Catherine's house in North Berwick. 'But farming was still big business then before the slump came.'

Mac's father, James Henderson, arrived in East Lothian from Angus in 1903 and farmed South Elphinston, near Tranent, and Buxley, later switching to the Knowes at East Linton. Both James and his wife, Catherine Grant McLaren, were of sound Scottish farming stock, Catherine being one of eleven children whose father farmed Balgillo (later renamed Broome), near Tannadice, and Balgarrock, near Aberlemno.

Mac's earliest memory is of being taken to Prestonpans Station by pony and trap. He said:

I suppose we were very fortunate in those days because there were always people around to do things for us. My father came of a generation where the men and the horses did the ploughing and the women and children picked the potatoes. All the threshing and cutting of the grain, stooking, stacking and haymaking was manual and provided the seasonal employment. Tractors were only just beginning to appear in the 1920s.

Which school you were sent to was also considered important among the East Lothian farming community and nearly all of the more prosperous farmers enrolled their sons at Edinburgh Academy, where Mac himself was a boarder. In common with the majority of them, Mac was a serious rugby enthusiast and played first for Dunbar, then the Edinburgh Academicals and Haddington. In 1933, he scored for Scotland against England, Wales and Ireland. He did not, however, score against France since, in those days, the Scottish Rugby Union objected to the French players being paid!

When his father died in 1936, Mac's brother Ian took over the Knowes but later moved to Newhall, later renamed Woodhead, at Gifford. In the meantime, the Knowes was taken over by John Cochran from yet another Edinburgh Academy and East Lothian farming clan.

'When I was a young man, farming techniques and an understanding of how land should be used were taken seriously,' Mac emphasised, not without irony. On leaving Edinburgh Academy, he was sent to visit relatives in New Zealand and worked on various sheep stations, earning thirty-three shillings a week with board and lodgings. On his return to East Lothian, he married and farmed Ugston, by Haddington, until his wife Janet bought the neighbouring Spitalrig Farm and set about launching a revolution in healthy eating.

Janet Henderson was a remarkable woman who, prior to her marriage, had travelled extensively in Europe where she became a confirmed vegetarian. By her mid-fifties, with seven children of manageable age, she decided to put her wholefood and organic ideas into practice and vegetarian produce from Spitalrig was soon finding its way into local households.

In 1962, she opened a shop in Edinburgh's Hanover Street, a year later transforming its derelict basement into a restaurant. Henderson's Salad Table rapidly acquired a legendary status. Those who remember it from the 1960s may recall the orange boxes for seating – a chic style statement that is not out of place half a century later. At one stage or another, all of the Henderson children – Andrew, John, Sara, Peter, Nicholas, Catherine and Oliver – worked behind the counter.

Janet's founding policy of providing good food at sensible prices rapidly gained momentum. Customer queues at Henderson's Salad Table often stretched into the street outside. Before long a bakery dedicated to brown loaves and bread rolls was launched in Canonmills, and, five years later, Henderson's Bistro in Thistle Street opened its doors.

Janet Henderson died in 1973 from an illness she contracted on a journey to the Far East but, although Henderson's Salad Table lost its founder, the sheer force of her personality ensured the business's survival under the continuing control of her family. Henderson's Salad Table and Bistro, selling organic and additive- and preservative-free produce, remain a staple of Edinburgh life – a fitting tribute to a woman with vision.

For a time, Mac continued to farm Spitalrig but eventually handed it on to his eldest son Andrew. 'Everything is so very different, though,' he said, with a touch of resignation. 'My son leases out most of the land and uses the buildings which once held cattle and machinery for commercial storage for Edinburgh law firms. It has to be an easier life. It certainly pays better.'[16]

There was a faraway look in his eyes. An easier life that pays better? That has to be true to some extent but, as commercial land use throughout the United Kingdom adapts to the demands of a global economy, the way in which our countryside once defined itself is in danger of being lost forever.

CHAPTER TEN

The Handsome Hays

On Monday, 3 April 1967, a memorial service took place at St Mary's Collegiate Church in Haddington. The 11th Marquis of Tweeddale had died after a prolonged illness following a fall in which he had suffered a broken leg. I only met him once but my father must have considered it appropriate for me to accompany him to pay our respects and we sat together solemnly in the centre pews of the west end of the kirk of our ancestors, surrounded by a full complement of mourners. That was several years before the restoration work on St Mary's began and, in a poignant twist in the passage of time, I was to find myself there thirty-nine years later in the fully restored church. On this occasion, I stood in the pulpit to read the eulogy for the Marquis's niece, Lady Marioth Hay who, in the intervening decades, had become a great friend.

My father first took me to Yester House, the Tweeddales' ancestral home at Gifford, in 1963, where I was introduced to Mr Brown, the gamekeeper. The Gifford Burn which runs through the Yester Estate is not much more than a trickle at times but it was here that I learned to fish, or rather how to cast a fly, under the benign eye of John Brown. Although illusive, there were certainly a few small brown trout to be caught if you knew where to look for them, but that was not the point of the exercise. It was yet another father-and-son diversion which led on to adventures on the River Tyne and in a small boat on Hope's Reservoir – excursions which, to my teenage mind, were infinitely more exciting than exploring old castles and graveyards.

The Hays of Yester, who became earls and marquises of Tweeddale, acquired their lands in 1397 through the marriage of Sir William Hay of Locherworth, Sheriff of Peeblesshire, to Jonet, heiress of Sir Hugh Gifford, whose direct ancestor and namesake was a man renowned locally for having made a pact with the Devil. Jonet herself appears to have been a lady of independent character, dispensing rough justice at her Baron Court and signing herself 'Gifford of Yester'.[1]

Hidden deep within the woods, a mile from Yester House, the building of which commenced in the late seventeenth century, is the pink sandstone ruin of the thirteenth-century Yester Castle. Encircled by the Hopes Water, during the summer months it is smothered with dense vegetation which makes it almost invisible. Below the rise on which it stands lies the fabled Goblin's Ha', a mysterious vaulted cavern which, according to local folklore, was built through necromancy. 'There never toiled a mortal arm, it all was wrought by word and charm,' wrote Sir Walter Scott six centuries later.[2]

A charter of William the Lion dated 1160 gives '[t]he Lands of Yestrith that Gamel held, by the bounds that he held them' to the first Hugh Gifford and refers to an earlier charter granted by Malcolm IV, which has since been lost.[3] Yester Castle is today maintained by Historic Scotland and, although there is a lock on the door to the Goblin Ha', it retains its fascination.

However, a certain amount of confusion exists surrounding the several Hugh Giffords who feature in the direct male line of succession until they come to an abrupt end in the fourteenth century. Sir Walter Scott further confounds the issue. In the section of *Marmion* entitled 'The Host's Tale', Alexander III of Scotland visits the wizard, Sir Hugo Gifford, in the hall of Yester Castle which he is alleged to have built in one night with the help of goblins. The King asks him to prophesy the outcome of the battle he is about to fight against the Danes. Sir Hugo sends him to confront the Phantom Knight at the foot of Redstone Rigg. Alexander defeats the Phantom, who obligingly prophesies victory. It makes for a good story but is entirely apocryphal.

Charters exist to confirm that 'Giffard' was the family name of Walter de Longueville, a cousin of William the Conqueror, who led the charge of the knights at the Battle of Hastings in 1066. On that basis, it can be assumed that the first of the Gifford name to appear in Scotland in the reign of David I was of this family, especially since the Countess of Huntingdon, King David's daughter-in-law, was closely related to the Longuevilles.

However, it proves impossible to verify the exact year in which Yester Castle was built, although it is known that a Sir Hugh Gifford was installed in such a place by 1250 and was in correspondence with his father-in-law, Thomas de Morham, about the extent of his park. Since a Broun of Colstoun witnessed a charter between the two men, this same Sir Hugh was, in all probability, the builder of the castle and, it follows, the wizard.

Writing at the time of *Marmion*'s publication in 1808, Sir Walter Scott makes a reference to the *Statistical Accounts of the Parishes of Garvald and Baro*, which gave the following account of the state of the castle and its apartments:

> Upon a Peninsula, formed by the waters of Hopes on the east, and a large rivulet on the west, stands the ancient castle of Yester. Sir David Dalrymple in

his Annals, relates that, 'Hugh Gifford de Yester died in 1267; that in his castle there was a capacious cavern, formed by magical art, and called in the county Bo-hall, ie: Hobgoblin Hall. A stair of twenty-four steps led down to this apartment, which is a large and capacious hall, with an arched roof; and though it hath stood for so many centuries, and has been exposed to the external air for a period of fifty or sixty years, it is still as firm and entire as if it had only stood for a few years. From the floor of this hall, another stair of thirty-six steps leads down to a pit which hath a communication with Hopes-water. A great part of this large and ancient castle is still standing. There is a tradition that the castle of Yester was the last fortification, in this country, that surrendered to General Gray, sent into Scotland by Protector Somerset.' I have only to add that in 1737, the Goblin Hall was tenanted by the Marquis of Tweeddale's falconer, as I learn from a poem by Boyse, entitled 'Retirement', written upon visiting Yester. It is now considered inaccessible by the fall of the stair.[4]

Of course, what we do know for a fact is that Yester Castle was abandoned after it was attacked by the English during The Rough Wooing of 1544–51. Following its surrender, the 4th Lord Yester did eventually get his castle back but from then on made Neidpath Castle at Peebles his principal residence. The earliest sign of the Hay family occupying a four-storey tower house at Bothans, a mile from Yester Castle, comes from the initials of William Hay and his wife Margaret Kerr and the date 1584. These are carved into the mantelpiece of the Laigh Hall of today's Yester House, which would then have been the Great Hall of Bothans.[5]

In the late seventeenth century, Father Richard Augustine Hay, author of a history of the Hay family, remarked of the Handsome Hays, 'It is to be observed that the whole fortune of this familie came by marriages, and whatever hath been purchased was by the selling of lands that had come that way.'[6]

Be that as it may, following Sir William's marriage to Jonet Gifford in 1399 their Hay descendants determinedly made all of the requisite moves to achieve pre-eminence in the Scottish peerage: fighting and falling with their King at the Battle of Flodden and being taken prisoners by the English at Pinkie. Having opposed the religious reforms of Charles I, John, 8th Lord Yester, was in 1646, in a curious turn-around, made Earl of Tweeddale. By then, of course, that unfortunate Stuart monarch was desperately looking for friends wherever he might find them and, in company with their Maitland neighbours, the ambition of the Hays knew no bounds.

In the next generation, John, 2nd Earl of Tweeddale, was, in 1692, appointed Lord High Chancellor of Scotland and, two years later, was created a marquis by William and Mary. Allegedly as bitterly opposed to the union of the Scottish and English parliaments as his neighbour Andrew Fletcher of Saltoun, it was nevertheless his leadership of the indecisive 'Squadrone Volante' which in the event carried the day. This was an outcome which, it has to be conceded, financially benefited all concerned.

The 4th Marquis became Secretary of State for Scotland in 1742. The 7th Marquis, while travelling in Europe, was taken prisoner by Napoleon and incarcerated in the fortress of Verdun while convalescing in France. His son, the 8th Marquis, was a hero of the Peninsular War. He served in the American War of 1812 and was, in 1842, appointed Governor General of Madras; his daughter, Lady Elizabeth Hay, became the wife of the 2nd Duke of Wellington.

On his return to Scotland from India, the 8th Marquis threw all of his energies into improving his inherited land, introducing drainage, deep ploughing and liming. Another of his domestic achievements was to transform Danskinebog, a swampy stretch of ground outside the south gate of Yester, into today's Danskin Loch. His heir, the 9th Marquis, fought in the Crimean War but also carried on his father's domestic improvements, although an attempt to open a copper mine on the Fasney Water, which rises on the farm of West Hopes, met with little success.

The rapid rise in the political fortunes of the Tweeddale family over the seventeenth century, not to mention the wealth they accumulated, brought to an end the village of Bothans, which then consisted of a fortalice, a tower, a kiln, a mill, church and manse. With the building work on Yester House commencing in 1708, the entire community was removed a convenient distance and their new hamlet given the name of Gifford, after the founding family.

In every way fulfilling the image of the perfect conservation village, the Gifford of today forms a sociable community which includes among its residents Sir William Kerr Fraser, a former Principal and Vice-Chancellor of the University of Glasgow, and his wife, Lady Marion who, in 1995, became the first woman to be appointed Lord High Commissioner to the General Assembly of the Church of Scotland. A further addition to the local economy arrived in 1987 with the opening of the Chippendale International School of Furniture which is housed in a steading at Myreside Grange on the Colstoun Estate. Founded by Anselm Fraser from Moniack in Inverness-shire, this provides courses in furniture restoration, design and manufacture.

Gifford is well served by two hotels – the Tweeddale Arms, formerly known as the Great Inn and dating from 1687, and the Goblin Ha', the oldest part of which dates from the same period. In 1899, the Gifford and Garvald Light Railway arrived, serving Humbie, Saltoun and Pencaitland, but curiously not Garvald, before joining the North British Line at Ormiston. It carried passengers until 1933, continuing to carry freight until 1948 when flooding swept away several bridges which were not replaced. Nowadays, visitors arrive and depart by bus or car.

Some of the older properties in Gifford have feudal title deeds which convey rights of grazing on the Common and the owners are known as the Feuars of Gifford. One of the clauses in these deeds is that a Feuar should 'attend the Marquis the space of two days yearly sufficiently mounted with horse and arms at his own expense and another two days at the Marquis's expense'.

Such obligations sound wonderfully feudal but were, by and large, taken for granted under the old order. Patronage does have a positive side. It was the 2nd Marquis of Tweeddale who financed the original courtroom and school and, in 1708, built the T-shaped post-Reformation Yester Kirk at the top of the Main Street. In so doing, he employed the services of Thomas Martine, who had earlier been involved in the building of Yester House.

This Thomas Martine was the son of Thomas Martine of Colstoun Old Myln and his first wife, Margaret Smyth. Nothing much more is known about him other than that he must have forsaken the farming life, thus clearing the way for his much younger stepbrother John to succeed their father. In 1697, he moved to live in Gifford, then in the early stages of being created, where he became a feu holder. Having first become an elder of the kirk at Gladsmuir, he was elected an elder of Baro Kirk and became its treasurer in 1700. When the parish boundaries changed in 1702, he became an elder of the newly built Yester Kirk.

Baro Kirk, with its dwindling congregation, fell rapidly into disrepair and was eventually dismantled. Meanwhile, Yester Kirk prospered. Records show that between 1712 and 1718, Thomas was responsible for the maintenance of its roof, along with those of the manse and school.[7] Unfortunately, I know nothing more of him.

Another casualty of the creation of the village of Gifford was the ancient and exquisitely beautiful St Cuthbert's Church at Bothans, today situated in woodland less than a hundred yards from Yester House. In pre-Reformation days, a dean or provost presided here with seven resident priests and two singing boys. Several of these priests were younger sons of the Hay family, as was the first post-Reformation minister Walter Hay, allegedly a son of the 5th Lord Hay.[8]

St Cuthbert's at Bothans was closed as a working chapel in 1710 and remained in a state of decay until tidied up during the Second World War for the marriage of Lady Georgina Hay, second daughter of the 11th Marquis, to Arthur Coleridge. It being a fine day, the reception for 300 guests was held on the lawn at the side of the house.

In 1723, the wife of the Reverend James Witherspoon, Minister of Yester Kirk, gave birth to a son, John, who, having followed in his father's Church of Scotland footsteps, emigrated to America with his family in 1768. Once established, he became President of the small Presbyterian College of New Jersey which later developed into Princeton University. He was the only clergymen to sign the American Declaration of Independence and from under his tutelage emerged thirty-seven judges, three of whom were elevated to the Supreme Court, twelve members of the Continental Congress, twenty-eight US senators and forty-nine US congressmen.[9] His best-known descendant today is the Hollywood actress Reese Witherspoon.

For upward of 200 years, my great-great-great-grandmother's family, the Carfraes, were tenant farmers on the Yester Estate. Primarily, they farmed Park, now forming part of Quarryford, but also Cairniehaugh, today absorbed into the larger holding of Long Yester, and Waldean, now part of Sheriffside. They married into the Hays of Duncanslaw, also on Yester, and other family members farmed Papple Lawhead on the Whittingehame Estate, now absorbed into the farms of Papple and Papple West Mains, at West Garleton, near Haddington, at Coates, near Gladsmuir on Lord Hopetoun's estate, at Hoprigg, near Cockburnspath, and the Brunt, near Dunbar.

The Carfraes were principally agriculturists but included among their ranks was the Reverend Patrick (1742–1822), Minister of Morham Kirk and the uncle of my great-great-great-grandmother Isabella. From his habit of preaching from manuscripts, he acquired the nickname 'Paper Pate'.

The farm of Morham West Mains, which today belongs to Peter de Pree (see Chapter 8), was then owned by John Dunlop of Dunlop in Ayrshire, whose wife, Frances Anna, following her husband's death in 1785, became a close confidant of Robert Burns. It was she who encouraged the Reverend Patrick to correspond with him over the works of their relative James Mylne, an amateur poet and farmer from Loch-hill, near Prestonpans. James Mylne was by then dead but Carfrae had been his life-long friend and sent Burns a tribute which Mylne had written to him. The bard, nothing if not direct, observed, 'The piece has a good deal of merit, but it has one damning fault – it is by far too long.'

The Reverend Patrick's brother, Captain John Carfrae of the Breadalbane Fencibles, fought in Germany during the Seven Years War and retired to farm Carniehaugh, today part of Long Yester. The Reverend Patrick's son John became a Major-General in the East Indian Forces (Indian Army) and retired to live at Bowerhouse, near Dunbar, a property he inherited through his mother, Mary Shirreff. The last of the Park line of Yester, yet another Thomas Carfrae, farmed Waldean and died in 1820. Around 1842, Joan Carfrae, a cousin in Edinburgh, married and emigrated to America with Allan

Pinkerton, the Glasgow-born founder of the Pinkerton Detective Agency. I realise that the connection is tenuous, but I confess to rather liking the link with a man who foiled a plot to assassinate President Abraham Lincoln.

In the summer of 1968, the year after the 11th Marquis of Tweeddale's death, Marjorie, his widow, opened Yester House to the public. It proved an inspired decision. Yester House was and remains an architectural masterpiece, built to enhance the image of an eighteenth-century Lord Chancellor of Scotland, son-in-law of the 1st and only Duke of Lauderdale. On top of this, an across-the-centuries amalgamation of the genius of James Smith, Alexander McGill, William Adam and his son Robert has created a prince's palace of elegant proportion – not too big, not too small. Moreover, there were paintings on the walls by William Delacour, Carlo Maratta, Gerard Soest and Sir Godfrey Kneller.

It was in the early days of country houses being opened to paying visitors in Scotland and it began in a haphazard fashion. Lady Daphne Stewart, third daughter of the 11th Marquis, compiled a guidebook. I was friendly with her daughter Vicky Fletcher and was recruited, along with my sister Patricia, to help out. Also co-opted were Lady Daphne's husband, Colonel Robin, Elizabeth Young, who had nursed the late Marquis during his illness and had stayed on as housekeeper, and Marioth Hay, then calling herself Lady Fox, who would sit serenely in the upstairs sitting room preoccupied with her needlepoint. The entrance fee for a tour of the house that summer was three shillings and six pence.

I had only recently left school and I enjoyed the experience of being a tour guide at Yester House, especially when it came to making up stories to answer some of the more obscure questions I was asked. I was allocated the staircase which had been designed and constructed by William Adam in 1745. I was also in charge of the ballroom, which had been decorated by William's son Robert during the 1750s. After one tour, Commander More Nisbett from the Drum at Gilmerton took me aside and said, 'I hate to tell you but you've got your Adams back to front. After all, I too live in an Adam house!' Happily, nobody else noticed or, if they did, they were too polite to say so.

One elderly lady showed a great deal of interest in the vast carpet which had also been much admired by Queen Mary, wife of George V, during a visit earlier in the century. 'What are those marks?' she demanded to know, pointing at some particularly vivid stains. 'Moët and Chandon,' I told her, fully aware that they were the work of Marjorie Tweeddale's poodles.

It was both sad and supremely difficult for the extended Tweeddale Family when Yester House was sold. After all, it had been in their hands for over seven centuries. The 11th Marquis had four daughters and, in the tradition of male-line inheritance, the title passed to his nephew, David Hay, who became the 12th Marquis. While he had five sons by two marriages, crippling death duties meant that Yester needed to be broken up. In the event, the estate was bought by Dr James Lumsden, already owner of the adjacent Quarryford Farm, formerly a Yester landholding. Retaining the agricultural land, he, in turn, sold Yester House and its surrounding park to Derek Parker and Peter Morris, owners of the successful Edinburgh-based interior design and antique business A. F. Drysdale. Ubiquitously known as 'The Boys', Parker and Morris had for some years lived at Hopes, the former dower house on the estate, and they generously allowed the dowager Marchioness to rent Yester House from them until she eventually decided to move on in 1969.

After that, I heard that she had gone to live in Gloucestershire but, on reading the memoirs of the English aesthete David Herbert two decades later, discovered that she had joined the British expatriate colony in Tangiers, where she died in 1977. Rubbing shoulders with the Woolworth heiress Barbara Hutton and American writer Paul Bowles must have proved strikingly different to her previous life in East Lothian – but perhaps not.

Having sold Hopes to John Martin, an Edinburgh-based design consultant, Parker and Morris moved into Yester House. However, in 1973 they were approached by the Italian-born composer and impresario Gian Carlo Menotti who, having left America where he had lived for over fifty years, was searching for a quiet retreat in Europe in which to work. 'I chose Scotland because I need peace and silence,' he announced, shrugging off comments about the rain. Even so, taking on an A-listed stately home of the size of Yester would have been quite a challenge for most people at the age of sixty-five. 'It was a form of madness,' he conceded later. 'But having had to live beyond my means keeps me working.' Quite so, with the overheads of Yester House to maintain.

In the autumn of 1992, I was invited to lunch at Yester by the maestro and Francis, his adopted son, who is known as 'Chip'. It was an irresistible opportunity to have a snoop at what they had done to the old place. The purpose of my visit, however, was for me to write an article for *Scottish Field* magazine about the opera school which they hoped to create in the former stable blocks.

Chip's wife Malinda, stepdaughter of the American multimillionaire and former American Vice President Nelson Rockefeller, was also present when I arrived. Presumably owing to the celebrity status of her parents, two burly, black-suited bodyguards lurked in the hallway as I was shown upstairs to the maestro's music room, which I had formerly known as Lady Tweeddale's sitting room. An arrangement of red and white tulips sat in a vase shedding petals on to the surface of a grand piano, which irritated the maestro who called for them to be replaced. This room, he told me, was where he found the inspiration to compose.

Born the youngest of seven sons at Cadegliano in Lombardy in 1911, the founder of the Spoleto and Charleston festivals looked impressively fit and handsome at the age of eighty-two, his profile only comparable to that of a Roman emperor. A child prodigy, he had composed his first mature work at the age of twenty-one for the Metropolitan Opera in New York.

His double bill, *The Medium* and *The Telephone*, was featured on Broadway in 1947, followed by *The Consul* in 1950 (for which he won a Pulitzer prize) and *Amahl and the Night Visitors* in 1951. Inevitably, though, there remained within the world of classical music an uptight faction who would never concede that his work was anything other than Hollywood, a burden Gian Carlo would have to carry for all of his life.

At the start of his career, he had been the librettist for the American composer Samuel Barber's famous opera *Vanessa*. The pair had been muse and critic to one another for well over three decades until Barber's death from cancer in 1981. As a final act of affection, Barber left instructions for a vacant plot to be kept next to his grave for the use of Gian Carlo when the time arrived, but intuitively had added the proviso that should Menotti decide to be buried elsewhere, a plaque would simply read 'To the Memory of Two Friends'.

While far from being an opera aficionado, I had encountered Menotti before at the Edinburgh Festival and had even seen Chip play Toby, the deaf mute, in the Washington Opera revival of *The Medium* in 1985. As we sat down to lunch, Malinda and her bodyguards departed to go shopping in Haddington and Gian Carlo and Chip explained their vision for an opera house of chamber proportions. Situated in the stables, a stone's throw from the mansion house, it would have a seating capacity of no more than 400. This would hopefully attract artists – musicians, actors, dancers, directors, stage and set designers, conductors, technicians and costume designers – from different countries and cultures. The composer Leonard Bernstein and the dancer Rudolph Nureyev were among the names who had guaranteed their support. The benefit to the local economy would be significant. The main house was to be used for chamber music recitals and receptions. Visitors and students would be found accommodation in the neighbourhood, while teachers and leading artists would stay in the house itself.

A design, based on Yester's existing nineteenth-century stable block, set on a rise beyond the two walled gardens and screened from view by mature trees, had already been drawn up by the English architect Quinlan Terry. A model by Simon Montgomery was on display, showing the proportions with baroque statues and rich pediments featured on an Italianate front.

'I know that I have no problems in finding an audience,' announced Gian Carlo confidently. 'I already have two festivals and an international following that will come to Scotland without hesitation. The local audience will develop.'

As an illustration of the goodwill engendered by his international audience, Società Finanziaria Telefonica PA, an Italian telephone company, had, the previous year, sponsored a performance at Yester House of the Mozart work *Apollo et Hyacinthus* in the presence of the Prince of Wales. Listed-building status and planning permissions had already been obtained and Lothian and Edinburgh Enterprise had given assistance with a business plan. 'All we need to do now is raise £7.5 million to finish the job,' observed Chip with a wry smile.

The Menottis' dream, alas, was not to be realised. Despite the £8 million that was raised annually to sustain the Festival of Two Worlds in Umbria, sufficient funding for the Menotti Opera School at Yester failed to materialise. Alas, it was largely the timing. With bank interest rates fluctuating dramatically to 12 per cent following the financial fallout of Black Wednesday that September, money, especially government money, was increasingly tight.

Six weeks later, I found myself at Gosford House where Lord Neidpath was hoping to create an art gallery in the sprawling unoccupied central block from which the roof had been removed during the Second World War (see Chapter 19). He too wanted to raise £8 million. Neither project found the required financial support, which left the Menotti School of Opera at Yester, if not the Gosford House gallery, out on a funding limb. Gian Carlo parted company with the Charleston Festival that same year but continued his association with the Festival of Two Worlds in Spoleto as founder, with Chip becoming its president and artistic director.

Four years before the arrival of the Menottis at Gifford, Marioth Hay had moved into a house in the village. Here she created a garden with terraces and corners of tumbling roses, with clusters of foxgloves, pansies, primroses and Fantin-Latour roses when in season, and she renamed the property Forbes Lodge. Built in the late eighteenth century for the factor of the Yester Estate and remodelled around 1841, it was previously known as Gifford Bank. Earlier in the twentieth century, it was owned by Ronald Fairbairn, the eminent psychoanalyst whose son Nicholas, a flamboyant Conservative Member of Parliament, became Solicitor General for Scotland in 1979. Shortly before his death in 1995 Sir Nicholas, as he had by then become, mused, 'I have seen one thousand marriages disintegrate and have defended seventeen people from the death penalty. All of them came out of it alive.' Immediately prior to Marioth's purchase, Gifford Bank was owned by the

Campbell Fraser Family, whose sculptress daughter Tessa married the television impressionist and comedian Rory Bremner in 1999.

Marioth was rather grand in the manner of the old British aristocracy. Imbued with a generous personality and infinitely kind, she nevertheless did sometimes reflect upon herself as a displaced lady of the manor and, with Yester on her doorstep, developed a mischievous, if innocent, habit of sometimes treating it as if it were still her family home. This was just about the same time as the BBC released its popular television sitcom *To The Manor Born* and, at times, it was almost as if the actress Penelope Keith's character of Audrey fforbes-Hamilton was modelled on Marioth.

Marioth was, after all, a granddaughter of the 10th Marquis of Tweeddale and a sister of the 12th. Her mother had died when she was five years old and her childhood was therefore divided between her father's home in Epping, England, and Yester, where she was surrounded by her Hay cousins and their nannies. She grew up in that watershed period between two world wars. For girls of her class, it was a leisurely, privileged existence of endless country house parties, but it was all to come to an abrupt halt in 1939. At her presentation at Court as a debutant in 1936, she and the other girls were told to assemble wearing white dresses and ostrich feathers in a collecting ring. 'When our names were called out we all had to trot along a red carpet and there was a large white arrow pointing to where the Duke of Windsor, then Prince of Wales, was sitting, just in case we didn't notice him and walked straight past!' It was a fast-vanishing era.

Marioth's father, Lord Edward Hay, was killed by a German bomb while reading the lesson in the Guard's Chapel at Wellington Barracks in 1944. By then, however, Marioth had married Lieutenant-Colonel George Trotter and was living in Berwickshire. They divorced in 1954 and she then became the second wife of Sir Gifford Fox, a Member of Parliament, who died in 1969. In those fifteen years of marriage, she and her husband travelled extensively and she told me that, on a visit to Cyprus, the Cypriot President, Archbishop Makarios, had pinched her bottom. She related this story with all the coquettish glee of a naughty schoolgirl.

Marioth's third marriage was to Sir John James, Controller of the Royal Mint, whom she divorced in 1971. Meanwhile, her brother had become 12th Marquis of Tweeddale so she reverted to her maiden name of Hay and took up her courtesy title.

I often used to look in on Forbes Lodge when passing through Gifford and there was always a warm welcome while she painted on an easel in her kitchen and boiled a kettle for a cup of tea. Like so many women of her generation and background, she was extremely accomplished. She had been an early friend of the poet John Betjeman and enjoyed the company of a circle of professional artists such as John Halliday, even holding an exhibition of his paintings in her garage. Sometimes, I would be invited to one of her lunch parties where she served up her staple dish of coronation chicken which, although subject to ribaldry from her family, was always delicious. It was at one of these lunches that I was first introduced to Gian Carlo Menotti.

In 2000, I had set off to take photographs of Yester Castle for a book I was writing about the supernatural. It was a Sunday in June and when I set off in the early afternoon the sky was azure blue but, by the time I reached Yester Mains, it was leaden grey. As I started to walk around the circumference of the golf course towards the little gate which opens into the woodland, the rain arrived in torrents. By the time I had clambered up the overgrown footpath and reached the castle courtyard, I was drenched.

I took my photographs, but decided not to venture through the small postern gate into the subterranean Goblin Ha', which I had explored so many times before. Instead, I retraced my steps along the pathway only to find myself completely lost. The rain was now really sheeting down and the woods became darker with every step. I started to panic. What made it worse was that I was fully conversant with the curses surrounding Hugh Gifford, the builder of the castle. I had told nobody where I was going. Nobody knew where I was. Images of demons and mythical beasts flashed through my mind.

From the castle forecourt I could even see where I needed to get to and, after an hour of walking around in circles, I decided to slide myself down the riverbank in order to cross over the Hopes Water. If I thought that I had been wet before, I was now soaked to the skin. Clambering up the opposite bank and over a fence, I encountered a bull. It stared at me with red eyes so I leapt over another fence and sprinted across the empty golf course to my car. Covered in mud and dripping wet, I finally arrived at Forbes Lodge and Marioth came to the door highly entertained. 'That'll teach you for going to that place on your own,' she chided, as I sat in the kitchen wrapped in a towel with my clothes draped over the Aga. 'A couple of years ago,' she told me, 'I gave a lift to a Canadian man who was living in the village and whose car had broken down. He told me that he'd been up at the castle earlier that day with a metal detector. Do you know, that very same evening he suffered a heart attack and died!'

To begin with, a strong friendship existed between Lady Marioth and Gian Carlo Menotti but sadly this ran into difficulties in 1996. When the Yester Estate was sold to Parker and Morris, the one piece of property retained by the Tweeddale Family Trust was St Cuthbert's Chapel (Bothans) in which generations of the Tweeddale Hays of Yester were interred. Shortly before the sale, Marioth and her cousin, Lady Georgina Coleridge, had applied to

Historic Scotland for a repair grant. They received £13,000 and this had been spent on rescuing the chapel from dereliction. However, part of the understanding with Historic Scotland was that St Cuthbert's Chapel should be open to visitors at least once a year. The majority of those who subsequently came to inspect the chapel – not exactly in great numbers, it has to be said – were invariably accompanied by Marioth. This, of course, made it all the more upsetting for her when, after twenty years had elapsed, she received a letter out of the blue from the Menottis' solicitor informing her that such visitors were not welcome. The Menottis, not unreasonably, objected to cars being parked in their driveway, but this, as it transpired, gave rise to another matter.

In 1982, Historic Scotland had handed over a £203,000 grant for the restoration of Yester House and, again, part of the deal was that it should, on occasion, be accessible to the public. Marioth was not going to take this lying down and she was certainly not going to be denied access to her family's chapel where not only her ancestors were interred but also generations of family pets. Not for nothing did the family motto carved into the sandstone crest above St Cuthbert's heavy oak door read 'Spare Nought'.

After a punchy article in the *East Lothian Courier* and complaints from Gifford Community Council, East Lothian's Member of Parliament John Home Robertson eventually raised the subject at Question Time in the House of Commons. The Menottis' response was that, since the repairs had been completed, ownership of Yester House had been transferred to another member of the family which made the Historic Scotland obligation invalid. As a gesture of goodwill, however, Gian Carlo did thereafter allow the local community to hold a one-off service at Bothans and he permitted Lady Daphne Stewart to be buried there in 2001. At the time of the community event, however, he was quoted as saying, 'I do not want this to be an excuse for Lady Marioth to have services every Sunday.'[10]

Marioth died in April 2006 and I was immensely flattered, if a trifle daunted, when, aware that the end was coming, she asked me to give the address at her service. She was like that, Marioth, always well organised and rather brave. In the event, there was a large turnout at St Mary's. In my address, I did my best to do her justice. As the sun streamed through glass windows on either side, the cookery and television personality Clarissa Dickson Wright read Rudyard Kipling's 'The Glory of the Garden'. It was an emotional and warm send-off for a much-loved individual, the last of the Hays of Yester to live at Gifford. After the service in Haddington, Marioth was interred in the family plot at Yester Kirk.

Malinda Menotti, who had died in October 2005, is also buried at Yester Kirk. Gian Carlo died in Monaco, in February 2007, on the eve of a production of his opera *The Medium*, directed by Chip. He had reached the age of ninety-five and, contrary to his friend Samuel Barber's proposal that he be interred beside him in a county cemetery in West Chester, Pennsylvania, Gian Carlo chose Yester Kirk instead, close to the Scottish home he had loved for thirty years. Appropriately, his funeral took place at Yester Kirk on the day Scotland played Italy in the Six Nations Rugby Championship at Murrayfield. Italy won.

The President of the Italian Republic sent a telegram to be read out by the Italian Consul General; the great Italian tenor Luciano Pavarotti, who was himself to die in the September of the following year, had written a letter which was read out by Gian Carlo's godson, the Marquis of Clydesdale. During the interment, in the sky above, Angus, 15th Duke of Hamilton provided the mourners with a five-minute fly-past and aerial acrobatic display in his Bulldog.

As all of us stood there in the cemetery of Yester Kirk, on that bleak February morning, a melancholy, if not ironic, thought crossed my mind. Now at peace, Marioth and the Menottis are still neighbours in Gifford.[11]

CHAPTER ELEVEN

Bob's Your Uncle

BOUNDED ON THE WEST by the Parish of Morham, to the south and west by Garvald, on the north by Prestonkirk, on the east by Stenton and on the south again by Cranshaws and Longformacus, the Whittingehame Estate, named after 'the Whittings, a tribe of Angles', has had a succession of lords and masters. Comprising half of the lands of the Parish of Spott, it passed from the earls of March to the Douglases of Dalkeith, and, in 1564, was ratified to their representative James Douglas, 4th Earl of Morton, by Mary, Queen of Scots.[1] It was, indeed, beneath the great yew tree at Whittingehame Tower that Morton and Sir Archibald Douglas, then its resident, the 14th Earl of Bothwell and William Maitland of Lethington conspired to eradicate Mary's errant husband, Lord Darnley. Writing of this remarkable tree in 1929, the Reverend Marshall T. Lang, Minister of Whittingehame, noted, 'It is 147 yards in circumference, its branches being turned downward and resting on the soil, thereby completely obscuring the central trunk which measures 11 feet in girth.'[2] In 2006, the girth of its trunk had reached 12 feet (3.64 metres).[3]

After Morton's downfall, the Whittingehame Estate passed through marriage to the Hays of Drumelzier but its heyday, if you will excuse the pun, was to come 200 years later when, in 1817, it was bought, along with a number of adjacent farms, by James Balfour, second son of John Balfour of Balbirnie in Fife, who had acquired a large fortune in India. James Balfour engaged Sir Robert Smirke, who was to be the architect of the British Museum no less, to build a mansion house on the grand scale. Balfour's brief for Smirke was very simple – 'Build me a house grander than the family home at Balbirnie.'

James had been despatched to India as the black sheep of the family and he wished to make an irrevocable statement about his own standing. Upon its completion, such was its scale and appearance that it was considered to be one of the finest neoclassical houses of its time. Unfortunately, much of its original classical simplicity was sacrificed in 1826 when William Burn was brought in to decorate the interiors and add on extensions. Nevertheless, no expense was spared. The gardens, a notable feature of the overall design, were laid out by William S. Gilpin.

In 1843, James Balfour's son, also James, married Lady Blanche Cecil, sister of the 3rd Marquess of Salisbury who, between 1885 and 1902, was to serve three times as British Prime Minister. Then, as now, such associations count in politics. James Balfour represented East Lothian in Parliament under the old system and, in 1831, polled forty old freehold votes against the eleven of his opponent, Sir David Baird of Newbyth. However, in 1854, at the age of thirty-six, he died of tuberculosis in Madeira, the same year that Hermann Brehmer opened the first sanatorium dedicated to curing the disease at Görbersdorf in Germany.

James and Lady Blanche's eldest son Arthur James Balfour inherited Whittingehame from his father at the age of sixteen. Having been educated at Eton and Trinity College, Cambridge, he was elected Conservative Member of Parliament for Hertford in England in 1874 and, four years later, became Lord Salisbury's parliamentary private secretary, the appointment giving rise to the expression 'Bob's your uncle'! Balfour's subsequent premiership, as heir to his uncle's Tory fiefdom, saw the end of the South African War, the passing of the Education Act to create local education authorities and the establishment of the Committee of Imperial Defence. In 1911, he resigned the leadership of the House of Commons owing to the constitutional crisis but he served under David Lloyd George as Foreign Secretary from 1916. In 1917, he was responsible for the Balfour Declaration which had originally been drafted by Lord Milner and promised Zionists a national homeland in Palestine, a policy keenly opposed by the League of Nations. The letter outlining the proposal was actually written at Whittingehame and sent to Lord Rothschild, a leader of the British Jewish Community. In 1920, it was incorporated into the Treaty of Sèvres between the Allies and the Ottoman Empire, an agreement which was to be superseded by the Treaty of Lausanne in 1923.

Earl Balfour, as he became in 1922, died in 1930 and was interred in the family's private burial ground at Whittingehame. Thereafter, his brother's family occupied the big house until 1935 when the running costs overtook them. Following this, the 4th Earl Balfour renovated Whittingehame Tower which is today occupied by his nephew Mackie Brander, grandson of the 3rd Earl Balfour.[4]

Between 1939 and 1941 Whittingehame House became a farm school, after which it was leased to Dr Guthrie's Institution for Boys until 1953. It was briefly utilised in 1956 as a home for Hungarian refugees. It then lay empty until 1963 when it was purchased, along with forty-five acres, by the Holt School for Boys. This lasted until 1980, when it was bought by

Mohammed Al-Abdaly, an Arab sheikh, who wished to create a seventy-five-bed private hospital for wealthy Saudi Arabians. However, planning permission was denied 'on the grounds that the development would have a detrimental effect upon the local Health Services and resources, particularly upon the availability of qualified and experienced nursing staff in the Lothian Health Board area'.[5] This decision was later reversed by the Secretary of State for Scotland but, by then, the sheikh's backers, Thamoud (Scotland) Ltd, had gone into liquidation. In the aftermath of this sadly all too typical bureaucratic affair, the surrounding land and buildings were sold off but Whittingehame House itself was seen by potential purchasers as a white elephant and sat empty, awaiting its destiny.[6]

I first encountered Paul Harris in the late 1970s, shortly after the closure of his first publishing venture Impulse in Aberdeen and before he set up his Paul Harris imprint in Edinburgh. Over lunch at The Tilted Wig, a local hostelry in the capital, he agreed to republish my first book, *The Swinging Sporran* (written jointly with Andrew Campbell and at that time out of print). In 1983, he commissioned me to write *Royal Scotland*, a history of Scotland's ruling dynasties. Wearing owl spectacles and with a penchant for loud suits, bow ties and cigars, Paul was the epitome of the twentieth-century publisher, astute in judgement but never afraid to take risks. This was a talent he developed to great advantage in later years. However, that is to jump ahead.

In the early 1980s, based in Edinburgh's New Town, Paul concentrated on re-issuing a series of limited editions which enabled him to publish a less profitable general list and the occasional play and volume of poetry which he considered important because they set the tone of his business. Alas, publishing is a fickle mistress and increased overheads finally persuaded him to abandon his city-centre offices in favour of the port of Leith at a time when the area was not yet fashionable. He was soon thereafter obliged to abandon publishing and returned to a mix of writing, publishing consultancy and issuing the odd book as and when funds allowed.

In April 1986, a discreet small advertisement appeared in the property section of the *Scotsman* newspaper announcing that Whittingehame House in East Lothian, situated in its own grounds with woodland, tennis court and fishing rights, was up for sale. Offers in the region of £120,000 were invited.

Now it just so happened that Paul had recently been approached by Charles Skilton, one of his publisher clients in the south of England, who was interested in purchasing a country house close to Edinburgh. Paul was initially puzzled as to why a house with eighty-six rooms should be on the market for such as modest sum but, on viewing the property and making a guess at the potential costs of renovation, it became obvious. But this was not sufficiently off-putting to deter either of them. 'Despite its vastness, its institutional green, the hardboard nailed to the walls, the water flowing through cracked and collapsed ceilings and the general air of abandonment which lay heavy in the rooms and corridors, we were excited by the atmosphere and potential for living in the building,' he wrote.

In his book *Life in a Scottish Country House – the Story of A. J. Balfour and Whittingehame House*, published in 1989, Paul later reflected that 'between 1875 and 1975, a recorded 318 Scottish country houses were destroyed and, of these, 190 disappeared after the Second World War'. He went on to observe that

> the toll of destruction, considering the relatively small size of the county, was particularly severe in East Lothian: Belton House (demolished 1967), Caponflat House (1947), Congalton (1927), Elphinstone Tower (1964), Smeaton Hepburn (1948), Smeaton House (1948) and Thurston (1952). There were especially significant losses at Dunglass House (1950) and Amisfield (1928) and many partial demolitions, notably at Biel House.

Undaunted, he and Skilton hatched a scheme and, on the basis of the enormous public rooms on the first floor being retained as one unit, the planning authority accepted their proposal for Whittingehame to be divided into six residential apartments. For all concerned, it seemed a logical way of saving an important historic building that had realistically outlived its purpose. Unfortunately, Charles Skilton was to run into financial problems and become ill. He would never come up with his share of the development funds and would die prematurely from cancer in 1989.

All the same, there were precedents for a somewhat unusual development by two amateurs. Not so very far away, Saltoun Hall had been divided up during the 1960s. In 1989, Tyninghame House, near East Linton, was similarly converted into nine vertically divided homes by the new developer Kit Martin (see Chapter 28). It made sense.

The redevelopment of Whittingehame House took place with Paul himself occupying the 'nursery wing' which had been so dubbed by the late Lord Balfour, who remembered being brought up and educated as a child in that part of the house. 'It was manna from heaven for me and I was able to buy my portion of the house and part of the top floor from out of the deal,' Paul said. 'I spent the following two years working on the restoration and that got me back on my feet again in business.'

The house also required to be furnished and he rapidly set about acquiring and rescuing various antiques, one of which ultimately turned out to be extremely providential at a time when he was feeling financially hard up. 'I was on my own one day when there was a loud banging on the door,' he recalled. 'Outside I found an American gentleman who had been visiting downstairs and been told that I had a desk.' This, of course, was the desk from the Whittingehame library upon which the Balfour Declaration had been signed. 'It was an undistinguished Regency writing table which I had just had restored by Whytock & Reid of Edinburgh,' he recalled. 'The provenance, of course, was purely anecdotal but, such as it was, it came from somebody who had once lived at Whittingehame and had exchanged it with me for another desk after reading my book on the house. I showed it to the American and he instantly produced a Bank Leumi chequebook and asked me how much I wanted for it. As it happened, I had recently had it valued at Phillips, the auctioneers, so I quoted him a sum around twenty-five per cent over the estimate and he wrote me out a cheque on the spot.

'He was Miro Weizmann, a nephew of Chaim Weizmann, founder of the State of Israel,' Paul explained. 'The table was then unexpectedly arrested in my hands by the temporary owners of downstairs who were, let us say, mysterious interlopers from Ireland and it was released when their bankers forced them to sell up. It was eventually shipped to Weizmann in Miami.'

But that is to jump ahead in time. Charles Skilton, a non-smoker for all of his life, died from lung cancer in 1989 but, by then, Whittingehame House had been successfully divided up and had attracted its full quota of occupants, including Jamie Swinton, a documentary film producer, and Alan Cope, who later purchased the George Hotel in Haddington. The main apartment is today owned by David and Mary McMillan, who were formerly at Seton House (see Chapter 19).

Paul had also started to write again and, on a visit to the Frankfurt Book Fair in 1987, he had met a group of printers from Yugoslavia who were looking for work. 'I proposed myself as their British representative and we subsequently built up a very good business,' he said. That was until 25 June 1991, when Slovenian independence was declared. Paul was over on a business trip and was just preparing to board his flight at Ljubljana airport, when it was destroyed in a bombing attack. 'It was truly a career change moment,' he said. 'Once I had got over the shock, I took some photographs and sold them to Reuters. Then the telephone calls started to come in and all of a sudden I was a photojournalist.'

Paul remained in the Balkans until the end of the Bosnian War in 1995, regularly flying backwards and forwards to the UK to process his pictures and sell his articles. When the peace agreement was finally signed, the then Deputy Editor of *Scotland on Sunday* newspaper, Brian Groom, for whom he had covered the war for almost five years, telephoned him and said, 'Paul, the war is over.'

'He would be wrong,' said Paul on reflection, 'but, by then, my heart had gone out of it. I needed to move on.'

Five years later, he would find himself in Kosovo during the NATO campaign and there he met some people from a village in the mountains who told him that something terrible had happened – a large number of women had been raped and their bodies stuffed down a well. 'Ben Brown of the BBC asked me to go up there with Vaughan Smith, who ran the famous Frontline Agency. When we arrived, the villagers, all men, opened up the well. The sky was filled with a black cloud of insects and I was stung by one of them.'

Not long afterwards, Paul began to feel queasy and realised that something was wrong. He immediately drove out of Kosovo through Macedonia and into Greece where, unable to walk, he was carried on to the ferry to Bari in Italy. Within days of reaching the hospital, he had lost half of his body weight and was treated with seven different antibiotics before the eighth one kicked in as he faced death. 'I was diagnosed as having a type of blood poisoning which had not been seen since the Great Plague!'

Paul's recovery was slow but recover he did and, once again, it was time to reflect upon his future. He had spent four years since the end of the war in Bosnia travelling the world – he calculated that he had covered more than a dozen wars and had datelines from more than fifty countries. But the country with which he still continued to feel a real affinity was Sri Lanka, the Indian Ocean teardrop of land ravaged by war.

Following the wind-down of conflict in former Yugoslavia, he had been covering the war in Sri Lanka. Paul arrived in Colombo on a Sunday morning at the end of January 1996 and, as if fate were once again orchestrating his life, his visit coincided with the Tamil Tigers, the Liberation Tigers of Tamil Eelam (otherwise LTTE), blowing up the town's business district just three days after his arrival. The following morning, his report featured on page one of the *Scotsman*. Over the years that followed, Paul would visit Sri Lanka thirteen times as a war correspondent and in November 2001 decided to settle there, leasing out his flat at Whittingehame and taking up residence in the celebrated Galle Face Hotel, the oldest hotel east of Suez.[7]

It was the beginning of yet another outlandish episode in his life. Within twelve months, working as the *Daily Telegraph* correspondent in Sri Lanka and for *Jane's Intelligence Review* in London, he had succeeded in antagonising both the Sri Lankan Prime Minister and the LTTE to the extent that he and his Chinese girlfriend Sulee were expelled from the country. Fortunately, his friend Ian Nimmo, a former editor of the *Edinburgh Evening News*, had been contracted to advise the Chinese government on newspaper development and offered him a job as a foreign expert on the *Shanghai Daily* newspaper.

In August of the following year, Paul married Sulee and, a year later, their daughter Lucy was born in Shanghai. It had always been Paul's intention to return to Whittingehame and, in November 2004, he and his family did just that. Shortly after they had settled in, however, he was contacted by MI5, the British Security Service, and informed that a directive had been issued by the LTTE ordering his assassination.

Although the probability of the LTTE striking at the heart of East Lothian was a remote and slightly farcical idea, such threats should never be taken lightly. A month after he returned to Whittingehame, a false alarm resulted in the Lothian and Borders Police Armed Response Unit being scrambled to the house, where they fanned out over the elegant lawns in flak jackets and helmets.

Terrorism has a long arm and, during the ceasefire of 2005, Paul's friend Lakshman Kadirgamar, Sri Lanka's Foreign Minister, was shot while climbing out of a swimming pool at his residence in Colombo. Paul now had the safety of his wife and child to consider. Nineteen years after he had instigated the restoration work at Whittingehame House, he therefore reluctantly decided that, yet again, it was time to move on. The 'nursery flat' was put on the market at the beginning of 2005 and was soon snapped up.

'It was always so useful,' observed Lady Evelyn Brander, daughter of the 3rd Earl of Balfour, who today lives at Whittingehame Mains with her husband Michael Brander, the well-known country sportsman and author. 'Whenever we wanted to amuse the children, we just sent them up Traprain Law.'

Since the Law squats almost on her doorstep and the views from the summit across the flat lands of coastal East Lothian are spectacular, it is easy to see what she means. Resembling a large pan loaf dropped from above, the 350-foot high Traprain Law (724 feet above sea level), anciently called Dunpender Law, has played with the imagination of Scottish historians since time immemorial. Writing in 1970, R. W. Feachem, the Archaeology Officer of the Ordnance Survey, noted that it had attracted settled and prosperous people as early as the first half of the first millennium BC. Situated close to the Firth of Forth, it enabled them to participate in a sea-borne trade with the richer south and to develop an elaborate, almost urban life which included industrial enterprises such as bronze-casting and working in iron. These early settlers built houses and other buildings on the Law and eventually erected great walls around it for their protection.

Alexander Curle and James Cree of the Society of Antiquaries of Scotland commenced excavations in 1914 and, over two summers, unearthed not only Stone, Bronze and Iron Age relics but also Roman coins dating from the reign of the emperor brothers Arcadius (reigned AD 395–408) and Honorius (reigned AD 395–423). However, they found no evidence to suggest Roman occupation of the hill and so concluded that the currency must either have been stolen by pirates on the Firth of Forth or given as a reward for services and hidden there.

In 1919, further excavation was encouraged by Dr Jimmy Richardson, who was, by then, closely involved with the Society of Antiquaries of Scotland. This revealed a pit containing 160 silver dishes, bowls and chalices. Although at first thought to be spoils from shipping plundered in the Firth of Forth, Richardson's considered opinion was that it must have originated from the Saxon monastery at Tyninghame. This treasure trove is on display in the Museum of Scotland in Edinburgh.

In popular mythology, there lived, around AD 518, King Loth of the Gododdin, a great Celtic ruler who administered Lothian from a compound on Traprain Law. Those who have explored the Scottish end of the Arthurian legends will know that Loth was allegedly the brother-in-law of King Arthur of the Britons. Sometimes magnanimous but more often than not a ruthless tyrant, Loth had the misfortune to have, in addition to his son Mordred, an only daughter called Thenu or Enoch, who, as so often occurs in such circles, fell in love with somebody her father considered entirely unsuitable – a shepherd lad, no less. Having failed to dissuade her from her folly, the King ordained that she be tossed off the cliffs on the eastern side of Traprain Law and, when this failed to dampen her ardour, set her adrift in a coracle on the Firth of Forth. Miraculously Thenu/Enoch once again survived. When her boat eventually washed up on the northern shore at Culross, she gave birth to a son whom she named Kentigern, who was later beatified as St Mungo and became the patron saint of Glasgow. To keep the story politically correct, Kentigern's biographer, a monk named Jocelyn of Furness, insisted that the shepherd must have taken advantage of Thenu/Enoch while she was unconscious, in other words that she was raped. It is also claimed that the broken-hearted shepherd boy was so wildly incensed by King Loth's cruelty that he took up his bow and arrow and shot him through his heart.

It all adds up to a good yarn, especially when a standing stone known as the Loth Stone can still be seen in a field at Standingstone Farm. However, this is not, apparently, where it was previously situated, it having been removed from the nearby Cairndinnis Farm to enable its original site to be ploughed over. Under the circumstances, the fact that it is still standing at all makes it worth a visit.

CHAPTER TWELVE

The Golf Coast

NIGEL TRANTER USED TO tell a story, which he insisted was true, of the Prime Minister of Denmark being taken to North Berwick while on an official visit to Edinburgh. On being asked by the Provost of North Berwick what he thought of East Lothian, the Dane politely replied that he was much impressed, having noticed that all of the land which was unsuitable for golf had been turned over to agriculture.

This raised a few laughs at the time but there can be no doubt whatsoever that golf, with the international tourism it attracts, is, alongside farming, the staple of East Lothian's economy and has been for a considerable amount of time. With its glorious coastline, brisk sea air and distant vistas, there can be few finer locations for enjoying the game, which explains why there are now twenty-two East Lothian golf clubs to choose from.

The Musselburgh Golf Club at Monktonhall was established within a wooded loop of the River Esk, overlooking Inveresk, in 1938. Beside Musselburgh Race Course is the Old Course of Musselburgh Links and, having been established in 1672, this is the grandfather of them all. An original venue for the Open Championship, the oldest of the four major championships in men's golf worldwide, it hosted the competition on six occasions between 1874 and 1889. Then, just to confuse those who are unaware of golf's enduring popularity in the region, there is the Royal Musselburgh Golf Club, which is centred on the mansion of Prestongrange House at Prestonpans. Founded in 1774, this ranks as the fifth oldest golf club in the world.

For over 150 years, Royal Musselburgh members played over the nine holes on Musselburgh Levenhall links. Then, in 1926, a new eighteen-hole course designed by the Fife-born James Braid, winner of the Open Championship in 1901, 1905, 1906, 1908 and 1910, was officially opened. When, in 1958, Prestongrange House was put up for sale, the Royal Musselburgh Golf Club was given first option to buy it. In the event, it was purchased by the Coal Industry Social and Welfare Organisation and was held in trust by the Musselburgh Miners' Charitable Society, the accommodation to be shared with the RMGC. In 1962, to some extent emphasising the strength of the relationship, James Bush, a miner, was appointed club captain.

Set in 130 acres of walled parkland which once formed part of the Amisfield Estate, the Haddington Golf Club was inaugurated in 1865 and, apart from a twenty-year period from 1881 when the land was given over to grazing and the club moved to Garleton Hill, it has remained at Amisfield Park ever since. The hamlet of Gifford offers two options – the Castle Park Golf Club was established in 1994, its principal challenge being the lake which splits the first fairway, and, on the west side of the village, the Gifford Golf Club, a nine-hole parkland course dating from 1904.

At Aberlady, the Kilspindie Golf Club was founded in 1867 and, ranking as the thirty-fifth oldest golf club in Scotland, retains its original features with several holes bordering the shoreline. The Longniddry Golf Club, built in 1921, is another Open qualifying location. At Aberlady, the Craigielaw Golf Club was established in 1998. It was designed by Donald Steel, President of the English Golf Union, and thrives with young talent. Since 2005, it has featured a golf school presided over by PGA Professional Eric Grandison.

Gullane Golf Club offers three courses, their numbering a reflection of their age. Gullane No. 1 has, since its creation in 1882, hosted the Scottish Amateur Championship, the Open Championship Qualifying, the Senior Open Amateur and European Boys Team Championships. Gullane No. 2, which opened in 1900, has also been used for Open Championship Qualifying and the Seniors Open Amateur. Gullane No. 3 was established in 1910 and, although the shortest of the Gullane courses, it is considered a challenging experience.

Next to the Gullane Professional Shop, run by PGA Professional Alasdair Good, I met Archie Baird, a former captain of Gullane who, in 1980, created the Heritage of Golf Museum which is housed in a section of the seventeenth-century building thought to have once been a toll house, before becoming a school, then a club-maker's shop.

'The first thing I did was to marry the right woman,' he announced, with a twinkle in his eye, as he showed me around his collection. Sheila Baird, Archie's wife, is a great-granddaughter of Willie Park, who won the first Open Championship in 1875 and went on to win the Opens of 1887 and 1889. As well as being a player, Willie Park was a club-maker and his son, Willie Park Junior, Sheila's great-uncle, not only laid out the Gullane No. 2 Course but also designed courses as far afield as Argentina.

'For the No. 2 Course, Willie Junior sent in a bill for 10 guineas,' said Archie. 'The Committee asked him to modify his account but he refused!

Look at that face!' he added, indicating a monochrome portrait of Willie Junior with full walrus moustache. 'That's not the sort of face to modify an account! Of course, it didn't mean that he wasn't asked to design the No. 3 Course as well.'

For many years, Archie ran a successful veterinary practice in Edinburgh. He and Sheila lived in a house in York Place and, while in the process of doing it up, became familiar with most of the antique shops in the capital. One day, purely by chance, Archie came across a long-nose golf club inscribed 'W. Park Musselburgh'. 'I had never realised what a beautiful object a club was,' he said and thus began a lifelong passion for collecting golf memorabilia.

'I started buying up every one I could find,' he continued. 'Then I came across clubs made by manufacturers I'd never heard of so I started buying books to find out more about them. Then Sheila gave me a little painting of golfers and I began to collect early golf paintings.'

It was around this time that Archie came across John Smart who, about 1889, painted golf courses throughout Scotland, starting at Dunbar. In 1893, John Aikman put together a collection of engravings of Smart's pictures and these were published in a book which enabled Archie to know exactly how many paintings were in existence. So far he has tracked down eighteen of the twenty recorded. The originals of Gullane and Luffness, for example, hang in the Luffness Club House.

Archie already owned Smart's painting of North Berwick but, given his wife's family connections, the one he really wanted was that of Musselburgh. Through a certain amount of detective work, he discovered that it had gone to Japan but then, quite suddenly, it appeared in a picture sale held at Gleneagles Hotel, with an estimated selling price of between £10,000 and £15,000.

Archie immediately set out to buy it but, in the event, it sold for £55,000 and he came away from the sale very disappointed. However, it later transpired that he knew the buyer who, coincidentally, lived at North Berwick and they had swapped pictures. 'The Musselburgh painting shows the bunker at "Pandy", short for "Pandemonium",' he said with glee as he showed me the copy on show in the museum.

The Heritage of Golf exhibition was opened in 1980, coinciding with the first edition of Archie's book *Golf on Gullane Hill*, now in its ninth edition. The opening ceremony was performed by American Masters champion Ben Crenshaw and, a quarter of a century on, the small space continues to encapsulate a veritable treasure trove of collectibles ranging from feathery balls and personality portraits to golf clothing and just a selection of Archie's 500 clubs. But take note – it is not open on a day-to-day basis so you have to book an appointment.

'Golf is terribly important to East Lothian,' insisted Archie. 'But the vast majority of golfers have no idea how the game started or where it comes from. All they need to do to find out is to come here and I will show them.'

The most recent addition to East Lothian's prolific golfing portfolio is at Archerfield, between Dirleton and North Berwick, where David J. Russell has created the Fidra Links and Dirleton Links for the Edinburgh-based entrepreneur Kevin Doyle. A pristine Archerfield Links Clubhouse now overlooks the ninth green on Fidra and the eighteenth green on Dirleton and historic Archerfield House (see Chapter 25) has been restored and renovated to become a fifteen-bedroom luxury hotel. Adjoining Archerfield Links on the east and Muirfield on the west is the 300-acre Renaissance Club, where a course and clubhouse have been designed by the American architect Tom Doak for Hamilton & Kinneil (1987) Limited, the Duke of Hamilton's family trust.

At the inland Whitekirk Golf Club, which opened in 1995, there is a heathland course designed by Cameron Sinclair, a past captain of Northamptonshire County Golf Club. At North Berwick there are two spectacularly situated clubs. On the East Links is the Glen Golf Club, which dates from 1906, and, on the Beach Road, the older North Berwick Golf Club, dating from 1832, also an Open qualifying venue. At Dunbar there is the Winterfield Golf Club, established in 1935, and the Dunbar Golf Club, which opened in 1856. The former has a headland reaching into the North Sea while at the latter, fourteen consecutive holes follow a testing narrow strip of land alongside the Firth of Forth.

Then, of course, there is the jewel in East Lothian's golfing crown, The Honourable Company of Edinburgh Golfers, next to Gullane, at Muirfield, the oldest golf club in the world. In company with the nearby Luffness New Golf Club, The Honourable Company of Edinburgh Golfers at Muirfield operates with an exclusively male membership (although women visitors are welcomed), a brave and fragile distinction in this unisex world. For this distinction both forfeit their charitable status, which seems unfair, but is probably worth it, as can be judged from Muirfield's 600 members and a waiting list of many years. Although not a member myself, I have in the past enjoyed the generous hospitality of two of Muirfield's outstanding club secretaries, Major Vanrenan and Group Captain John Prideaux, and my most recent visit was to meet the present Secretary, Alastair Brown, who took up the post in 2003.

Relaxing both before and after lunch in the spectacular clubroom with its sweeping vistas over the links to the Firth of Forth, it is easy to comprehend why Muirfield tops the poll of the hundred best golf clubs and courses in Britain and, some would say, the world. Not only that – since its course was completed in 1892, it has welcomed the Open sixteen times. Muirfield is the only course to have hosted all of the great tournaments – the Open, the British Amateur, the British Mid-Amateur, the Ryder Cup, the Walker Cup and the Curtis Cup. Moreover, The Honourable Company of Edinburgh Golfers has records which date back to 1744, when the Club wrote the original Thirteen Rules of Golf for the first competition played for the Silver Club. At that time, members played on the five holes at Leith Links, moving, in 1836, to Musselburgh's nine-hole Old Course and then to their current home in 1891.

My host on the occasion of my visit this time was the caricaturist and artist Hugh Dodd, who has become one of the top painters of golf courses in the UK, his oil and watercolour landscapes reaching out to an international clientele. In addition, he has the distinction of living with his wife Sarah and two daughters in the house, complete with putting green, that Ben Sayers built in North Berwick.

It was interesting to take note of who else was lunching at the long tables on that Friday – a veritable who's who of East Lothian life ranging from Sir Garth Morrison, the Lord Lieutenant, and Simon Stodart from Kingston, to Andrew and Nicholas Henderson of the Spitalrig farming family, and Sir Francis Ogilvy, whose family had previously owned the land upon which the links course was originally created.

Hugh is also a director of the Luffness New Golf Club which was designed by 'Old' Tom Morris, celebrated for having either created or altered in the region of seventy courses throughout the British Isles. Luffness New, which was first completed in 1872, he re-styled in 1894 (hence the 'New') and it runs adjacent to the three Gullane courses. The original membership was made up of '102 gentlemen as life-members on the payment of six pounds each'. Today, it is used as a final qualifying course whenever the Open is played at Muirfield.

Later on that same September day, Hugh took me on a tour of inspection and, through the windows of the panelled clubroom of Luffness New, only eclipsed in outlook by those at Muirfield, we watched flights of migrating greylag geese winging their way over the links against a big sky. 'There's no better place in the world for links golf,' mused Hugh.

On the panelled walls there hung a portrait of the Edinburgh-born Freddie Tait, friend of John E. Laidlay (see Chapter 27), winner of the Open in 1896 and 1897 and who died ridiculously young at the age of thirty while fighting in the Second Boer War.

When it comes to East Lothian's golfing heroes, however, no essay could possibly be complete without inclusion of the name Ben Sayers, father and son. By the time of his death in 1924, the elder Ben had won twenty-four tournaments and, although he failed to win the coveted cup, he played in every Open championship from 1880, when he was twenty-three, until 1923. His son, also Ben, born in North Berwick in 1884, was to build spectacularly on his father's legacy.

Ben Sayers senior arrived from Leith to live in Haddington in 1869 at the age of twelve, where, as he grew up to become a diminutive five foot three inches tall, he was encouraged to play golf by an uncle. In 1879, he went to live in North Berwick, where he began winning competitions and manufacturing golf equipment, clubs and balls, at a time when feathery balls were being replaced by the gutta-percha ones. He also began providing golf lessons for a glittering client list which included Edward VII and Queen Alexandra, the Prince of Wales, the future George V, the Grand Duke Michael of Russia and King Alfonso XII of Spain. In 1906, in a celebrated Medal Competition at North Berwick, he partnered A. J. Balfour, the prime minister of the day.[1]

Golf was certainly in the blood. Ben's nephew, Jack White, became the professional at Sunningdale, in England, and won the Open in 1904. His brother-in-law, David Grant, also began making balls in North Berwick.

As the popularity of golf continued to gain momentum, it was Ben Sayers Junior who, having himself become a professional golfer in 1908, truly expanded the family business. From premises in Station Road, then a shop at the first tee of the West Links, he sent clubs and accessories overseas to all the countries of the golfing world. In 1931, he moved to a larger space in the High Street and opened a retail outlet. Doreen, his daughter, was put in charge of stock control, costings and advertising.

After the Second World War, Doreen's husband Dick Stephenson, a farmer from Duns, joined the firm and new premises were opened in North Berwick's Tantallon Road. However, with the death of her parents in 1961, Doreen sold the business to Grampian Holdings of Glasgow. In 1998, Ben Sayers Ltd was bought by the Caledonian Golf Group and, in 2002, the company was acquired by Tandem plc, a Devon-based sports and leisure equipment supplier. The following year, the North Berwick unit was closed and the manufacture of all Ben Sayers' equipment was transferred to China. It was the end of a remarkable and rather special episode in the story of East Lothian golf. Doreen died in 2003.

CHAPTER THIRTEEN

Honest Goings-On

WE EACH OF US HAVE memories of a specific place in time and, in my case, Musselburgh will always be associated with Scappaticcio Luca's ice-cream shop, which was established here in 1908. When Luca and his wife Anastasia arrived in Edinburgh in the 1880s from Cassino, in Italy, he worked first as a barber and then as a pastry chef at the North British Hotel (later the Balmoral Hotel). By 1908, he had saved enough money to rent a shop to sell home-made ice cream in Musselburgh.

As his business grew, Luca launched a small fleet of ice-cream vans which travelled around East Lothian villages. Despite the setback of the Second World War, when their patriarch was interned as an enemy alien, the family opened a second shop in North Berwick in 1950. Although this has now closed, several members of a third generation continue to run the business, which today includes a shop in the Edinburgh suburb of Morningside.

With the advent of the Edinburgh bypass, it was no longer necessary to drive through the main street of Musselburgh when travelling south down the east coast but, in the 1960s, there was no alternative. On every one of our early East Lothian excursions, my father and I would stop off for Luca's delicious two-tone ice-cream chocolate slabs and, whenever this comes to mind, I have a childishly unkind image of my father's old school friend, J. G. Stewart Macphail, a civil servant with the Scottish Office, and a former district officer in the Sudan.

The Macphails lived in a fine stone villa called Overton on Haddington's West Road. I was at school with Stewart's son Ross and occasionally partnered his daughter Mary to teenage dances during the school holidays. For better or worse, a lot of things were by then starting to change in the Honest Toun but not Luca's ice cream and, one afternoon, my father and I encountered Stewart MacPhail standing in the doorway of Luca's with vanilla ice cream dripping all over the front of his immaculately tailored suit. Somehow I have never been able to expunge the image of this distinguished and dignified man so obviously enjoying an illicit treat.

Musselburgh and adjacent Inveresk are only recent recruits to the county of East Lothian, if you can call the local government reorganisation of 1975 recent. It amuses me that Wikipedia, the free online encyclopedia, asserts that, although border changes saw several villages on the outskirts of Edinburgh transferred, many residents of 'Haddingtonshire' still do not regard them as part of the same county. It takes time to accept incomers. It was ever thus.

However, Musselburgh is a small town that has grown to become considerably larger than Haddington itself. Its name originates from the mussel beds which once proliferated here offshore but which, long ago, were decimated by coastal erosion and pollution. With a greater environmental awareness and improvements in sewage treatment, there is talk of the shoreline being re-seeded and farmed once again to meet a growing demand.[1]

Musselburgh's reputation as the 'Honest Toun' dates from 1332, when Thomas Randolph, 1st Earl of Moray and Regent of Scotland, died after a long illness during which time he was devotedly cared for by the townsfolk. His successor as Regent was Robert the Bruce's nephew, Donald of Mar, who offered the townsfolk a reward for their loyalty. It was declined on the basis that they were only doing what was expected of them. Hence, the 'Honest Toun'.

But, in 1547, honesty meant little to the former Earl of Hertford, now Duke of Somerset, who was still intent on forcing the five-year-old Mary, Queen of Scots to marry his nephew, the ten-year-old, recently crowned King Edward VI of England. Having failed in his first attempt, the 'Burnt Candlemas' of the previous year, he this time bypassed Dunbar and Tantallon and marched to confront the Scottish army at Musselburgh. In the ensuing Battle of Pinkie Cleuch, fought on the banks of the River Esk, 10,000 Scots were slain and 1,500 taken prisoner. Then, as fast as he had arrived, Somerset withdrew. At home, his enemies were plotting against him and by the following year he had been ignominiously dismissed.[2]

Pinkie Cleuch, the gorge where the battle was fought, was overlooked by a sixteenth-century tower house which belonged to the Abbey of Dunfermline. Thirty years after the Duke of Somerset's carnage, this estate was acquired by Alexander Seton, 1st Earl of Dunfermline, who was James VI's Lord Chancellor. In 1603, when James moved to London to become King of England, he and Queen Anne left their children behind in Scotland to be brought up by the Countess of Dunfermline.[3]

Lady Dunfermline, the Earl's third wife, was Margaret Hay of Yester. When her husband decided to expand the existing building of Pinkie House with a wing to the south, her brother, the 1st Earl of Tweeddale, stood surety for his borrowing. Unfortunately, the debts rapidly mounted and

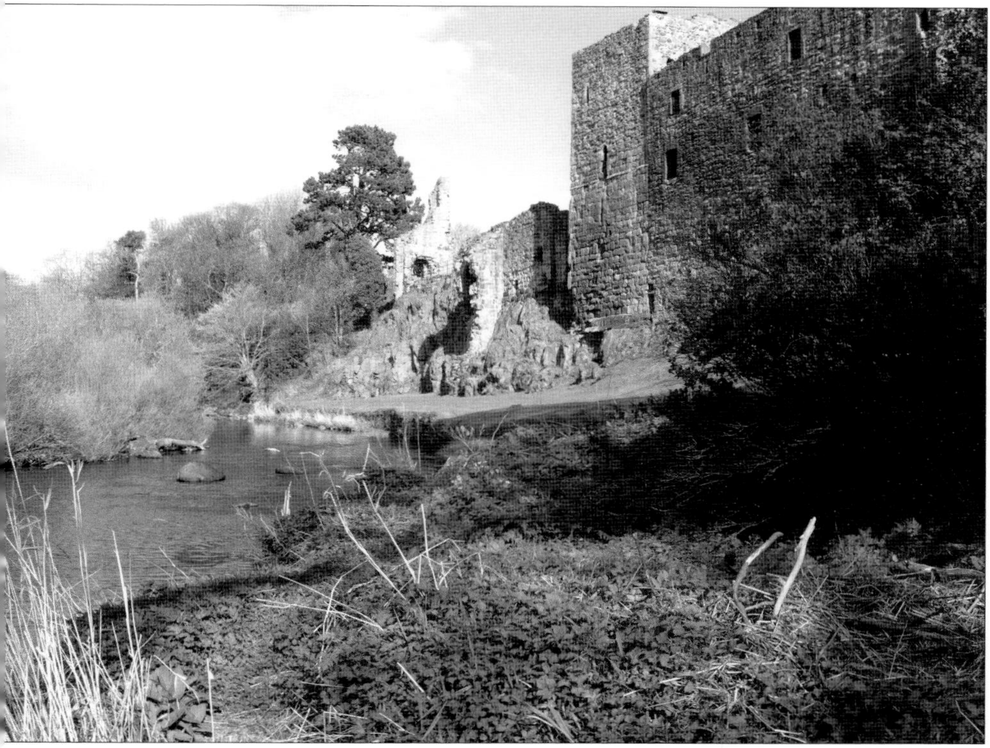

:s Castle, Morham.

view across the River Tyne towards Over Hailes, from a window at Hailes Castle.

LEFT. John Knox (c.1515–1572). (Courtes
East Lothian Local History Centre)

BELOW. A fine oak tree, planted in 1881, stands on the site of the house in which J
Knox's family is alleged to have lived.

Sir Peter Laurie, born at Sandersdean on the Colstoun Estate in 1778, became Lord Mayor of London in 1832. From the original portrait by Thomas Phillips, RA. (Courtesy of East Lothian Local History Centre)

Welsh Carlyle (1801–1866). (Courtesy of
Lothian Local History Centre)

Morham Kirk.

St Martin's Chapel, Haddington.

Stones from the grave of Sir James Stanfield, who was murdered in 1687.

:uthbert's Kirk at Bothans on Yester estate.

:toun Mill.

St Mary's Parish Church, Haddington, seen from across the River Tyne.

Carvings of the Three Kings of Cologne are displayed on the wall of the Lauderdale Aisle, St Mary's Parish Chu

Town House of Haddington sits between the divide of Back Street and the High Street.

dington House.

The River Tyne flooded its banks on many occasions. These photographs were taken in 1931.

ft to right: Silhouette of the first Provost John Martine (1725–1812); Alison Forrest and her husband, the ond Provost John Martine (1767–1849). (Courtesy of Alison Campbell Kinghorn)

eft to right: Janet (Jessie) Forrest (1785–1868) and her husband Peter Martine (1775–1865) (courtesy of laine Meeks); their cousin John Martine, brewer, farmer and author (1811–1891).

A tennis party at Weston, Haddington c.1890.

John Black with Dr Robert Martine in the 2-Seater Renault 8HP, plated SS28.

Dr Howden, who owned the first car in Haddington, with a later vehicle plated SS40.

ıes Croal (1848–1883) and David Croal (1819–1904), founders of the *Haddingtonshire Courier*.

William Gillies (1898–1973).

Hugo Andrew of Acredales (d.1948).

George McVie, Town Clerk of Haddington (d.2006). (Courtesy of Fiona Sheldon)

Richard Burdon Haldane, Viscount Haldane (1856–1928).

Gosford House, Aberlady.

ɩbeth Trevelyan (d.1891)
.ırtesy of Hugh Buchanan)

Arthur Trevelyan (d.1878)
(Courtesy of Hugh Buchanan)

ɛholm, Pencaitland. (Courtesy of East Lothian Local History Centre)

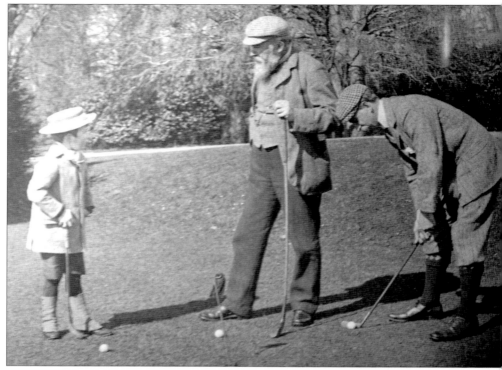

ABOVE. John Christopher Laidlay with four-time Open Championship winner Tom Morris Snr (1821–1908) and two-time British Amateur Champion John E. Laidlay (1860–1940) at Invereil House at Dirleton in 1898. (Courtesy of Sya Simpson)

RIGHT. Archie Baird and Hugh Dodd outside the Heritage of Golf Museum, Gullane.

Golf on Musselburgh Links, c.1900.

Old Tower at Whittingehame.
urtesy of East Lothian Local History Centre)

Arthur James Balfour (1848–1930).

ittingehame House. (Courtesy of East Lothian Local History Centre)

ABOVE. Winton Castle, Pencaitland.

RIGHT. Sir Francis Ogilvy.

View towards Morham with North Berwick Law in the distance.

noxlove, Haddington.

er House, Gifford.

LEFT. Peter Forrest (1753–1836). (Courtesy of Virginia Fitzwilliams)

BELOW. Ian Middlemass at Northrig, 2008. Over o[ne] third of the farm is today planted with wheat.

The Flag Heritage Centre at Athelstaneford.

Northfield House, Prestonpans.

kenzie Power Station.

uel Burns & Co., Prestongrange.

Elizabeth, Duchess of Hamilton with Gian Carlo Menotti. (Photograph by Patrick Douglas-Hamilton)

Lady (Edith) Broun-Lindsay. (Courtesy of Ludovic Broun-Lindsay)

Shelagh, Countess of Wemyss and the 12th Earl of Wemyss and March.

Lady Marioth Hay.

Henderson with his daughter Catherine in 2008.

Portrait of Janet Henderson by William Crosbie, 1949. (Reproduced courtesy of the Henderson family)

ldred's Chapel, Tyninghame.

Sir Timothy and Lady Clifford at Tyninghame.

Members of the East Lothian Antiquarian and Field Naturalists Society at Broxmouth Park, Dunbar, 2007.

North Bewick and Fidra.

aw Abbey, Garvald.

on House, Prestonpans.

'Dog fight over Yester', a painting by John Spencer Churchill (1909–1992), who witnessed the scene. (Reproduced courtesy of Simon Kesley)

The German Heinkel plane shot down over the Lammermuirs on 18 September 1939.

ess House, Aberlady, c.1900.

mes Smith Richardson (1883–1970).

Nigel Tranter (1909–2000).
(Courtesy of Mrs Joan Earle)

Michele and Robert Dale at Lochhouses, Dunbar, 2007.

Robert Louis Stevenson (1850–1894).

Seacliff House, North Berwick following the disastrous fire of 1907. (Courtesy of Sya Simpson)

ew Fletcher of Saltoun (1653–1716).
rtesy of East Lothian Local History Centre)

Archibald Skirving (1749–1819). Portrait by George Watson. (Courtesy of East Lothian Museum Services)

drew's Old Church, Gullane, c.1900.

Archerfield House, Dirleton.

Mrs Jackson Young's saloon car is pulled from North Berwick Harbour, September 1943.

nghame House, by Dunbar. Print by T. Allen, J.B. Allen. (Courtesy of East Lothian Local History Centre)

glass Castle, by Dunbar, c.1813. Drawing J.P. Neale, engraving J.R. Hay. This was demolished following a n 1947. (Courtesy of East Lothian Local History Centre)

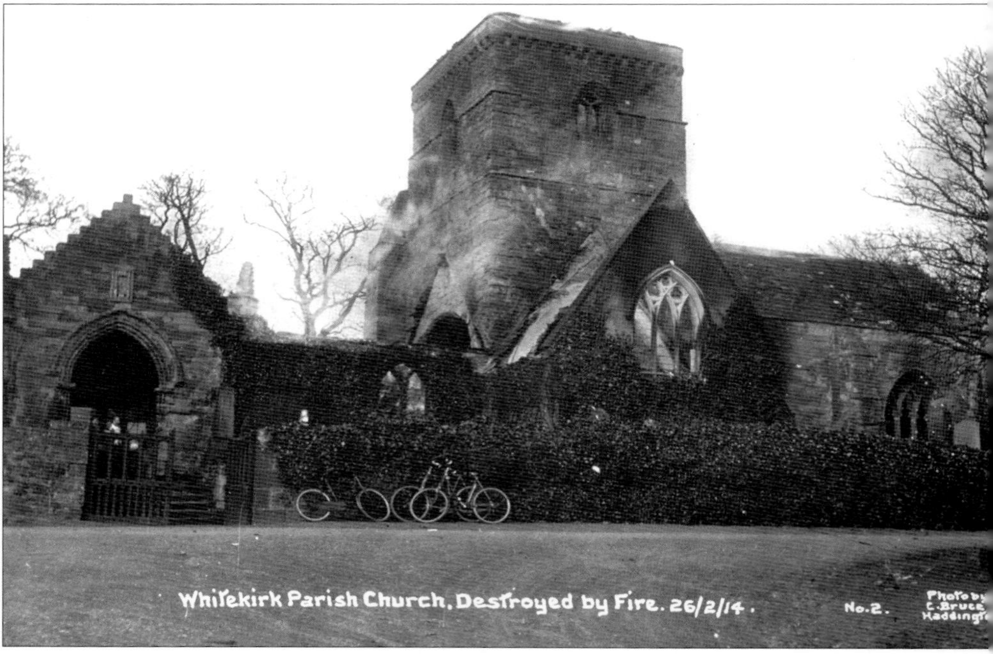

Whitekirk immediately after it was burned by the Scottish Suffragette Movement in February 1914. (Courtesy of East Lothian Local History Centre)

Torness Nuclear Power Station.

ain Patrick Grant, DSO with his sisters Constance, Margaret and Blanche at Beil House, c.1935.
rtesy of Richard Blake)

allon Castle and the Bass Rock by moonlight, c.1900.

Fenton Tower.

George Hope of Fenton Barns (1811–1876).

ABOVE. Phantassie House, East Linton. (Courtesy of East Lothian Local History Centre)

RIGHT. Keith Chalmers-Watson at Fenton Barns, 2008.

when Tweeddale was approached to bail out his brother-in-law, he got Pinkie House in return. It was at Pinkie House that he mostly lived during the building of Yester House, seeing the results only shortly before his death in 1712.[4]

This was just under three decades before Prince Charles Edward Stuart arrived here with his Jacobite army and, following the Prince's victory at nearby Prestonpans, the Pinkie Estate was requisitioned as a Jacobite field hospital. In 1778 it was disposed of to Archibald Hope of Craighall. Then, after 179 years, it was bought by Loretto School, an independent boarding establishment for boys, which is now co-educational. Among Loretto School's star pupils at the end of the twentieth century were the future champion racing driver Jim Clark, the Conservative Chancellor of the Exchequer, Norman Lamont, the Labour Chancellor of the Exchequer, Alistair Darling, and the television broadcaster Andrew Marr.

Brunton's Wire Works, founded in 1870, was, up until its closure, the largest employer in the town. With engineering structures throughout the world, including the Forth Road Bridge, making use of its products production soared but, when competition from abroad caused a price war, wire manufacturing in Musselburgh came to an end. Musselburgh's paper-making industry began at Inveresk Mills in 1871 and, by 1922, the Inveresk Paper Company Limited operated sixteen mills throughout Scotland. For several decades it prospered, with Inveresk writing and cartridge papers known in almost every household in the land but, by 1971, with falling demand, the Inveresk Mill too was closed.

In a final gesture to the town, however, John D. Brunton, son of the founder of the wire works, seed-funded the Brunton Theatre, which was officially opened in 1971 by Queen Elizabeth, the Queen Mother. This in turn gave birth to the Brunton Theatre Company, whose first artistic director was Sandy Neilson.

In 1961, Musselburgh was officially twinned with the French town of Champigny-sur-Marne, chosen principally because it was where the town clerk's daughter had a pen pal. In 1983, a similar twinning was organised with Rosignano Marittimo in Italy. Every autumn, representatives from Musselburgh, Champigny and Rosignano meet to agree a programme of shared activities for the coming year. The county of East Lothian itself is twinned with the Spree-Neisse district of Germany.

In terms of local and visitor diversions, Musselburgh has them in abundance. Members of the Royal Company of Archers (the Queen's Bodyguard in Scotland), founded in 1676 as a private archery club, annually compete for the Musselburgh Silver Arrow, the oldest sporting trophy in the world. Musselburgh Race Course, opened in 1816, continues to flourish, hosting twenty-six race days throughout the year – both Flat racing and National Hunt meetings. The latest incomer to the area is the massive campus of Queen Margaret's University and the full impact of this is still to be felt.

Two miles south of the town is Carberry Tower, first mentioned in the eleventh-century writings of the monks of Dunfermline. In 1480, it was occupied by Hugh Rig, an Edinburgh advocate whose descendants continued to live here until 1669. The next owner was Sir Adam Blair of Lochwood who, in 1686, became Commissioner of Supply for Edinburgh. From Sir Adam it passed on to Sir Robert Dickson of Inveresk and from him to Sir John Fullerton. Sir John's niece married William Elphinstone, third son of the 10th Lord Elphinstone. This title was created for an old Stirlingshire family in the reign of James IV and was eventually inherited by William's descendant.

The Elphinstones took up residence at Carberry in 1802 and, in 1910, the 16th Lord Elphinstone married Lady Mary Frances Bowes-Lyon, whose sister, Lady Elizabeth, is best remembered as Queen Elizabeth, the Queen Mother, the wife of George VI.

Lord Elphinstone died at Carberry Tower in 1955 and his widow lived on there until her death in 1961, when it was gifted to the Church of Scotland Youth Centre. In 1996, it was bought by the Carberry Trust which, in 2004, became part of the Gartmore Trust. Aside from hosting an annual Christian Arts Festival and providing self-catering visitor accommodation, the house provides facilities for day and residential conferences.

I first visited the neighbouring Newhailes House in 1985, accompanied by the Edinburgh-based photographer Brodrick Haldane. Brodrick, brother of the Laird of Gleneagles and scion of the one-time Haddington Haldane family, was a childhood friend of its then owner, Lady Antonia Dalrymple, the petite and engaging sister of the 13th Earl of Galloway.

Newhailes was built as a small house by the architect James Smith in 1686 but, in 1709, bad investments obliged him to sell it to Sir David Dalrymple, brother of the 1st Earl of Stair. A partial refit by William Adam took place in 1720, with additional interiors and decoration added in 1757.

The most celebrated occupant of Newhailes was Sir David's grandson, another Sir David, who gained distinction as a lawyer, antiquary and historian and took the legal title of Lord Hailes. His first wife was Anne, a daughter of Sir George Broun, Lord Colstoun, yet another Court of Session judge; his second, Helen, was the daughter of Sir James Fergusson of Kilkerran in Ayrshire. The one consistency about the Scottish aristocracy is that it was always de rigueur to marry strategically.

When the celebrated English lexicographer and critic Dr Samuel Johnson and his acolyte biographer James Boswell visited in 1773, Boswell lamented afterwards that such was the hospitality that he remembered very little about it.[5] Johnson was perhaps too blasé to comment upon the house, although he did concede that it contained one of the finest libraries in Britain.

Following the death of Lord Hailes's great-great-great-grandson, Sir Mark Dalrymple, who was Lady Antonia's husband, this 'greatest surviving contemporary collection of books and manuscripts of the Scottish Enlightenment' was accepted by the British Treasury in lieu of death duties in 1971.[6] The contents of the library are therefore now in the possession of the National Library of Scotland. In 1995, Newhailes was acquired by the National Trust for Scotland.

Atmospheric and faded, the darkly painted interiors of Newhailes struck me at once as exquisitely elegant and so, when I came to put together *Living in Scotland*, a coffee table book of Scottish homes photographed by Fritz von der Schulenberg, I insisted that it be included. When published, the book was reviewed for *World of Interiors* magazine by the English interior decorator Nicholas Haslam, who announced that, of the twenty-four illustrated chapters, his favourite was that showing Lady Antonia Dalrymple in her drawing room, 'shelved with old books and masses of un-showy porcelain'. He goes on to describe her as sitting on a slate-coloured, slip-covered sofa, against baggy apricot silk cushions. Her feet are firmly on the ground, her 'slacks crisply pressed, her cardie cheerful, her smile enchanting. Lady Antonia Dalrymple would not have turned back at Derby'.[7]

The village of Inveresk sits upon a ridge on the north bank of the River Esk above the sprawl of Musselburgh and, during the first and second centuries AD, was occupied by the Romans, giving rise to the claim that it is the oldest continually inhabited place in Scotland. Today, the main street of substantial houses forms the nucleus for an eclectic neighbourhood with occupants including: Sir Malcolm Rifkind, a former Secretary of State for Scotland and British Foreign Secretary; the artist Harry More Gordon and his wife Marianne; Clarissa Dickson Wright, the celebrity cook and countryside activist; Philip and Mary Contini of the Edinburgh-based Italian Valvona & Crolla dynasty; and Sir Charles Fraser, former purse bearer to the Lord High Commissioner to the General Assembly of the Church of Scotland.

In his 1727 book *A Tour through the Whole Island of Great Britain*, vol. III, Daniel Defoe, the government spy and author of the novels *Robinson Crusoe* and *Moll Flanders* wrote:

> At that part of the town called Inner Esk are some handsome Country Houses with Gardens, and the Citizens of Edinburgh come out in the Summer and take lodgings here for the Air, as they do from London at Kensington Gravel Pits, or at Hampstead and Highgate.

Not much has altered since. All of the land here once lay within the confines of Inveresk House, which was built as a manse in 1597 by Adam Colt, youngest son of a Perthshire magistrate and the second minister of the parish to be appointed after the Reformation. His property comprised over 1,000 acres, including the entirety of Inveresk Hill, with the exception of the old monastery and nunnery upon which Inveresk Lodge stands. During excavations in the nineteenth century, the remains of some Roman baths and a passage were discovered under the house. Within the passage were found the remains of a cavalier in full suit of armour and clutching what appeared to have been a full keg of gunpowder.[8]

For the Colts, St Michael's Church at Inveresk was seen as something of a family business which, in the political and religious turmoil of the age in which they lived, required a certain amount of intellectual dexterity. In due course Adam's son succeeded him as minister but, in 1641, conformed to Episcopacy and later became Rector under the Archdiocese of St Andrews.

When Oliver Cromwell invaded Scotland in 1650, however, Adam Colt fled to Dundee while the Lord Protector used his home as a headquarters during the time his troops were camped in Musselburgh. It is thought that the skeleton found in the secret passage below the room in which Cromwell lodged is that of Adam Colt's younger brother George, who disappeared at the time. Following the Restoration the Duke and Duchess of York, while in residence at the Palace of Holyroodhouse, dined here with Sir Robert Colt, by then the Solicitor General for Scotland.

For a ball held in the house in the mid eighteenth century, Neil Gow, the Scottish fiddler, composed a French peasant dance which he named the 'Inveresk House Gavotte'. The property remained in the Colt family until 1890, when it was sold to John Park, a seed merchant. During the 1920s, a healing centre based on natural methods was established here by Dr Andrew Gold and next to the church was an enclosure where residents were encouraged to sunbathe. Around this time, it was rumoured locally that Inveresk House had become a nudist colony.

The property is now divided into two dwellings. The unconnected west wing is known as Rowan House. Linden House, the extension section, is owned by Ian Leitch while John Chute owns the main house. Both men are retired Writers to the Signet. Encouraged by the impresario Richard Demarco (see Chapter 30), John Chute's wife, under her maiden name of Alice Beberman, gained a certain notoriety with her art installations during the 1970s. One of her projects was to position a giant breast on the summit of Arthur's Seat but, although the television presenter Esther Rantzen arrived with a film crew to record the event, planning permission was denied. More recently, John and Alice's daughter Daisy Chute has won national acclaim as a jazz singer and makes up one quarter of the classical singing group All Angels.

The St Michael's Parish Church of medieval antiquity is supposed to have been built on the site of a Roman temple to Apollo. However, by the eighteenth century changes were afoot. By the time of the Very Reverend Dr Alexander 'Jupiter' Carlyle's death in 1805 a splendid, larger church had begun to emerge. Nicknamed 'Jupiter' for his striking appearance, Carlyle was born in 1722 and brought up in Prestonpans, where he witnessed the battle of 1745 at first hand. Having followed his father into the ministry, he was inducted at Inveresk in 1748 and remained there until his death fifty-seven years later. Over the ensuing period, known as the Scottish Enlightenment, Jupiter Carlyle collected around him a brilliant coterie of friends which included the philosopher David Hume, the economist Adam Smith and the novelist Tobias Smollet. Early on in his career he caused a scandal by attending a performance of *Douglas*, which was written by his friend, the dramatist John Home. Although this work was considered blasphemous by the Kirk, he survived the censure and, in 1770, served as Moderator of the General Assembly of the Church of Scotland. Perhaps his most significant achievement was to introduce Sunday Schools to Musselburgh and the adjoining district of Fisherow.[9]

In 1761, the land on the far side of the Musselburgh road from Inveresk House was purchased by Sir David Rae, who took the judicial title of Lord Eskgrove and whose son, the second Sir David Rae, in 1785 married Helen Colt from Inveresk House. For a while thereafter, Eskgrove House was leased out, its most illustrious tenant being the writer John Galt, who published biographies of Lord Byron and Benjamin West. Unfortunately, Galt's involvement with speculative land ventures in Canada all but ruined him and he retired to live in Greenock.

In 1990, the policies of this mini-estate were divided to allow for further housing development. Shortly afterwards, the mansion house was purchased by Sir Malcolm and Lady Rifkind.

That planning permission for new housing was granted in the first place seems surprising but, with a burgeoning capital on its doorstep, nobody can take the future for granted. An Inveresk Preservation Society has therefore been in existence since 1957 and has proved a formidable force in protecting the village's rural and architectural character, notably the properties of Eskhill, Catherine Lodge, Rose Hill, Rose Court, the White House, Shepherd House, Halkerston and the Manor House.

And that is why I prefer to think of Inveresk in terms of a delightful time warp and hope and pray that it remains as such. In the late 1970s, I well remember visiting the romantically named Rose Hill, an early eighteenth-century laird's house, when it was the home of Alasdair Campbell of Airds, Unicorn Pursuivant at the Court of the Lord Lyon, King of Arms. Next door, at Rose Court, lived George Burnet, another retired Writer to the Signet, whose wife Jane, in 1999, compiled and published a lovingly researched and thought-provoking history entitled *A Reason for Inveresk.* For several years, Catherine Lodge was occupied by the headmaster of Loretto School. It is today the home of the Younger family. At the Manor House are the artist Harry More Gordon and his equally talented wife, Marianne. His insightful contemporary image of Gian Carlo Menotti at Yester and a group portrait of eight Secretaries of State for Scotland in front of the drawing room fireplace of Bute House are in the collection of the Scottish National Portrait Gallery in Edinburgh.

Inveresk Lodge, at the far end of Inveresk Village Road, was completed prior to the death of Sir Richard Colt in 1699. In 1775 it was bought for £1,000 by James Wedderburn, who owned plantations in Jamaica, and thereafter was sold by his son to Robert Skirving, of the East India Company, and his sister Grizel, widow of their cousin Robert Ainslie. The Skirvings were brother and sister of the artist Archibald Skirving, who died there in 1819 (see Chapter 20). The lodge was subsequently bought back in equal ownership by James Wedderburn's cousins, Colonel Alexander, Mary and Susan Wedderburn, and remained in their family until 1911, when it was sold to a member of the Brunton Wire Works family. In 1959, both lodge and garden were gifted to the National Trust for Scotland by Helen Brunton.

An intriguing footnote is that in 1762, back in Jamaica, James Wedderburn had fathered a child by a slave girl called Rosanna. When Rosanna was sold prior to James's return to Scotland, it was stipulated that their son be freed. The boy grew up with the name Robert Wedderburn and converted to Christianity, whereupon he travelled to London and became not only an ardent political activist but, in 1826, wrote a book entitled *The Horrors of Slavery.* However, when he decided to pay a social call on his father at Inveresk, he was sent away with 'some small beer and a bent sixpence'.

This story was told to me by the writer Douglas Sutherland, one of the most entertaining and impossible characters I have ever known. From 1979, for two relatively chaos-free years in their eventful existence, Douglas and his wife, Diana, were the National Trust for Scotland's tenants at Inveresk Lodge.

Douglas, a portly Winston Churchill look-alike, was a decorated Second World War hero who had worked on the staff of Field Marshal Viscount Montgomery of Alamein and been selected as an observer at the Nuremberg War Crimes Tribunal. When he returned to civilian life in London, he embarked upon a career as an investigative journalist and produced a string of successful books. These included his co-authoring of *Burgess and Maclean*, about the British diplomats who spied for the Soviet Union during the Cold War. Published in 1965, he obliquely but accurately identified their co-conspirator Anthony Blunt, some fourteen years before his public exposure by Prime Minister Margaret Thatcher.

At the time of the Sutherlands' occupancy of Inveresk Lodge, it was Douglas's books on the eccentricities, real or imagined, of the English gentleman which were propelling him towards fame and fortune – or so he thought. Although the *English Gentleman* series grossed over a million in sales, the royalties, for reasons which remain a mystery, failed to materialise and he and Diana spent their final years in penury, embroiled in a series of desperate and stressful legal disputes.

However, this did not deter either of them from living the high life and, for a brief and unforgettable period, Inveresk Lodge became a meeting place for public figures and socialites from across Britain – that is, until the money finally ran out and the Sutherlands were obliged to move on. Their hurried departure inevitably caused disapproval but typically their loudest critics were among those who had previously been only too happy to join in the fun. Such is life. No doubt Douglas and Diana would have gained some comfort from knowing that their daughter Jojo has since embarked upon a career as a professional stand-up comedian.

Since 1994, Inveresk Lodge has been the home of Robin Dow, former chief executive of Levi Strauss Europe and head of the Addison Consultancy Group. His Swedish wife Sophie is the driving force behind the charity Mindroom.

CHAPTER FOURTEEN

Siege and Salvation

WAS IT A CRISIS OF faith or the direct consequence of the events of a dark winter night in 1546 that transformed the thirty-one-year-old John Knox from devout Catholic into Presbyterian zealot? I believe it to be the latter. As far as Knox was concerned, it was not he who left the Catholic faith but the Catholic Church which had sold out to corruption. It only required for something deeply traumatic and personal to trigger his final disaffection. And all of the evidence points to Ormiston and the fate of his friend George Wishart.

Wishart was much of an age with Knox. A charismatic preacher, he had, by the age of twenty-five, attracted a devoted domestic following until he was charged with heresy and forced to travel abroad. He returned to Scotland in 1543 and that was when he encountered Knox and the two men were soon inseparable. Indeed, following two assassination attempts, Knox was to be found at Wishart's side at all times armed with a two-handed sword.

The Cockburn family had occupied Ormiston Castle, near to Tranent, since 1368, when John Cockburn, second son of Sir Alexander Cockburn of Clerkington, married into the incumbent Lindsay family.[1] These Cockburns of Cockburn and Clerkington were yet another family who served as constables and sheriffs of Haddingtonshire and thus carried significant influence throughout the territory.

On 16 January 1546 Wishart, having lodged with David Forrest in Haddington, preached a sermon from the pulpit of St Mary's Church.[2] He was afterwards invited to spend the night at Ormiston Castle as the guest of the laird, John Cockburn, whose son Alexander was being tutored by Knox, in company with George and Francis Douglas, the sons of Sir Hugh Douglas of Longniddry Castle.

Rumours concerning Wishart's safety had already begun to circulate and Knox was determined to accompany him until his friend stopped him with the words, 'Nay, return to your bairns [meaning his pupils] and God bless you. One is sufficient for a sacrifice.'[3]

Knox therefore set off for Longniddry Castle, while Wishart went to Ormiston, where he dined with his host and Cockburn's brother-in-law, John Sandilands, before retiring to bed. However, shortly after midnight, a contingent of the 3rd Earl of Bothwell's men arrived at the gate and demanded that he be turned over to them. Cockburn at first refused but was warned that both the Governor of Scotland and Cardinal Beaton of St Andrews, Wishart's sworn enemy, were on their way to arrest the cleric. Bothwell reassured Cockburn that, if Wishart came with him immediately, his safety would be assured. But it was not to be the case.

To be fair, Bothwell initially honoured his promise and escorted Wishart the four miles to Elphinstone Tower and then on to Hailes Castle.[4] But the Cardinal was resolved to silence his enemy once and for all. Under immense political pressure, Bothwell handed over Wishart, whereupon he was taken to St Andrews, sentenced to death by an ecclesiastical court and semi-hanged before being burned at the stake.

A pervasive sense of disgust reverberated throughout Scotland. Wishart's ashes were barely cool when a pro-Protestant faction seized St Andrews Castle and murdered the Cardinal. As chaos ensued, the Queen Regent summoned a fleet of French gunboats to bombard St Andrews with cannon until the castle surrendered. In the event, among those taken prisoner by the French was John Knox. With him was David Forrest from Haddington (see Chapter 3), who somehow managed to escape the confinement. Not so Knox, who was despatched to France as a galley slave, a humiliation he endured for the following year.[5]

David Forrest's descendant, Martin A. Forrest, provides an insight into the conflicting loyalties of the age. Following a meteoric rise in the established Episcopal Church, David's brother, Alexander Forrest, had become secretary to John Hamilton, Cardinal Beaton's successor as Archbishop of St Andrews. He must have used his influence to free his brother because David was certainly back in Haddington in time for Hertford's invasion of the following year. Moreover, within months, David was to find himself embroiled in yet another siege – that of Haddington itself.

For fifteen months between 1548 and 1549, Haddington was occupied by the English army, at which time Ormiston Castle, its Cockburn laird not unsympathetic to an English Protestant alliance, came under the full assault of the Earl of Arran acting on behalf of the Queen Regent of Scotland. When Cockburn surrendered, he and his brother-in-law were arrested and taken to Edinburgh Castle, but both later escaped.

With Cockburn banished from the kingdom, his wife and son Alexander took refuge at Winton Castle, between Tranent and Pencaitland, where Alexander's education continued under the supervision of Adam Wallace, a colleague of Knox.[6] In 1550, Wallace too was seized and incarcerated in Edinburgh Castle. Not so fortunate as his pupil's father and uncle, he was tried for heresy and summarily executed. However, violence only serves to fan the flames of disaffection. Writing seven years later from Dieppe to the 'Lords and Others Professing the Truth in Scotland', Knox passionately reminded them of 'Mr George Wishart, Simpill Adame Wallace and of uthris whilk died suffer for Chrystic cause'.[7]

Two remarkable attributes of the Scottish nobility have been their resilience and their ability to bounce back when seemingly everything had been lost. The Cockburns were no exception to the rule and, within a decade or so, their lands had been retrieved intact. However, it was a commitment of a very different kind that would ultimately deprive them of their good fortune.

In 1679, another John Cockburn of Ormiston was born, the son of Adam Cockburn, Lord Justice General of Scotland. A member of the old Scottish Parliament, this John went on to become a member of the Westminster Parliament and it was while travelling between East Lothian and London that he began to notice how land in England was in the process of being enclosed for crop rotation. A benign and astute landlord, he also came to the conclusion that long leases encouraged tenants to make more of the land and, to this end, granted a thirty-eight-year lease to Robert Wight, his tenant at Muirhouse Farm.

As his benevolence gained momentum, Cockburn next embarked upon creating one of Scotland's first planned villages at Ormiston. By granting leases only for buildings which conformed to strict guidelines, he located housing for artisans and cottage industries (spinning and weaving) around the original 'mill hamlet', and laid out the main street with trees. A linen mill was established and workers from Ireland were imported to teach their skills to local people. He introduced a bleach works, the second in Scotland, and built a brewery to make use of local barley. While all of this was taking place, he also founded the Edinburgh Society of Improvers, a predecessor of the Highland Agricultural Society.

With such far-sightedness, Cockburn should have died rich but instead it bankrupted him. In 1747, he was obliged to sell everything, including Ormiston Hall – located approximately 200 yards from where its predecessor, Ormiston Castle, once stood – to the 2nd Earl of Hopetoun. Thus ended four centuries of Cockburns at Ormiston, but not everyone was a loser. Following their benefactor's lead, his tenants Robert Wight and Alexander Wight, his son, had by then enclosed their farmland, dug ditches, introduced land drainage and planted hedges around their fields, thus revolutionising farming concepts for others to follow.

Encouraged by the 6th Earl of Haddington, grass and clover were cultivated from seed to improve the quality of pastureland for cattle and sheep. Turnips and potatoes were planted with immediate success. None of this would have taken place without Cockburn, whose agricultural legacy would, in time, benefit the whole of Scotland.

The remains of the Ormiston Hall of 1745 can still be seen, surrounded by trees. In 1948, one of the biggest oak trees ever recorded in Scotland, 20 feet high and 47 inches in girth, was felled. Fortunately, the Ormiston yew, which rises in close proximity to another tree of similar stature, survives. In 1792, it was claimed that the spread of its branches covered one fifth of an acre. In 1897, it was believed to be among the largest of its species in Scotland.[8]

When the park of Ormiston was sold during the 1970s, it attracted a group of like-minded academics who made their homes in close proximity to one another. These included the artist John Busby, the scientist Murdoch Mitchison and his wife Professor Rosalind Mitchison and the ecologist Doctor Ulrich Loening. The old Tower of Ormiston is the home of Professor Aubrey Manning, the zoologist and author and a recent addition to the compound is Paddy Scott, who runs Scotland's Gardens Scheme.

War is the great vandal. Prior to the Battle of Pinkie Cleugh in 1547, Fawside Castle, from its hillside vantage point overlooking the coastal plain, was set on fire and it was to be 400 years before it was fully restored. From 1976, it was occupied by Tom Craig, then James and Charmie Douglas and is currently owned by the architect Ian Brash.

The settlement of Humbie sits at the march of East Lothian with Midlothian, where the Southern Uplands meet the Lammermuirs. In such close proximity to the A68 and to the rise of Soutra Hill, I frequently become confused as to which Lothian it actually belongs to. This is made even more complex by John Martine's *Reminiscences* including the old parish of Soutra, when it had been firmly situated in Midlothian since 1618.

Yet the adjoining parishes of Keith Marischal and Keith Hundeby, which in that same year amalgamated to form the parish of Humbie, were definitely in East Lothian and, for the 400 years before that, were the domain of yet another of Scotland's all-powerful Norman-Scots families, the Keiths.

There is a tradition among members of the Highland Clan Keith that they are descended from the Catti, a Germanic tribe, one of whose number emigrated to Scotland. For slaying the Danish General Camus at the Battle of Barrie in 1010, Robert, Chief of the Catti, was made Marischal of the Kingdom and Custodian of the Royal Regalia, with responsibility for the Monarch's safety within Parliament. When I interviewed the 12th Earl of Kintore, Chief of Clan Keith, for *Scottish Field* magazine in 1988, he laughed. 'I always say that I'm a cousin of everybody in Scotland. The Keiths fought all the men and slept with all the women!'

By the twelfth century, the lands of Keith in Lothian and Aberdeenshire had passed into the hands of a Norman called Harvei, who carried the title of King's Marischal, and it was his progeny who adopted the Keith surname. At Keith Marischal, there is evidence of a previous construction beneath the original L-shaped tower house which dates from 1589 and earthworks in the adjoining meadow suggest that it was once a medieval settlement.

Having won his great battle against the English at Bannockburn in 1314, Robert Bruce's dying wish fifteen years afterwards was to atone for having murdered his cousin John Comyn eight years earlier. His greatest desire had been to take part in a Crusade to the Holy Land but it had simply not been possible. On his death, therefore, his friends and admirers decided to honour his memory and a group of them set off on a foray against the infidel, taking with them the King's embalmed heart. Among this group of well-meaning and noble knights was Sir William Keith of Keith Marischal.

They got as far as Teba, in Andalucía, where, rather too carried away with their task, they were virtually wiped out. In a confrontation with the forces of Mohammed IV, Sultan of Granada, Sir James Douglas, Sir William St Clair and his brother John St Clair of Rosslyn, Sir Robert Logan of Restalrig and his brother Sir Walter, were all killed but Sir William Keith and Sir Simon Lockhard of the Lee survived to tell the tale and to return Bruce's heart and the bodies of their comrades home to Scotland. In the graveyard of Keith Marischal's Chapel is the tombstone of a crusading knight which is thought to cover the valiant Sir William's final resting place.

Along with the Setons, the Keiths were among the great losers of the early eighteenth century, their titles and lands attainted for backing the Jacobite cause. Seizing the opportunity, as they did throughout East Lothian, the Hopes of Hopetoun stepped in to buy Keith Marischal. In the late nineteenth century they sold it to George Fraser Tytler, who had previously been Secretary of the Bank of Scotland and who employed the Edinburgh firm of architects Peddie & Kinnear to build on an extension to the original tower house. In 1953, the estate was once again put up for sale and this time it was bought by Dennis Cadzow, who farmed Duncrahill, by Pencaitland. Cadzow was one of three remarkable farming brothers who, fifteen years earlier, had introduced the celebrated Luing breed of beef cattle. Having no use for the mansion house, as such, it was sold on to the architect Sir Robert Matthew, who had by then returned with his family to work in Scotland.

'My father went to England in 1948 to become Chief Architect of London City Council. Having completed the LCC Development Plan and built the London Festival Hall, I don't think he had any intention of staying there,' said Aidan Matthew, who now lives at North Berwick.

As Professor of Architecture at Edinburgh University and Edinburgh Art

College, where he had previously trained, Robert Matthew discovered, much to his delight, that he was also allowed to practice architecture in a private capacity. His first commission was for the all-wooden Edinburgh Airport and this was followed by Cockenzie Power Station (see Chapter 17), then the power stations at Longannet and Kincardine, both double the size of the ones before.

'With various relatives also moving in, Keith Marischal became something of a Matthew family settlement,' recalled Aidan. Sold in 2003, it is today owned by Colin and Clare Roger, and within a development of the old stable block are eight dwellings which include the home and studio of Sir Robert's daughter Jessie Ann, a painter and photographer, and her artist husband Jonathan Gibbs.

A short walk from the castle are the ivy-strangled remains of a thirteenth-century Norman Gothic chapel, where the burial ground has been colonised by badgers – either that or the dead have walked. I only hope that the bones underfoot and the skull shelved on a branch of a tree did not belong to Sir William Keith. Even if his mortal soul did depart this world 900 years ago, it seems an ignominious fate for his cranium to be so visibly exposed to the elements. Or perhaps there are darker forces at work?

In 1589, James VI travelled to Oslo to collect his bride, Princess Anne of Denmark, and on their return journey to Scotland, the royal couple encountered a great storm at the mouth of the Firth of Forth. James, riddled with superstition, immediately attributed this to the work of the occult. In the notorious North Berwick witch trials that followed, one of the accused was Agnes Sampson, a local midwife from Nether Keith, a quarter of a mile from Keith Marischal. This unfortunate lady was taken to Castlehill, at the top of Edinburgh's Royal Mile, where she was garrotted and incinerated. For centuries since her ghost has been seen on the wooded banks of the Humbie Water late at night.

Malcolm Kirk, known as the East Lothian Mole Catcher and who lives with his wife Avril in 'the highest house in Humbie', has often encountered strange phenomena when going about his business at night. 'Sometimes I have heard what sounds like a wee lassie crying,' he says. 'There are very few country sounds I can't identify, but that one is a complete mystery.'

On moonlit nights he has often noticed the shadows of figures hurrying swiftly past. He once saw an old lady with a hood standing beside a cottage only to discover later that she had died several years earlier. 'There is nothing you can do about badgers,' he says, 'apart from moving them, which is not necessarily such a good thing as they always go back. They are a protected species and thrive in graveyards because of the rich soil.'

Malcolm's father Andrew Kirk was the shepherd at Johnscleugh on the

Garvald Road to Duns across the Lammermuirs. His elder sister Mary, whose poetry is published in the *Southern Reporter* under the name of Mary Lammermuir, was the shepherdess.[9] 'My father moved there in 1952 when I was fifteen and a half,' he says.

Johnscleugh was part of the Earl of Haddington's estate and was rented to the Eliotts of Blackhough at Clovenfords. Malcolm was therefore brought up in the depths of the real, rolling Lowland countryside and learned all of the tricks of snaring vermin and shooting from the local rabbit catcher William Ritchie. As a youngster, he worked first at Nunraw Barns as a pigman and tractorman, then at Long Yester for James Hogg. For a brief period, he was employed at Glenkinchie Distillery before going to Duncrahill to work for Dennis Cadzow.

Today, self-employed Malcolm is East Lothian's jack of all trades. When not in pursuit of vermin, he is either sorting out molehills or turning his hand to mending motor cars, tractors or anything else mechanical that needs attention. His workshop is a veritable Aladdin's cave of equipment, featuring everything from electric drills to angle grinders. He even owns an old brass turning lathe.

Centuries and generations move on. In 1905, several acres of land at Humbie were allocated to a village for children from deprived Edinburgh homes. This came to an end when the nine houses and four plots of land were sold for development in 2006. However, the immensely pretty nineteenth-century Humbie Church remains much as it was in 1883 when John Martine made reference to it and Stobshiel House, today the home of businessman Max Ward and his family. At Humbie House, long in the possession of the Hepburn-Scotts who became the lords Polwarth, is the Laing family. Chesterhill is the home of Donald Hardie, a former Chief Executive of the Institute of Directors in Scotland, and his American wife, Sally.

In 1967, the innovative contemporary architect James Morris, whose own pioneering modern home is just over the Midlothian county boundary at Fala, was commissioned to design Scadlaw House for Sir Peter Balfour, then Chairman of Scottish & Newcastle Breweries. Of an L-shaped plan, with mono-pitch roof and cedar cladding, it won a Civic Trust award in 1971. Around this time, even the village's eighteenth-century lectern-shaped doocot was cleverly converted for residential use. Having been transformed into a country house hotel during the 1980s, the fine seventeenth/eighteenth-century mansion of Johnstonburn, which literally sits on the borderline of East Lothian and Midlothian, has once again reverted to private ownership.

CHAPTER FIFTEEN

Home of the Patriot

AT THE TIME OF MY writing this, Scotland has had ten years of devolved government under its very own elected and reinstated Scottish Parliament. Furthermore, over a year and a half has passed since a minority Scottish National Party administration was voted into power. Where this ultimately leads remains to be seen but it is perhaps pertinent to remember that, despite radical advances, Scotland is not so fundamentally different in temperament from the way it was 300 years ago when the Act of Union ignited widespread protest throughout the land. It therefore seems an apposite moment to consider the life and times of East Lothian's most revered Nationalist, Andrew Fletcher of Saltoun. I have often wondered why the Scottish Nationalist Party has never made more of him but I suspect that it is because he is, for them, that most politically incorrect of role models – an articulate landowner with attitude.

Saltoun Hall is yet another resplendent East Lothian mansion house steeped in the ground plan of Scotland's story, but its name will forever be coupled with that of this seventeenth-century Scottish patriot. Originally held within the feudal grasp of the Norman de Morevilles, a family which, by the thirteenth century, had totally vanished from Scotland, Saltoun passed to the Abernethys, another curiously extinct dynasty. The tower, which they built and occupied, is now incorporated within today's Saltoun Hall, the manor of which in 1643 was purchased by Sir Andrew Fletcher of Innerpeffer. A senator of the College of Justice, Sir Andrew had twenty years earlier been created Lord Innerpeffer, a judicial title which he derived from his northern roots in the County of Angus.

Lord Innerpeffer died in 1650 and his grandson, born three years later, was eleven years old when his own father, Sir Robert, also died. But, by then, his education and that of his younger brother Henry had already been consigned to the astute Gilbert Burnet, minister of Saltoun Church.[1]

Although immensely principled, Andrew Fletcher, champion of the underdog and fiercely proud of his native land, was not, I suspect, an entirely likeable character, unless, of course, you were a non-smoker. In exile in Holland, he found himself on the deck of a boat standing next to the pipe-smoking Dutch skipper of the vessel. When the Dutchman refused to desist from his vice, Fletcher threw him overboard.[2] This violent temperament, coupled with an absolute intolerance of anyone who disagreed with him, won him no favours in negotiating the snake pit of Anglo-Scottish politics. 'A low, thin man, of a brown complexion, full of fire, with a stern, sour look',[3] Fletcher was first elected to the Scots Parliament in 1678, having defeated, against all expectations, the all-powerful Duke of Lauderdale's chosen candidate. Re-elected three years later, he remained unequivocal towards Charles II's attempts to re-establish the Church of England in Scotland. 'Better yet a republic than a blood bespattered tyrant waxing gross and tyrannical upon the throne of Scotland,' he wrote in one of his pamphlets. It was only a matter of time before the Duke of York, the King's Commissioner for Scotland, charged him with sedition.

With his estate forfeited to the Crown, Fletcher fled to The Hague where, suppressing his often extreme republican leanings, he joined his fellow exiles in plotting the Duke of Monmouth's rebellion, convinced that overthrowing the recently crowned James VII was in the best interests of both civil liberty and the Protestant faith. He got as far as Dorset but, once again, his temper got the better of him. In a trifling quarrel over a horse, he shot and killed the mayor of Taunton, a loyal Monmouth supporter. Providentially, as it turned out, this necessitated a hasty withdrawal to Bilbao although, following Monmouth's defeat and execution, he was tracked down and arrested by King James's agents. Once more he escaped, this time to Hungary, where he signed on as a mercenary to fight for the Duke of Lorraine against the Turks.[4]

In this universe, fortune favours the bold and, three years later, he was back in England with William of Orange, a rather more resolute and steely character than his previous choice of champion. True to his word, King William reinstated him at Saltoun but, as the incoming monarch took possession of his fractious realm, Fletcher's frustration only increased.

With a total population of one and a half million, Scotland, at the dawn of the eighteenth century, had become little more than an economic backwater. Andrew Fletcher was determined to remedy the situation and, ever conscious of a bigger picture, sought out William Paterson, an ambitious, Dumfries-born Scot who, in 1694, had founded the Bank of England. It was a liaison that everyone concerned would come to regret.

William Paterson's personal fortune had been accumulated in foreign trade and, coinciding with the formation of a Bank of Scotland, he had developed a plan for a Scottish colony at Darien on the Isthmus of Panama in South

America. Darien offered opportunities for opening up trade routes to the Far East. The same thinking was to lead to the building of the Panama Canal two centuries later but, even then, it was to claim the lives of over a quarter of a million operatives.

Cajoled along by Fletcher, the Scots Parliament in 1695 passed an Act to grant a patent to a Scottish company with interests in Africa and the Indies to develop the project. This Act also committed King William III, as occupant of the throne of Scotland, to provide the company with protection should it be attacked by an alien power. Subscriptions to fund the venture were initially raised among Scots merchants in London but, when it emerged that there was a conflict of interest with an earlier patent for the English-controlled East India Company, investors hastily withdrew. More to the point, England was at war with France, and Spain, England's ally, had already claimed the Panama territory as part of New Granada. Nobody among the ruling English elite wanted to upset Spain.

William Paterson next turned to Edinburgh for finance and, in an act of collective defiance towards England, £400,000 was raised, approximately one third of Scotland's total wealth. On 14 July 1698, five ships carrying around 12,000 passengers set sail from Leith.

As fate would decree, the venture was a total catastrophe. Colonists who did not die at sea succumbed to malaria. The lack of supplies and repeated attacks from hostile Spaniards made it impossible to continue. Of the 136 Darien Scheme subscribers domiciled in Scotland, twenty-four were Scottish aristocrats, thirty-nine landed proprietors, forty-one merchants, fourteen lawyers and judges and, unusually for that time, seven women. Many of them were ruined.[5] Fletcher himself had promised £1,000 and lost it all. Among the East Lothian investors were: the 2nd Marquis of Tweeddale, whose total family contribution was £3,000; Sir Robert Sinclair of Stevenson and his brother and nephew, who gave a total of £600; John Cockburn of Ormiston – £1,200; his brother, Patrick Cockburn of Clarkington – £300; their kinsman, George Cockburn, merchant of Haddington – £200; William Nisbet of Dirleton – £1,000; Sir John Baird of Newbyth – £1,000; and William Johnston, postmaster in Haddington – £100. I was amazed to discover that even Robert, the eldest son of Thomas Martine's first marriage, donated £200.[6] Fortunately, his siblings had more sense.

By the time Andrew Fletcher was once again re-elected to the Scottish Parliament in 1702, the full scale of the Darien disaster was starting to unravel. Faced with financial meltdown, the Estates of Scotland searched desperately for a solution. England and Scotland already shared the same monarch and, in England, it was widely promoted that a merger of the Scottish and English parliaments would guarantee the Protestant royal succession, both north and south of the Border. For England, political union secured the survival of the Church of England. For Scotland, it simply offered a way out of debt.

For Andrew Fletcher, who fought valiantly against it, the Treaty of Union was the ultimate betrayal but, with substantial sums of money having already changed hands among the hierarchy, the odds were heavily stacked against him. This did not, however, deter him from standing in the general election of the following year. As might have been foreseen, he was soundly defeated by William Morison of Prestongrange (see Chapter 17). Fletcher may have believed that the fight to retain a Scottish parliament was not yet over but, by then, his constituents were ready to move on.

Andrew Fletcher's active political career came to an abrupt end when he reached fifty but, as an enlightened activist for land reform, it continued in another form. Five years earlier, one of his pamphlets had carried the following observations:

> Were I to assign the principal and original source of our poverty, I should place it in the letting of our lands at so excessive rates, as makes the tenant poorer even than his servant, whose wages he cannot pay; and involves in the same misery day-labourers, tradesmen and the lesser merchants who live in the country villages and towns, and thereby influences no less the great towns, and wholesale merchants, makes the master have a troublesome and ill-paid rent, his lands not improved by enclosure, or otherwise but for want of horses and oxen fit for labour, everywhere run out, and abused. The condition of the lesser freeholders or heritors (as we call them) is not much better than that of our tenants; for they have no stocks to improve their lands, and living not as husbandmen but as gentlemen, they are never able to attain any. Besides this, the unskilfulness of their wretched and half-starved servants is such that their lands are no better cultivated than those by beggarly tenants.[7]

It was Andrew Fletcher's considered opinion that all of Scotland's endemic ills derived from bad land management. Having lost then retrieved his birthright, he determined to put his own house in order and, from 1708, he devoted his energies almost exclusively to Saltoun.

When asked why he remained unmarried, his stock reply was that his brother already had the woman who should have been his wife. Regardless of what this implied, Margaret Carnegie, who had married Henry Fletcher while his brother was abroad in 1688, was undoubtedly an invaluable asset to the team.

While at The Hague, Andrew had come across mills for the production of pearl barley and fanners for winnowing corn. In 1710, he returned to

Holland accompanied by Margaret and James Meikle, a local millwright, to acquire the necessary ironwork to build such a mill at Saltoun. This created constant employment and helped to offset his personal financial losses accrued from the Darien embarrassment. Margaret, meantime, not only managed the mill but also an office in Edinburgh, as she rapidly emerged as an immensely capable businesswoman.[8]

When Andrew Fletcher died in 1716, Saltoun passed to Henry and Margaret and their son, who was named Andrew after his uncle, inherited it from them. This Andrew became a Court of Session judge, taking the judicial title of Lord Milton, and his compassionate manner in dealing with Jacobite prisoners in the aftermath of the 1745 Uprising greatly helped to heal the wounds of a divided nation.

In 1954, the farms of East Saltoun and East Mains and, two years later, Greenhead and Barley Mill were sold to Hamilton & Kinneil Estates.[9] Today, stately Saltoun Hall is divided up into nine individual apartments. The present-day Andrew Fletcher, great-great-great-great-great-nephew of the patriot, lives with his wife Valerie in the elegantly converted stable buildings and continues to farm Saltoun Home Farm and Middlemains.

In 1968, Provost G. F. McNeill of Tranent and his fellow East Lothian councillor, Admiral Sir Peter Reid, Vice-Lieutenant of East Lothian, visited Herdmanston House at East Saltoun to decide its future with Anderson R. Waddell, the farmer of Herdmanston Mains. Their conclusion was that, if this venerable old property were allowed to deteriorate any further, it would become a serious danger to health and safety. Provost McNeill and Sir Peter reported back to the County Planning Committee. Shortly afterwards, Herdmanston House was blown up by 104 (City of Edinburgh) Field Squadron, Royal Engineers demolition team. In a single morning, 800 years of history were obliterated. Did anybody really care? Did it matter? Doubtless there were some who thought so among the throng who turned out to watch the explosion.

In 1068, a young Norman knight, Sir William St Clair, arrived in Scotland with Prince Edgar Atheling, the fugitive Saxon claimant to the throne of England, and his twenty-one-year-old sister Princess Margaret. Having disembarked from a boat on to the Fife coast, Margaret was swept into the arms of the Scottish King Malcolm III and became his second wife. For his loyalty and support, William 'the Seemly' St Clair, so called for his fair good looks, was given the lands of Rosslyn in Midlothian.

Two generations later, Henry St Clair, his grandson, was appointed sheriff to the Anglo-Norman Hugh de Moreville, Constable of Scotland. In 1162, de Moreville granted him the lands of Herdmanston at East Saltoun, where he built a tower house which, in the centuries that followed, formed the nucleus of the imposing mansion that was occupied by his descendants. Among them was Sir William St Clair of Herdmanston who, for having supported Robert the Bruce at the Battle of Bannockburn in 1314, was rewarded with the gift of a sword. On the side of this were engraved the words 'Le Roi me donne, St Clair me porte'.[10]

Until the dawning of the twentieth century, the Herdmanston St Clairs – or Sinclairs, as their name came to be spelled – were acknowledged as the oldest landed family in East Lothian.[11] However, since its owners were largely of a military persuasion and serving overseas, the house was left unoccupied for long periods of time and, in the mid eighteenth century, it was leased to the Honourable Adam Gillies, a distinguished historian and Senator of the College of Justice. Successive generations of Sinclair nevertheless returned to be buried in the adjacent small thirteenth-century Chapel of St John's, which was only built after permission was granted by the canons of Dryburgh who first had to be convinced 'that it would not detract from the mother church of Saltoun'.[12] Ironically, when the old house was demolished in 1968, the chapel was left intact.

On a summer afternoon in 2007, Bridget Ellwood, Marioth Hay's daughter, and I collected the large iron key from Annise Waddell, whose son, Archibald, today farms Herdmanston Mains. Still standing in the extensive parkland are the stable block, a small lectern-type doocot and some astonishingly large yew trees, their lower growth nibbled away with sculptural efficiency by hungry cattle.

Neither Bridget nor I had been there before so it proved pretty impossible for us to work out where the house had once stood. Nevertheless, the interior of St John's Chapel, albeit steeped in a film of dusty neglect, appeared to be in remarkably good condition given that nobody had set foot inside for a year or so. On the floor, two flat tombstones cover the remains of William and Sibilla de St Clair, 1598; on the walls are inscriptions relating to rather more recent family members, including the Crimean War Veteran, Charles, 15th Lord Sinclair, who died in 1922.

As we closed the stout oak door with its vast hinges behind us and beat a path through the forest of nettles and thistles engulfing the chapel on all sides, I was still trying to work out exactly where the great house must have stood. It was then that the Border legend of the two daughters of a fifteenth-century Herdmanston laird came to mind.

It was around the year 1470 that Sir John Sinclair of Herdmanston expired, leaving his two daughters, Margaret and Marion, as heiresses to his Kimmerghame and Polwarth estates at Duns in Berwickshire. Sir John's greedy brother Patrick inherited Herdmanston but was also covetous of his nieces' inheritance. He therefore invited them to stay on the pretext that he could introduce them to eligible suitors. However, as soon as they arrived, he locked them in a room.

Now, as fate would have it, Margaret Sinclair was already enamoured of her Berwickshire neighbour Sir Patrick Hume of Wedderburn Castle. But how could she possibly get word to him? Well, as we all should know, good triumphs over bad. On the morning of the fourth day of imprisonment, they awoke to the sound of Northumbrian pipes. Below their window was Johnny Faa, King of the Gypsies. To him they related their plight and he vowed to seek out the bold Sir Patrick.

On being brought the news, Sir Patrick was outraged and, accompanied by his brother George, immediately set off across the Lammermuirs with a hundred retainers. On reaching Herdmanston, a great tussle took place with much bloodshed on the very ground upon which Bridget and I were standing. Despite Sinclair's inferior numbers, it looked at first as if he might still triumph but then Johnny Faa and his men arrived with the cry, 'Fight, ye Humes! Fight! There is a prize before ye worthy of a clout on the crown or even a stab through the brisket!'

The sisters were rescued. Margaret became the bride of Sir Patrick, while her sister Marion fell into the arms of George Hume. On their joint wedding day, Johnny Faa and six of his followers played the pipes 'without fee, favour or reward'.[13]

CHAPTER SIXTEEN

Lowland Scotch and Tattie Howkin'

A FAMILIAR FACE FROM my teenage years was Angus Ogilvy, the handsome nephew of Sir David Ogilvy, 13th Baronet of Inverquharity and owner of Winton House at Pencaitland. Angus's parents, John and Margaret Ogilvy, lived at East Linton and, since his uncle remained unmarried and was by then into his fifties, it was widely understood that Angus would one day inherit Winton. But in 1966 Sir David married and, three years later, Francis Ogilvy, now 14th Baronet of Inverquharity, was born.

I never asked him about it but Angus, I suspect, was relieved to be free of the responsibilities. He married twice. I was an usher at his first wedding at St John's Church in Edinburgh in 1967 and, after his second marriage in 1980, he moved to live near Stirling, where he opened a novelty card shop before dying tragically young in 1989.

It was a Phillip de Sayton, yet another Norman acolyte of David I, who built the original Winton Castle around 1150. Perched on a steep embankment above the River Tyne as it winds its way from the Moorfoot Hills towards Haddington, Winton withstood the full onslaught of the Earl of Hertford's English army in 1544. Battered and virtually uninhabitable, it was rebuilt in the following century by William Wallace, Master Mason to James VI, emerging as one of the finest surviving period examples of Scottish Renaissance architecture.

In 1715, George Seton, the Jacobite-supporting 5th Earl of Winton, was captured by the English at the Battle of Preston in Lancashire. Taken to the Tower of London, he was condemned to death but escaped by cutting through the window bars of his cell. After taking ship to Europe, he found refuge among the Jacobite community in Rome. Thirty years later, it was claimed that he had given permission for the Jacobite army to pitch its camp at Winton before the Battle of Prestonpans. Still in exile four years later, he died at the age of seventy.

The 5th Earl of Winton having been attainted for his Jacobite sympathies, the Winton Estate (which included Seton Castle and the fishing village of

Cockenzie – see Chapter 17) was acquired by the York Buildings Company of London. To begin with, the policies were leased to a market gardener but, when the York Buildings Company filed for bankruptcy in 1779, Winton House, as it had become known, was purchased by Mary Hamilton Nisbet of Archerfield, Belhaven and Pencaitland for her second son, Colonel John Hamilton. After enlargement by the architect William Paterson, it passed to Colonel Hamilton's sister, another Mary.

Her daughter, also Mary, became the wife of James, Lord Ruthven, and it was she who built the village of New Winton and greatly enhanced the local community by financing a new school building.[1] When Lady Ruthven died in 1885, the Winton Estate passed to her cousin Constance Dundas Christopher Nisbet-Hamilton. In East Lothian alone, Constance now owned three mansion houses, four villages and over thirty-five farms (see Chapter 25).

Constance's husband was Henry Ogilvy, an advocate and the second son of Sir John Ogilvy, 9th Baronet of Inverquharity in the County of Forfar. They married in 1888, when Constance was forty-five and he was fifty-one. For most of their lives together, they resided mainly at Biel but, after Henry's death in 1909, Constance moved permanently to Winton and, in 1920, bequeathed the estate to Gilbert Ogilvy, her nephew by marriage.

When Gilbert died in 1953, the estate was inherited by his eldest son David, who came into his uncle's Inverquharity baronetcy in 1956. Sir David died in 1992 and Winton House is today the home of the 14th Baronet, Sir Francis, a chartered surveyor, his wife Dorothy and their children. Situated in close proximity to Edinburgh and the golf coast, it serves as a popular venue for conferences, weddings, corporate dinners and product launches.

Winton House also contains some remarkable furniture and features which date back to its occupancy by the Seton family. On the walls are portraits of Charles I and various Hamilton, Nisbet, Ogilvy and Bruce ancestors, including an engaging likeness of Mary Ferguson (see Chapter 25) by John Hoppner, showing her to be, by any standards, an outstanding beauty.

Sir Francis Ogilvy is deeply conscious of his inheritance. 'Whatever your personal history, there is much to be gained from an awareness of it in order to assist in how you relate to what is going on in the world around you,' he says. He sometimes finds it perplexing to watch one of those period dramas on television where all of the cast members are wearing formal dress under glorious plasterwork ceilings. 'All of a sudden your realise that your own surroundings are almost identical and that you are wearing old jeans and a jumper.

'I remember puzzling over what I wanted to do and a cousin saying to me, "Isn't it obvious?" ' he continues. 'But my parents never put any pressure on me to go into land management. It was entirely my decision to train as a chartered surveyor and it seemed like a neat fit when I returned to East

Lothian and teamed up with Stewart Chalmers. When he retired in 1999, I took over the running of the professional firm.'

Stewart Chalmers had first come to East Lothian in 1961 to factor the Lennoxlove Estate on behalf of John Sale & Partners. Around 1980, when John Sale & Partners was sold, he left Lennoxlove and took over the firm's Haddington office under his own name to provide general surveying and land management expertise to estates throughout the county. Today, Chalmers & Company, based in Haddington, provides a full range of chartered surveyor, land agency and architectural services. Sir Francis now works with an eleven-strong team across East Lothian, Midlothian, the Borders and the west of Scotland – all of this in addition to managing the Winton Estate and bringing up a young family.

After a recent visit to Winton House, I looked in on Jenny Black, a cheerful and gentle widow who lives in the lodge. Jenny arrived at Winton from Newton Stewart in 1934 with her mother, who had come to work in the big house and, within days, was sent to Prestonpans Secondary School, which seems quite a distance for a child to travel to school, even now. 'Of course, that was long before the Ross High started in Tranent,' she recalled. 'In those days, you either walked or caught the school bus which stopped at the War Memorial in the village and you paid a shilling a week for your lunch, or took sandwiches with you.'

When she left school at the age of fourteen, Jenny was at first employed at Winton House over the Christmas period then, at her mother's request, and unbeknown to Jenny, Gilbert Ogilvy put her name down with an employment agency in Edinburgh. The next thing she knew, she was offered a job with the Earl and Countess of Crawford at Balcarres in Fife, then with the Earl of Lichfield at Shugborough Hall in Staffordshire. There was no stigma attached to being in domestic service in that era, she confirmed. 'The majority of household staff considered themselves protected and extremely fortunate. And don't forget that the big houses provided a lot of work for local people.'

Having served as a Wren during the Second World War and married her husband, Norman, a shipwright, Jenny returned to work at Winton House in 1952. She has been living in the lodge ever since – half a century that has witnessed great changes in the style of country house occupancy. For example, 'None of the employers ever cooked for themselves; most of them didn't know how to,' she said, before confiding that the Ogilvys at Winton were always enormously kind and much more informal than in the other big houses she worked for. 'At Shugborough Hall, the countess liked us to wear mauve uniforms,' she recalled with a shudder.

Tyneholm House, which marches with Winton, was built in 1835 by William Burn for Patrick Dudgeon of Eastcraig, who purchased the land of

Wester Pencaitland from the Saltoun Estate. The property, with the neighbouring Woodhall and Wolfstar estates, was subsequently acquired by Arthur Trevelyan. The Trevelyan Family were well-connected landowners in Somerset and Northumberland and, had he survived his elder brother, Sir Walter Trevelyan of Nettlecombe, Arthur would have inherited the Trevelyan baronetcy, which passed instead to a cousin.[2]

A staunch supporter of the Temperance Movement and bitterly opposed to the Game Laws and vivisection, Arthur Trevelyan was nothing if not unconventional – perhaps a trifle more than East Lothian was used to. A follower of phrenology, the study of personality traits through the shape of the head, he believed in social equality. Assiduously he, late in life, married Elizabeth, a housemaid from an Edinburgh hotel – a lady who, it appears, sympathetically indulged her husband's many foibles. Forty years after the event, we find him writing to Cardinal Newman to complain that the Battle of Waterloo had been fought on a Sunday. Among his many dislikes were: soldiers – he called them 'man butchers and moral lunatics'; racing; the aristocracy – he referred to its members as 'antichrists'; and, for no explicable reason, ploughs. In one particularly memorable letter, he wrote to Prince Albert to complain that he spent too much time racing and shooting and that Queen Victoria wore too much jewellery. In one of his more obscure jottings, he suggested that the villagers of Pencaitland should wear Turkish national costume, which he considered to be an immensely colourful and sensible attire. 'Trousers should be tied at the ankle whenever possible,' he proposed.[3]

In the *Haddingtonshire Courier* of 8 February 1878, Arthur Trevelyan's obituary stated that he was found in his bedroom:

> There being no noise, and the door being locked, the gardener gained access by means of a ladder. Mrs Trevelyan slept in a separate room. He appeared to have been unconscious for some time. He had been in good health the previous day . . .
>
> The deceased, despite many eccentricities of character, possessed sterling qualities of disposition which will make his sudden removal a cause of deep regret in the parish and neighbourhood. He was an ardent social reformer taking an active and energetic part in every movement that appeared to him calculated to improve the well being of his fellow men . . .
>
> His opinions on theological matters were peculiar, but they were not offensively obtruded on those who differed from him . . . He carried literature about with him to disseminate liberally.

This might explain why his will specifically demanded that no clergyman of any denomination was to be allowed onto the Tyneholm Estate. Under the conditions of his having left funds for the creation of lunatic asylums, he also stipulated that dance classes were essential.[4] In 1884, the Arthur Trevelyan Memorial Hall was built at Pencaitland at a cost of £12,000 and gifted to the village.

Six years after Arthur's death, his widow Elizabeth married William Black, an architect, despite his being forty-seven years old and she being seventy-one. At her request, apparently, he acquired the additional name of Trevelyan. However, prior to their marriage, he was obliged to sign what would nowadays be termed a pre-nuptial arrangement, allegedly on the promise that ample provision would be made for him in her will.

As the family doctor, my great-grandfather, Dr William Martine, was in attendance when Elizabeth died in 1891.[5] Her remains were taken to the Trevelyan burial ground at Cambo, near Wallington 'drawn by four Belgian horses, and followed by two mourning coaches'.[6] The Victorians certainly knew how to put on a show. She left the bulk of everything to her cousin James Reid, an Aberdeenshire schoolmaster, but among her bequests was provision for the Sick Kids, the Robertson Orphan Homes in Edinburgh, the Ragged School, the Arthur Trevelyan Scholarship, the Refuge for the Destitute, Canongate, Edinburgh, and the Edinburgh Public Soup Kitchen. One hundred pounds was gifted to the Home for Imbeciles at Larbert and a sum of money allocated to supply coal to the poor in Pencaitland.

But Elizabeth's story did not conclude there. Three years later, William Black Trevelyan unsuccessfully raised an action against James Reid to claim half of the estate, which was valued at £32,734. It was an unpleasant dispute. In Reid's defence, it was argued that his cousin had been induced to marry the pursuer in the belief that he would assist her in the management of her affairs. Disagreements had occurred soon after their marriage and their life together became increasingly unhappy. William Black Trevelyan claimed £17,000, while under the terms of Elizabeth's original will he had already received £3,000 on the condition that he left the house immediately!

James Reid took up residence at Tyneholm and in 1903 set up the Woodhall Coal Company which employed over 120 men and prospered into the 1940s. He built several miners' cottages in the village which are still in use to this day. When he died aged eighty-nine, in 1947, the estate was divided between his nephews. Until 1985, Tyneholm House was run as a Dr Barnardo's Home and then as residential retreat for the elderly until it was bought by the present owners, Edward and Henrietta Gimlette.

'The tendency is to make fun of Arthur because he was such an eccentric,' says James Reid's great-nephew Angus McGregor, who lives at Tyninghame. 'But this overlooks the fact that he was extremely generous and a lot of the interests he espoused are now being taken seriously.'

Fountainhall at Pencaitland was previously known as Woodhead House and, before that, as Penkaet Castle, a tower house dating from 1550. It was bought from Sir George Cockburn by Robert Pringle in 1635, then acquired by Sir John Lauder, a leading Scottish jurist who took the legal title of Lord Fountainhall. He was one of the advocates chosen by the Duchess of Monmouth to defend her interests during the trial of her husband in 1686.

Lauder descendants continued to live at Pencaitland until 1922, when they moved to their house in Edinburgh's Grange and Woodhead House was purchased from them by Professor Ian Holbourn, a survivor of the RMS *Lusitania* when it was torpedoed off Old Head of Kinsale in Ireland in 1915. In 1957, the property was bought by Iain Cowe, who returned its name to Fountainhall. It is today the home of Robert and Alison Cowe.

At Woodhall, which was built as a hunting lodge for the Sinclairs of Herdmanston, lives the painter Hugh Buchanan, whose romanticised architectural works are in the collection of Her Majesty the Queen. Hugh has exhibited in London, Spain and America and, in 1987, was approached by the Prince of Wales to paint a series of interiors at Balmoral, followed in 1994 by those of Highgrove. In 2002, he was commissioned by the House of Lords to commemorate the lying-in-state of Her Majesty Queen Elizabeth, the Queen Mother at the Palace of Westminster.

Hugh, his wife Ann and their three strikingly attractive daughters love their life at the heart of East Lothian. 'Being in such close proximity to some of Robert Adam's greatest masterpieces inspires me greatly,' he says. Ann, meantime, lectures extensively on European art and architecture.

In passing through Pencaitland, it would be impossible for me as a published author on Scotch whisky to overlook the only surviving single malt distillery in the Scottish Lowlands. Next to the village are the farms of Milton, Lempockwells, Huntlaw and Peaston Bank which, from the nineteenth century, were occupied by the brothers John and George Rate. In 1825, the Rates established a distillery at Milton and, in 1837, they emerged as licence holders of the Kinchie Distillery at Pencaitland, where they grew and malted their own barley. This they mashed with the water of the Kinchie Burn, which flows from the Lammermuirs into the River Tyne, and distilled it to create a distinctive Lowland malt whisky.

With the end of the Rates' tenure in 1853, the manufacture of whisky stopped. For twenty-seven years the premises was used as a sawmill before being reinstated as the Glen Kinchie Distillery in 1880. By 1914, it was one of only five Lowland malt distilleries controlled by Scottish Malt Distillers, forerunner of United Distillers, and now Diageo. Of these, only Glen Kinchie, now Glenkinchie, survives.

In 1968, Glenkinchie's floor maltings were closed but the discarded equipment now forms the nucleus of the collection of a visitor centre, which was modernised in 1997. With the well-cared-for bowling green exclusive to distillery workers and villagers, Glenkinchie retains a close relationship with the local community and, at one stage, was famous for its sideline of breeding Clydesdale horses.[7] During the 1950s, the manager also ran the Glenkinchie beef herd which, over three successive years, won the fat stock Supreme Championships at Smithfield, Birmingham and Edinburgh, as well as many other individual show championships.

Avril Kirk, wife of Malcolm the Mole Catcher at Humbie, was brought up on the farm of Peaston Bank where her grandfather, John Peaston Bryson, was the grieve for George P. Gibson. 'The Gibsons grew peas and raspberries and kept ducks and hens,' she recalled. 'They also had two ponies, Court and Jester, the black one. My granny bought me a lovely pair of blue gloves and Jester ate one. I never forgave him.'

Peaston Bank and the surrounding countryside provided an idyllic playground for young children. One day, Avril's grandfather caught her and her sister pilfering peas. 'I was eight at the time and we hid them in our jumpers and sun hats. I'm sure my grandfather must have known but he didn't say anything. When I was very young, my father, Jim Bryson, used to plough with two Clydesdale horses. Around 1954, tractors were starting to be used and I can remember a Grey Ferguson model. My dad had a David Brown two-seater in the school holidays, and I would sit beside him when it was "Tattie Week".[8]

'I was allowed to drive it along the drills while Dad emptied the baskets of potatoes. It certainly beat having to be bent over in your stent (or stint), which was the set area between two sticks where you had to lift the tatties, frantically trying to pick them up before the digger came around.

'It was 1956 before we had electricity but, up until then, we managed with tilley lamps and were totally self-sufficient. My mother baked bread, preparing the dough with a rolling pin. The paper man came on a Sunday and brought dry batteries for the radio. In those days, you had to have two batteries and one would be taken away to be recharged. On Friday, my dad liked to listen to Scottish country dance music and football on Saturdays, so it was important to have enough battery power left.'

Before Humbie Station closed in 1963, a train delivered coal and loaded up with grain at Humbie. Avril and her school friends used to go down to the railway track at West Saltoun and the guards would allow them to climb on board and travel down to Humbie and back. 'It was a great treat,' she recalled, 'especially as our parents never knew about it. Can you imagine what a fuss there would be nowadays?'

CHAPTER SEVENTEEN

Bookends

Mining has been a feature of East Lothian since the thirteenth century when Robert de Quincy and his son, Sayer or Saer, lords of the Manor of Tranent, granted 'in free alms' the rights to quarry an extensive seam of coal at Preston down to the low water mark to the Cistercian monks of Newbattle.[1]

From this arrangement emerged the name Prestongrange. Preston means 'Priest's town', and the farmhouse in which the monks lived was the 'grange'. Around the same period, the monks also introduced salt-panning, hence the early settlement's name of Saltpreston. In the sixteenth century, a harbour was built which, in 1562, was known as Acheson's Haven, after Alexander Atkinson, a local trader. Now landlocked, it operated successfully for a hundred years, at one stage rivalling Leith in importance.

Meanwhile, under the auspices of Mark Ker, Abbot of Newbattle, ancestor of the marquises of Lothian, the estate of Prestongrange effortlessly made the transformation from a Catholic to a Protestant seminary. Ker's son succeeded his father as Commendator of Newbattle Abbey, taking over as of hereditary right. In 1584, in what would nowadays be considered a highly irregular transaction, both Newbattle and Prestongrange were confirmed by royal command upon Ker's heirs male. And they got away with it!

Then, early in the seventeenth century, the landholdings of Prestongrange were restructured into two baronies, Prestongrange and Preston. The former was granted to Sir George Morison who, around 1609, had purchased the Prestongrange Estate; the latter, about the same period, was bestowed upon Sir John Hamilton, brother of Thomas, 1st Earl of Haddington.

In 1700, the harbour was renamed Morrison's Haven after Sir George's descendant, William Morison.[2] This gentleman, who stood against Andrew Fletcher of Saltoun in the general election of 1707 and won, soon ran into financial problems created by a gambling debt of £14,305 owed to the notorious Francis Charteris (see Chapter 6). On his death in 1745, Prestongrange, including adjacent Dolphingston, was sold to pay off his liabilities.

The property was next purchased by William Grant, Lord Advocate of Scotland, who, in 1754, took his seat in the House of Lords as Lord Prestongrange.

After his death, the estate was inherited by his elder daughter Janet Grant, the wife of John Carmichael of Castlecraig, 4th Earl of Hyndford. When she died in 1818, the Grant of Prestongrange baronetcy was inherited by their nephew, Sir James Suttie of Balgone (see Chapter 27) and it was Sir James's son, Sir George Grant-Suttie, who, in 1848, with his estate manager Edward Yule, got the colliery up and running again.[3]

The Prestongrange Coal and Iron Company was formed in 1873 but ran into trouble after a series of strikes over pay and conditions. Sir George's death in 1878, followed closely by that of his heir, Sir James, forced the company into liquidation. In 1894, it was sold by Sir James's 24-year-old son, another Sir George, to the Summerlee and Mossend Iron and Steel Company.

For the workforce, it brought about a new lease of life. By 1910, the Summerlee Company, run by the Neilson family from the West of Scotland, employed over 4,100 miners and operated eight mines. Then came the First World War, in the aftermath of which there was more unrest over working conditions, culminating with the National Strike of 1921.

It was the beginning of the end for the coal-mining industry in Scotland. Between the mid 1920s and the outbreak of the Second World War, the workforce at Prestongrange Colliery was systematically broken up. Throughout Scotland, heavy industries such as iron and steel manufacture and shipbuilding – both major consumers of coal – were in a state of collapse. As part of its postwar reconstruction programme, the incoming Labour government placed the coal industry under state control but, by 1953, the workforce at Prestongrange had fallen to 660. By 1962, the Prestongrange Colliery was branded 'surplus to national requirements' and shut down.

If there was any consolation to be had from the sorry demise of East Lothian's coal legacy, it is that the story does not end there. After the closure, a committee comprising East Lothian Council, the National Coal Board, the National Museum of Mineworkers, the East Lothian Antiquarian and Field Naturalists' Society, the Institute of Mechanical Engineers and the Royal Museum of Scotland was set up to create the Prestongrange Industrial Heritage Museum. The inspiration of David Spence, former manager of the Wallyford Group of Collieries, this continues to provide a spellbinding tribute to a thousand years of Scotland's industrial history.

Towering behind the trees, half a mile inland from the sea, can be glimpsed the mansion house of Prestongrange which, although it dates from the sixteenth century, benefited from lavish embellishments by the architect William Playfair in both 1830 and 1850. Although a monumental building, the Grant-Sutties appear to have favoured and, from 1909, mainly occupied their more modest house of Balgone, further down the East Lothian coast.[4]

Prestongrange House remained empty until 1924, when it was leased to the Royal Musselburgh Golf Club (see Chapter 12). In 1958, it was sold to the Coal Industry Social and Welfare Organisation. Since then it has been held in trust by the Musselburgh Miners' Charitable Society, the accommodation being shared with the RMGC. During renovation work in 1963, a painted ceiling dating from 1581 was discovered under plasterwork and, because of its historic importance, it was moved to Napier University's Merchiston Tower for preservation. It is the earliest dated example of a Renaissance painted ceiling in Scotland.

Feudal baronies are a curious aberration. Despite the popular trend against hereditary honours and titles, such ennoblements are eagerly bought and sold, meaning very little in most cases but, in the case of that of Prestoungrange (the baronial spelling), it meant rather a lot. On the death of Philip, the 8th Grant-Suttie Baronet, in 1997, the remaining baronial lands of Prestoungrange – the foreshore of Morrison's Haven and Cuthill Rocks – were sold to Dr Gordon Wills, a successful marketing expert from Northamptonshire, whose maternal grandfather, William Park, had been a miner at the Prestongrange Colliery in 1900.

With this territory came the feudal Prestoungrange barony and Dr Prestoungrange, as he is now styled, has reintroduced the Prestoungrange Baron Court to revive some of the rather more beneficial traditions of the feudal concept. Most notably, he has financed a series of well-researched and invaluable historic booklets on the area.

The Gothenburg Tavern, one of three such establishments set up in 1908 to help the local mining communities of Danderhall, Newtongrange and Prestonpans, has also been restored. Pioneered by the Aberdeen-born artist Jim Cursitor, a series of murals and sculptures depicting local characters and historic events was commissioned to decorate the walls and buildings of Prestonpans, Cockenzie and Port Seton.

In 1947, Samuel Burns, a firewood merchant, opened up a yard in a whin quarry that had been owned by W. Baxter & Sons, Quarrymasters. 'He had been working for Presonpans Co-operative and began to suffer from angina, so he had to retire,' explained his son John. 'He was an awful man for always wanting to be doing something, so somebody suggested he set up on his own.'

His yard being strategically situated on the coast road, behind the high walls of the Prestongrange Estate, Sam Burns soon discovered that there was an even greater demand for the old wardrobes and wooden furniture which he acquired from house sales to transform into kindling. Thus Samuel Burns & Co, Second Hand Goods Merchant, came into being. As the demand increased, Sam applied for planning permission to erect a shed but, being against the prevailing green-belt policy, the request was turned down. As a consequence, therefore, he created makeshift shelters and stacked his furniture and bric-a-brac under trees for protection against the elements. Sam's son John remembers planning officer Frank Tindall visiting the yard on several occasions and shaking his head. 'It's a good job you have a big high wall around this place,' he told him.

With the entire stock exposed to the elements, Sam was obliged to keep his prices low in order to achieve a quick turnover but, as the word spread, the yard prospered. Many a young couple furnished their first Edinburgh home with bargains from Burns' Yard. 'All of the family helped out,' recalled John, who joined his father having completed his National Service in the 1950s. Today, Burns' Yard is run by his sons, Gordon and another John.

The Burns family have lived in Prestonpans since 1763 when Alexander Burn, a seafarer from Monifieth, settled there with his wife Margaret Wilson and raised a family of six children. It was Alexander, their youngest son, who added the 's' to the surname and it was his seventh child and fourth son, John Burns, who emigrated to New Zealand.

John's profession is listed in the national census as 'gardener' and, in 1844, he married Margaret Craig, daughter of the grieve at Long Yester. They had eleven surviving children (three sons having died young) and, of these, seven sons, one daughter and eight grandchildren joined their parents in New Zealand, while their second son Samuel remained in Prestonpans. In 1988, a reunion of the descendants of John and Margaret Burns was held in Dunedin, New Zealand. It numbered into the hundreds.[5]

In 1701, a young man of the name of William Cadell arrived in Haddington to seek work as a journeyman and found employment with James Hogg, burgess of the town. Hogg's sister, coincidentally, was married to David Martine, a son of the first marriage of my direct ancestor Thomas, who was then farming at Sandersdean on Colstoun. Not long afterwards, Cadell married his employer's daughter Anna and, setting up business in a warehouse in the small fishing village of Cockenzie, successfully launched a trading venture with the ports of Baltic countries such as Russia and Sweden.

From then on, the fortunes of the Cadells prospered dramatically, their commercial interests eventually embracing salt manufacture, mining, shipping and heavy manufacturing throughout Scotland's central belt. William Cadell's third son, also William, was a founder director of the Carron ironworks near Falkirk and, while he sent one of his sons, yet another

William, to manage this project, his younger son John was obliged to remain behind to manage the family interests in East Lothian.

In 1732, William Cadell took a lease out on the coal pits and salt pans of Cockenzie, Cockenzie Harbour and Cockenzie House, which had been forfeited thirteen years earlier by George Seton, 5th Earl of Winton (see Chapter 16). At the time they were held by the York Buildings Company of London but, when that company went into liquidation in 1777, John Cadell purchased them along with the barony of Tranent.

The Cadell Family were to occupy the substantial Jacobean mansion of Cockenzie House, which had been built for George Seton, Salt Master and Baillie of Tranent, for 200 years. John Cadell of Cockenzie's youngest son, Hew Francis, married Janet Buchan-Sydserf from Ruchlaw on the Whittingehame Estate and they had eleven children. John Martine describes his relative as:

> a man of mark and note in this day. He made salt, and wrought the Tranent coal-field to a large extent; was a shipowner, exported coals to foreign ports to a large extent, and imported into Cockenzie harbour, cargoes of linseed cake, bones, &c, for manure.

In 1834, Hew Francis employed Robert Stevenson, the engineer grandfather of Robert Louis Stevenson, to create Cockenzie Harbour at a cost of over £6,000. Hew Francis died in 1873 at the age of ninety-four.

Hew's third son, Francis, was born at Cockenzie in 1822 and, having set off to Australia in search of gold, he formed the Murray River Navigation Company. In 1867 he led an expedition to the Northern Territory to identify areas suitable for settlement on behalf of the Australian government. At a later stage in his career, he became financially involved in whaling and pearl fishing but was murdered when his crew mutinied in the Dutch East Indies in 1879. In Northern Australia, he is commemorated by the Cadell Strait and by a settlement on the Murray River.

Robert Cadell, one of Francis's younger brothers, served in the British Army during the Crimean War and Indian Mutiny of 1857 and rose to the rank of general. Their youngest brother, Thomas, was also stationed in India and was awarded the Victoria Cross at the age of twenty-one for rescuing two wounded soldiers under heavy fire. From 1878, until his retirement in 1892, he was Chief Commissioner of the Andaman and Nicobar Islands. The Scottish colourist, Francis Boileau Cadell, born in 1883, was another well-known descendant of this family,

On the death in 1959 of Marion Cadell, the last of Thomas's five unmarried daughters, Cockenzie House became the home of Donald Ross, owner of the fashionable L'Aperitif Restaurant in Edinburgh. After this, it was occupied by Michael Murgatroyd, National Treasurer for the Scottish National Party. It is currently a nursing home and the building has a Historic Scotland A-list status.

Rowland Wallis, a prolific portrait painter now living in France, was surprised, but equally challenged, when one of his sitters specifically asked him to paint her against the backdrop of Cockenzie Power Station. For her, the 500-foot-high twin chimneys of Cockenzie were the gateway to her childhood. In company with the coastal box of Torness Nuclear Power Station, to the south of the county, they form, on leaving Musselburgh, the bookends of coastal East Lothian.

It was in 1952 that the South of Scotland Electricity Board took the decision to build a 1,200-megawatt coal-fired power station, 800 feet long and 200 feet high at Cockenzie, on the site of the Preston Links Colliery, to replace the ageing and increasingly inefficient one situated at Portobello. The project was undertaken by consultant engineers Kennedy, Donkin, Strain and Robertson, employing architects, Robert Matthew, Johnson Marshall & Partners, with job architect Chris Carter. Even the Country Planning Officer Frank Tindall, who had at first pressed for the station to be built at Prestongrange, eventually conceded that it was a masterpiece of design.

Officially opened in 1968 by the then Secretary of State for Scotland, William Ross, Cockenzie Power Station won a Civic Trust Award in 1972. Under the privatised utility group, Scottish Power, it has since moved with the green agenda to drastically reduce its carbon emissions. Watch this space!

CHAPTER EIGHTEEN

Battlefields of One Kind or Another

IT HAS TO BE IMPOSSIBLE for those who have never known conscription or national service to imagine the scale of the outcry that occurred when the British government, at war with France in 1797, passed the Scottish Militia Act. Since the ruling classes of the day were convinced that an invasion was likely to take place at any moment, the legislation called for a body of 6,000 young men to be urgently enlisted to defend their native soil. Not unreasonable, you might think, but it was the way in which the recruitment was to be carried out that caused the furore.

Candidates were required to be between the ages of eighteen and twenty-three and schoolmasters throughout Scotland were instructed to draw up lists of former pupils within that age bracket. Those who were married with more than two children were exempt. Others were subjected to a ballot but could be excused if they were prepared to pay for a substitute to take their place. Recruitment was, therefore, very much focused on the lower echelons of society and this understandably caused a groundswell of resentment. What made matters worse was that Europe, at the end of the eighteenth century, was still reverberating from the atrocities of the French Revolution. In certain quarters, the degree of protest levelled against the Scottish Militia Act suggested that a similar uprising against the British ruling classes was imminent.

As I drive through the small town of Tranent in the second millennium, I often wonder if any of its current inhabitants are even remotely aware of the shocking incident that took place there on 29 August 1797. But then, why should they be? There was nothing even remotely to be proud of.

On the evening before the schoolmasters' ballot lists were to be examined, a cavalry dragoon, accompanied by his servant, just chanced to be riding through Tranent when he was assaulted by a group of townsfolk. Whether or not he provoked them or they him will never be known since the subsequent evidence was widely contradictory. However, the incident was sufficient to inflame the entire local population, many of whom marched on the house of Robert Paisley, the Tranent schoolmaster, to demand that he hand over his list. Parish schoolmasters in Saltoun, Pencaitland, Ormiston and Gladsmuir were similarly harangued and David Anderson, the Deputy Lieutenant of East Lothian, became sufficiently alarmed to summon help from the Commander of the Cinque Ports Cavalry stationed at Haddington.

When the local yeomanry assembled the following morning, they were therefore joined by twenty-two horsemen of the Cinque Ports and eighty members of the Pembrokeshire Cavalry quartered at Musselburgh. On their arrival about mid morning at John Glen's Inn at Tranent, where the ballot papers were to be collected, the officials found themselves surrounded by an angry mob comprised largely of women. John Cadell, the owner of the local coalmine, attempted to read the Riot Act but his words were drowned out.

As a warning, the dragoons were first instructed to fire off a volley of blanks and then told to load their guns. What happened next was that eleven of the protesters were killed, including two women, Joan Crookston and Isabel Rodger, aged nineteen.[1] Eight onlookers were wounded and thirty-six taken prisoner.

Writing on the subject from a distance of forty-seven years, the historian James Miller observed that, accepting the military had suffered much provocation:

> they exercised barbarities worse than any used by the highland caterans against the Covenanters of the west, and which would not now be tolerated. Parties of cavalry armed with pistols, carabines and swords rode through the fields and high roads to the distance of one mile or two around Tranent and, without the smallest provocation, wantonly and barbarously fired upon or cut with swords many persons at that distance, and actually put to death several decent people who were going about their ordinary business, and totally unconcerned or unconnected with what was going on.[2]

It was a shocking debacle, only superseded by the efforts to apportion the blame afterwards.[3] Six rioters were summoned to appear in court but only two turned up – Robert Mitchell and Neil Redpath. The latter was defended by a young Walter Scott, soon to embark upon a writing career. Both men pleaded not guilty and a verdict of not proven was returned.

In 1995, a statue of Joan Crookston with a child was unveiled in Tranent's town centre – it is a rather idealised image by the sculptor David Annand, considering what had taken place. In the aftermath of the violence, the shame invoked among the wider public was largely covered up by the authorities and, as memories became more distant, it became more politic to sentimentalise over the rather more bloody but equally divisive military event that had taken place earlier in the same century.

On the morning of 21 September 1745, the 1,400-strong Jacobite army of Prince Charles Edward Stuart emerged from the high ground of the farms of Myles and Birsley in the Parish of Tranent to cross the morass which is, however, situated in the Parish of Prestonpans. Hence, the ensuing Battle of Prestonpans is sometimes referred to locally as the Battle of Tranent or Battle of Gladsmuir but, in the long run, Prestonpans has a more evocative ring to it.

Romantic historians sometimes give the impression that the colourful Highlanders and their Bonnie Prince were universally popular during their incursion into southern Scotland. This is simply not the case. The reality is that there was remarkably little enthusiasm for any sort of confrontation among Lowland Scots, as was evidenced by the Jacobites' almost effortless seizure of Edinburgh.

When Alexander Martine and his fellow heralds read out the Young Pretender's 'Proclamation of Regency' at the Mercat Cross (see Chapter 5), the crowd which assembled was largely made up of women hoping to catch a glimpse of the handsome Prince. Most of their menfolk stayed indoors for fear of being forcibly recruited to the cause.

As the Jacobite army moved onwards, its following certainly increased but not in East Lothian, as can be judged from the large number of Presbyterian clergymen who volunteered for the Government cause. Among such recruits were: John Home who, the following year, was ordained as Minister of Athelstaneford; his friend Alexander Carlyle, afterwards Minister of Inveresk; and the Reverend John Brown, Minister of St Mary's, Haddington.

Post-Reformation, it became abundantly clear that the East Lothian majority preferred to keep faith with authority and the status quo. The county had suffered enough from the wars of the past. When the Hanoverian succession was established in 1714, Haddington celebrated along with the rest of Scotland. When, in the following year, the then Jacobite general William Mackintosh of Borlum landed his troops at Aberlady, Gullane and North Berwick, the response was pitiful.

Large numbers of spectators, however, did turn out in 1745 to watch the Government army under Sir John Cope set up their encampment on the rising ground west of Haddington, but few were inclined to take sides. Many years later, Robert Herkes of Muirtown Farm remembered his father holding him up as a child to see the King's Army pass on the road leading above Abbey Mains by Barney Mains to Yellowcraigs. It was something to tell his grandchildren, he said, but his father had not even the slightest intention of becoming involved.[4]

Conflicts create their own heroes and casualties and the Battle of Prestonpans is synonymous with the names of the losers – General John Cope and Colonel James Gardiner, the latter commander of a regiment of dragoons which had previously fought heroically against the French in Flanders. Colonel Gardiner has an additional status in the folklore of East Lothian in that he was the owner of Oliestob (also known as Holy Stop), a picturesque seventeenth-century mansion house which, by sheer coincidence, just happened to be situated on the fringe of the battlefield.

The Battle of Prestonpans was over in less than fifteen minutes. Hundreds of Government troops were killed and wounded and 1,500 taken prisoner. The Highland army, in comparison, suffered less than one hundred killed or wounded.

In preparation for the approaching confrontation, Colonel Gardiner had placed a guard of seventy dragoons around his home and put his two daughters in the care of his friend Andrew Wight of Ormiston. The following day, Wight rode over to Prestonpans and, finding his friend stripped naked and mortally wounded, approached the Jacobite Duke of Perth, whom he knew, for permission to remove the body.

Permission was granted and, having wrapped the Colonel in a plaid purchased from a Highlander, Wight removed it to the home of his brother-in-law, the Reverend Charles Cunningham, Minister of Tranent. It speaks volumes as to the divisive nature of the times that Andrew Wight, who remained neutral, James Drummond, Duke of Perth, one of the Prince's staunchest supporters, and Colonel Gardiner were all three members of John Cockburn of Ormiston's Edinburgh Society of Improvers.[5] As a further act of compassion, the Duke deployed a guard of Jacobite soldiers to Oliestob to protect it from being looted.

For over a century, a thorn tree marked the spot where the fighting was at its fiercest and where the brave 'Christian' Colonel Gardiner fell. There were originally three stems, standing out so markedly from each other that local author Peter McNeill writes of it as a clump of trees.[6] Today the thorns are long gone but, in 1853, a memorial to the Colonel was erected in front of his house. In 1932, a cairn to the dead designed by William Davidson FRIBA was commissioned by the Society for the Preservation of Rural Scotland. It is situated on a triangular piece of ground at a fork in the Edinburgh to North Berwick Road.

Following Colonel Gardiner's death, Oliestob was purchased by the Scottish judge Lord Bankton, from whom it derives its current name. In the twentieth century, the surrounding land was acquired by the Scottish Coal Board to service the adjacent Bankton Colliery. Bankton House soon deteriorated into a roofless shell but, in 1998, it was rescued and converted into flats by the Edinburgh-based architect Nicholas Groves-Raines.

Built in 1596, Prestonpans Parish Church claims to be one of the first post-Reformation places of worship in Scotland. A century and a half later, the brief, enfolding drama of the Battle of Prestonpans was watched from the church tower by the Reverend William Carlyle, father of the rather more famous Reverend Alexander Carlyle. In the aftermath, a melancholy gravestone was erected in memory of Captain John Stuart of Physgill who was 'barbarously murdered by four Highlanders near the end of the Battle'.

Preston Tower, 90 feet high with walls almost seven foot thick, is now part of the portfolio of the National Trust for Scotland and is maintained by the council. On top of the original tower is an extension, the thinking no doubt being that its occupants would be safer high above their attackers than below. At the time of the Battle of Prestonpans it was already a ruin but it too must have afforded an unparalleled view of the battlefield.

The Preston Estate came into the hands of the Hamilton family in the fifteenth century with the marriage of Sir John Hamilton to Jane Lyddell of Preston. The castle, which occupied an extensive area, was set on fire during the incursions of both the Earl of Hertford and Oliver Cromwell, and only the keep remains.

At the centre of the village is Hamilton House, built for Sir John Hamilton, a brother of the 1st Earl of Haddington. Implicated in the abduction of James VI in the Ruthven Raid of 1582, he was later pardoned and, in the years that followed, became a staunch supporter of the Covenant, the confession of faith of the Kirk of Scotland. Above the entrance to his home he placed the inscription 'Praised be the Lord My Strength and My Redeemer'.

A two-storey house of double L-plan format forming three sides of a courtyard, Hamilton House was, in the course of time, split into tenements and, in 1937, was one of the earliest acquisitions of the fledgling National Trust for Scotland. Restored as a single dwelling, it was occupied for ten years by the architect Robert Matthew and his family. When Matthew was appointed Chief Architect of London County Council, it became the home of Jo Grimond, leader of the British Liberal Party. Until 2008 it was tenanted by the late David Lumsden of Cushnie, a monarchist of Jacobite persuasion, who, during the 1980s, helped to set up the Castles of Scotland Preservation Trust. One of his more idiosyncratic pursuits was to campaign against the wearing of white socks with the kilt.

Northfield House, less than 100 yards away, was also owned by the Hamiltons of Preston in the sixteenth century but was acquired from a George Acheson and Barbara Congleton, his wife, along with the lands and house south of the village of Salt-Preston by Joseph Marjoribanks, an Edinburgh merchant. Over the garden doorway are the date 1611 and the initials of Marjoribanks and his wife, Marion Simpson. It was they who expanded and remodelled the existing mansion.

In 1703 the house was sold to the Symes, an Edinburgh legal family, who subdivided the great hall into more fashionable panelled rooms and plastered over the brightly painted ornate ceilings. In 1896, the house passed to James McNeill, a mining engineer, whose daughter, in 1953, sold the property to the architect Walter Schomberg Scott, who lovingly restored it. Owing to the rapid decline in his family's fortunes, however, by the time of his death it had deteriorated into much the same state as when he had bought it.

I had just left school when I was invited to a party at Northfield House. From attending a tutorial college in Edinburgh, I had got to know Schomberg Scott's son Mark. Known as 'Isie', he was an exotic creature who was rumoured to smoke illicit substances – it was the 1960s, after all. We were all very naive about such things, it has to be said, but I shall never forget Isie opening the door to let us in, wearing a multicoloured kaftan, while his parents and younger brother were in a room upstairs listening to Beatles records. His was, I regret to say, a tragic ending.

Isie was very much a child of the sixties and, as the sixties became the seventies, it became increasingly hard for him to find a niche in life. I was told that he drove a lorry in England for a time but eventually returned to live at Northfield. Eventually, in 1997, a combination of alcohol and substance abuse culminated in an altercation with his girlfriend and he was stabbed to death. His father was, by then, in a nursing home and died shortly afterwards.

However, buildings such as Northfield House survive through attracting those who love them and, since purchasing the by then totally run-down property from the executors in 1999, the current owner Finlay Lockie and his partner, Kirsten, have embarked upon an astonishingly dedicated commitment towards bringing the old place back to life.

Finlay is one of that rare breed who believe passionately in rescuing the past and almost all of the remedial work at Northfield, from the plumbing to the roofing, has been stoically undertaken by him and Kirsten, with occasional help from family members and friends. That work extends into the semi-formal garden to the south side of the house which Schomberg Scott himself had so successfully reinstated but which, by the time of Finlay's arrival, had become a jungle. When I looked in on them last summer, Kirsten was preoccupied with cutting the grass, a monumental task.

'There was one afternoon after I had been working all day on window sashes when I sat down exhausted and almost burst into tears,' Finlay confessed. 'But, after a bit of contemplation, I began to see what I was achieving and it all seemed so important and worthwhile.'

CHAPTER NINETEEN

Beaked Fishermen and Airheads

THE FORMER FISHING village of Port Seton straddles the coast road from Cockenzie to Aberlady Bay and, in 2005, the artist John Bellany, painter of fishermen with abstract puffin beaks and angst-ridden herring girls, was honoured as the first Freeman of East Lothian. Born in Port Seton in 1942, Bellany now lives and works in Cambridge, Edinburgh and Barga in Italy but proudly retains close links with his birthplace.

It was at a charity auction held on HMS *Ark Royal*, anchored in Leith Docks in 1992, that Sir Alistair Grant (see Chapter 7) purchased one of Bellany's paintings. Since he was on his way to London, he asked me to look after it until the following week when he would be able to take it to his home at Tyninghame. Entitled *Woman with Cat*, it sat on the sideboard in my dining room for seven days, an evocative image of such powerful presence that neither of my own two living household kittens would enter the room.

Seton Palace was where Mary, Queen of Scots would often retreat in search of solace and privacy during her short reign – hence the designation of 'Palace'. And it was on his triumphal progression south to claim his English kingdom in 1603 that her son, James VI, unexpectedly encountered the funeral procession of the 1st Earl of Winton, his mother's loyal supporter. Impulsively, he signalled his retainers to stop and positioned himself on the south-west turret of the palace where he remained still and silent until the cortège had passed.[1]

Not far from where he sat is the Collegiate Church of Seton, which was built in the fourteenth century at the instigation of Catherine St Clair of Herdmanston, widow of the 1st Lord William Seton. In the following century, an age when Scottish nobles competed for the attention of the Almighty, some elaborate interior decorations were introduced, said only to be comparable with those at Rosslyn Chapel. Sadly, these were desecrated in 1544 when the chapel was ransacked by the English. Later acquired by the Wemyss & March Estates, the church today serves as a mausoleum for the Charteris family.

In 1719, the last Earl of Winton was attainted for his support of the Old Pretender and his lands were confiscated so that Seton Palace then became the property of the York Buildings Company of London. In 1790, following the Society's collapse, the estate was purchased by Lieutenant-Colonel Alexander Mackenzie of the 21st Dragoons, who pulled down what remained of the old building and commissioned Robert Adam to design the present house. Mackenzie died five years later from, as local gossip would have us believe, a curse inflicted by an old lady whom he had evicted from her cottage.

Thereafter, Seton House was acquired by Wemyss & March Estates and, from the 1960s to the 1990s, was leased to Captain Tony Stevenson, owner of the fashionable Prestonfield House Hotel on the outskirts of Edinburgh. His daughter, Sue, was a friend while I was at college and often, after parties there, we would watch the sun rise from the battlements. In 1972 she married Peter Orton, who helped to build the enormously successful *Muppet Show* on British television and launched HiT Entertainment, producers of the children's television programmes such as *Bob the Builder* and *Thomas the Tank Engine*. Peter died of cancer in December 2007.

In 2003, Seton House was sold for £1.5 million to Mary McMillan, a mother of six who had been brought up in a Loanhead miner's cottage and had accumulated a fortune through property development. A year later, following a lavish restoration, she put it on the market again for £15 million. In 2007, it was bought by Internet entrepreneur Stephen Leach for an undisclosed sum. The McMillans thereafter moved into the main apartment at Whittingehame (see Chapter 11), which they bought from its then owner Lady Melissa Brady.

From Aberlady, the coastal road skirts to Gullane past the impressive walls of the Gosford Estate, affording occasional peeks of the great dome of the main house which appears almost to float on a carpet of treetops. Situated on the west side of the estate is Eventyre which, in the latter half of the twentieth century, was occupied by the family of Sir Max Harper Gow, chairman of the transport and shipping company Christian Salvesen. At some distance, between the road and the water's edge and hidden behind another wall of dense trees, are two other houses – Greencraigs which, up until recently, was run as a hotel and Hairstaynes, for many years leased to Sir Jamie Stormonth Darling, the founder director of the National Trust for Scotland.

It was Sir Jamie, a lawyer, who successfully transformed the fledgling Trust from a shoestring affair to the major landowner that it has since become. Before his death in 2000, his wife Mary, a talented architect, designed and built Westerlea, a modern house at Dirleton, with an entrancing garden. I shall always think of Sir Jamie with affection since, at the very start of my career, he summoned me to his office to offer me a job as his assistant. I often wonder how my life might have turned out had I accepted.

The original sections of Gosford House, which overlook Aberlady Bay and provide breathtaking views across the Firth of Forth towards Edinburgh, were begun in 1790 by the architect Robert Adam and completed in 1800, on the instructions of Francis Charteris, de jure 7th Earl of Wemyss (see Chapter 6). Although Charteris was principally installed at Amisfield on the outskirts of Haddington, Gosford provided him with a more convenient access to his enduring passion – the game of golf.

Charteris's grandson, who inherited the estate as 8th Earl of Wemyss, was less of a golfing obsessive and disliked the style of Adam's wings, which he pulled down, leaving the mansion as a solitary main block. However, his son, in turn, had other ideas and, in 1890, commissioned a new design from the architect William Young. It was also Young who created the spectacular Italianate hall with its staircase of pink alabaster in the south pavilion and, to add to the exterior impact, Sir William Arrol was engaged to create the steelwork for an enormous central dome.

At the time of the publication of John Martine's *Reminiscences* in 1883, Gosford House was uninhabited. He does, however, refer to 'a grand collection of pictures, most of them by masters of the highest merit' adorning the walls. Well over a century later, some, if not all, are still there, adorning the walls alongside the family portraits, notably works by Murillo, Poussin and Rubens.

Francis, 10th Earl of Wemyss, served as the Whig Member of Parliament for Haddingtonshire from 1847 to 1883 and was the first Commanding Officer of the London Scottish Regiment. Affording perhaps a glimpse of family eccentricities to come, he became President of the London Homeopathic Hospital and, living to be ninety-eight, attributed his physical well-being to his having been treated with homeopathic medicine throughout his life. He died in 1914 and was succeeded by his son, Hugo Charteris, whose son and heir, Lord Elcho, known to his friends as 'Ego', was killed in the Sinai desert in 1916 during the Great War.[2]

Francis David Charteris succeeded his grandfather as 12th Earl of Wemyss and 8th Earl of March in 1937 and, with Gosford and the Peeblesshire holdings (Amisfield had by then been demolished), came the manor house of Stanway. A classic Jacobean property in the Cotswolds, it was regarded by The Souls, that turn-of-the-last-century intellectual and aesthetic coterie who numbered among their membership the 1st Marquis Curzon and A. J. Balfour, as the most beautiful house in England. Judging from the number of times Stanway has been a backdrop for period televisions dramas such as the BBC production of *The Buccaneers*, The Souls were on to something. But then the pink marble staircase of Gosford too has featured in the 2000 film adaptation of Edith Wharton's 1905 novel *House of Mirth.*

During the Second World War, Gosford House was requisitioned, much to its detriment, by the army and, during its occupation, a fire broke out and destroyed a large proportion of the central block. The ensuing outbreak of dry rot meant that a major section of the roof needed to be removed and it was not until the early 1950s that the 12th Lord Wemyss, his wife, two sons and daughter made Gosford their principal home. Then tragedy struck in 1954 when Lord Elcho, their eldest son, aged eight, was killed in a car accident in Ayrshire. Following this, their surviving son James adopted the peerage's secondary courtesy title of Lord Neidpath.

In his youth, Lord Neidpath was appointed a page of honour to HM the Queen Mother. A gifted student at Oxford University, where he achieved a first in Philosophy, Politics and Economics, he at one stage tutored Bill Clinton, the future President of America. For his doctoral thesis, he chose the Fall of Singapore, published in 1981 as *The Singapore Naval Base and the Defence of Britain's Eastern Empire, 1919–1941.*

With a penchant for Regency coats and floppy bow ties, possibly a throwback to when he was a royal page, Jamie Neidpath, now 13th Earl of Wemyss, has consistently cut a flamboyant figure in aristocratic circles.

From his first marriage to journalist and author Catherine Guinness, daughter of Lord Moyne, he has a son and daughter. In 1995, he married Amanda Fielding, an enthusiast for trepanation, the centuries-old practice of drilling holes in the head which is said to decrease depressions and increase creativity. Having followed her example, he told the *Washington Post* in 1998 that a hole in his head 'seemed to be very beneficial'.

In November 1992, I was among a group of guests invited to lunch at Gosford House by Lord Neidpath. The party consisted of Peter Palumbo, then Chairman of the Arts Council of Great Britain, Lord Prosser, a Court of Session judge and Chairman of the Scottish Historic Buildings Trust, Timothy Clifford, Director of the National Galleries of Scotland, Sheena McDonald, the broadcaster, and various other luminaries from the worlds of heritage and conservation. I was then a columnist with the *Sunday Times Scotland* and was presumably expected to write on the subject.

Gosford House was built to showcase a collection of art. Lord Neidpath's proposal was that the disused area behind the mezzanine of the entrance hall should be reinstated as an art gallery and opened to the public. There was only one thing stopping him. He needed £8 million to cover the costs and that was the purpose of Peter Palumbo's visit – to discuss the possibility of a British Arts Council grant. Walking through the central part of the house still open to the elements and seeing legions of pictures stacked against the walls proved an unexpectedly surreal experience.

Afterwards, it became apparent that the availability of public funding was unlikely. In 1999, Botticelli's *The Virgin Adoring the Christ Child*, which had hung largely unnoticed on the mezzanine wall at Gosford, was acquired by the National Galleries of Scotland for a sum in the region of £10 million, having fought off a bid of £15 million from a museum in Texas. With the proceeds, Wemyss & March Estates were therefore able to restore Gosford's central block to its former glory.

Following the death of his first wife Mavis, known as Babs, in 1988, the 12th Earl of Wemyss, three times Lord High Commissioner to the General Assembly of the Church of Scotland, had cut a solitary figure pursuing his many public commitments, notably as President Emeritus of the National Trust for Scotland. For a time, he courted Eola Wood-Gush, a gentle, intelligent widow who rented a lodge in the driveway of Barns House, a Wemyss & March Estates property near Peebles. When she died in 1994, he touchingly insisted that her obituary notice include the words 'Betrothed of the Earl of Wemyss'.

Then in 1995, at the age of eighty-three, he married for a second time, shrugging off comments about the age difference between him and his Canadian bride, Shelagh Kennedy (née Thrift). 'There is a precedent,' he told me with obvious pleasure when I interviewed him on the subject. 'My great-grandfather was married for the second time at the age of eighty-two to a Miss Grace Blackburn, a much younger lady. They were extremely happy together and he lived to be ninety-six.'

The formula appears to have worked. Following a complete renovation of the central block, conducted tours of Gosford House were personally supervised during the summer months by Countess Shelagh who, before her marriage, was manager of the National Trust for Scotland's Georgian House in Edinburgh. Lord Wemyss died in December 2008, almost exactly one month short of his ninety-seventh birthday.

CHAPTER TWENTY

Flying the Flag

MARGARET AINSLIE OF THE Abbey Farm had ten brothers and sisters, whose progeny in due course fanned out to participate in a variety of enterprises other than farming. With her untimely death in 1733, followed by that of her husband John Martine three years later, it was her brother John, Town Clerk of Haddington, and their brother Robert, who stepped in to safeguard the interests of her orphaned children. The links between our two families were therefore strong and, in the following century, Ainslie relatives featured regularly in my family's affairs.

Over this same period, the firm of William & James Ainslie had begun to trade in wines and spirits in Leith. With premises in the Broad Wynd, later moving to Walter Lane, this enterprise soon became extremely lucrative. By 1888, John Martine records that the Ainslies had gained possession of 2,000 acres of fine arable land in East Lothian.[1] He also refers to the Butterdean Woods, the finely timbered parks of the Elvingston Estate, and 'the sheltering places around the various farm steadings which added a sylvian appearance to what would otherwise be a bleak-looking exposed ridge'.[2] It was at Elvingston that its then owner, William Law, first introduced the harrowing of wheat lands in the spring months, thereby giving rise to the system of sowing seeds with grain.[3] Having entered the Scottish Bar as an advocate and been Sheriff of Haddingtonshire for fifty years, Law died in 1806 at the age of ninety-two.

His son James, a fellow of the Royal College of Surgeons, died in 1830 and, thereafter, the estate passed through marriage to a Robert Ainslie. It was he who, in 1837, built the Jacobean baronial Elvingston House which today belongs to the American industrialist Dr David Simpson and his wife Janice.

Supported by Scottish Enterprise, East Lothian Council and Napier University, the Simpsons, some years ago, launched the Elvingston Science Centre to provide purpose-built facilities for technology and research. It has obviously filled a void in the market and, over the past decade, has generated over 150 technology-based jobs.

The lands immediately to the north-west of Haddington were granted to the Church in the early twelfth century by the Countess of Huntingdon and, for two centuries, served as a religious retreat known as Nunland. A house was built here c.1561 by a gentleman of the name of Adam Carkerhill and the estate was passed on to his niece Margaret, who sold it to Robert Dougall, a prosperous merchant whose family were fiercely anti-Jacobite and appear to have committed their not-inconsiderable fortune to opposing the cause.[4]

This Dougall family occupied Nunland for four generations until 1712 when it was acquired by Alexander Hay, an advocate, who already owned the neighbouring Alderston Estate. It was he who changed the name to Huntington, presumably with its original benefactress in mind, but was unable to spell her title. When his lawyer son, Thomas, was appointed to the Court of Session in 1755, he took the legal courtesy title of Lord Huntington.

The property was next occupied by David Robertson, late of Culcutta, and, in 1761, by Dr George Gray, also from Culcutta. From the latter it passed to his son Lieutenant Charles Gray of the 31st Foot, and then, in 1802, to Admiral Robert Deans, whom John Martine describes as a member of one of the oldest families in the county.[5] Although the ownership of many of East Lothian's prime properties regularly changed hands through the centuries, Huntington House does seem to have had more than its fair share of occupants. After Admiral Deans came Farquhar Campbell, who sold it to William Ainslie, whose brother was, around the same time, establishing himself in the neighbouring Elvingston Estate.

Thereafter, Huntington House was sold to Dr Greenlees of Loretto School and then, in 1953, to Commander Wilfrid Crawford and his wife Patricia.[6] As a young naval officer, Commander Crawford had been capped five times for playing rugby for Scotland and was a member of the famous 1938 team which won the Triple Crown. During the Second World War, he served in the Fleet Air Arm, making more than 1,000 aircraft carrier landings. When invalided out of the navy because of a back injury, he took up farming and, following a passion for point-to-point racing, took out a permit and later a licence to train racehorses. Thereafter, he and his wife went on to train for themselves and close friends and, in the ensuing years, accumulated an impressive list of over 100 winners. Lothian Princess, for example, the founder of a highly successful jumping blood line, they bought for only £125. Later in life, Patricia took up carriage driving and was Scottish Champion in 1987.[7] Growing up with such close equestrian ties, it was hardly unexpected that their daughter Susan should emerge as one of the world's most sought-after painters of horses. Although she now lives in Ireland, she continues to exhibit regularly at the Tryon Gallery in London and, in addition to featuring horses, her portfolio contains portraits of the

British royal family, the Sultans of Oman and Brunei and the jockey Lester Piggott. Susan's elder brother George now lives in France, while her younger brother Charles catches lobsters at Scoughall in partnership with Jack Dale. Charles's wife, Cathie, runs one of the county's most successful home catering operations.

In 1993, Huntington House was sold to John and Sarah Brownlie, whose previous connection with East Lothian comes about through John's family business, A. & R. Brownlie, now BSW Timber plc. After the Second World War, the Brownlies operated sawmills at Gifford and Stottencleuch, beside Oldhamstocks, and cleared swathes of timber from Binning Wood at Tyninghame, Ormiston and Lennoxlove. In those days, it was an arduous, labour-intensive process, with trees felled by axe and cleared by horse and cart, long before the introduction of power saws and logging techniques.[8] By the twenty-first century, BSW Timber plc had become the largest sawmilling operation in the United Kingdom.

Most of what we know about the dark and medieval ages of Scotland is tainted with make-believe and oral tradition. Given my elusive ancestor Alexander St Martine's tenure of Athelstaneford during the early part of the thirteenth century, I suppose that I should feel some sort of special affinity towards the place but suffice it to say that everything in the present village dates from long after his time. There is nothing even to indicate where he might have lived. Perhaps it was at East Garleton, where the earls of Winton raised a keep on the moated site of a building from the previous millennium – but that can only be speculation.

> Ada the Countess, mother of the King of Scots, grants to Alexander de St Martine, the lands of Elstaneford, by these same marches by which King David gave the same Elstaneford to him. She moreover, gave Barowe, Donecaeslaye, Bangelave, and that land which Uhtred son of Gilise held,[9] and that land which is on the east side of Seton, by those marches by which her men walked the lands and delivered them to him: also the site of the mill on the Tyne, and one carucate of land in Carelsira, to wit, in Petollin, and one full toft in Hadintun, and another in Carel, all to be held in fee and heritage for service of one knight, with sake and sok, tol and theam, infandthef and other liberties.[10]

Now it would appear that Alexander had a brother called Adulf or Edulf who accidentally killed Malcolm de Moreville while out hunting.[11] As the de Morevilles were the all-powerful Hereditary High Constables of Scotland, this was presumably not considered to be a particularly career-enhancing deed at the time.[12]

Alas, nothing additional is known about him and my only reason for mentioning him at all is that, given that Alexander had only a daughter, it must have been Adulf's Martine descendants who later emerged in Haddington, St Andrews and Edinburgh. The other tantalising link is Athelstaneford's secular link with the Culdee Priory of St Andrews, which possibly explains how and why the name of Magistro Alexandro do St Martino should appear in that town around 1219. Was he Adulf's grandson?

From a traditional and far more important perspective, of course, Athelstaneford retains a unique significance in Scotland's story, although I am inclined to wonder how many Scots are actually aware of it. The legend tells us that on or around the year 832, the Picts of the east and the Scots of the west formed a coalition to defend themselves against an invading army of Northumbrians led by the Saxon King Athelstane. The two armies confronted each other across the Cogtail Burn.

On the morning of battle, a diagonal cross of white cloud, symbolic of that upon which St Andrew was crucified at Patras in Greece, appeared in the clear blue sky over the fields of Markle in the east. According to the legend, the impressionable Scots vowed that should victory be granted to them, the saltire of St Andrew would be adopted as the flag of Scotland.

It was a profoundly superstitious age. A few of St Andrew's body parts – a tooth, an arm bone, a kneecap and some fingers – were already in Scotland, washed ashore on the Fife Coast four centuries earlier with a Greek monk called St Rule. It was through this occurrence that the spot where the shipwreck occurred came to be known as St Andrews. Other relics associated with the saint followed in the seventh century and, by the ninth century, a Culdee religious community was well entrenched here, with St Andrew well on his way to becoming Scotland's patron saint. It only needed a victory over the Saxons to make it official.

As tradition has it, King Athelstane was killed during the conflict. Afterwards, his head was cut off and displayed on a pike on the island of Inchgarvie in the Firth of Forth – not, it has to be observed, the most accessible place for it to be seen. His body, it is rumoured, was buried near the ford of the Cogtail Burn. John Martine writes that, in 1840, when a quarry was opened on the spot, the workmen unearthed a stone coffin formed of five handsome freestones, and that it contained a human skeleton with the jawbone in a very decayed state. Since the skull itself was missing, rumour had it that this was none other than King Athelstane of Northumbria himself. Although John Martine writes that the find was promptly removed for safekeeping by Sir David Kinloch, the 9th Baronet of Gilmerton, his descendant, the 13th Baronet, has no idea what became of it. It sounds as if somebody opening a cupboard might be in for a shock.

Following the Reformation, the lands of Athelstaneford passed from the Culdee Priory of St Andrews to the Chapel Royal of Holyrood but the flag in the sky and Scotland's victory over the Northumbrians were not to be ignored. In 1965, a large plaque was erected by public subscription in the churchyard of the sixteenth-century Athelstaneford Parish Church. To its rear, is the Doocot Flag Heritage Centre, a sixteenth-century lectern doocot which, in 1996, was imaginatively restored to provide an interpretation centre complete with animated sound track.

The churchyard itself is well worth exploring, if only to see the memorial to the Reverend Robert Blair, author of the best-selling poem *The Grave*. With its fourteen cheery verses, much of its content is as pertinent today as it was during his lifetime:

> When Self-Esteem, or others' Adulation,
> Would cunningly persuade us we were Something
> Above the common Level of our Kind,
> The *Grave* gainsays the smooth-complexion'd Flatt'ry,
> And with blunt Truth acquaints us what we are.

Blair was ordained as Minister of Athelstaneford in 1743, the very same year that his Gothic masterpiece was published. *The Grave* ran to forty-nine editions and was illustrated sixty-four years after his death by the English painter William Blake. There must have been some strain of literary wizardry in the Athelstaneford air as, in 1746, Blair was succeeded as minister by the Reverend John Home, who promptly set about composing his equally successful but rather more challenging play *Douglas*.

Other inmates of the cemetery here are Adam Skirving, the farmer-poet, and his son Archibald, the portrait painter, whose memorial stone from 1819 carries the inscription:

> To beauty, virtue, talent he would bow
> But claims of birth and rank would not allow,
> Kept friends and foes at almost equal distance,
> Knew how to give but not to take assistance,
> At three score ten when scarce begun to fail
> He dropped at once without apparent ail.

Archibald Skirving, who was Adam's eldest son, is best remembered for his posthumous red chalk study of the poet Robert Burns, now in the collection of the Scottish National Portrait Gallery. Yet his miniature portraits were immensely fashionable and much sought after in his lifetime.

Adam Skirving was the tenant farmer of East Garleton, whose own not inconsiderable claim to fame is that he was the author of the popular ballad 'Hey, Johnnie Cope, Are ye Walking yet?'.

On a more personal level, however, Adam's wife and Archibald's mother was Jean, a daughter of Robert Ainslie of the Abbey Farm at Garvald and therefore a cousin of my direct ancestor Peter Martine and of his brother, Provost John.

Having attracted early patronage from, among others, John Rennie of Phantassie and Lord Elcho, son of the 7th Earl of Wemyss, Archibald Skirving was to rapidly emerge as a prodigy. Unfortunately, his was a volatile genius much prone to insecurity. A typical incident involved Sir John Dalrymple who, having encouraged him, complained to a fellow member of the Edinburgh-based Poker Club that he was 'unable to get rid of him'. Word of this soon got back to Skirving who, as a result, fell into a deep depression.[13]

In 1785, he travelled to Rome and, over the following seven and a half years, produced a series of outstanding portraits of the Italian-Scottish community. At this juncture, Britain was at war with France and, on his journey home, Skirving was seized at Gibralter and accused of spying. There followed several months of imprisonment at Brest, an indignity from which he never fully recovered. Back in Edinburgh, his behaviour is said to have become increasingly eccentric but he found at least one champion in Thomas Carlyle, whose wife, Jane Welsh, had previously taken drawing lessons from him. And I personally think that Carlyle's written description of him paints as detailed a portrait as any visual image:

> An altogether striking man, wiry, elastic, perpendicular and of good inches, still brisk-looking though perhaps 70 odd, spotlessly clean, his linen white as snow, no neck-tie but a loosish-fastened black ribbon, hair all gray, now white over long; face, neck, hands of a fine brown tint – one of the cleanest old men I ever saw – and such a face as you would still more rarely see. Eagle like, nose hooked like an eagle's bill, eyes still with the something of the eagle's flash in them; squarish, prominent brown, under jaw ditto-ditto, cheeks and neck thin, all betokening impetuosity, rapidity, delicacy, and the stormy fire of genius not yet hidden under the ashes of old age.[14]

Skirving's demise is rather less colourfully documented in a contemporary letter – 'Poor man, he was nailing some boards in an old pigeon house in his sister's garden when he fell down and instantly expired.' In 1999, the Scottish National Portrait Gallery held an extensive exhibition of his work, the credit for which goes to Stephen Lloyd, the gallery's senior curator, who entitled the show *Raeburn's Rival.* Although the commercially adept and widely lionised Sir Henry Raeburn was Archibald's contemporary and rose to rather more spectacular heights in Scotland's artistic establishment, it would be a shame were his equally brilliant 'rival' to be forgotten.

In 1653, Francis Kinloch, a wealthy merchant and former Lord Provost of Edinburgh and Member of Parliament for that city, purchased the Gilmerton Estate at Athelstaneford. For lending a substantial sum of money to the Duke of York, he was rewarded with a Nova Scotia baronetcy. A century later, however, his Jacobite-supporting great-grandson James was disinherited by his father and sailed to America with his brother David, assuming the title upon his father's death in 1778.

In America, James's grandson, another Francis Kinloch, aged eleven, along with his younger brother, became wards of Thomas Boone, Governor of New Jersey, who sent them to England to be educated at Eton College. This Francis married twice, first to Maldred Walker, whose father Thomas was a guardian of Thomas Jefferson, and second to Martha, daughter of the Governor of South Carolina. By the time of the American War of Independence, he had become a secessionist and was taken prisoner, by pure chance, by his first cousin from Scotland, who was also named Francis.

Captain Francis Kinloch from Georgetown, South Carolina subsequently went on to become a member of the Continental Congress, America's first independent government, while his Scottish cousin Francis Kinloch, in 1795, aged forty-six, became the 6th Baronet of Gilmerton. Alas, that inheritance was to be short lived. Two months after succeeding to his title, Francis was shot on the front stairs by his deranged brother Major Archibald Kinloch, who had only recently returned from the West Indies. Sir Archibald, as he then became, was charged with fratricide and taken to the Tolbooth in Edinburgh for trial, whereupon he was released into the custody of his family on the grounds that he was a lunatic. This is held to be one of the earliest examples of a plea of insanity being accepted as proven.

Gilmerton House today remains a dignified stately home and is owned by Sir David Kinloch, the 13th Baronet, and his wife Maureen.

CHAPTER TWENTY-ONE

Airfields, Turkeys and a Retail Park

When Barry and Sarah Laird moved to live at West Fenton and heard that I was researching this book, they thoughtfully hosted a lunch party to introduce me to their immediate neighbours, Sir Garth Morrison and his wife Gill, who farm West Fenton, and John Gray, who farms East Fenton.

It was a typically kind gesture by Sarah, who has been a dynamic organiser from the days when she worked in London for *Vogue* magazine; indeed, when we first met she was closely involved in the management of the department store Debenham's and was about to become a central figure in the creation of the government agency Scottish Financial Enterprise. Since then, she has proved indomitable in raising funds for charitable causes. Barry is a six-handicap golfer so their retirement to live at the heart of the golf coast was, in many ways, a foregone conclusion.

I had also known John Gray and his wife, Denise, since her parents lived at Gullane and her father, Campbell Reid, owned the Edinburgh-based interior designers and cabinetmakers Whytock & Reid. John was brought up at Smeaton Hepburn (see Chapter 23) and, in 1972, took over the management of the farm of East Fenton, with its fine outlook over to the coast. An astute observer of the changing face of the countryside, he remains a resolute sportsman.

Sir Garth Morrison, a patrician figure, has been farming West Fenton since 1973, when he returned from serving as an engineering officer in the Royal Navy. His family having moved from Berwickshire to West Fenton in 1916 and their having bought the farm in 1922, he began by going into partnership with his father, Courtenay Morrison. Since then his part-time interest in and involvement with the Scout Movement has seen him become Commissioner of East Lothian, Chief Commissioner of Scotland, Chief Scout of the United Kingdom and a member of the World Scout Committee. In 2001, he was made Lord Lieutenant of East Lothian and in 2007 he became a Knight of the Thistle. Since 1999, he has been Chairman of The Lamp of Lothian

Collegiate Trust (see Chapter 7), as well as becoming a founder trustee of the Battle of Prestonpans (1745) Heritage Trust. His wife Gill is the founder of the Muirfield Riding for the Disabled Group.

The Parish of Dirleton serves as the perfect rural location for those in need of ready access to Scotland's capital since the central village of Drem is still blessed with a railway station on the Edinburgh to North Berwick line. During the First World War, the West Fenton Aerodrome was established here and, between 1916 and 1917, provided the base for No. 77 Home Defence Squadron, Royal Flying Depot. In 1922 it was renamed Gullane Aerodrome and became a training depot. In 1939, the grass airstrip was resurfaced to become RAF Drem, home to the No. 13 Flying Training School. With the outbreak of the Second World War, it served as the air defence fighter unit for the City of Edinburgh, encompassing the shipping area around the Firth of Forth.[1]

The German Luftwaffe made its first attack in October 1939 and the following year a lighting system was introduced for defensive night landings. In 1945, the unit was handed over to the Admiralty as HMS *Nighthawk* and then decommissioned when it was returned to the Air Ministry the following year. The hangars now form the nucleus of the East Fortune National Museum of Flight, under the umbrella of the National Museums of Scotland. Exhibitions show how air travel has developed from the Wright Brothers back in 1909 to the present day. A major attraction is the retired supersonic Concorde donated by British Airways in 2003.

The early history of the farm of Fenton Barns is covered in Chapter 9 but its subsequent story is of equal importance. For the duration of the First World War, the tenant farmer there was James Glendinning, who had previously farmed at Samuelston. In 1921, when his resources made it possible, he bought Fenton Barns which had, by then, been inherited by Gilbert Ogilvy of Winton Castle. On James's death in 1923, he bequeathed it to his nephew Dr Douglas Chalmers-Watson, a medical practitioner in Edinburgh, with the codicil that 'in due course his son Rupert, and possibly his older brother Irvine, will find the fascination of farming as I have done'.[2]

'It was a complete surprise,' says his grandson Keith Chalmers-Watson. 'My grandfather was the youngest of four boys and was left the farm by his bachelor uncle. My father was a doctor not a farmer and, from then on, his brothers never spoke to him again. Of course, what nobody mentioned at the time was that the farm was heavily mortgaged.'

James Glendinning must have known what he was doing. Although continuing to practise medicine, Douglas moved rapidly to take control of Fenton Barns, reassuring the elderly grieve Mr Simpson, that the farm employees – one grieve, one woman grieve, nine ploughmen, two boys (for single horses), five orramen, six women workers and one blacksmith – would be looked after. The next occurrence was that the government's Disposal Board offered him the land and all the buildings which had made up the First World War aerodrome.

For some time prior to this, Douglas and his wife, Mona, had talked about selling 'certified' milk in Edinburgh and, with their inheritance, this now became a possibility. Mona Chalmers-Watson, the first woman to graduate in medicine from Edinburgh University, took over the farming activities and the first large-scale dairy enterprise in the east of Scotland began. Two of the old hangars were adapted, one for cows and one as a storage shed for food. Grain crops grown on the farm were allocated to another hangar and threshed under cover by the travelling steam mill, which had just been introduced in the Lothians. Soon afterwards, the first fifty pedigree heifers arrived.[3]

At first, the establishment of a milking herd in East Lothian was considered folly by the majority of the surrounding farmers but then the Chalmers-Watsons also introduced pigs and soon after that a poultry farm was underway. Meanwhile, both Irvine and Rupert had left Edinburgh Academy. Irvine first trained as a mud student at an Ayrshire dairy, then attended Reading Agricultural College. Rupert enrolled at the East of Scotland Agricultural College.

Then came the Second World War, when 250 acres of land and the buildings purchased in from the government in 1923 were requisitioned back by the Air Force. It was a shock but the family persevered and swiftly relocated their operation, with Irvine training as a pilot officer and forming 603 Squadron of the Auxiliary Fighter Squadron at Turnhouse Aerodrome. Rupert, meanwhile, continued the farm and formed an attachment with Margaret Holloway, the administrative officer of the WAAF. The couple were married in 1944.

When the war ended, it was back to basics at Fenton Barns. Douglas died in 1946, and Irvine and Rupert went to the company safe to extract his will, which left everything jointly to both sons. Death duty exemption was outside a seven-year period and, much to their amazement, they discovered that their father had survived for exactly seven years and four days. 'He must have known,' said Rupert's son, Keith. 'The liability otherwise would have been £40,000 and the farm would have had to be sold.'

Instead, negotiations began with the Air Ministry to re-purchase the land and buildings that had been used by the Royal Air Force. This was more or less accomplished by 1949, except for the hangars and buildings, which the Air Ministry and Public Works Department decided to keep under their control.

Soon a company named Chunky Chicks Limited was formed with D. B. Marshall, a small poultry farmer at Ratho. The venture was a great success and was absorbed into Sterling Poultry Products before being taken over by the Ross Group of Grimsby and ultimately swallowed up by Imperial Tobacco Co. (Foods Division).

In 1947, Irvine and Rupert established a turkey farm at Bankrugg, Gifford, and, as demand increased, they developed it further at Newbyth, which they bought in 1948. In 1953 they sold the Fenton Barns dairy herd and turned the byre and dairy buildings over to full-time turkey production. In 1962, three small turkey breeders, John S. Lintern Limited, Hockenhull Turkeys and Fenton Barns, combined to form British United Turkeys Limited. It proved a phenomenal success although, in 1977, the year of Rupert's death, British United Turkeys removed its production from Scotland.

Keith remained on the board of BUT until its sale in 1979 to a multinational pharmaceutical company. The group was ultimately acquired in 2005 by Aviagen, the world's leading poultry breeding conglomerate. In 1981, Keith formed a new company still retaining the name Fenton Barns Scotland Limited in partnership with two cooked meats entrepreneurs, Henry Ackroyd and Peter Humble. New technology was starting to emerge and the company prospered. In 1999, it was acquired by Brown Brothers, an established business in the cooked meats sector. Brown Brothers have since invested heavily in Fenton Barns and still retain the brand.

Towards the end of the twentieth century, the smaller surviving buildings on the Fenton Barns landholding were converted to form the Fenton Barns Retail and Leisure Village, a major visitor attraction which includes an archery centre, farm shop and cafe. Today, there are ninety storage or retail workshop units within the Fenton Barns complex and new-build premises are planned to meet the increasing demand for space.

All of this has allowed Keith to concentrate on his great love of breeding pheasants and he presently has the largest collection of game birds in the United Kingdom and is Vice-Chairman of the World Pheasant Association which has among its objectives, the return of game bird species to their countries of origin.

In 1890, John Martine refers to Sydserff, on the North Berwick road, as 'a fine old place, once the property of the "monks of old" '. In 1296, the names of William de Sytserf and Marjorie de Sytserf are to be found paying homage to Edward I on the Ragman's Roll but little is known of this family until 1513, when Alexander Sydserf fell with his monarch on the battlefield of Flodden. In 1541, his son Patrick, having married a daughter of Sir Robert Lauder of the Bass, acquired the lands of Ruchlaw on Whittingehame.[4]

For better or worse, East Lothian has seen many a fine old place ruthlessly adapted to meet the demands of twenty-first-century living. However, on my way from Fenton Barns to Fenton Tower, I could not help but notice what had taken place at Sydserff, as sympathetic an example of well-thought-out development as I have come across. It began with the architect Nicholas Groves-Raines, who had already drawn up plans, persuading both the landowner Ian Simpson and East Lothian Council that a major restoration, coupled with a steading development, would greatly enhance what was, in effect, an important historic property. With the support of Historic Scotland this led to Dunglass Limited, a small-scale developer focusing mainly on East Lothian, collaborating in the creation of six dwellings.

Fenton Tower, which also sits on land belonging to the Simpson's Highfield Farm, is a small fortification originally built by the de Vaux Family in the twelfth century. At that time it would have been constructed in wood but, by the late fifteenth century, it had been replaced by the present tower, which was built for Patrick Whytelaw. After this, it was lived in by Sir John Carmichael, Warden of Scotland's Middle March, whose duties included the policing of the Scottish Border.

James VI briefly sought refuge here in 1591, having escaped across the Firth of Forth from an uprising led by his natural kinsman, Francis Stewart, whom he had unwisely created Earl of Bothwell after his stepfather's forfeiture. At the time of Oliver Cromwell's invasion in 1650, Fenton Tower was held by Sir John Maxwell of Innerwick. It then passed to Sir John Nisbett, becoming part of the Biel and Dirleton Estates, and, in 1920, Highfield Farm was purchased by the Simpson family who had been its tenants since the 1850s.[5]

By this time, Fenton Tower had fallen into serious disrepair but, in 1998, Ian Simpson and his Edinburgh-born childhood friend John Macaskill, then Managing Director of the Chase Manhattan Bank in New York, decided that it was time for a major restoration. John was convinced that, properly marketed, a sensitively renovated Fenton Tower would attract worldwide interest as a golf destination. Again employing the skills of architect Nicholas Groves-Raines and under the watchful eye of Historic Scotland, the shell of the old building has been transformed into a comfortable modern residence specifically designed to accommodate up to twelve overnight guests.

The village of Kingston appears in the records of Dryburgh Abbey in 1221 and, for centuries, supported a thriving agricultural community with two smithies, a roadside inn and a large windmill on Kingston Farm. Owned for over two centuries by the Hepburn family, the land then became part of the holdings of the Nisbets of Dirleton. Writing in 1890, John Martine mentions that the 400-acre Kingston Farm and its mansion house, which twenty years earlier had been valued at £27,000, had 'recently been sold to George Watson, Esq, for £16,500 after being on the market for a long time'. This was a prime illustration of the great fall that had taken place in the value of agricultural land at that time – sub-prime mortgage lenders take note.[6]

In the early 1900s, Kingston was bought from a Squire Anderson by Thomas Stodart, a colonel in the Indian Medical Service. When he died in 1934, the farm was left to his eldest son William but, when William decided to join the army, Kingston was managed by his younger brother Anthony. Having contested Berwick and East Lothian seat in 1951, Anthony Stodart was elected Conservative Member of Parliament for Edinburgh West in 1959 and subsequently served in the governments of both Sir Alec Douglas Home and Edward Heath. From 1975 to 1987, he was Chairman of the Agricultural Credit Corporation and, in 1981, was created Baron Stodart of Leaston.

In the meantime, Colonel Thomas's brother, Charles, had purchased the 800-acre farm of Leaston, at Humbie, which was looked after for him by his nephew, William, when he left the army in 1947. William continued to run Leaston until 1968 when his uncle died and Leaston was inherited by Anthony. It was at this point that William and Anthony took the view that they should both occupy and run their own farms, so a swap took place. William was then at Kingston in partnership with his son Simon but, in 1985, his share was transferred to Simon's son, another Anthony.

Simon and his wife Jane have recently moved into a sunny and spacious cottage–smithy conversion on Kingston Hill, while their son Anthony now occupies Kingston House. Simon has also followed in his uncle's footsteps in becoming one of the fifty High Constables of the Port of Leith, while Jane is both a Deputy Lieutenant of East Lothian and the Lothian Representative for the National Art Collections Fund.

CHAPTER TWENTY-TWO

Linton on the Great North Road

FROM RESEARCHING THE East Lothian sasines of 1842, I have now discovered that, in addition to his business premises in Haddington and Maryville, the small mansion house he purchased on the northern approach road to that town, Peter Martine owned two dwelling houses, a shop and a bakehouse in East Linton, which is an indication of just how prosperous the Post Master of Haddington had become at this stage.

But whichever properties the family once owned in East Linton, they have long since been disposed of and, in rather more recent times, my principal port of call in the town has been the Drovers Inn on Bridge Street, both before and after it was owned by Jim Findlay. Having been born at Kingston, Jim is yet another scion of East Lothian farming stock which, he claims, makes him no stranger to hard work. In 2002, having in addition turned around the fortunes of the Waterside Bistro in Haddington, he and his family moved to the Rocks Restaurant at Dunbar, which they have since transformed into a warm and welcoming hostelry.

For centuries, the bridge at East Linton was part of the Great North Road leading directly from England towards Haddington and Edinburgh and, because of this, by the middle of the eighteenth century, bustling weekly corn and cattle markets had become a major feature of the main square. During Peter Martine's lifetime there were fifty shops, an inn and twelve pubs. There was even the Linton Distillery established by George Rennie, which employed fifty men with twelve excise officers on call. This was demolished in 1846 to make way for the railway line.

An extract taken from an early file of the *Haddingtonshire Courier* gives a picture of life in the town.

> Linton, from its central position, had from an early date, a weekly established port every Monday morning during the harvest season, for hiring shearers and fixing the wages. Very large numbers of workers, mostly Irish, assembled to be hired, and sometimes it was no easy business for farmers and them to come to

> terms. Frequently riots and disturbances took place, and when Linton Whisky began to operate, fighting took place. Farmers had their coats torn off their backs, and were knocked down. Mr Rennie's authority as Justice of the Peace, aided by Baillie Ballantyne, was often set at defiance. On one occasion Ralph Plain, the constable at the place, got his big red nose nearly cut off with a hook; and very often the ringleaders had to be bound hand and foot and sent up to Haddington jail in carts. For some seasons, 12 dragoons were sent early every Monday morning from Piershill to keep the shearers in order.

Some believe that this was the reason that East Linton was designated a Police Burgh, proudly maintaining its status until the 1970s. Statistically, there are still large numbers of policemen living in the village.

In 1887 a clock was erected by public subscription in honour of Queen Victoria's Golden Jubilee. Officially it was called the 'Victoria Clock' but a local lad called Bob Sharp, son of the owner of the Railway Hotel was smitten by a local girl called Jessie Cowe and romantically named it 'Jessie's Clock'. Alas, his ardour was not reciprocated and Jessie emigrated with her family to Australia. However, the name stuck. In 1988, the first century of Jessie's Clock was celebrated with a local exhibition.

Five mills once stood close to the Linn Falls on the River Tyne, with a further two located downstream. The remaining Preston Mill, which claims to be the oldest working water mill in Scotland, was handed over to the National Trust by George Gray in 1949 and continued in commercial use until 1959. Today, it is surrounded by well-maintained detached residences which quietly reflect the contemporary affluence of the neighbourhood.

With such tranquil surroundings, it was inevitable that a turn-of-the-century colony of artists should flourish here. Notably, these included: John Pettie RA, whose father ran a grocery shop in the Square; Charles Martin Hardie RSA whose family owned a joinery business; and Arthur Melville ARSA, RSW, RWS, whose father was a coachman on the Smeaton Estate. A later addition to the fold was Robert Noble, a popular exhibitor at both the Royal Scottish Academy in Edinburgh and the Royal Academy in London.

No exact provenance exists for the exotic place name of Phantassie, that of an estate adjoining Traprain Law to the east of the town of East Linton. Some claim it has a Greek association – others, French. Somebody has even hijacked it for a computer game. In all probability, its origin lies in the Gaelic *Fan-t-Easan* loosely interpreted as meaning 'gentle slope at a small burn', being situated on the last fall of land before the sea, a surface riddled with natural water sources. From Pencraig, higher up on the terrain, spring water was piped through the fields providing household supplies until as late as 1928. On the Great North Road, a Phantassie horse trough was similarly replenished.

In the latter half of the eighteenth century, the Phantassie Estate was part of the dowry of Charlotte, daughter of William Baird of Newbyth. In 1782, she married George Gordon, Lord Haddo, heir to the 3rd Earl of Aberdeen and the Gordons being at that stage an impecunious dynasty, the property and land were soon after sold to her tenant farmer, George Rennie, who made the name famous. In the churchyard at Prestonkirk is Rennie's memorial stone, which reads:

> he corresponded with, and was visited not only by the leading agriculturists of England and Ireland, but many noblemen and gentlemen from France and Russia, Germany, Poland, Hungary and other European states, seeking information to improve their domains.

This gives an indication as to the worldwide renown enjoyed by East Lothian 'improvers' at this point in history.

Prior to George purchasing Phantassie, the Rennies had been established as agriculturists in East Lothian for generations. George had already taken over the Phantassie lease from his father in 1767, when their neighbour on Gurly Bank, part of the estate, on the south-east side of the Post Road, was Thomas Forrest, my great-great-grandmother's great-uncle. Thomas also owned a mill here which was swept away when the River Tyne flooded in 1775.[1] After his death, Gurly Bank passed for a short period to his son Peter Forrest who, when the Phantassie Estate was sold, moved to Northrig at Morham (see Chapter 9).

More than in any previous century, Britain during the 1780s was in the grip of an unprecedented era of innovation which was almost entirely pioneered by Scots. In Glasgow, James Watt was in the process of developing the steam engine; the Ayrshire-born John Loudon McAdam was experimenting with tar for road surfacing; and Thomas Telford, a stone mason and civil engineer from Dumfriesshire, was building bridges, canals and docks both north and south of the Border.

Before 1787, several attempts had been made to separate corn from straw with a threshing machine but it was at George Rennie's Houston Mill on the Phantassie Estate that Andrew Meikle, the mechanical engineer son of the equally innovative James Meikle, millwright at Saltoun (see Chapter 15), first made the breakthrough. Sponsored by George, Andrew had already partaken of an extensive tour of the Low Countries, which then was the European centre for expertise in land irrigation and agricultural innovation. In 1750 he invented the 'fantail' which kept mill sails rotating at right angles to the direction of the wind. He later devised the 'spring' sail, which counteracted the effect of sudden gusts. What made this all the more remarkable when it came to the threshing machine was that the basic concept was simple enough. Sheaves of corn were fed through fluted rollers onto a revolving drum equipped with a beater to remove the grain. The outcome was revolutionary.

Andrew Meikle's first installation was worked by horses, but soon afterwards harnessed to a powerful windmill. With this great achievement, the production of grain throughout Britain was transformed. As it transpired, Meikle made little money from his groundbreaking invention himself but, to maintain him in his old age, a subscription fund was launched to which every proprietor and tenant farmer in East Lothian, as well as twenty Scots counties and several in England, made a contribution. On his tombstone, his patron, George Rennie, paid him the following tribute:

> Descended from a race of ingenious mechanics, to whom the county for ages has been greatly indebted, he steadily followed the example of his ancestors, and by inventing and bringing to perfection a machine for separating corn from straw (constructed on the principle of velocity and furnished with fixed beaters or scutchers), rendered to the agriculturists of Britain and of other nations a more beneficial service than any hitherto recorded in the annals of ancient or modern science.

Nor was there any lack of genius in George Rennie's own family. By then John Rennie, the youngest of George's four brothers, having first trained with Andrew Meikle, then with James Watt in London, had become one of the most celebrated engineers of his generation. The list of his many projects is inspiring, among them the Crinan Canal, the Bell Rock Lighthouse, the docks at Leith and Waterloo Bridge.[2] He also designed London Bridge, which was not constructed until after his death but was supervised by his sons, another George and Sir John Rennie, both having followed their father into the partnership.

George Rennie Senior, however, remained at Phantassie, where he channelled the same level of pioneering brilliance into land husbandry – erecting kilns and burning limestone extracted from the south side of his farm. Heavy crops flourished on the fertile soil and, in 1806, the Linton Orchard was planted. He died on 10 October 1828, aged seventy-nine.

Alas, time takes its toll and the splendid legacy which George bequeathed to his eldest son, yet another John Rennie, was soon dissipated. To be fair, this was not through lack of ability but the outcome of a series of speculative disasters. A clever individual, this John Rennie was, at times, just a little too clever for his own good.

On a Monday in 1829, a great and sudden rise in the price of wheat was announced in London's Mark Lane market and, chancing to be there at the time, John Rennie knew that the news would not reach Scotland until the following Wednesday. He instantly took the night coach north and, on passing the farm of Skateraw, east of Dunbar, borrowed a horse and pressed on. At East Linton, he acquired a fresh horse and, from Haddington, took a post-chaise to the market in Leith. Before going to bed that night, he had secured a sizeable quantity of wheat at the price of the day. When news of the increased value in London broke the following morning, John Rennie was a rich man.[3]

Alas, such early bonanzas only spurred him on to less successful dealings in grain and cattle until, at the end, to quote an extract from the *Haddingtonshire Courier*, 'his affairs were involved'. His end too was tragic. He had gone to Shetland to buy cattle and the vessel upon which he embarked with his purchases to return to the mainland was sunk without trace.

After being managed for a few years by his trustees, the Phantassie Estate was at last sequestered and, in 1840, purchased by William Mitchell-Innes, a wealthy banker who lived at Ayton Castle in Berwickshire, for his second son, Thomas.[4] 'The new owner further improved this show farm, and so arranged for the consumption on the holding of the enormous crops of turnips it produced – from 80 to 130 acres a year – that colossal quantities of manure were always available.'[5]

The Mitchell-Innes Family remained at Phantassie for the ensuing century, the house being occupied after her husband's death by Julia Mitchell-Innes and their daughter Isabella. From 1904 it was leased to William Weston Hope of the Knowes at East Linton.

In 1847, the writer John Martine's sister Janet Carfrae Martine became the wife of Thomas Ronaldson, whose family, at the time, farmed Morham Mains. The Ronaldsons had married into the Shirreff Family of Easter Broomhouse at Spott and had their own East Lothian origins at Gladsmuir. However, during the 1780s they moved to Ireland with their son Peter, eventually returning to Scotland to farm in Fife before moving to Morham. When Thomas and Janet wed, they at first set up home in Ireland but, by 1852, had also returned to East Lothian to farm South Belton, by Dunbar.[6]

In 1886, Thomas's second son John Martine Ronaldson, became Chief Inspector of Mines in the West of Scotland and, around 1906, his eldest daughter Mary was sent to act as housekeeper for her uncle, George Ronaldson, at Kilduff Mains.[7] There she met and soon afterwards married Lieutenant-Colonel Robert Waugh Tweedie, an officer with the 8th Royal Scots.

The Tweedies at that time farmed Coates, part of the Hopetoun Estate at Longniddry, but, in 1919 Colonel Robert bought the Phantassie Estate from where he indulged his great passion for owning racehorses. His horse Mr Jolly took part in the Grand National of 1927 and with Ballybrack, ridden by his son Reg, he won the famous Foxhunters' Steeplechase at Liverpool in 1932.[8]

The Colonel's oldest son Alexander, known as Lex, served with 8th Battalion The Royal Scots during the Second World War. His mother's family, the Waughs, having farmed there for generations, he bought Eweford at Dunbar, West Barns Mains and part of the Lochend Farm from the Warrender family in 1946, selling the property in 1967. The Colonel's second son, Robert, known as Reg, was, like his father, a keen horseman and, between 1932 and 1949, rode 128 winners. He farmed Middlethird, at Gordon in Berwickshire, and became Chairman of Kelso Race Course.

The farm at Phantassie was sold to the Hamilton family in 1946 and they are now in the third generation, with William Hamilton at Phantassie and his brother Gavin at Garvald Mains and Waldon on Sheriffside. Douglas Tweedie, Lex and Reg's younger brother, however, continued to live at Phantassie House until he died in 1982. 'He was rather more a lawyer than a farmer,' said his niece Patricia Stephen. 'But he did open a market garden, which was known as the French Garden because he was among the first to import garden cloches from France.'

A bachelor, Douglas sold Phantassie to his sister, May, wife of Robert Stephen of the Standard Literature Company of London, Calcutta and Ceylon, who had gone on to become a successful stockbroker. Robert died in 1994 and May in 1995. Having successfully launched her own business, Canterbury Wholefoods, their daughter Patricia returned to live at Phantassie in 1992, which she today runs as an organic farming enterprise with her partner Ralph Curry.

Natural compost and manure, comfrey and seaweed, using crop rotation, green manuring and companion planting, ensure the strength and fertility of the soil. No chemical sprays, fertilisers or pesticides are employed. Phantassie vegetable boxes, fruit and fresh eggs are much in demand throughout the county and beyond. 'As the granddaughter of a farmer, I never set out to follow in his footsteps,' says Patricia, 'but I now find I have a passion for small-scale food production. It must be in the blood.'

More recently she and Ralph have bought back the old Phantassie steading from William Hamilton who, with the proceeds, has built himself and his family a fine new farmhouse. 'The steading is the largest in the east of Scotland,' said Patricia. 'It is huge – approximately a hundred yards long with a footprint of over one hectare. We bought it with the express intention of finding a use for it as an engine to create local employment, as it was when it was built.'

Today it is an A-listed building and they have plans to develop it as an upmarket retail centre to serve the surrounding community. They also hope to include an exhibition telling the story of the Rennies of Phantassie.

CHAPTER TWENTY-THREE

The Garden of East Lothian

IN AN ADMIRABLY well-researched lecture delivered at Preston Kirk in 2007, David Affleck of the East Lothian Local History Society outlined the visionary importance of seventeenth- and early-eighteenth-century landowners and the impact their ideas had on succeeding generations. It was an event organised by the East Lothian Antiquarian and Field Naturalists' Society and, in particular, David singled out Sir George Buchan-Hepburn of Smeaton. Such men as Sir George were not simply content in holding down the legal career which led to his being appointed a Baron of the Exchequer. Multifaceted in his talents, it is for his *General Agricultural View of East Lothian*, published in 1794, that he is nowadays principally remembered.

The Buchan-Hepburns of Smeaton Hepburn are yet another of the old East Lothian families which eventually dispersed elsewhere but, before doing so, left their indelible mark. Between 1838 and 1847, Sir George's grandson, Sir Thomas, was Haddingtonshire's Member of Parliament. On the home front, however, he created a lasting memorial with the large conifers and deciduous trees which he and John Black, his gardener of fifty years, planted around the man-made lake which they also created. Sir Archibald, the 4th Baronet, also a keen botanist, simply added to his father's vision and the lovely orchards and plantings they orchestrated survive for all to see. All to their credit, George and Anne Gray, the subsequent owners of Smeaton Hepburn, have sensitively maintained and developed the garden traditions of their predecessors.[1]

Today, the 7th Buchan-Hepburn Baronet, Sir Alistair, lives in St Andrews where he has campaigned vigorously for the return of the remains of his ancestor, the 4th Earl of Bothwell, currently interred at Fårevejle Church, Zealand, in Denmark.

In the early 1880s John R. Gray, whose father farmed at Hareburn at Avonbridge, in Stirlingshire, moved to Edinburgh, where he took a lease of the good arable land at Gorgie Mains, on the western approaches to Edinburgh. Twenty-six years later, when Gorgie was about to be swallowed up by the city and built upon, he took a lease of Niddrie Mains, then a 400-acre farm at Craigmillar. 'They had dairy cows, arable crops, pigs, horses and grew potatoes,' says his grandson, another John R. Gray (see Chapter 21). 'They sold their produce locally to Edinburgh. That was just the way it was done then.'

Nearly thirty years passed and history repeated itself. Niddrie Mains was vacated and the Grays bought Smeaton Hepburn with its 800 acres. The farm of East Fenton, between Drem and North Berwick, was bought in 1937 and farmed by George Gray until 1962, when he and his wife Anne, a daughter of Jack Dale of Auldhame, moved to Smeaton.[2]

A member of East Lothian Regional Council, George soon found himself Chairman of the East Lothian Area of the National Farmers' Union. Convenor of the Union's cereals committee, a member of the Pig Industry Development Authority and a variety of offices in the Scout Movement culminated in 1991 with his being awarded the OBE. A much-loved personality, he died in 2008. For seven years, Anne Gray served on East Lothian County Council's Education Committee.

Despite the gardens having been lovingly retained, major changes took place at Smeaton Hepburn in the early 1950s when the thirty-six-bedroom, eighteenth-century mansion house was demolished. Over the Second World War, it had been requisitioned by Edinburgh Corporation as a minor ailments hospital for children. When it was eventually returned, the cost of repairs proved to be prohibitive and, very reluctantly, George and Anne agreed to its being pulled down. The centre part of their present house, however, is older than its predecessor. Originally built in 1715 as the garden cottage, it was extended for the Gray family and totally renovated in 1962 by Frederick R. Stevenson, the senior lecturer in architecture at Edinburgh University.[3]

Among George Rennie of Phantassie's contemporaries in the churchyard of Prestonkirk is his close friend Robert Brown, farmer first at West Fortune, then at Markle and finally at Drylawhill which today is owned by the Dale Family, with George Gray's sister Gladys Dale having inherited it as part of the Smeaton Estate.

In 1793, Brown and Rennie, with John Shirreff of Captainhead, were commissioned by the Board of Agriculture and Internal Improvements to produce an agricultural survey of the West Riding of Yorkshire. Over five weeks, these three men visited thirty-nine towns and accumulated statistical agricultural information on sixty-four English parishes.

In 1800, Brown established and edited *The Farmer's Magazine*. His classic work *A Treatise on Agriculture and Rural Affairs*, published in 1811, became a standard source of reference.

On a rocky mound about three quarters of a mile from East Linton are the remains of Markle or Merkhill Castle, long ago a stronghold of the Hepburns of Hailes, which became yet another victim of the Earl of Hertford's 1544 invasion. In August 1830, nineteen-year leases for the farms of Markle, Markle Mains and Crauchie on the Gilmerton Estate were advertised in the *Edinburgh Evening Courant*. In addition 'a Steam Engine, made by Sked, of six horse power – equal to nine – with a thrashing machine attached, a second very substantial Thrashing Machine with Wind-power attached, two pairs of Fanners, and sundry other implements' were sold by public roup at Markle.

In the event, the lease for Markle was signed by William Christie, Crauchie by David Sanderson and Markle Mains by David Hardie, seventh child and fifth son of John Hardie of Broomie Knowe in Fife. The Hardies were to hold the tenancy of Markle Mains for fifty years so it comes as no surprise when their overseas descendants turn up in search of their roots.[4]

Markle House, the core of which dates from the sixteenth century, is today owned by Jim McGuinness, formerly owner of Edinburgh's Engine Room Restaurant, and his wife Carinna. 'We had been visiting friends in Dunbar and had seen Markle House advertised,' says Jim, 'so we made a detour to have a look at it. It had been inherited by Ian Kinloch, who wanted to sell and it was just what we were looking for. From the bottom of my heart, I have to say this is the most wonderful place to live. It has everything anyone would want – easy access to Edinburgh and we are surrounded by glorious countryside.'

There were fourteen farms in the Parish of Prestonkirk and, in the last twenty years, half of these have been dismantled, with farmhouse cottages and steadings being sold off for housing.

'You can't fail to notice the number of steading developments all over East Lothian,' says Tom Middlemass who with his wife Marion and their son William are the latest generations of Middlemasses to own Markle Mains. 'When I was a boy, only my father and the farm manager at Markle had cars. Since the steadings at Crauchie and Markle have been developed, every household has at least two cars, the last count being seventy-two along our wee countryside road.'

The Middlemass story at Markle Mains begins with Thomas Middlemost from Jedburgh, whose grandson William took on the tenancy in 1892, by which time his surname had changed to Middlemass. Of this William's three sons, Thomas and another William both helped their father on the farm, although the former moved south to West Bearford, near Morham, in 1898. Meanwhile their third brother, John, was proving himself a successful businessman. Having become a successful livestock dealer, he settled at Dale House in Haddington in 1892 and, following his brother Thomas's premature death in 1908, not only managed West Bearford until 1919 but bought the farms of Collielaw and Bowerhouse unseen. In 1914 he took on the tenancy of Northrig at Morham (see Chapters 1 and 9) for his son Finlay. Northrig is today farmed by Ian Middlemass, great-grandson of John and Tom's second cousin once removed.

When the Gilmerton Estate sold Markle Mains in 1921, it was bought by William Middlemass for £5,000. A year before his death in 1924 it was taken over by his nephew, yet another William, who was born at West Bearford. By then this William had already proved himself as an invaluable help to his uncles who, at this stage, had grazings all over East Lothian. Between the wars he also tenanted Berryhill, a hill farm near Methven, and Findoglen, on the Ardvorlich Estate on the south shore of Loch Earn.

Over the Second World War period much of the grassland at Markle Mains was ploughed up to make way for wheat, oats and potatoes. This required a far greater casual workforce so William employed off-duty airmen from East Fortune Airfield. Before long, prisoners of war were being brought in to help out with the harvest, potato lifting, singling and shawing. Help also came from the Women's Land Army, a number of Land Girls being based in a large house at North Berwick.

William himself enrolled as a member of a secret army platoon based in 'a hole in the ground' in Smeaton Wood which, in the event of a German invasion, was expected to 'hinder' enemy progress. As it transpired, they only had flying incidents to contend with.[5]

William died in 1967 and great changes have since taken place. Up until fifty or so years ago, the steading at Markle Mains remained exactly as it had been since the 1830s. The original farm buildings formed a large square with open cattle courts in the centre but, in the 1970s, new buildings were blended with old and, while the steading exterior remained unchanged, its interiors were comfortably renovated for modern workday practices.

Ten farm cottages had been altered during the 1930s to make seven. Each was fitted with an indoor lavatory, considered a great luxury at the time, but, since these opened into the kitchens, they were condemned under the health and safety regulations of the 1970s. The seven cottages were then renovated to become four cottages and are currently rented out to provide a useful boost to farm income.

'Would I say that it was better or more satisfying to have been a farmer in the good old days?' reflects Tom. 'There is no doubt that things are very different but we are still trying to achieve the same ends – to produce food for us all to eat and, at the same time, earn a living. I know that my forebears enjoyed being farmers through the good and the lean years and I certainly wouldn't want to do anything else.'

Off the A1, equidistant from East Linton and Dunbar, is the village of Stenton which, in 1969, was awarded the status of an Outstanding Conservation Area. Once an agricultural settlement – the name means 'Stone Town' – between 1681 and 1862 it was the scene of weekly cattle and sheep markets. At one end of the Main Street is a surprisingly large Gothic parish church designed by the architect William Burn in 1829.

The lands of Biel, Stenton, Pitcox and Belton long ago formed part of the earldoms of Dunbar and March and the name 'Bele' is taken from the stream which also gives its name to the village of Belhaven. Biel was the portion allotted to Sir Patrick Dunbar, son of the 10th Earl of Dunbar, whose son, Hugh, sold it to Sir Robert Lauder of the Bass in 1489. The estate later passed into the hands of Sir John Hamilton who, in 1647, was elevated to the peerage by Charles I as Lord Belhaven and Stenton. In 1777 the 5th Lord Belhaven died unmarried and Biel was inherited by his cousin Mary Hamilton Nisbet of Pencaitland, wife of William Nisbet of Dirleton (see Chapters 16 and 25).

John Martine waxes lyrical about the stone breastwork and buttresses of the flower terraces which were overgrown with shrubs and evergreen creepers. On inheriting the property from his mother in 1797, William Hamilton-Nisbet commissioned the architect William Atkinson to create substantial Gothic additions and, judging from old photographs, the 1902 description of it being ranked as 'one of the finest of the great houses in Scotland' was well deserved. Centred on the original tower, Atkinson's additions ranged an impressive 593 feet in length. However, they were largely demolished in 1952 when 4,000 tons of rubble were removed at a cost of £16,000. What remained was the rather more modest yet equally stately dwelling that exists today.

Until 1909 Biel was the principal home of Henry and Constance Hamilton-Nisbet-Ogilvy (see Chapter 16) but, on Constance's death without children in 1920, it was left, along with the Archerfield Estate, to her cousin once removed, Lieutenant-Colonel John Patrick Grant of Kilgraston. Legacies are not always what they might appear. Along with his inheritance, Colonel Grant faced £116,000 of estate duties and mortgages of £220,000. To meet these debts he sold sixteen farms, the Archerfield Estate and Muirfield. At Biel there was a small summerhouse in which stood a statue of Constance. In recognition of the minimal efforts to which she had gone in order to try to avoid passing assets to her heir in entail, it was turned to face the wall.

In 1917, the Kilgraston Estate in Perthshire was also broken up. The mansion house passed to the nation and was subsequently sold and converted into the present Kilgraston School. The Colonel, who had latterly lived in Drummonie, the Kilgraston Dower House, moved to Biel with three of his unmarried sisters and they lived there throughout the twenties and thirties but, during the Second World War, the house was opened up to those in need. Writing to one of his cousins in February 1941, Colonel Pat's tone is ironic:

> Biel has passed through many vicissitudes – hoards of very dirty carcases followed by detachments of troops, refugee relations, etc, etc. On more than one occasion we have provided accommodation for fifty-four souls. Now almost all are gone and, as all the servants are giving notice to quit in order to see something of the gaiety of the war, we shall have to shut up the house, all but half a dozen rooms.
>
> That is just as well because there will soon be no money to pay anyone's wages with. I for one don't mind a bit. All rather fun.

In 1946, his sisters having pre-deceased him, the Colonel, also unmarried and without a direct heir, realised that it was time for him to put his affairs in order and he therefore gifted the estate to Vice Admiral Basil Brooke, his cousin once removed. What particularly intrigued me about this, having myself been born in Sarawak in south-east Asia and indeed written on the subject, was that Admiral Brooke was a grandson of James Brooke Johnson Brooke, nephew of Sir James Brooke, Sarawak's first White Rajah.

In 1828, Lady Lucy Bruce, daughter of Thomas, 7th Earl of Elgin and his first wife, the heiress Mary Hamilton-Nisbet of Dirleton, Biel, Innerwick, Pencaitland and Alford and Bloxholm in Lincolnshire, had married John Grant of Kilgraston, the brother of the well-known artist Sir Francis Grant. It was their daughter Annie who married Brooke Brooke, as he was generally known. Brooke Brooke had been in line to succeed his uncle as Rajah but, in 1860, an altercation over the possibility of Sarawak becoming a Dutch protectorate led to his uncle demoting him from Tuan Muda, the heir apparent, and passing him over in favour of his younger brother Charles Johnson Brooke.[6]

Admiral Basil Brooke had already achieved distinction himself in the Royal Navy and, in 1946, agreed to take early retirement and run the Biel Estate. It was an enticing legacy and everything might have run smoothly if the Colonel had lived for another five years. As it was, he died a few months before the death duty exemption would have been triggered and, as it transpired, Basil was obliged to sell eight farms to pay the requisite £87,000 tax.

Out of the three mansion houses, four villages and over thirty-five farms inherited by Constance Ogilvy, there now only remained Biel House with its 2,000 acres, part of North Berwick Golf Course, Dirleton Castle, some feus and Pressmennan and Spott reservoirs. It sounds a lot but was, in effect, a mere fraction of what the family had owned in the past. 'These figures show how estates that have taken centuries to build up can be destroyed,' the Admiral wrote sadly in his accounts.

By 1958 it had become even more difficult to continue to maintain the family's inheritance, especially when the Admiral's eldest son, who had gone to Rhodesia to farm, showed reluctance to return to Scotland to take on the burden. So the 'magnificently timbered, small compact agricultural and sporting estate of Biel' was advertised for sale.[7] It was bought by Charles Spence who, with his father before him, had farmed Tynefield for many years.

Part of the agreement was that several paintings and other items directly associated with Biel should remain in the house for future generations to enjoy and, to mark the colonial association, a collection of Sarawak memorabilia was left behind in the tower room. This had been collected by Colonel Pat's father, Charles Grant of Kilgraston, who had served as the private secretary to the first White Rajah of Sarawak and who was the brother-in-law of Brooke Brooke.

However, the majority of the spectacular contents listed in John Martine's *Reminiscences,* those not already gifted to the National Galleries of Scotland by Constance Ogilvy or sold at auction, were dispersed among the immediate Brooke family. Of unimaginable value was the 2,000-year-old Gymnasiarch Chair, carrying the owl of Minerva on one arm. This had been presented to William Hamilton-Nisbet by the Archbishop of Athens when on a visit to his daughter and son-in-law, Lord and Lady Elgin, in 1802. Having stood for many years on the upper terrace at Biel, it was removed to England in 1958. It can now be seen in all its splendour in close proximity to the Elgin Marbles in the British Museum.

CHAPTER TWENTY-FOUR

Overblown with Sand

ON THE OUTSKIRTS OF Longniddry is Quarry House which fronts onto the coastal road of Aberlady Bay. For many years this was the home of Nigel Tranter, whose prolific literary output embraced subjects ranging from St Columba to the French Emperor Napoleon Bonaparte. However, it was his passionate interest in medieval Scottish castles that continually inspired Nigel to write, albeit his earliest ambition was to become an architect. Since there was then no requirement to attend college in order to study architecture, he was apprenticed at the age of nineteen to the firm Jamieson and Arnott in Glasgow. 'I worked for them during the day and went to evening classes,' he told me when I asked him why he had given it up. 'Unfortunately, I didn't get paid and my mother simply couldn't afford to keep me when my father died.'

Nigel therefore went to work for his uncle, who had founded the Scottish National Insurance Company, but he still found time to write about his beloved castles. Between 1962 and 1971, he published the landmark five-volume book *The Fortified House in Scotland*. This covered the history and structure of every stronghold and similar structure in Scotland – 663 buildings in all. Then he moved on to imagining what might have taken place within their walls.

Throughout his career, Nigel drew his creativity from the Scottish landscape. When he and his wife and young family moved to live at Aberlady, he would set off around ten o'clock every weekday morning to cross over the slender footbridge opposite his home, after which he would follow the footpath through Aberlady Bay Bird Sanctuary towards Gullane Beach. As he progressed, he took notes using a waterproof pen and paper. 'They get typed out later,' he told me in 1986.

His wife May had, by then, died and he was living alone, although every Sunday, having fastidiously attended church at Athelstaneford in the morning, he would go to his daughter's house for an evening meal. His only son

Philip had tragically died on a mountaineering trip to Turkey in 1966. This had affected the family deeply.

A gentle and self-effacing personality, Nigel Tranter lived to be ninety-one and latterly formed a close friendship with a near neighbour, Joan Earle, whose husband had also died. It is Joan who, more than any other, has striven to keep his memory alive. With more than 140 published works, including children's books and Western fiction, Nigel left a lasting legacy to Scottish literature.

In 2000, a commemorative cairn was unveiled at Aberlady Bay Nature Reserve by his daughter, Frances May Baker. In 2003, a Nigel Tranter Centre was inaugurated at Lennoxlove House and, in 2008, it was transferred to Athelstaneford at the invitation of the Reverend Kenneth Walker, Minister of Athelstaneford Parish Church.

On the northern spur of the Garleton Hills stands a stone pillar erected in memory of General Sir John Hope, who became 4th Earl of Hopetoun. This serves as a very visible reminder that the Hopes of Hopetoun House, that stately William Bruce/Robert Adam masterpiece at South Queensferry in Midlothian, were intrinsically involved in the affairs of East Lothian, despite their barony originating from Leadhills, a mining village in Lanarkshire. As was customary with the Scottish aristocracy, they married strategically. They made unions with the Bennets of Wallyford and the Foulis family and, not long afterwards, made two marriages with the family of the earls of Haddington, inheriting and purchasing parcels of land along the way (see Chapter 14).

The castle of Luffness, half a mile east of the village of Aberlady and today an elegant country house surrounded by woodland, has a long and remarkable history. During the nineteenth century, when the floor of the entrance hall was lowered, three skeletons, buried as in the womb with their bodies doubled up, were found.

These have always been considered to be the remains of Norsemen but archaeologists state that the Norse did not bury their dead like this. They are, therefore, most probably much older and, in the opinion of George Hope, the current owner, this confirms that the site has been inhabited for thousands of years. In all probability it was one of a series of strategically positioned fortified wooden camps used by Viking invaders as they plundered up and down Scotland's eastern seaboard. The wooden palisades must have made them look very similar to those Wild West forts so often depicted in films.

With the arrival of the Normans after 1066, everything changed. Following William the Conqueror's courtesy call on the Scottish king, Malcolm

Canmore, in 1068, a very substantial stone-built coastal fortalice was built at Luffness by the earls of Dunbar and March specifically to protect Haddington and its busy port of Aberlady from coastal attack. In the following century the castle here was acquired by the powerful Lindsay lords for the same purpose.

In an essay published in the transactions of the East Lothian and Field Naturalists' Society in 2006, Chris Tabraham suggests that Sir William Lindsay, Lord of Luffness, had three sons and that it was not, as has often been presumed, his eldest son, Sir David, but his second son who inherited the property. When he died without an heir, the estate passed to their younger brother Gerard and, when he too died without a male heir, it passed to their sister Alice, who had married Henry de Pinkeney, Lord of Weedon Pinkeney in England.[1] The de Pinkeneys were loyal supporters of King John Balliol and returned to England when his fortunes waned. After their departure, Luffness became a royal castle held by, among others, Sir John de Bickerton and his descendant, Squire Bickerton, who acted as constables.

On the Luffness Estate stand the ruins of a Carmelite chapel. Under an archway in the north corner is a horizontal life-size statue of a knight with a shield on his breast, his right hand grasping a sword. For a long time nobody was able to identify who this was until a visit during the 1980s by Nigel Tranter, accompanied by the 29th Earl of Crawford, Chief of the Clan and name of Lindsay. Lord Crawford asked for a photograph of the effigy and it was noticed on the negative that the edge of the shield had the same fess-chequy (dicing) as the Lindsay coat-of-arms. This led to the conclusion that the effigy must be that of Sir David Lindsay of Crawford and the Byres, the High Chamberlain of Scotland, who, in 1270, embarked upon a crusade to the Holy Land. Sir David died there, not in battle but of sickness and, during his last illness, was nursed by Carmelite friars, including Kentigern Lauder, a Scot. As his dying wish, he asked that they build a monastery in his garden at Luffness. Friar Kentigern and his brethren duly fulfilled his request, making this the first Carmelite house in Scotland.

On a moonlit August night in 1388 there took place in Northumberland the Battle of Otterburn. On the one side were the English led by Harry 'Hotspur' Percy, son of the 1st Earl of Northumberland and on the opposing side, the Scots under James, 2nd Earl of Douglas. The ensuing carnage ended in victory for the Scots but, in the heat of battle, Douglas was killed. At his side was his squire, Bickerton of Luffness, who afterwards was accused of having failed to fasten Douglas's suit of armour properly, while others claimed that he himself had assassinated his feudal superior.

Either way, Bickerton was far from popular and only made matters worse when he fled from the battlefield to Luffness, where he hid away for several months in a small closet off the stairway. He emerged in the following spring on the assumption that it would at least be safe for him to visit the monastery but the Douglases were lying in wait for him. In the pleasant spring sunshine he went to sleep and, although he was on Church land, he was done for.

When Colonel Archibald Hope and his wife Mary, parents of the current owner, arrived to live at Luffness in 1939, Mary set off for a walk in the grounds and caught sight of a strange figure wearing medieval dress moving slowly through the trees. When she described what she had seen to Grassick, a forester who had been employed on the estate since the age of sixteen, he shook his head. 'Ah, that'll be Bickerton. That was where he was killed,' he informed her.

The fortress of Luffness was further strengthened during the Rough Wooing period and the French commander, de Thermes, by denying the English the use of the port of Aberlady, effectively prevented them from advancing any further than Haddington. Then Lord Hertford tried a different approach, advancing over the Soutra Pass to utterly defeat the Scots at the Battle of Pinkie Cleugh in 1547. However, he had not forgotten Luffness so, when it came to the peace negotiations of 1552, he insisted that it be 'utterly thrown down'.[2] The curtain walls were therefore demolished and the site remained derelict for several decades thereafter. The earthworks and the moat from this period are still visible, the latter having been drained during the 1840s.

It was always rumoured that there was a subterranean passage connecting the original stronghold to Aberlady. However, it was not until the mid twentieth century, when farm machinery became heavier, that a dip in a field revealed its probable whereabouts.

After the departure of the Lindsays in the late sixteenth century Sir Patrick Hepburn of Waughton, a cousin of the 4th Earl of Bothwell, built a central tower house on the site of the demolished fortress and subsequent generations have continued to add on to this. In 1739, the estate was purchased by the 1st Earl of Hopetoun and it was his grandsons, Sir Charles and Sir Alexander, who employed first William Burn, then David Bryce, to add on Georgian and Victorian additions.

Luffness House has since been the private home of the Hope Family for almost three centuries, albeit having been leased for nineteen of those years to William Thomson of the Ben Line shipping dynasty. It was then requisitioned to house the Mayfield Royal Navy Orphanage during the Second World War.

When occupied once again by the family, Colonel Hope's four eye-catching daughters – Catherine, Margaret, Caroline and Cecilia – took social Scotland and London by storm during the 1960s. Since their marriage in

1996, Colonel Hope's son, George, and his wife, Anna, from Holland, have made their own contributions to the future of the house, including the renovation of much of the existing building and the commissioning of a stylish conservatory extension designed by Ben Tindall, architect son of Frank and Mary Tindall.

During the nineteenth century Luffness Mains was farmed by James Skirving, a nephew of the painter Archibald Skirving (see Chapter 20). Three generations of the Stevenson Family have now been there since 1911, when Allan Stevenson first arrived in East Lothian from Ayrshire. His son John took over in 1935, handing over to his son Allan, a chartered accountant, in 2001. 'It can be confusing,' says John Stevenson (see Chapter 25). 'For nine generations, the family Christian names have alternated between Allan and John. My grandson is also a John.' That seems to be the way with most farming families.

At the heart of Aberlady village is the Kilspindie House Hotel, which in 2004 was transformed by the celebrated Edinburgh restaurateur Malcolm Duck. Follow the signs and they will take you to the Myreton Motor Museum, opened in 1966 by farmer and motor transport enthusiast Willie Dale (see Chapter 9) and taken over by his son Alex in 1991. Visitors are welcome daily from March until November.

Inside are more than fifty cars, including a 1927 Rolls Royce, a collection of motorcycles belonging to the 15th Duke of Hamilton and a vintage *Edinburgh Evening News* aluminium van used to deliver papers on the Border run for twenty-five years.

There is also a 1925 15.9 h.p. Morris Oxford (Bull Nose) that was found in a sale and bought by Willie Dale for £15. It was only when he was cleaning it out and came across a letter that had slipped behind the back seat that he realised it had once belonged to his father. Back in the 1920s, the family had christened the car Susan, after the legendary French tennis champion Suzanne Lenglen – 'Suitable for long rallies and fast returns!' explained Alex with a laugh.

A hospital dedicated to St Cuthbert existed at Ballencrieff in the twelfth century.[3] In 1507, a tower house was built and, despite being another casualty of the Earl of Hertford's soldiers in 1547, was rebuilt forty years later and continuously occupied for almost 400 years by a branch of the Murray family. In 1643 Charles I rewarded his Master of Works, Sir Gideon Murray, by making him Lord Elibank. When, over a century later, Dr Samuel Johnson stayed at Ballencrieff for two nights with the 5th Lord Elibank, the creator of the English dictionary observed of him, 'I can find in books all that he has read; but he has a great deal of what is in books, proved by the test of real life.'[4]

Ballencrieff House was burnt down in a fire in 1868 and the ruins remained in a sorry state until 1989, when they were bought by Peter Gillies and Lin Dalgleish. It took them eight years to complete the task but, with Gillies's contacts and his past experience as a civil engineer, the tower house, with its twenty-three rooms, has been splendidly brought back to life again. It is now owned by George and Joy Sypert from Florida who, for a brief period, owned an apartment at Whittingehame.

The land at Saltcoats, south of Aberlady on Archerfield, was gifted by the Crown to Patrick Levingtown in the sixteenth century for destroying a wild boar. Between 1634 and 1750 it was farmed by my Forrest ancestors who, at one stage or another, also had the tenancies of West Fenton, Stevenson Mains, Linton, Linton Miln and Gurly Bank on the Phantassie Estate.[5]

Their provenance in the Parish of Dirleton (Gullane), however, dates from much earlier, as is evidenced from research compiled in 2002 by Martin A. Forrest. Although the family were in Haddington from about 1450, the name Fourhouse, later Forrest, occurs from the early fifteenth century in the Dirleton, Gullane and West Fenton areas of East Lothian. For instance, on 16 April 1438, William Fourhous of Lucasland, Dirleton, was a witness to a sasine involving land at Muirfield, Gullane.[6]

Indeed, it seems that the family was originally based at Dirleton and took part in the civic affairs of North Berwick from the time of the earliest records. There is also an indication that the wealth of the family was built on their participation in the wool trade as evidenced by entries in the Exchequer Rolls of Scotland which show a Walter Forehous being responsible for the paying of duties on wool and woollen cloth to the Crown from North Berwick from 1460 to 1474. By 1498 the Exchequer Rolls record a David Forhous paying duties for Haddington, presumably as Burgh Treasurer. David seems to have been the originator of the Haddington branch of the family, although the Forrests remained in the Dirleton area until well into the nineteenth century. There is an interesting record in the Exchequer Rolls for 6 December 1505 of lands owned or rented by the Dirleton Forrests. It is recorded that Edward, Drew, David and George Forehous all owned land within the town of Dirleton at the time.

Moving forward two centuries, James Forrest of the Dirleton/Gullane family, born in 1744, married a Helen Smith and had seven children, with two of their daughters marrying John and Peter Martine of Haddington. The former is my great-great-great-uncle, the latter my great-great-grandfather.

As was the pattern with the Martines and the Carfraes, the Dirleton/ Gullane Forrests also inter-married with the Yules, another prosperous farming family from the same parish. It paints a picture of the flexible interlinking strands of agricultural life over the seventeenth and eighteenth centuries that the Yules too moved around extensively, farming, for example, Fenton Barns and East Fenton for two generations, then Blackdykes, near North Berwick.

By the early seventeenth century both the Forrest and Yule families owned private burial aisles at either end of Gullane's Old Parish Church of St Andrews, the ruins of which are set back from the curve of the road as it enters the Main Street. In 1827 James Yule, while living at Luffness Mill, approached the Dirleton Parish Heritors and Kirk Session for the re-use of the virtually complete aisle as a private burial ground. A metal lockable gate has therefore been installed with a massive key which is kept locally. Today, there are seventeen memorial plaques on the walls listing over fifty members of the Yule Family, eleven of whom are buried there.[7]

Originating from hardy East Lothian farming stock, these Yules provided three major-generals, seven lieutenant-colonels, two colonels and a major – an impressive contribution to the British Raj. Two of James Yule's brothers, Major William Yule and Colonel Udny Yule, saw service with the East India Company; Colonel Udny's son Patrick reached the rank of Major General. George Yule, a Lieutenant of Marines, was lost at sea when the naval sloop *Dispatch* sank off Sable Island, 100 miles south-east of Nova Scotia. Other family members included Sir George Udny Yule who served with the Bengal Civil Service for thirty-eight years and retired to live at Beech Hill House (see Chapter 8). Lieutenant Robert Abercrombie Yule commanded the 9th Lancers and was killed in 1875 during the Sepoy Revolt in Delhi.[8]

Local records indicate that a church dedicated to St Andrew stood on this spot as early as the ninth century, three centuries before the simple Norman-style place of worship which succeeded it. However, owing to this building being 'continewallie over blawn with sand', an official decree of the Scots Parliament in 1612 transferred its congregation to Dirleton, thus causing the church to fall into disrepair. In time, Gullane's popularity as a golf and holiday resort in the nineteenth century soon led to the building of St Peter's Church, now disused, Gullane Parish Church and St Andrew's Scottish Episcopal Church, the latter two still in use.

Should I be passing through Gullane, I sometimes pause to contemplate the melancholy state of the old Church of St Andrew, whereupon I feel a twinge of guilt at the condition of the neglected and overgrown Forrest aisle. Such is the way with all mortality as it passes through the generations.

After the dawn of the eighteenth century, the Dirleton/Gullane Forrest family transferred their allegiances almost exclusively to St Mary's in Haddington. However, the Yule aisle survives and is still in use for interment. In 1994, Lieutenant-Colonel James Yule, domiciled in Essex, gave a donation towards its upkeep to the Gullane and Dirleton History Society. In 2002, his younger daughter Clare arranged for the removal of shrub and weed growth and the lowering and levelling the subsoil. Once this had been done, a membrane was laid and it was then covered with coarse gravel.

Gullane today, flanked by its golf courses and the sea, comprises a handsome huddle of small Georgian villas overlooking an expanse of common land known as Goose Green. In a small courtyard off the main street is the restaurant La Potinière, which in French means 'the gossip place' and has been the recipient of many an accolade since it first opened in 1969. From 1977 it was run by husband and wife team David and Hilary Brown and became so popular that bookings often had to be made two years in advance. A quarter of a century on, it is run with equal aplomb by Mary Runciman with Keith Marley and, although bookings are now taken on a rather more realistic basis, its popularity has by no means diminished.

In 1979, carrying on the bakery tradition pioneered by her mother, Catherine Henderson (now Catherine Home), of the Spitalrig farming dynasty, took over the Goose Green Bakery on Stanley Road, its previous owner having been killed in a plane crash. Six years later, she decided to lease it out and it is currently Falko's Konditorei, a tearoom with German-style baking. Not without merit has it been designated one of the best cake shops in Britain.

Travelling towards the coastline of the Firth of Forth, parallel roads slope over towards expansive dunes. During the 1980s these were a favourite exercise ground for Jock Wallace, the tough-talking boss of Glasgow Rangers, to test his players' fitness. With five top-of-the-range golf courses in close proximity to each other, it was inevitable that Gullane should emerge as a residential Mecca for devotees of the game and among those who have a home here are the Edinburgh-born comic genius Ronnie Corbett and his actress wife Ann Hart.

Some years ago, Ronnie contacted me in connection with an article he had been asked to write for a magazine and we arranged to meet in a London restaurant. Identifying him from the moment he walked in the door, the restaurateur seated us at a window table and it was only when we had reached the main course that I noticed a small crowd had gathered outside to watch us eat. 'You must always remember not to wave to them before they wave to you,' said Ronnie wisely. 'Otherwise, they'll think we want them to come in and join us.' Such is fame.

Greywalls is the next-door neighbour of the Honourable Company of Edinburgh Golfers at Muirfield (see Chapter 12) of which Ronnie Corbett is a member. The house dates from 1901 and was designed as 'a small, albeit dignified, holiday home'[9] by the great Victorian-Edwardian architect Sir Edwin Lutyens, with the garden created by his equally celebrated colleague,

Gertrude Jekyll. Its first owner was the Hon. Alfred Lyttelton, a famous cricketer, keen golfer and nephew of William Ewart Gladstone, the Victorian British Prime Minister. In 1895, he became a Liberal Unionist Member of Parliament and served as Colonial Secretary between 1903 and 1905 in succession to Joseph Chamberlain. His first wife was Laura Tennant, the sister of Margot, Countess of Oxford and Asquith (see Chapter 26).

In 1905 Alfred Lyttelton sold his small, albeit dignified, holiday home to the American railroad millionaire William James, who added on the lodge gates and commissioned Sir Robert Lorimer to create the nursery wing. William James's wife was a close friend of Edward VII and her son Edward, a patron of the arts and surrealist enthusiast, was the King's godson. In 1924, Greywalls was purchased by Lieutenant-Colonel Sir James Horlick. When he and his wife moved to Achamore House on the west-coast island of Gigha in 1948, Greywalls was transformed into a top-class hotel by their daughter Ursula and her husband Colonel Weaver. More recently, it has been run as an exclusive-use venue by their son Giles and his wife Ros.

My favourite anecdote concerning Greywalls was when the late Princess Margaret, Countess of Snowdon, had been lunching there. Afterwards, she had settled down in the television lounge to watch a golf tournament and was joined by another guest. 'Do you play golf?' she inquired of him.

'Yes,' he said.

'So did my father,' she informed him.

'Who was your father?' he asked.

'The King,' she replied.

The other guest was Tom Weiskopf, the American golfer, who had failed to recognise her and, under the circumstances, the Princess had no idea who he was either.

CHAPTER TWENTY-FIVE

The Spoils of Time

Dirleton Castle, the weathered ruins of which create a striking centrepiece for the adjoining village, was built in the thirteenth century for the Norman de Vaux family. In the following century it was annexed by the wealthy Halyburtons; a century later, the Ruthvens took it over and then it was bought by Sir Thomas Erskine, who sold the estate to Sir James Douglas.

In 1650 it was used as a base for Scottish moss-troopers to attack the supply chain of Oliver Cromwell's invading army, the result of which is that it suffered severely from General Monk's cannon. After being used as a field hospital during the final gasps of the Civil War, it was left in ruins.

Then came deliverance of a sort. In 1663, the Dirleton Estate was purchased by Sir John Nisbet, a rising advocate who, on becoming a Lord of Session, took the judicial title of Lord Dirleton. Among the farms situated between Dirleton and Gullane was Saltcoats, where my Forrest ancestors were his tenants,[1] but, to provide a less personal timeline, in 1641 he was one of the three advocates chosen personally by James Graham, 1st Marquis of Montrose, to defend him against the accusations of treason levelled against him. Such charges were negated but failed to save Montrose when he was sent to the scaffold nine years later.

Sir John liked nothing better than persecuting Covenanters – largely, it is thought, because a number of his own relatives supported the cause. As you might imagine, his personal life was far from happy and he sounds, by all accounts, a thoroughly disagreeable man. In his will of 1687, he bypassed his only daughter Jean in favour of their kinsman William Nisbet, Younger of Craigentinnie, a gesture which led to months of unhappy and ultimately unsuccessful litigation.

But it has to be observed that the Craigentinnie Nisbets went on to do extremely well for themselves. In 1747, their direct descendant, another William Nisbet, married Mary Hamilton, daughter of Alexander Hamilton of Pencaitland, which proved an immensely profitable liaison for all concerned.

In 1797 William Hamilton-Nisbet, their only son, inherited the properties of Dirleton and Innerwick from his father; from his mother, a grand-niece of the 2nd Lord Belhaven, he acquired the Biel Estate, while Winton Castle at Pencaitland was purchased by their mother for his younger brother John (see Chapter 16).

By then, an original design by William for Archerfield House had already been put into effect by John Douglas, with new ceilings and fine marble chimneypieces added in later by Robert Adam. These were the opulent surroundings in which Mary, William Hamilton-Nisbet's only daughter and, through her mother, a granddaughter of the 2nd Duke of Rutland, spent her childhood.

With such connections and a fortune at her disposal, there was no shortage of suitors for Mary's hand but, at the age of twenty-one, she chose Thomas Bruce, 7th Earl of Elgin. They were married and, shortly afterwards, sailed for Constantinople where he had been appointed British Ambassador to the Ottoman Empire which, at that time, included both Turkey and Greece.

While in Athens, Elgin, an admirer of all things Byzantine, became obsessed with the rescue of Greek antiquities from the neglect of the Turks. His wife's fortune helped, of course, and he set about amassing an important collection of carvings, saved – although some might insist plundered – from the Parthenon and adjacent historic sites. These were shipped back to England and eventually sold to the British Museum where, controversially, they remain on display to this day.

Elgin suffered from ill health and seemingly acquired a flesh-eating virus from the then common practice of applying mercury powder to the skin. With the approach of the first Napoleonic War in 1803, while they were returning to Britain through France, Lord Elgin was arrested as a foreign national and possible spy. In the hope of finding somebody to intercede on his behalf, Lady Elgin set off on a fateful trip to Paris where she met, for the first time, Robert Ferguson of Raith, an aspiring diplomat and Whig politician. Her husband was released from captivity but, within two years, Lady Elgin had become Ferguson's mistress.

With our twenty-first-century obsession with Regency promiscuity, it might be imagined that such behaviour was commonplace among the upper classes of that era. But, in 1807, during the reign of George III, it took an Act of Parliament to bring about a divorce and the consequences for a wife could be dire. And so it proved. With Elgin taking the moral high ground, Mary was refused the right to see their four children ever again. Of course, what everyone forgets is that children eventually grow up and make their own decisions.

Under such circumstance, however, wealth helps and it was not an entirely unhappy outcome for Mary and Robert Ferguson. Having married, he was elected Whig Member of Parliament for Kirkcaldy Burghs in 1832 and again in 1837, with two years in between as the MP for Haddingtonshire. Elgin too remarried and had a second family.

Despite his tenure being brief, by any standards, Ferguson's political presence in East Lothian did not go unnoticed. Two years after his death in 1841 and one month after that of Lord Elgin, a statue was unveiled on the top of a soaring forty-five-foot-high memorial column situated at the corner of Knox Place and Station Road in Haddington. It was designed at a cost of £650 by Robert Forrest.[2] The inscription on his plinth describes its subject as 'a kind landlord, a liberal dispenser of wealth, a generous patron of literature, science and art'. I wonder how many passers-by have any notion of the passion and scandal that this man created in Regency Britain, not to mention Fife and East Lothian.

With Lord Elgin, Mary had one surviving son and three daughters but their son George, Lord Bruce, was an epileptic who never married and, in 1840, he predeceased his parents. On Elgin's death, his family titles and Fife estates passed to the eldest son of his second marriage. However, it was to their eldest daughter, Lady Mary Bruce, by then the wife of Robert Christopher Dundas, that the Dirleton, Belhaven and Biel Estates were bequeathed. These, in turn, passed to her daughter, Constance who, in 1888, married Henry Ogilvy (see Chapter 16). With such an inheritance, it was not difficult to persuade the spouses of either daughter or granddaughter to acquire the additional surnames of Hamilton and Nisbet.

By the end of the nineteenth century, however, Archerfield House was being increasingly abandoned by the Hamilton-Nisbet-Ogilvys in favour of Biel and Winton. Over the first decade of the twentieth century, it was seasonally leased out to, among others, Herbert Asquith, the British Prime Minister, and his second wife, the clever and outspoken Margot Tennant. This was a particularly convenient arrangement for the Asquiths since the Prime Minister's son by his first wife had married Lady Cynthia Charteris, daughter of 11th Earl of Wemyss, whose Scottish home was at Gosford. And it is widely conjectured that it was while staying with the Balfours at Whittingehame in 1911 that Winston Churchill was invited to dine with the Asquiths at Archerfield House and was appointed First Lord of the Admiralty.

Two years after Constance Ogilvy's death in 1920 the Archerfield Estate was sold by her beneficiary Colonel Grant to meet death duties (see Chapter 23). It was purchased by the industrialist Jackson Russell but it was a tenure that would end in tragedy.

In 1936, Mrs Russell had taken her niece, Mrs Boyd, her fourteen-year-old great-niece Patricia and her nephew Thomas Boyd, aged eleven, on an excursion to North Berwick and she had parked the car in a bay on street level opposite the harbour. On their return, however, she turned on the ignition and the vehicle accelerated forward into the water and turned upside down. Standing nearby was Jack Stewart, a twenty-one-year-old upholsterer, who gallantly removed his jacket and plunged after them, closely followed by George Lawson, Robert Small, Ian Melville and Richard O'Halloran. Ben Millar, a local boat hirer, also took part in the rescue operation, the group securing the safety of Mrs Boyd and the children but they were sadly unable to save the unfortunate Mrs Russell.[3] Her husband was understandably devastated by the loss.

In common with Gosford House and other substantial East Lothian mansions, Archerfield House was requisitioned for the duration of the Second World War by the War Office. Yet again, the damage incurred through the billeting of soldiers within its walls left it virtually uninhabitable. In 1944, the estate was purchased by Alexander Milne, a market gardener, who sold it on to the tenant farmer George Mitchell and his son Ian.

With its Adam interiors already wrecked, the mansion house was soon relegated to storing farm equipment including a grain dryer. By then, it was of no use to its next owner, the 14th Duke of Hamilton whose son, the Marquis of Clydesdale, employed the Edinburgh architect Law and Dunbar-Naismith to convert the home farm to accommodate his growing family. When the estate was advertised for sale in 1960, Stewart Chalmers, who had only recently been appointed factor at Lennoxlove, remembers the Duke asking him to find out the details. 'He had come across Archerfield when the air force were installing search lights and defence equipment there,' he said. 'He already owned a house in North Berwick and saw it as a good investment.'

At some point during the 1970s I remember exploring the rapidly deteriorating interiors which were then open to the sky. Then, in 2001, they were miraculously saved. The greater proportion of the estate, including the shell of the house, was sold by Hamilton & Kinneil Estates to Caledonian Heritable, a company controlled by Kevin Doyle, owner of Edinburgh's Dome Restaurant and Ryan's Bar. Archerfield House has since been re-roofed to become a luxurious hotel, the centrepiece of an exclusive £55 million golfing development. Although the modern street lighting is, to my mind, entirely out of place and I did have to blink in disbelief when I saw some of the luxury homes that have sprung up nearby, it is undoubtedly a triumph.

In the summer of 2007, the 15th Duke and Duchess took me for a drive around the section of the estate which is still owned by his family trust, thus enabling me to catch a distant glimpse of Marine Cottage and the coastal sands from where Alan Breck Stewart takes ship to France in Robert Louis Stevenson's novel *Catriona*.

Burial cists uncovered from time to time along this section of coastline indicate that there was once a sizeable Iron Age settlement on the seashore here. In 1908 two caves, about 15 feet above the high water mark, were excavated. Hearths and fireplace ovens were discovered recessed into the walls, along with a hoard of relics – a quern stone, an iron knife, a spindle whorl of deer horn, a small iron spearhead, a bone button and a bracelet made of coloured glass.[4] All of these items can now be seen in the Museum of Scotland.

It was not the first time I had been for a spin in a car with Angus Hamilton. A former air force test pilot, he became a non-executive director of Supacat, a company which manufactures off-road vehicles for developing countries. Next to flying in his Cessna aeroplanes, there was nothing, therefore, that he enjoyed more than a rough terrain challenge. On another occasion, having recently returned from a trip to Australia, he took me on a hair-raising cross-country ride through the Archerfield woods to inspect a pond beside which he had just erected a sign which read 'Beware of Crocodiles'.

In close proximity to their home he has a grass airstrip, with an aircraft hangar. Inside are stored several of the planes he has collected over the years, including the scarlet Bulldog he tested for Scottish Aviation in 1971. To describe them as his pride and joy would be an understatement.

Facing on to the green of Dirleton village is The Open Arms Hotel. During the Second World War Patricia Gibson, whose husband George Gibson farmed Peaston Bank at Pencaitland (see Chapter 16), was appointed Land Army Commissioner for East Lothian and, almost every day, would travel to visit the land army girls' hostel in North Berwick. The journey, in those days, involved her driving through the centre of Dirleton village, where she noticed an attractive-looking boarding house called Rockville. When the war ended and the land army girls were looking for employment, it occurred to Pat that Rockville would make an ideal hotel. The opportunity to purchase the property arose in 1947 and a remarkable chapter in Scottish hospitality was launched.

To start off with, George Gibson offered £5 to anyone who could come up with a suitable name for the venture and Rupert Chalmers-Watson from Fenton Barns suggested 'The Open Arms', based on the image of a beautiful woman with her arms extended in welcome. This proved doubly appropriate since, until the early 1950s, The Open Arms was entirely managed and staffed by women. It is hard to imagine what a daringly innovative concept that was in those days.

Then, in February 1954, a young man of twenty-four, fresh from working in the Bellevue Palace Hotel in Berne, arrived. This was Arthur Neil and he would go on to create catering history in Scotland but says that he only went for the interview because, when he answered the advertisement, Pat Gibson had offered him lunch. Arthur had started young as a hotelier. His father, a soldier in the 51st Highland Division, had been taken prisoner in Germany during the Second World War and his mother had been forced to close the family's sweet-making business in Falkirk. Arthur still treasures a jar which carries the Neil & Sons label.

'It was my father's idea that I should go into the hotel business,' he said. 'When he was released from the army, he came home to Falkirk and immediately sent me off to a hospitality school in France. I then applied to the Hotel School in Glasgow. I was the youngest person there as most of the other students had come straight from the army. I was then called up myself and served in the Army Catering Corps. That also proved to be an invaluable experience.'

Afterwards, he wrote to the famous hotelier Otto Goring who, after grilling him in an interview, sent him to Switzerland. When Pat Gibson invited him to lunch, Arthur had been undecided about his future. 'After working at the Glasgow Central Hotel and the Bellevue Palace, I was not at all sure about being confined to a village in East Lothian,' he said.

Needless to say, Pat Gibson was determined to take him on and talked him into it. By this stage, The Open Arms had not only become fashionable as a small country hotel but its outside catering business had also started to mushroom throughout Scotland, a demand mostly created by its owner's force of personality. Then disaster struck. On a visit to Edinburgh, Pat was killed in a car accident.

'On that same day, The Open Arms sign fell down,' recalled Arthur. 'I went outside to put it up again and Gerry Gibson was so impressed by this that he asked me to stay on and brought me into the business.'

In due course, Arthur not only bought out all of the shareholders but he married Romy Gibson, George and Pat's daughter. 'I carried on very much as I expect that Pat would have done,' he said. 'The outside catering business became even more successful. Then it struck me that there was a gap in the market for the supply of fresh food produce.'

With John Stevenson, who farmed Luffness Mains (see Chapter 24), he launched Shieldhouse Produce. Soon the company had depots in Newcastle, Manchester and Bo'ness. Next came a training school at the Grange Inn at St Andrews. Arthur was appointed Catering Industry Training Board Officer for Scotland and, from the 1960s until the mid 1980s, presided over a dramatic and long-overdue overhaul of standards in both the hotel and outside catering industries throughout Lowland Scotland. In 1984 he bought a guest house in Edinburgh called the St Christopher and transformed it into the Howard Hotel. This was sold in 1989 and, having reached the age of sixty-five, Arthur finally decided to sell The Open Arms and retire to live in Gullane.

'East Lothian was far more cliquish when I arrived here in the 1950s,' he reflected. 'For example, none of the farmers would have anything to do with the people who bought houses here and commuted into Edinburgh for work.'

He jogged my memory. 'Do you remember that there used to be an East Lothian Ball? It was usually held at the Marine Hotel in North Berwick, although I can remember a couple of years when it took place at Saltoun Hall. To acquire tickets you had first to be approved by a lady in Dunbar. If you were not on her list, there were none available. That was what it was like then.'

CHAPTER TWENTY-SIX

The Miracle of the Bass

A NOVEL WHICH AFFORDED me an enormous amount of enjoyment when I first came across it was *Father Malachy's Miracle* by Bruce Marshall. First published in 1931, it concerns the trials of a humble Benedictine monk who is sent to Edinburgh to instruct the curates of St Margaret's of Scotland in the performance of the liturgy. Adjacent to St Margaret's is a rowdy dance hall known as The Garden of Eden and Father Malachy is soon prevailed upon to pray to the Lord Almighty for its removal. Within days, his prayers are answered. The Garden of Eden, with full complement of chorus girls and the Lord Bishop's wayward brother, rises high into the air and is transported to the Bass Rock. As a result of Bruce Marshall's hilarious romp, this 100-metre-high offshore carbuncle became for me, at an impressionable age, far more than just a striking icon of East Lothian's coastal landscape – it embodied a curiously unfulfilled naughtiness.

According to Henry the Minstrel, also known as Blind Harry and certainly not the most reliable of sources, the first stronghold on the Bass Rock was built by Robert de Lauder of Congaltoun and Bass who, in the thirteenth century, accompanied the patriot Sir William Wallace on his escapades against the English. He died in 1311 and was buried in the Auld Kirk graveyard at North Berwick. Six centuries earlier, St Baldred, a disciple of Kentigern, who was also known as St Mungo (see Chapter 11), kept a cell on Bass Rock but, disappointingly, the small Culdee chapel on the island that bears his name was built almost a millennium later, around 1491. With its strategic situation at the entrance of the Firth of Forth, the rock was understandably coveted by a string of Scottish monarchs but not until 1671 was it finally annexed by the Duke of Lauderdale for the Crown. It then became a state prison. Today, it provides shelter for an estimated 40,000 pairs of gannets.

Fortunately, I was blessed with blue skies and calm waters on each of the three occasions when I have set foot on it. At the time, somebody remarked to me that, if only Scotland had as much sunshine on a regular basis, the Bass

Rock might become as popular a holiday destination as Bora Bora or the Maldives. Judging from the topping of guano deposited by the seabirds, I think not but it is nevertheless an exhilarating place to visit.

Nowadays there are excursions on *Sula II*, a passenger boat belonging to the Marr family who trace their North Berwick ancestry back twelve generations. My first excursion was I cannot think how long ago with Fred Marr, who retired in 2004. Now the boat is run by his son Chris and daughter Pat MacAulay. However, the majority of visitors to North Berwick nowadays settle for seeing the seabirds on the live webcam at the Scottish Seabird Centre based in the town's harbour.

It may be more environmentally friendly but I cannot imagine it offering the same thrill. In medieval times North Berwick was the southernmost terminal of a ferry service which transported up to 10,000 pilgrims a year travelling between Haddington and Whitekirk, and Earlsferry and St Andrews on the far side of the Firth of Forth. As more immediate ferry crossings were introduced at Leith and South Queensferry, all of this changed. When the railway arrived in 1850, North Berwick was nothing more than a small fishing village. Of course, then everything really changed as urban Victorians flocked to the seaside to embrace the fresh air and abundant scenic beauty. Hotels and fashionable shops opened their doors. Spacious dwelling houses were created on the seafront, bringing with them that curiously Victorian snobbery in regard to which end of the town people occupied. As a result, those who inhabited the east end rarely dined with those in the west end. What is it about east and west ends?

'The prevailing winds,' explained Caroline Lawrie who, for several years, meticulously catalogued the contents of the *Haddingtonshire Courier* for the East Lothian History Society. I had never thought of this before. It must have been those same prevailing winds in an age of sea routes which persuaded the Augustinians of St Andrews to build their Parish Church at Haddington.

Among those who took advantage of the fashionable summer exodus to North Berwick were the three Edinburgh-based sons of Robert Stevenson, builder of harbours and lighthouses. All Robert's sons – David, Alan and Thomas – were to become successful engineers in their own right but it was Thomas's only son, the author Robert Louis Stevenson, who brought international celebrity to the name.[1]

Their father having earlier been involved in the restoration of North Berwick Harbour, it became the practice of the Stevenson brothers and their families after 1860 to rent properties for the months of August and September in North Berwick, in particular Anchor Villa on West Bay Road.[2] As a child, Robert Louis suffered from mild lung congestion so the sea air proved a perfect tonic and, in North Berwick, he could play along the sands with his young cousins under the watchful eyes of nannies and nurses. Sandy bays and ruined castles, with the offshore islands of Fidra, Craigleith and the Lamb, not to mention the Bass Rock – there was a wealth of material on tap for the future author of *Treasure Island*, *Catriona* and *Kidnapped*.

Almost a century later, I too played along those sands for I also had a North Berwick connection. It was where the Little Aunt lived.

My grandfather, having inherited the family medical practice in Haddington in 1895, married two years later and caused considerable consternation among older family members by purchasing a modest house at No. 4 The Quadrant, North Berwick, where he settled his three unmarried sisters – Jessie, Aimee and Isabella.[3] The sisters named their new home Lindores, after the Grange of Lindores, their mother's old home in Fife. Although they were probably unaware of it, the house next door at No. 5, The Quadrant, and another along the street, at No. 1, had, four decades earlier, been rented for holidays by the parents of Robert Louis Stevenson.

Most of what I know about the three Martine sisters is from snippets of conversation I overheard when young. Great-Aunt Jessie painted in watercolours, three of which I now own, and her sister Great-Aunt Aimee suffered from ill health. However, I recently received a letter from Derick Mills, a retired lawyer living in Haddington, who vividly recalled being taken to visit them as a boy with his sister and parents. 'I remember afternoon tea being served by a maid in full afternoon maid's dress and having to be on my best behaviour,' he wrote. 'That wasn't difficult as my sister and I loved going there.'

Both Jessie and Aimee died before I was born but I did know Great-Aunt Isabella. A tiny individual with a big personality, she refused to be confined by the constraints of her generation and took up nursing during the First World War. Two decades later, she ended her career as matron not only of the City Hospital in Hull but of the nearby fever hospital at Cottingham. A photograph of her exists, five foot tall, wearing a starched cap and uniform, a diminutive figure of authority surrounded by her hospital staff of a hundred or more.

Isabella's independence of character must have been formed at an early age. As the youngest of eight children, she grew up in the limited confines of Haddington but, in 1901, was summoned to Kansas to nurse her brother Patrick's recently born son who had become ill. Great-Uncle Patrick had, ten years earlier, at the age of eighteen, set off to America. Landing in New York, he worked his way south to New Orleans in the State of Louisiana. When his funds ran out, he found employment as a cowpuncher in Texas, moving on to Kansas City where he became a cashier with the Fowler Packing Company.

In 1897 he married Janet Wise from Lincoln, Nebraska.[4] It was not long after the birth of their son, William Tod, that Isabella was sent for in 1901.

No ruby slippers for Isabella. Her journey to America involved a sea voyage and an overland rail, stagecoach and horseback journey of 5,000 miles. To put it into historical context, President William McKinlay had just been assassinated while attending the Pan-American Exhibition at Buffalo, Texas, and Theodore Roosevelt was being sworn in as America's youngest president to date. Later that same year, Guglielmo Marconi signalled the first Morse code letter 'S' across the Atlantic by wireless telegraph. It was to be another two years before the first coast-to-coast automobile trip, from San Francisco to New York, took place.

I deeply regret having been too young to interrogate the Little Aunt about her adventures in Kansas and she left no written record of them. However, on a visit to Charlotte, North Carolina, in 1983, I met Cousin Bill whom she had made her epic journey to nurse. She and I were the only relatives from Scotland he had ever met, and he told me that her name, coupled with her two-year sojourn in the USA, had become part of the folklore of his particular branch of the family.

Back in Scotland, there was talk of a suitor in the years immediately prior to the Great War but the whisper was that he fell at Flanders. Like her sisters, Isabella never married and, in 1956, died at the age of eighty-one at St Baldred's Tower, a nursing home in North Berwick where she had regularly helped out after her retirement from Hull.

Before becoming a nursing home, St Baldred's Tower had been the home of Robert Chambers, of the well-known Scottish publishing family. Those were the days when prominent members of British society who were not stalking the deer in the Highlands appeared in North Berwick for the months of August and September. Not without reason did the town become known as the Biarritz of the North. As Field Marshal Lord Kitchener played golf on the West Links in 1903, HMS *Dreadnought*, sailing past on its way to Rosyth, fired a ten-gun salute.[5]

And among those who owned properties around the town were the wealthy Astor, McAlpine and Coates families. Lady Astor, the American wife of the 2nd Viscount Astor, was the first woman to become a Member of the British Parliament and once addressed the House on the perfect happiness of nine days in North Berwick. The perfect happiness she referred to involved, of course, eighteen holes of golf a day.[6] A fine oil painting by Sir John Lavery of 1920 shows her in full swing.[7]

Francis Tennant, brother-in-law of H. H. Asquith, the pre-First World War British Prime Minister, owned Hyndford House on Fidra Road, which was inherited by his son Hugh. It has now been divided into seven apartments. Asquith's son by his first marriage married Lady Cynthia Charteris, daughter of the 11th Earl of Wemyss, and Francis's niece, Lucy Tennant, married the 11th Earl's second son, so there were close connections with Gosford House.

Moreover, it was Alfred Lyttleton, husband of Asquith's deceased sister Laura, who built Greywalls at Gullane (see Chapter 24). In a prime situation overlooking the seventh hole of the West Golf Course, Sir Patrick Ford, Solicitor General for Scotland and patron of the artist Sir John Lavery, occupied the imposing mansion of Wester Dunes. The small and delightful formal garden, which Lavery designed for him in the early 1920s, remains intact.

The East Lothian coast continued as a holiday retreat for the great and the good throughout the first half of the twentieth century and a great time was had by all. In 1933 the Reverend Hector Macpherson of Wardie Crescent, Edinburgh, felt obliged to write a letter of complaint to the Countess of Oxford and Asquith concerning the behaviour of a group of her house guests on North Berwick Golf Course. These included her granddaughter who, when he had remonstrated with her about her conduct, spat at him.[8]

The North Berwick of my childhood I remember as a windy place of unpredictable sunshine and frequent rain which largely kept me and my sisters indoors to complete endless jigsaw puzzles. So far as I can tell, not much has altered in the intervening years apart from the car parking problems, which are ubiquitous. The Little Aunt's house in The Quadrant being small, my parents, sisters and I would stay at the Marine Hotel, where she would join us for lunch.

Sometimes my sisters and I would climb to the top of North Berwick Law to marvel at the 23-foot-high arch of whale jawbones which have now been removed. First placed there in 1789,[9] they were replaced in 1860 and then again in 1933.[10] In the summer of 2007, to draw attention to their absence, somebody unknown created an arch of old drainpipes but these were rapidly removed by the authorities. Happily, replica jawbones, cast in fibreglass, wood and steel from the ones that were removed in 2005, were airlifted by helicopter and planted on top of the Law in June 2008. I suppose this is better than nothing as, for me, North Berwick was never the same without them.

Glancing through Doreen Sayers' *Scrapbook* tribute to her father and grandfather, I came across a photograph of Ben Sayers with a group of friends in America. On the left-hand side stands a fair, good-looking young man. Underneath has been inscribed 'Jimmy Richardson, exBS, NB'. My immediate reaction was that this must have been the Jimmy Richardson I had known as a child but further investigation proved him to be a North Berwick-born contemporary of the same name – one of Ben Sayers' club-makers who emigrated to America in 1921. It struck me then how little I knew about my father's friend – or rather the friend of my Great-Uncle Harry whose death in 1905 at the age of thirty-two had deeply affected his family. A small watercolour portrait of Harry by Jimmy has survived and shows that the latter possessed a very considerable talent. He especially loved to draw cartoons and ruthlessly parodied the foibles of the Provosts, Town Clerks and Councillors of North Berwick from the turn of the century.

James Smith Richardson – architect, artist, archaeologist, antiquarian, writer, historian and teacher – was born in Edinburgh in 1883, the second of the five sons – John, James, David, Adam and Arthur – of Dr James T. Richardson. Dr Richardson, who studied both at Edinburgh University and in Vienna, did not practice medicine and appears to have had independent means. He and his wife Christina, a sister of Arthur Thomson, the first Professor of Anatomy at Oxford University, brought their family, which also included a daughter, Mary, to North Berwick in 1887.

After schooling at the Abbey School, North Berwick, Jimmy studied drawing at the old Royal Scottish Academy Institute and architecture in the office of Robert Lorimer. In 1906 he travelled to England with the conservationist and writer Aymer Vallance, absorbing a lasting knowledge and love of woodcarving.[11] His appreciation of craftsmanship had already shown itself by 1910 and his design for the carved wooden chancel screen at St Baldred's Church in North Berwick was favourably reviewed in *The Studio*, the leading contemporary magazine of applied and fine art.

Jimmy became a Fellow of the Society of Antiquaries of Scotland in 1912 and, in 1914, was appointed the first (part-time) Inspector of Ancient Monuments for Scotland under Sir Charles Peers. However, with the outbreak of war he was commissioned into the local battalion of the 2/8 Royal Scots, which meant he was obliged to give up work and spend the duration of the war in England, Ireland and France. His youngest brother Arthur was killed while serving with the Argyll and Sutherland Highlanders at the Battle of Loos in 1915.

John Richardson served in the 8th Royal Scots in the trenches and was wounded at the Somme and Passchendaele. His brother David had already enlisted as a doctor with the RAMC and served in Aden and India, then afterwards in Jamaica and London, retiring in 1945 as Director of Hygiene for British and Empire Forces.

On being demobilised, Jimmy formed an architectural partnership with John Ross McKay who had also worked for Lorimer. In 1920, the post of Inspector of Ancient Monuments in Scotland was made full-time and, two years later, he was invited by John Begg to become a part-time lecturer in architectural history at Edinburgh College of Art. The following year he married Frances Stevenson, widow of Lieutenant-Commander David Douglas who had been killed at the Battle of Jutland in 1916. Frances was a granddaughter of David Stevenson and therefore a first cousin once removed of Robert Louis Stevenson.

'They did have a happy time to begin with but it was a difficult marriage as they were both strong characters,' said Jean Leslie, Frances's daughter. 'My sister Bettina Thomson and I were immensely fond of him and he was tremendously good with us when we were children.' The couple separated in the early 1940s.

Throughout the 1920s and 1930s Jimmy travelled Scotland from end to end and, working with Sir John Stirling Maxwell, Chairman of the Ancient Monuments Advisory Board, set the wheels in motion for the Crown to acquire Scotland's best-known tourist attractions. Under his guidance, many great projects of excavation and restoration, from Shetland to the Mull of Galloway, were undertaken. Assisted by Frances, he wrote the official guide books for literally dozens of Scotland's abbeys, castles and ancient monuments and it was he who first located a Stone Age dwelling at Skara Brae on Orkney, a discovery which later led to the village being excavated by Professor Vere Gordon Childe.

In 1948 the University of St Andrews conferred upon him the degree of Doctor of Law, honoris causa. That same year he delivered the prestigious Rhind Lectures, choosing as his subject the medieval stonemason in Scotland. By this stage his reputation was such that, when Queen Elizabeth, the Queen Mother purchased the Castle of Mey in Caithness, it was to Jimmy that she turned for advice.

A Richardson family story relates to Her Majesty visiting him at his home and being shown around the house, which was an Aladdin's cave of treasures. The kitchen was out of bounds because of the state it was in but she insisted on putting her head around the door for a look. Her comment was, 'Oh, Dr Richardson!'

Some months later, he was waiting for the ferry at South Queensferry when he was summoned over to speak to the Queen Mother, who was also travelling north. 'Is your house as untidy as ever?' she enquired.

Jimmy's local contribution was equally valuable. He designed the North Berwick War Memorial and excavated the ruins of the town's twelfth-century parish church. In September 1961, my father and I joined him at Gourock, where we embarked upon a National Trust for Scotland cruise around the Scottish coastline on the SS *Dunera*. Also on board, as I recall, were the Earl of Wemyss, Lord MacLeod of Fuinary, founder of the Iona Community, the well-known ornithologist Henry Douglas Home and the novelist Eric

Linklater. Circumnavigating Scotland, we visited St Kilda, Inverewe, Orkney and Shetland and Jimmy lectured on our architectural heritage, auctioning off some of his impromptu sketches for charity. In my files I have an eight-millimetre ciné film I made of the trip which I have always intended to have made into a DVD. Perhaps now I will have this done. Sheila Richardson, the wife of Jimmy's nephew Arthur, remembers the Richardson family being instructed to line up in the front garden of Tantallon Terrace to wave as the ship sailed up the Firth of Forth to dock at North Queensferry on its return. Naturally, it was far too far away for them to be noticed.

'When one stood behind him and watched the keenness of his eye and listened to his tentative comments and speculations, it was almost as though the long-departed masons and the stones themselves spoke to him,' remembered North Berwick's Provost J. C. Fowler.[12]

That was exactly how I felt when I began this journey standing in front of a window at Hailes Castle. The old man did not talk down to you – he shared his sense of fun and encouraged you to think for yourself. David Richardson, his great-nephew, concurs. 'Uncle Jimmy died when I was twelve,' he said, 'but, as my family lived downstairs on the ground floor at Tantallon Terrace and he had the two upper floors, I spent a lot of time looking through old things with him. As he did not own a television, he would also come downstairs most evenings to watch the news. When he did, I would get him to draw things for me – Vikings being my particular favourite. It was because of him that I went on to study archaeology at university.'

And it was through his knowledge and under his guidance that the North Berwick Museum was officially opened in 1957 by Provost Gilbert. Ten years later, North Berwick Town Council conferred upon him the Freedom of the Burgh, making him the town's youngest Burgess. At the time he noted that, if any of the promises he was obliged to make under the terms of the oath were broken, he would be expected to pay £100 Scots or to remain in prison until that sum was paid. 'It is comforting to know that this sum is no longer legal tender and that there is no longer any prison under the direct control of North Berwick Town Council,' he informed the 500 townsfolk who assembled for the ceremony.[13]

Jimmy ended his days at Tantallon Terrace, his childhood home, part of which his nephew's family still owns. There cannot be many families in North Berwick still living in the house that their forebears bought over 120 years ago.

'Tantallon Terrace with its upstairs window, looking over the lovely bay with its rocks and yellow sands and ever-changing tides and restless waves, the room behind so crowded with collected treasures, carved wood figures, porcelain bowls and oil paintings,' wrote Provost Fowler in a tribute published on Jimmy's death in 1970 in the *East Lothian Courier*.[14] In May 1971 a plaque was unveiled in his memory at the North Berwick Museum by the Lord Lieutenant Sir Hew Hamilton-Dalrymple.

In collating this information on Dr Jimmy, I must add that I am immensely grateful to Norma Buckingham, a local historian, who had been preparing a biography on him before her untimely death in 2007. The file which she compiled is full of compelling late-Victorian and early-Edwardian photographs. They evoke an era when life, at least for the residents of North Berwick, appears to have been infinitely more gentle than in the decades that were to follow.

As I write this, the North Berwick Museum, housed in the commodious rooms of the former Burgh School, in School Road, has been closed for some time. The building also houses the library, which remains open. Happily, in response to a petition of over 7,000 names, the Friends of the Museum and other community groups have now pledged to find ways of re-opening the museum section.

Today, North Berwick is still a favoured retreat for the wealthy and successful, as property prices confirm. Wester Dunes is owned by the American businessman John Inslay. Lord Macfarlane of Bearsden, the Glasgow industrialist and President Emeritus of the international drinks giant Diageo, has a home here, as does the 15th Duke of Hamilton's brother, Lord Douglas of Selkirk, formerly Lord James Douglas-Hamilton, who, in his long political career, served as both a Member of Parliament and a Member of the Scottish Parliament.

To the east of the town there is Tantallon Castle, which squats defiantly on a high cliff top, overlooking the Bass Rock slightly to the north. The greater part of this formidable stronghold is in a ruinous state, although it has to be observed that the approach road and encroaching verges are neatly manicured with Historic Scotland's usual obsessive meticulousness.

As the fourteenth-century stronghold of the Red Douglas, Tantallon was considered impregnable – that was until it fell first to the stealth of the Covenanters in 1638, then to General Monck thirteen years later. Given its dark and turbulent history under siege, there is a certain charm in its having derived its name, not from any great Pictish or Roman territorial provenance, but from its original superintendents, Thomas and Allan, who carved their names on the walls – 'Tam et Allan'.[15]

CHAPTER TWENTY-SEVEN

Shipwrecks, Saints and Sandy Beaches

ORAL TRADITION HAS IT that, in either the seventh or eighth century, St Baldred made the shoreline of Auldhame and Scoughall (pronounced the same as 'skull') his headquarters, bequeathing his name to a rock formation in the bay known as St Baldred's Boat. Nine hundred years later, there is yet another equally potent, but largely forgotten, figure associated with this area – John Mair. Some historians, including John Martine, insist on referring to him as John Major – not to be confused, of course, with the late twentieth-century British Prime Minister, although it is quite entertaining to speculate on their being related.

John Mair (I prefer to use the less conflicting surname) was born on the farm at Glenhornie in 1469 and, after schooling in Haddington, studied in Paris and Cambridge, later becoming Canon of the Chapel Royal in Glasgow. In 1518 he penned an important early history of Scotland but, more significantly, seven years later he took up the post of teacher of theology at St Andrews University where he coached not only the young John Knox but also the humanist scholar George Buchanan and George Wishart.

Mair was nothing if not forthright in his views of the Roman Church and its abuses. More controversial still, he dared to dismiss the Divine Right of Kings. He was prepared to accept that monarchs were chosen by God but ultimately their authority derived from the people they governed and they, he insisted, were perfectly entitled to get rid of them should they fail in their duties.[1] In medieval Europe such opinions were considered inflammatory and therefore made a significant impact on Mair's students, many of whom were to become champions of the Reformation. As fate would have it, Mair died in 1550, just at the time that his ideology was starting to gain momentum.

In his *Reminiscences*, John Martine writes of Seacliff House and grounds as having 'command of some of the finest sea views that are anywhere to be met with. The land is of the best quality, much of it stretches along the coast to Peffer Side and is light, sandy and benty.'

Three storeys high, with turrets at each corner, Seacliff House was built in 1843 for George Weir, a merchant in Leith, by architects Francis Farquharson and David Bryce. Twenty years later, along with the farms of Scoughall and Auldhame, the estate was bought by John Watson Laidlay, who had made a fortune manufacturing dye from indigo in Calcutta. It next passed to his eldest son, Andrew Laidlay, a scientist, who constructed a small harbour on the Gheghan Rock in the bay and, on the South Car Rock, rebuilt St Baldred's Beacon, a warning tower surmounted by a cross that had been erected by medieval monks.

Andrew's brother, John E. Laidlay, was a celebrated golfer, a two-time British Amateur Champion and runner-up in the 1888, 1890 and 1893 British Opens. In 1899, at Invereil House at Dirleton, he built himself his own miniature golf course, overlooking the eighth fairway on the West Links. A uniquely versatile man, he played cricket for Scotland, pioneered wildlife photography and carved wood.[2]

There are some disastrous events where it is often best simply to refer to the newspaper accounts of the time and that is what I have chosen to do here. In July 1907, the following report appeared in the *Haddingtonshire Courier*, under the headline 'Seacliff Mansion Destroyed By Fire. Mr Andrew Laidlay's Tragic Fate':

> A more tragic event has seldom occurred in the annals of East Lothian than the destruction by fire early on Saturday morning of the beautiful mansion house of Seacliff, accompanied as it was by the death of its popular proprietor Mr Andrew Laidlay, who fell a victim to the flames and was buried amid the ruins. The mansion house occupies a lovely site east of Tantallon, about four miles from North Berwick, and the family have long been associated with the county.
>
> It appears that shortly after two o'clock on Sunday morning the table maid and kitchen maid were awakened by a crackling sound in their bedroom, and thereafter some article of furniture was heard to fall. They rose to acquaint the housemaid, who slept in another apartment, that something was seriously wrong. By this time the smoke was issuing from parts of the house, and the housemaid went outside and threw gravel at the windows of Miss Laidlay's bedroom, which was on the top storey, to alarm her. Miss Laidlay, at once taking in the situation, went to apprise Mrs Laidlay, and both escaped from Mrs Laidlay's bedroom, also on the top storey, by means of knotted sheets tied to the knob of the window, climbing hand over hand and reaching the balcony on the second storey in this way. A ladder was then procured by someone and they reached the ground safely from the balcony by means of it. The fire had spread so rapidly that they were glad to escape from the doomed building in

their nightdresses. A gallant attempt was early made by the housemaid, Miss Effie Hamilton, to get inside her master's bedroom. She was forced back by the smoke and heat, and compelled to retire.

It was now noticed that the fire was evidently spreading up from the library below and situated on the second floor, the incidents mentioned having happened in less time that it takes to fall. Meanwhile, one of the servants having telephoned to the gamekeeper, Mr Forsyth, he in turn telephoned to North Berwick Coastguard Station and on North Berwick Fire Brigade being communicated with, they were very promptly at the scene of the conflagration. Firemaster W. Ross Young and his staff were at the fire about half an hour after being summoned shortly after 4 a.m. There was, however, great scarcity of water, as, beyond a few gallons in one of the wells, the only source was the sea, which is at a very considerable distance off, and between one hundred and two hundred feet below the site on which the mansion house was built.

Owing to the precipitous and rocky nature of the ground, the fire engine was only with great difficulty pulled along the sand and gravel to the edge of the water, and had repeatedly to be shifted over the rocks with the receding tide. Mr Ross Young and his firemen had been hard at work since their arrival, the leading of the hose right over the cliff towards the sea occasioning some difficulty in itself. But even if there had been quite a plentiful water supply, the brigade could have done practically nothing to save the mansion house as the main block was belching forth flames, and the roof was, indeed, fast falling in ere their arrival, the fire having evidently broken out hours before the household was alarmed. The safe was afterwards recovered intact.

The fire probably originated about the library, at the west end of the building, and must have sped at a rapid pace through the corridors until it reached the extremity of the western block, a freshening westerly wind prevailing. Under the circumstances, the firemen's attention was chiefly confined to preventing the fire spreading to the kitchen and laundry block, and in this they were partially successful in cutting off the fire about the middle of the kitchen block.

The cause is shrouded in mystery, but a not unlikely conjecture is that Mr Laidlay had been reading late in the library and had turned the light of his paraffin lamp on the table too far up and had possibly dozed over, the silk and lace lampshade probably catching fire and igniting the curtains close by.

In 1914, such accommodation as survived was requisitioned by the Royal Navy and became known as HMS *Scottish Seacliff*. Following the end of the Great War, the estate was purchased by John Robert Dale, who had been the tenant of Scoughall Farm since 1848 and of Auldhame since 1834 (see Chapter 9). In 1871, John Robert's son Thomas married Joanna Smith, the daughter of an indigo planter in India. A woman of immense character, as is revealed in a paper she wrote entitled 'Scoughall Jottings', she lived continually at Scoughall for seventy-three years, latterly carrying an ear trumpet suspended around her neck since, without it, she could hear nothing. Born in India in 1851, her family had skirted the Cape of Good Hope before the Suez Canal was created and, since the voyage took six months, by the time they reached Britain, the six-year-old Joanna had learned to read, write, recite poetry, do sums and even to knit.[3]

Some years into her marriage, she recalled a visit from John Martine, then in his eighties, who told her of his having seen George IV ride up the Canongate of Edinburgh on his celebrated visit of 1822. John Martine was eleven years old and the old lady of the house had leaned over his shoulder and said to him, 'Ah, my boy, I can remember looking out of this very same window to see Prince Charlie ride past.' That would have been in 1745.[4]

Joanna's father was the youngest brother of Robert Louis Stevenson's maternal grandmother, who was married to the Reverend Dr Lewis Balfour of Colinton Manse. Although her father was the uncle of Stevenson's mother, Joanna and Robert Louis were only a year apart in age and therefore spent much of their childhood together. When Joanna married Thomas Dale in 1871, it was Robert Louis who proposed the toast to the bridesmaids.[5]

And it was a letter from Joanna that inspired him to write *The Wreckers*, his last book, co-authored with his stepson Lloyd Osborne. A great many vessels used to come ashore on the Scoughall coast before the Barns Ness, Bass and Fidra lighthouses were built between 1901 and 1903 and her letter had described such an event. Her husband was the first officer of the Volunteer Rocket Apparatus and, as the tide retreated, crowds of men searched the rocks for bodies. Thomas described it as a weird scene, reminiscent of olden times when the 'pagans of Scoughall' tied a horse's head to its knee and attached a lantern to the rope before driving the horse slowly along the cliff tops. Vessels in the Firth of Forth would think that they were seeing a ship riding at anchor and, coming closer inshore, were wrecked and plundered.

Elsewhere, she refers to a vessel carrying brandy; £3,000-worth of the liquor was recovered and sealed up in a barn but a number of men died from drinking an excess of it combined with the seawater that had penetrated the leaky casks.

Around 1700, a colony of weavers occupied Halfland Barns, on a small ridge south of Tantallon. In her 'Scoughall Jottings', Joanna Dale mentions that a Laird of Lochhouses fought at the Battle of Dunbar in 1650 but, when it became apparent that the Scots were being routed, he slunk home unaware that he was being followed by an English soldier who shot him dead on his doorstep. His house was then occupied by field labourers, among them a family called Gloag. When the Gloag father was carried off by a press gang, his wife supported their family by growing flax which she then steeped in the Peffer Burn and wove into linen. The Gloags were much valued by their employers at Auldhame and Glenhornie and Joanna writes that a web of the mother's weaving was bequeathed to her when the last of the sons died. A piece of it was sent by her to the 11th Earl of Haddington who, in acknowledging it, told her that, before its arrival, he and his factor had been going over the old leases and had come across one which stipulated that no more flax was to be grown at Lochhouses as it impoverished the soil.

Lochhouses in the twenty-first century is farmed by Robert Dale and his wife Michele and produces potatoes, wheat and barley, Brussels sprouts and turnips. They also keep cattle on the grassland slopes near the sea. This area is also managed as a wetland for wading birds such as ducks, oystercatchers, swans, geese and moorhens. Lochhouses supports the wild grey partridge replenishment scheme and, in 2007, Robert became the first recipient of the Dodseed East Lothian Grey Partridge Trophy. In keeping with the diversification necessary in every landed venture nowadays, he and Michele provide tented holidays close to the beach through Feather Down Farm Days. Inside a small boat that has been recycled for use as an administrative office, they have a display telling the story of the Dale family.

South of North Berwick lie the two landed estates of Balgone and Leuchie. Reputations are fairly or unfairly earned. In retrospect, I find it difficult to decide if Sir Philip Grant-Suttie, 8th Baronet of Balgonie, who died in 1997, deserved his or not, although I suspect that at times he rather enjoyed it. The reason I feel sensitive on this subject is that I fell into a trap when writing his obituary for the *Scottish Daily Mail* and, having done so, opened the paper to discover my name over a largely edited chunk of copy into which had been inserted extracts from several of that newspaper's cuttings files. The opening paragraph, for example, read, 'Fast cars, private planes, glamorous women and the faintest whiff of notoriety were all part of the life of one of Scotland's last playboy aristocrats.' Well, it was the *Scottish Daily Mail*. What else would you expect?

Inserted into my restrained and sensitively written text, which I had mercifully read to his former wife Elspeth over the phone before filing my copy to the paper, were details of his facing a charge for driving while nearly four times over the legal drink limit, of his having boasted of keeping ten women on the go at the same time and of his abandoning his Cessna 172 light aeroplane on a sandy beach on the Ayrshire coast after having radioed for help over Loch Fyne. A massive sea and air rescue search was launched but Philip and his two passengers had already made their way back to East Lothian unaware of the panic they had created. The latter story I had known about but tactfully omitted. Nor had I mentioned the dozens of women of my acquaintance who were utterly besotted by him. Believe me, many a frustrated bachelor at the time was desperate to know the secret of his infallible magnetism.

The Grant-Suttie family of Balgone, Sheriffhall, have played an influential role in East Lothian since the early eighteenth century. Balgone House, however, dates from the fifteenth century when it belonged to the Nunnery and Prioress of North Berwick. After the Reformation, the estate passed through several owners, including the Hepburns of Wachton to Marion, daughter of John Semple, Writer to the Signet, and his wife Anna Sydeserf who, in her widowhood, succeeded Janet Dalrymple, the real-life 'Bride of Lammermoor', as the second wife of Sir David Dunbar of Baldoon, in Wigtownshire.[6]

In 1680, Marion married George Suttie, the representative in Edinburgh of an eminent Dutch mercantile house and who, in 1701, became one of the last Baronets of Nova Scotia to be created. His son, Sir James Suttie Bt, married Agnes Grant of Prestongrange in 1818 and, in order to inherit that property, assumed the surname Grant-Suttie (see Chapter 17). In the nineteenth century, the 2nd and 4th Grant-Suttie baronets represented Haddingtonshire in the Westminster parliament. In his *Reminiscences*, John Martine writes of a well-known North Berwick character called Matthew Cassie who lived in that century and, when asked by a traveller the name of the Grant-Suttie estate, replied in the vernacular, 'Begone, Sir.' The traveller asked again and received the same reply.

'You are a very impertinent fellow,' the traveller informed Matthew.

Philip Grant-Suttie was born in Canada in 1938, son of Major George Grant-Suttie, a grandson of the 2nd Baronet, who died in 1940. Seven years later he succeeded his uncle, who had died childless and, in 1960, having finished his education in New Brunswick, the 8th Baronet of Balgone set off to conquer Scotland.

With his rakish charm, good looks and Newfoundland drawl, Sir Philip rapidly made a favourable impact on the social circles into which he was thrown and it was no exaggeration that women found him irresistible. In 1962 he married Elspeth, daughter of the Second World War *Bridge Too Far* hero, Major-General Sir Roy Urquhart. The marriage ended in 1969 and Elspeth became the wife of Sir Menzies Campbell who, in 1987, was elected Liberal Member of Parliament for North-East Fife and, from 2006 to 2007, was leader of the Liberal Democrat Party.

Following his divorce, Sir Philip did become a bit of a wild card but that did not mean that he was a bad landowner – quite the opposite. On taking over Balgone and Sheriffhall, he took over the estate farms which had previously been tenanted and set about creating a thriving agricultural business, a legacy which his son James, the 9th Baronet, continues, although Balgone itself was sold in 1989 to Alan Dean, whose son Marcus removed the Victorian extension in 1992. Balgone House, the North Lodge and the Coach House are today B-listed.

Sir Philip's fascination with flight earned him the sobriquet of 'The Flying Bart' and, for a time, he ran a sideline in selling helicopters. A remarkably well-read man, he would proudly boast that through his Nova Scotia ancestors he was a genuine descendant of the Míkmaq people – 'Míkmaq' meaning, in the tribal language, 'My Friends'. Perhaps that was the secret of his attraction.

At a time when I contributed on a regular basis to a Scottish lifestyle magazine, I was approached by the then editor to write a historic feature on the Dalrymple family. I jokingly began my essay with 'In the modern age he would have been sent to The Hague and charged with crimes against humanity. Instead, they gave him an earldom.' When the editor, a friend of the family, read this, he looked uncomfortable. The article remained unpublished.

I was, of course, referring to John Dalrymple, the Master of Stair (eldest son of the 1st Viscount Stair) who, in 1692, in his capacity as King William's joint-Secretary of State for Scotland, signed the order for the Massacre of Glencoe. On his instructions, forty Highlanders of the Clan MacIan Macdonald who had provided overnight hospitality for a regiment of government troops were put to the sword in the winter snows of the north-west Highlands. The official charge was that the MacIan Chief had been late in swearing an oath of allegiance to the incoming British monarch.

Memories of wrong-doings linger long in the Scottish psyche, particularly in the Highlands, but in the Lothians, among those who favoured the arrival of a Protestant monarch on the British throne, the dispatch of a few troublesome savages located in a remote and largely inaccessible region far to the north, was viewed by many at the time as good riddance, regardless of the circumstances. Only a few, such as Andrew Fletcher of Saltoun, who chanced to be dining with Stair when the report of the murders was delivered, were outraged.[7]

A judicial enquiry followed but Dalrymple and his alleged fellow conspirator Sir Thomas Livingstone, who had commanded the armed forces in Scotland, were exonerated. In 1703, Queen Anne created him 1st Earl of Stair. Only eleven years earlier, his third son, Sir Hew Dalrymple, had purchased the North Berwick Estate, including Tantallon Castle and the Bass Rock. In 1698, he succeeded his father as Lord President of the Court of Session, taking the judicial title of Lord North Berwick.

It was a privileged little world but it worked if you had the right connections, leaving Sir Walter Scott to observe that the family of Dalrymple had, within two centuries, produced 'as many men of talent, civil and military, political and professional eminence, as any house in Scotland'. A fervent supporter of the 1707 Act of Union, the Lord President planted several now substantial beech trees on North Berwick Law to commemorate the occasion.[8] The eldest of his five sons married twice and had seven sons and three daughters; the second son, Lord Drummore, a Law Lord, had twelve children. Through marriage, the dynasty acquired the Bargeny Estate in Ayrshire and adopted the surname Dalrymple-Hamilton, while east-coast family members retain that of Hamilton-Dalrymple.

The A-listed Leuchie House has been the ancestral home of the North Berwick Dalrymples since 1699. In 1960, the family moved to a smaller property in the walled garden, designed by the architects Law and Dunbar-Naismith. The main house was used as a convent for nine years, next becoming a Richard Cave Holiday Home and then a Multiple Sclerosis Society hospice.

In 1982, Sir Hew Hamilton-Dalrymple, 10th Baronet, was appointed Lord-Lieutenant of East Lothian. Of his four sons, Hew, the eldest, manages the family interests, Father Jock is a Catholic priest, Robert runs a successful print design business in Edinburgh and William Dalrymple is the author of a series of best-selling travel and history books which include *From the Holy Mountain: A Journey in the Shadow of Byzantium*, *In Xanadu: A Quest* and *The Last Mughal: The Fall of a Dynasty, Delhi, 1857*.

It would appear that Sir Walter Scott's observation still holds true.

CHAPTER TWENTY-EIGHT

The Village of those Dwelling by the River Tyne

THE VILLAGE OF Whitekirk owes its early celebrity to a visit from Aeneas Sylvius Piccolomini, the future Pope Pius II who, in 1435, having survived a fearful storm in the Firth of Forth, was put ashore at Dunbar in the depth of winter and declared that, to give thanks for his survival, he would walk barefoot to the nearest shrine dedicated to Our Lady. Had he known that this would involve a ten-mile hike across the frozen fields to Whitekirk, he might perhaps have changed his mind. As it was, after fulfilling his avowal, he suffered from gout and damaged feet for the remainder of his life. I have as much sympathy for him as I have for cyclists who wear Lycra shorts during the midge season.

Aeneas Sylvius was sent to Scotland by the papal legate Cardinal Albergati, although the purpose of his mission remains a puzzle. However, it must have been considered of some significance since a fresco survives in the library of Siena Cathedral depicting his audience with James I, despite the artist Bernadino Pintoriccio's backdrop looking suspiciously Italian.

That Aeneas Sylvius was a ladies' man becomes apparent in his autobiography when he remarks that the Scottish women were 'good looking and comely and gave their lips as freely and readily as Italian women did their hands'.[1] Oh that Pope Benedict XV1 should make such a statement!

Whitekirk's first house of prayer was constructed in the twelfth century under the jurisdiction of the Abbey of Holyrood. When the waters of a nearby well were found to cure infertility, Whitekirk emerged as an important medieval spa for pilgrims. A shrine to Our Lady was erected and, by the following century, was attracting in the region of 16,000 pilgrims a year. This was sufficient for James I to give orders for hostels to accommodate them.

But, under constant threat of an English invasion from the south, Whitekirk needed to be defended and, by 1537, Whitekirk Castle had been built on top of the hill. This was held by the St Clair Family of Rosslyn until it was destroyed in 1544 by the Earl of Hertford's soldiers. Its remains are today incorporated in a tithe barn dating from the seventeenth century. The holy well, alas, has long since dried up as a consequence of agricultural drainage during the nineteenth century.

Between 1913 and 1914 the Scottish Suffragette Movement claimed responsibility for twenty-nine acts of arson and these included an attack on Whitekirk Church in the early hours of 26 February 1914. Four days later, the *Scotsman* newspaper published the following report: 'All smouldering portions of burning material have now been extinguished and the roofless and scorched walls stand a melancholy proof to the success of the outrage.'

And an outrage it certainly caused. Burning country houses and public buildings was barely excusable but the destruction of a House of God was sacrilege. What exacerbated the situation was that no reason was given for Whitekirk's being chosen although, days earlier, a non-militant suffragette deputation had been snubbed by the Haddington Presbytery. If the Scottish Suffragette Movement had wanted publicity it certainly received it, but large numbers of its own followers were alienated as a consequence. In 1917, the architect Sir Robert Lorimer was employed to oversee a sympathetic restoration, both inside and out, and further repairs were instigated in 2005.

Search deep into the past and the placename of Tyninghame emerges as 'the village of those dwelling by the River Tyne', which does seem appropriate despite there being several other sites with an equal call upon such a distinction. Situated between North Berwick and Dunbar, the estate occupies a swathe of pretty pastureland that was much coveted by first-millennium Angles invading from Northumberland. Give or take a century or two, St Baldred, in oral tradition, founded a monastery here. At that time, the territory fell under the feudal possessions of the monks of Holy Island, otherwise known as Lindisfarne, so it is probable that Baldred originated from Northumberland.

In folklore, he is described as being a hermit who lived on the Bass Rock. There he built a chapel where he died on 6 March in either 603 or 606. The eleventh-century English monastic chronicler Symeon (or Simeon) of Durham was convinced otherwise, insisting that the year of his death was 756. So what's in a century or two when you become a saint?

Of course, if, as some insist, St Baldred was a contemporary of St Kentigern (otherwise known as St Mungo, which has always puzzled me), the founder of Glasgow, it would have had to have been the earlier option. But, regardless of which century either he or his namesake actually did occupy, it was undoubtedly Baldred who nourished the early Christian tradition of this particular corner of Scotland. Someone who actually managed to die in triplicate, leaving three corpses to be interred at Prestonkirk, Tyninghame and Auldhame, must have had something going for him.

From the end of the eleventh century, the lands of Tyninghame were held by the Lauders of Bass under feu to the Abbey of St Andrews. In 1628, the estate was purchased for 200,000 merks (approximately £1,100) by Sir Thomas Hamilton, Keeper of the Privy Seal of Scotland, a loyal supporter of James VI and I. Appointed Secretary of State for Scotland in 1613, he was created 1st Earl of Haddington by Charles I.

Things were shaping up rather well for this particular branch of the Hamilton Clan when, in the next generation, Thomas, 2nd Earl of Haddington, a staunch supporter of the Covenanters, was killed in the massive explosion which destroyed Dunglass Castle (see Chapter 30). Not much thereafter was achieved by his descendants but, around 1719, Charles, Lord Binning, son and heir of the 6th Earl, married Rachel Baillie and, as a result, Mellerstain House, near Kelso, thereafter became the family's principal seat. The village of Tyninghame was established as a planned estate community in 1761 and remained as such until 1950. The elegant, red sandstone Tudor-style Tyninghame House of today was extensively rebuilt as a second home for the 8th Earl of Haddington by William Burn in 1829. The 9th Earl was appointed First Lord of the Admiralty in Sir Robert Peel's government. When he died without a male heir, the earldom passed to his kinsman George Baillie, a descendant of the 6th Earl, who took the surname Baillie-Hamilton.

After the death of the 12th Earl of Haddington in 1986, his Canadian widow took up residence at Tyninghame while her son, the 13th Earl, and his family occupied the Mellerstain Estate. At Tyninghame she created a spectacular garden which she regularly opened to the public as one of the pioneers of the Scotland's Gardens Scheme. Following her death in 1987, a sale of Tyninghame House's contents – English and continental furniture, Gothic tapestries, English and Scottish silver and European and oriental ceramics – was overseen by the auction house Sotheby's and the mansion house sold for £250,000 to the property developer Kit Martin.

Kit Martin renovated and divided the property into nine apartments – his philosophy being to create a mixed community of different sized properties – and the house is divided vertically, with each section having its own entrance. Among those who moved into the house conversion were: Lord Briggs, the historian and author; Sir Timothy Clifford, director of the National Galleries of Scotland from 1984 until 2005; and Sir Alistair Grant, the industrialist (see Chapter 7). Others, equally diverse and creative, soon followed to take up other residences on the estate: David Gillon and the late James Thompson, who had acquired the Edinburgh-based interior decorating firm of

Drysdales from Derek Parker and Peter Morris at Yester House (see Chapter 10); Willa, Lady Elphinstone, widow of the Queen's cousin, the 18th Lord Elphinstone, who is also one of Scotland's top interior decorators; and Nick and Priscilla Parry, who run Clock House Furniture in the Old Stables at Overhailes.

Lord Briggs, better known as the historian Asa Briggs, served in the British Intelligence Corps, working at the British wartime code-breaking station Bletchley Park. Post-war, his academic career embraced Worcester College, Oxford, Nuffield College, the Institute for Advanced Study, Princeton Township, New Jersey, the University of Leeds and the University of Sheffield. Having been made a Life Peer in 1976, he returned to Oxford to become Provost of Worcester College and was Chancellor of the Open University from 1978 to 1994. His best-known literary work is his trilogy, *Victorian People*, *Victorian Cities* and *Victorian Things.*

Timothy Clifford arrived in Scotland amid much excitement in 1984 to transform the National Gallery of Scotland. He began by double-hanging old master paintings against rich colours and, causing a considerable amount of controversy, added marbles, bronzes, Renaissance medals, prints and drawings to the gallery collection. As Director-General, he was additionally responsible for running the Scottish National Gallery of Modern Art, the Scottish National Portrait Gallery and 'outreach' galleries at Duff House in Banffshire and Paxton House in Berwickshire. A gregarious and often outspoken champion of his own beliefs, it was through his seemingly boundless energy that the money was found to acquire such treasures as Antonio Canova's *Three Graces*, Sandro Botticelli's *Madonna of the Rose Garden* (from Gosford House) and Gian Lorenzo Bernini's *Bust of Monsignor Carlo Antonio dal Pozzo.*

Since his retirement in 2005, Sir Timothy and Lady Clifford (he was knighted in 2003) have been renovating a property in Italy but their garden accommodation at Tyninghame remains a coup de théâtre. When I visited them in August 2007 we strolled gently down the avenue of lime trees at the rear of the house to admire the remaining Norman arches and enclosure of the twelfth-century Chapel of St Baldred, close to where their grandson, Mungo Curwen, was christened out of doors during a high gale in the spring of 2004. Happily, the spectacular gardens created by the Dowager Countess of Haddington in the last century are still maintained in all their glory.

In 2003, following a failed community woodland bid, a consortium, comprising the Dale and Gray farming families, succeeded in purchasing the 689-acre Lawhead Farm, Binning Wood and a sea-trout and salmon beat on the River Tyne.

The Bairds of Newbyth, close to Tyninghame, were yet another of East

Lothian's most remarkable families, emerging in the seventeenth century when James Baird from Auchmedden in Aberdeenshire was made a Commissioner of the Ecclesiastical Court. His son, Sir John, having acquired the Newbyth Estate, married Margaret, a daughter of Sir William Hay of Linplum, a brother of the 1st Marquis of Tweeddale. On becoming a Lord of Session he took the legal title of Lord Newbyth. In 1695, his son William was created a baronet of Nova Scotia, the title passing to his son John. Then, on his death without children in 1745, the baronetcy became extinct and the Newbyth Estate was inherited by his second cousin, another William.

'A gallant, hard-headed, lion-hearted officer' is how his commanding officer Arthur Wellesley, later 1st Duke of Wellington, described the surviving son of this William Baird. David Baird was born at Newbyth in 1757. Having entered the British Army as an ensign in the 2nd Foot Regiment in 1772, he rose to the rank of lieutenant and sailed to India as a captain in the 73rd. On his arrival in Madras in 1780, he was instantly plunged into the British offensive against Hyder Ali, the Shia Muslim leader of Mysore of southern India. It was a classic example of Empire politicians being naively unaware of what they were up against. The British forces were totally unprepared for the ensuing onslaught and, following the massacre of his soldiers, Baird himself was seized and held prisoner in one of Hyder Ali's fortresses.

On being released four years later as part of a prisoner exchange, Baird rejoined his regiment, now styled the 71st, and, after a two-year leave of absence, returned to India as a Lieutenant-Colonel. Having, by 1799, become a Major-General, he was in command of the storming party for the assault on Seringapatam, defended by Hyder Ali's brilliant and ruthless son, Tipu Sultan.

It was the final and most brutal confrontation of the fourth Anglo–Mysore War, which ended with Tipu Sultan being killed and Major-General Sir David Baird emerging as the hero of the hour. In recognition of his valour, he was formally presented with Tipu Sultan's sword as a souvenir.[2]

But his career did not end there. After leaving India, Sir David led the successful British expedition against Napoleon's forces in Egypt in 1801. Four years later he helped to capture the Cape of Good Hope in South Africa from the Dutch. Severely wounded at the Battle of Corunna in 1809, he retired to Scotland, where he died in 1829. For his achievements, he was created a baronet, with remainder to his brother Robert and heirs male, taking the territorial designation of Newbyth, as had his forebears in their previous baronetcy.

The British army remained in the Baird blood. The 2nd Baronet, Sir David's nephew, a captain in a cavalry regiment, fought at the Battle of

Waterloo and was severely wounded. Both the 3rd Baronet, another Sir David, and his brother William fought in Africa – the former in the Kaffir War, the latter in the Ashantee War.

In 1864, the 3rd Baronet, another Sir David, married Ellen Stuart, second daughter and co-heir of the 12th Lord Blantyre, and thus the Bairds acquired the Lennoxlove Estate (see Chapter 2). With the death of the 4th Baronet in 1941, the Baird baronetcy along with the Lennoxlove and Newbyth Estates was inherited by his nephews.

During the Second World War Newbyth House was commandeered as an army hospital and then converted into a convalescent home. In 1946, concurrent with his brother Robert Baird selling Lennoxlove to the 14th Duke of Hamilton, Sir David Baird, the 5th Baronet, who had made his home in Perthshire, sold the Newbyth and Whitekirk farms to his tenants, James Gardner and William Main. The remaining land was disposed of to Irvine Chalmers-Watson of Fenton Barns who, in an exchange arrangement with Gardner, consolidated his holding with Kamehill.

In 1949, Chalmers-Watson built a second Newbyth House and used the land and the orchard for his family's turkey business. In 1972, just as work began on dividing it into flats, the old Newbyth House was severely damaged by a fire. Since then, the stable block has been converted into four apartments by the developer Christopher Weeks and the steading into seventeen houses by David Gallacher.[3] Among those who have their home here is Patrick Bourne, proprietor of the Bourne Fine Art Gallery in Edinburgh.

CHAPTER TWENTY-NINE

Instant Sunshine

SOMEWHERE IN MY subliminal consciousness, I recall it being said that Dunbar enjoys more sunshine hours than anywhere else in Scotland. All I can conclude from this is that my early visits to the town must have been badly mistimed. For me, Dunbar will forever be associated with the now closed open-air swimming pool. In family holidays of half-a-century ago, it always rained – not just the occasional gentle sprinkle but a repetitive, relentless drizzle that seemed to go on and on and on throughout the summer months.

Needless to say, we all thought this perfectly normal and swam in the pool regardless. So perhaps it is true what the pessimists say about global warming. On a visit to Belhaven Hill School sports day in the summer of 2007 to watch my godson Henry Dobson win the Victor Ludorum School Cup, I definitely acquired at least the basis of a suntan. Besides, there is no longer any reason to shiver on the diving board. Twenty-first-century Dunbar boasts a brand-new indoor leisure centre with pool, multi-gym and squash courts.

Of course, the town has grown beyond belief since I first knew it back in the 1950s. Yet seagulls still wheel and shriek over the waterfront where, in living memory, the herring fleet would gather between August and September. Despite the encroachment of housing, the reassuring ruins of the once-formidable Dunbar Castle can still be seen beside the harbour. It still seems so churlish that it should have been dismantled by order of the Scottish Parliament simply because Mary, Queen of Scots took refuge here in 1567.

The town centre, despite the rash of new building that encroaches upon it, still conjures up the period charm of the old coastal fishing town that I remember. An enjoyable diversion is still to lunch at the Rocks Bar and Restaurant on Marine Road, today owned by Jim Findlay (see Chapter 22), and I was gratified to discover that the Fishermen's Memorial of 1861 had been sensitively restored by the stone carver Michelle de Bruin in 1998. Yet another example of immortality at a cost, it was originally the work of the Musselburgh-born sculptor Alexander Handyside Ritchie, who died penniless.

In 1719, the Burgh of Dunbar levied a local tax on brewers to fund civic improvements but, providentially, the Belhaven Brewery was situated immediately beyond the town boundaries. Over the first half of the eighteenth century, it was known as Johnstone's, then Dudgeon's and, at one stage, had more than twenty-four competitors. Only three breweries – Dunbar, West Barns and Belhaven – kept going into the nineteenth century, the latter being the sole survivor. By 2005, Belhaven had become the largest and oldest independent brewery in Scotland and, that same year, ownership was acquired in a £187 million takeover by the Suffolk-based Greene King PLC.

At the end of Dunbar's High Street is Lauderdale House, formerly known as Dunbar House, which was built around 1740 by Captain James Fall, Member of Parliament for Haddington Burghs from 1734 until 1742. The Fall Family claimed descent from Johnny Faa, the King of the Gypsies (see Chapter 15), and, when Robert Burns visited Dunbar, riding into 'this neat little town like the Devil', he dined with Provost Robert Fall, Captain James's son.[1]

The Falls' wealth was accumulated from merchant trading activities through which they built up an empire encompassing the Baltic Ports, the Americas and the Low Countries. Accordingly, the family dominated Dunbar for most of the eighteenth century. Provost Charles Fall, for example, introduced the town's first fresh water supply from Spott in 1766. Provost Robert persuaded the council to build the harbour battery and a dry dock for the cleaning and repair of ships.

But, as political upheaval in Europe and the American Revolutionary War gained momentum, trade links fractured and the Fall family fell on hard times. In 1788, Dunbar House was sold to James Maitland, 8th Earl of Lauderdale, who commissioned the architects Robert and James Adam to remodel and extend it. As an admirer of the French Revolution and personal friend of the doomed activist Jean-Paul Marat, the 8th Earl was considered by many to be a contentious figure. Having led the Whigs in Scotland, in 1832 he crossed over to the Tory party and voted against the Reform Bill.

Lord Lauderdale died in 1839 at his principal seat of Thirlestane Castle and Lauderdale House at Dunbar was sold to the government as a military barracks. It was later appropriated by Dunbar Town Council and has, more recently, been divided into private apartments.

Given Lauderdale's Francophile sympathies, it was fitting that, following pupil exchanges between Dunbar Grammar School and the College of Lignières in France, Dunbar and the French town should be twinned. Through its John Muir association, Dunbar has also since been twinned with Martinez in California and Kingston, Massachusetts, both in the USA. Regular exchanges now take place between all three locations.

Situated four miles south of Dunbar, the village of Innerwick can appear pretty remote although, with the A1 a distance of less than a mile away, the old schoolhouse is today a centre for the promotion of countryside studies and outdoor activities.

For forty-seven years until 1967, Lizzie Patterson and her brothers Jockie and Nelson ran the 'midnight bakers of Innerwick'. From a black-leaded oven and spotlessly scrubbed wooden tables, deliveries were door-to-door, at first by horse and cart and then by van. 'We were never off the road, morning, noon and night, to get round our customers,' recalled Jockie, when interviewed at the time of the bakery's closure.

'During the war years, people just let us know where they kept their purse and, if they were out or perhaps asleep in bed, we would just walk in and take a look at their order on a piece of paper. They trusted us to go into their purses and take what was necessary and leave a note of it,' he said. 'I'll be sorry to see the bakery go,' he added, 'but you can't find young people to take an interest in the early starts. I don't suppose the oven will ever be used again but I've made an arrangement with an outside firm and they are going to base a van here.'[2]

Some years after the bake-house and shop closed, the property was bought and transformed into living accommodation. Close by, in a similar conversion, is the elegant home of Annabel Younger who came to live here from Baro at Gifford in 2005. 'I love being in Innerwick,' she said. 'There is a real sense of community. The house is at the top of the village and, looking north, I have views right over to the Fife coast.'

Designated a Conservation Area, Innerwick once formed the fulcrum for two great estates – Thurston, belonging to the Hunters, descendants of the old Ayrshire family of Hunter of Hunterston, and Innerwick, which was a landholding of the Hamilton-Nisbet-Ogilvys of Biel and Archerfield (see Chapters 16 and 23). Not a great deal has radically altered since John Martine wrote affectionately of the area over 100 years ago and highlighted its magical attributes:

> The geological structure of the hill tract of the parish is composed of a coarse conglomerate or plum-pudding stone, an off-shoot of the old red sandstone formation, interspersed with masses of greywacke, traversed by projecting dykes or veins of trap. The masses are most numerous on the farms of Aikengall and Elmscleuch, where the appearances present themselves in curious and fantastic shapes, which gave rise to the old popular idea that the 'Fairies' once upon a time had their dwelling place here. These distorted masses are still known in the neighbourhood as 'The Fairies' Castles'.

In 1938, my uncle David Martine married Janet Gregor. Her mother was Janet Wyllie, daughter of James Wyllie, who farmed Pathhead at Cockburnspath, Innerwick and Thurston Mains (see Chapter 2). In 1898 she had married Charles Gregor who, in due course, took over the running of Innerwick and Thurston Mains.

From 1926 Thurston Mains was taken on by Clunie Gregor, one of their twin sons. A hands-on career in farming, however, was not the destiny of his twin brother James who, having qualified as a botanist, became director of the Scottish Plant Breeding Centre at Pentlandfield, Roslin, from 1950 until 1956. The Gregor family nevertheless retained the Innerwick farm until Charles's death, after which it was sold in 1944 to Sir James Hope, who farmed Eastbarnes.[3] Clunie continued to farm Thurston Mains until a hip injury obliged him to retire in 1951.

Standing at the side of the Thurston Road as it leaves Innerwick village is the Jubilee Horse Trough designed by Walter Macfarlane & Co. of Glasgow. It was placed there in 1887 and carries a universal message to every lover of our four-legged friends:

> A man of kindness to his beast is kind
> But brutal actions show a brutal mind
> Remember he who made thee made the brute
> Who gave thee speech and reason made him mute
> He can't complain but God's all seeing eye
> Beholds thy cruelty and hears his cry
> He was designed thy servant not thy drudge
> Remember his creator is thy judge.

In 1989, the quarterly county magazine *East Lothian Life* was launched by Pauline Jaffray. Pauline's grandfather, Andrew Jaffray, was one of three brothers and a sister, all of whom were born at Braidwood, near Innerwick, and, as a family, operated smallholdings between Innerwick and Oldhamstocks.

When her father took up a job with Rank Hovis McDougall, Pauline found herself moving to England but hated it so much that, at the age of fifteen, she was allowed to move back to Scotland to live with her grandparents. 'Even though we lived in such a remote area, it was a blissful childhood,' she recalls. 'Routine was the norm. Up at 6 a.m., the fire was always ablaze and breakfast being prepared. We did our chores, came back for breakfast and caught the school bus. Dinner was always at twelve noon and consisted of healthy and substantial meat and two veg with a milk pudding to follow. Tea and biscuits at 3 p.m., tea at 5 p.m. and supper at 8 p.m.

'I always awoke to the wireless with my grandparents and parents listening to the farming programme. We did have a television which was switched on for the weather and news, Saturday wrestling and football results, when my granddad patiently checked his coupon and for a Saturday-night *Bonanza* treat. But, to be honest, we spent most of our time outdoors.

'A number of vans called each week, the "Store" butcher, the "Store" grocery van, the local baker, Dixon's hardware, Willie Sanderson with his boots and shoes, the fish man and so on. We were very well served and travelled by post bus or the Saturday bus which did the country trip to Dunbar for other requirements.

'Friday evening was when everyone visited and chattered, discussing, as well as local issues, the price of crops and whether the hens were laying well. Also the trick of how to make good girdle scones and who had won what at the local shows and markets. But it was only when my grandfather, dad and other family members died that I found all of the local folklore was disappearing.

'My grandfather kept a journal and drew illustrations in the margins. I also remember him reading a local magazine which kept him informed about what was going on. Since it no longer existed, I thought I'd start one myself. So much was changing. I just wanted to try and hang on to some of the past before it was lost forever. The hard work, the variants of the weather, the peace and quiet, the noise and confusion, the sadness and joy and, above all, the love of a land and the respect for its people provided everybody with a close bond and a tremendous enjoyment of life.'

In 1986, Pauline launched PJ Design, her own public relations, marketing and design company, based in Dunbar. *East Lothian Life* has since become a popular feature of many an East Lothian household.

Up until the end of the eighteenth century, the hamlet of Spott was, by all accounts, a great gathering place for witches. Almost every parish in East Lothian was infested with warlocks and witches of one kind or another but it is common knowledge that rather a lot of them met their ends on the summit of Spott Loan.[4] To the west of the village, on the roadside in front of a hawthorn hedge, is the Witches' Stone, almost unnoticeable within the railing that surrounds it. Marion Little, known as the Rigwood Witch, was dispatched here in 1698 but quite what part this rather unprepossessing chunk of rock played in her demise is not recorded.

Spott House is another property that long ago belonged to the Hays of Yester. A dwelling house stood here on the south-west spur of Doon Hill as early as the thirteenth century but the Tudor and Jacobean detailing of the present building is attributed to the architect William Burn in the early nineteenth century. John Martine, a friend of the builder James Dorward who was employed for the renovation, enthuses greatly over the views, garden and grandly wooded glen.[5]

At that time, the Spott Estate, comprising 1,000 acres, belonged to James Sprot. It must have been something to do with the annunciation because, by the end of the nineteenth century, the estate passed, believe it or not, to his adopted niece Miss Adeline Watt. On her death, the estate reverted to James Sprot's great-great-nephew Kenneth Sprot.

'Adeline also inherited an estate in England called Speke,' explained Kenneth's niece, Louise Ramsay. 'In the early days of outgoing telephone calls, it was necessary to go through the local exchange and there was a lot of confusion.'

On one occasion Louise's grandmother telephoned and said, 'Hello, this is Mrs Sprot. Can you put me through to Miss Watt of Spott?'

'Miss What?' came the response.

'Yes, Miss Watt.'

'What?'

'Yes, you know. Miss Watt of Spott and Speke.'

'This is Miss Watt speaking.'

After the Sprots, the property was sold to Sir James Hope, then to the Laurie Family. Spott House is currently owned by Lars Foghsgaard from Denmark.

Bowerhouse is a small country house of great charm in this vicinity, occupied over the nineteenth century by the Shirreff and Carfrae families (see Chapter 10). After them, it was owned by the Andersons and Johnsons until 1946, when it was bought by Roley Fielding Scovell.

Given charge of the Leith, Hull & Hamburg Steam Packet Co., owned by his Cambridge University contemporary James Currie, Scovell had, during the Second World War, changed the company name to the Currie Line Ltd. Roley's son Kerry Scovell, who lives in Gullane, remembers the Currie Line office parties held at Bowerhouse during the summer months. Especially vivid is the image of the gardener, John Whitson, being transported home to his wife in a wheelbarrow by Sir Charles Norton, who worked for the company and later became the first Lord Mayor of Westminster. 'They were immensely enjoyable occasions,' he says. In 1970, Bowerhouse was sold by the Scovells and today is the home of Edinburgh businessman Mark Tyndall.

Around 1626, Thomas Martine, tenant of Colstoun Old Mill, married Margaret Home, daughter of the Reverend James Home, a graduate of St Andrews University who died in 1634. Reverend Home's wife was Mary Lauder, the daughter of yet another family who, through the generations, have been closely associated with my own. However, where the Reverend James arouses my curiosity is that his grandfather, George Home, is described in family papers as the Laird of Broxmouth.[6]

Taking its name from the Brocks or Badger Burn, Broxmouth was part of the thirteenth-century fiefdom of the earls of Dunbar, passing to a branch of the Borders family of Home, presumably that to which the Reverend James belonged. In 1644, the tower house and its land were acquired by William Ker, 2nd Earl of Roxburghe and, six years later, Oliver Cromwell pitched his camp here in the park. Standing on a rise and fearing the vulnerability of his position, Cromwell observed, to his amazement, the Scottish Covenanter Army under General David Leslie descending from their vantage point of Doone Hill. 'The Lord Hath delivered them into my hands,' he announced.

The Scots were decimated and among the many killed at this Battle of Dunbar[7] was Sir William Douglas of Kirkness, who was buried close to where he fell in today's woodland, less than a hundred yards from the house. A plain stone slab bearing his name was placed across the spot and remains there to this day.

The present mansion house, known as Broxmouth Park, was built in 1775 as a dower house for the 3rd Duke of Roxburghe's mother by James Nisbet of Kelso. It thereafter became the Roxburghe family's second Scottish home after Floors Castle and, as with Floors, the estate was enclosed by a high stone wall. The Duchess Anne, mother of the 8th Duke of Roxburghe, was a close friend of the widowed Queen Victoria, who came to stay for four days in 1878. Just south of the house, the Queen planted a cedar tree in memory of her husband, Prince Albert.

Thereafter, the Roxburghe family became noticeable by their absence and Broxmouth Park was leased to various tenants. Among these was the shipping millionaire Sir William Burrell, whose great art collection was bequeathed to the City of Glasgow in 1944. In 1960, following the 9th Duke of Roxburghe's divorce from his first wife, Broxmouth with seven acres was bought by Major-General Sir John Kennedy, a former Governor General and Commander-in-Chief of Southern Rhodesia (today Zimbabwe). The remaining land was purchased by Robert Hope, brother and heir of Sir James.

Sir John lavished a fortune on the property but, after the death of his wife in the early 1970s, he summoned Ella MacGregor, her brother Tom and sister Ina to dine with him. The MacGregors owned the neighbouring farms of East and West Meikle Pinkerton and the Brunt and he said to them, 'I want you to have Broxmouth.'

'It was his custom to sit at the centre of the table, not at the top,' Ella recalls. 'He told us he was prepared to sell at a favourable price and he genuinely wanted us to have it. After dinner, he took me to have a look at William Douglas's tombstone in the wood in front of the house and asked if my brother, sister and I would have any objection to his also being buried there beside his wife when his time came.'

Shortly afterwards, Sir John died. His ashes were scattered in the wood and a small plaque pays tribute to him as 'one who loved this place'.

After Tom MacGregor sold Broxmouth Park in 1975, the house passed through several hands, including those of the Barclay brothers, the Island of Sark-domiciled property and newspaper tycoons. Today, it is owned by Simon Flame, an accountant from Cheshire, and his Australian wife Susan, from Adelaide. With other properties in London and across the north-west of England, Flame Estates specialise in the renovation of period buildings and, although they make use of it as a holiday home, it is also available for parties and corporate events.

Meantime, Ella MacGregor, as one of Scotland's top horse breeders, owns the Pinkerton Stud which, over the years, has nurtured a string of stallion bloodlines. 'I've had horses since I was nineteen,' she says. Among her champion racehorses are numbered White Domino, Kayen and Bridge Pal. Bridge Pal has recently been on a visit to one of His Highness Sheikh Mohammed bin Rashid Al Maktoum's stallions at Dalham Hall Stud at Newmarket.

Moving on to the East Lothian coastline again, I am inclined to wonder what John Muir, the celebrated American conservationist, would make of the country park named after him on Belhaven Bay – or, for that matter, his name being attached to the headquarters of East Lothian Council in Haddington. Considering that he was only eleven years old in 1849 when his parents emigrated to Wisconsin, I am sure he would be immensely flattered, if a trifle bemused, by the road bumps and East Links Family Park with its tea room and agricultural discovery centre. I also suspect he would be astonished to learn that he had become such a hero so far from the Yosemite Valley where he spent the greater part of his remaining sixty-five years.

But then, with the exception of tarmac roads, things are not so very different here from when he and his eight brothers and sisters played together alongside the River Tyne estuary. 'When I was a boy in Scotland I was fond of everything that was wild,' he wrote wistfully in his biography, published in 1913. 'I loved to wander in the fields to hear the birds sing, and along the shore to gaze and wonder at the shells and the seaweeds, eels and crabs in the pools when the tide was low; and best of all to watch the waves in awful storms thundering on the black headlands and craggy ruins of old Dunbar Castle.'[8]

His words might just as easily have been penned today. In 1997, a statue by the Ukrainian sculptor Valentin Znoba, depicting John Muir as a boy, was unveiled in front of Dunbar's Town House. The following year, the John Muir Birthplace Trust (JMBT) was formed to secure a future for his birthplace in Dunbar's High Street.

CHAPTER THIRTY

Cottage Tales and Art Installations

In 1969, my mother purchased a burnt-out cottage on the main street of Oldhamstocks with the intention of restoring it as a weekend retreat. Architects' plans were drawn up but, infuriatingly, they were turned down at the first hurdle by the planning authority on the basis that they included dormer windows on the first floor. The fact that photographs of the building before the fire showed dormer windows on the first floor was summarily dismissed. After two years of wrangling, inaction and indolence from the planning department, my mother gave up the good fight and sold the property complete with architects' plans. It still rankles with me when I visit Oldhamstocks to find that the cottage, now perfectly compatible with those on either side, was eventually restored with dormer windows on the first floor. Alas, such are the whims of planning and conservation authorities that it is no wonder there are so many derelict, abandoned properties scattered about our countryside.

But, if anything good came from that summer of camping out in the roofless cottage on the main street in Oldhamstocks, it was that it encouraged me to explore its glorious and undulating surroundings, as rustic a landscape as is ever likely to be found anywhere.

The village, which forms a terrace and swathe of community ground, is situated above the Oldhamstocks Burn in the extreme east of East Lothian as it tumbles into the Lammermuirs. Its most famous son is John Broadwood, the piano maker, who was born here in 1732. Several of his family are interred in the churchyard in company with other old farming families from the area – the Dods of Stotencleuch, Stoneypath Tower, the Brunt and Cocklaw; the Wauchhopes of Stotencleuch, Fenders and Fernilee; and the Sleighs of Thorntonloch and Crowhill.[1]

John Broadwood's father and grandfather before him were joiners and cabinetmakers but, while the family business prospered, there were two other brothers and plainly the enterprise would not support them all. So John set off for London and, by the age of twenty-nine, he had found employment with the harpsichord-maker Burkat Shudi, a friend of the German-born British composer George Frideric Handel. In due course, John married Shudi's daughter Barbara and inherited the business when his father-in-law died in 1773.

By patenting the invention of piano and forte pedals to replace knee dampers and extending the length of the keyboard, John Broadwood revolutionised piano design. By the time of his own death in 1812, he numbered everyone from royalty to the Duke of Wellington among his clients.[2]

Bordering East Lothian and Berwickshire is the Dunglass Dean, a richly wooded ravine which extends north-north-eastward to the North Sea. Spanning this is a fine, five-arched railway viaduct, the middle arch of which rises 125 feet from the bed of the stream below to the top of the parapet and is 135 feet in span.

Long ago this was Home territory, descendants of the earls of Dunbar whose titles, following a foray to London by the 11th Earl, were confiscated by James I, who considered him a threat. However, the barony of Dunglass, which had been acquired through marriage to the heiress in the fourteenth century, was retained. In 1473, Sir Alexander Home, a descendant of this line, was created Lord Home, his descendant, the 6th Lord, being created Earl of Home in 1605. Tradition has it that, close to Dunglass, the carriage of James VI of Scotland broke down on his journey to London, thus necessitating an overnight stay at the castle.

Later in the same century, Dunglass was held by the Covenanting Army under the 2nd Earl of Haddington, who was responsible for monitoring the movements of the Royalist garrison at Berwick. On 30 August 1640, while the Earl and his council were assembled in the castle court, an English page, allegedly incited by a taunt against his countrymen, thrust a red-hot iron into a powder barrel. The full force of the ensuing blast not only killed the page himself but the Earl and many others. There were only four survivors, the force of the explosion having catapulted them into the surrounding undergrowth.[3]

Towards the end of the seventeenth century, the barony of Dunglass was acquired by John Hall, a baillie of Edinburgh who had become the city's Lord Provost. His grandson, Sir James Hall, was a distinguished geologist and chemist and also an amateur architect who, having contracted the landscape artist Alexander Nasmyth to create drawings, saw the potential for exploiting the dramatic scenery of the Dunglass Dean by building a new house on the site of the former keep, at the edge of the ravine. The building work was undertaken by the architect Richard Crichton between 1807 and

1813, and the house subsequently occupied by the Hall family until sold in 1918. Its new owner, Frank Usher, a scion of the Scottish Brewery family, introduced extensive modernisations but, during the Second World War, the mansion house was requisitioned as a boys' school. Afterwards, having suffered a considerable amount of damage and neglect, it was deemed to have deteriorated beyond repair and blown up, a smaller house being built on the site.[4]

I now realise that I have known Professor Richard Demarco OBE, CBE for more than forty years, a startling thought which came to mind when I attended his seventy-sixth birthday party, thrown for him by Andrew Murray Threipland at Fingask Castle, near Dundee, in 2006. This was a memorable occasion taking the form of a slightly chaotic picnic lunch in the castle grounds – but then there have been many, many unforgettable, slightly chaotic occasions associated with Scotland's longest serving impresario.

During the early 1970s, the Richard Demarco Gallery, with its basement restaurant in Edinburgh's Melville Crescent, was a beacon for anyone interested in the visual arts. Among those who exhibited there alongside Scottish artists such as Sir Robin Philipson, Elizabeth Blackadder and Ian Hamilton-Finlay were David Hockney, Fleur Cowles and John Piper. But that was not enough for its flamboyant owner. In 1970 he imported forty Düsseldorf-based avant-garde artists to take over the Edinburgh College of Art for three weeks, turning the Scottish Arts establishment on its head. In 1972 and 1975, he brought the Polish theatre director Tadeusz Kantor to the Edinburgh Festival. His friendship and regular collaborations with the German conceptual artist Joseph Beuys proved inspirational, until Beuys's death in 1986.

In 1980, Demarco used his Scottish Arts Council grant, intended for gallery exhibitions, to charter a sailing ship and engaged the Orcadian author George Mackay Brown to steer it through waters he had only previously written about. During the Edinburgh Festival of 1989, Ricky produced Shakespeare's *Macbeth* in the open air on the island of Inchcolm in the middle of the Firth of Forth. It rained constantly.

A few years later, he took the 'Scottish Play' to Ravenscraig Castle on the Fife coast, where a cast of Belarusians enacted the tragedy on the ruined battlements, once again in pouring rain. Those of us who huddled together, wrapped in blankets, on that windswept cliff top above the linoleum town of Kirkcaldy, will never forget the experience. It was extraordinary.

But then the word 'extraordinary' features regularly in the vocabulary of this Edinburgh-born Italo-Scot – as does the 'Road to Meikle Seggie', a mythical 7,500-mile journey which begins in the Mediterranean on the island of Malta and connects eastern Europe with western Europe and ultimately Scotland. Meikle Seggie is the on-going theme of every one of the exhibitions of his own work, delicate watercolour and pastel journeys through Europe and the mind.

All roads, in Demarco's mind, lead to Scotland, and to promote this somewhat esoteric vision, the Demarco European Art Foundation was set up in 1992. But there have been many ups and downs along the Road to Meikle Seggie. Constantly plagued by a lack of public funding, the Demarco Gallery was regularly forced to relocate, eventually coming to rest at the Royal High School, the rejected site for the Scottish Parliament. Then it moved again – this time to somewhere which, as you might expect, can only be described as extraordinary.

Four miles north of Dunbar, the Demarco collection was up until February 2009 housed in a vast grain store situated at Skateraw. To the east is the North Sea. To the north are East Barnes, the John Muir Country Park and a substantial cement works which periodically sprinkles an eerie coating of white powder across the surrounding landscape. Ironically, this is situated on the site of Oxwell Mains, a farm once tenanted by the son of George Hope of Fenton Barns (see Chapter 9).[5] Adding drama to the situation, the box of Torness Nuclear Power Station lies to the south.

During the 1970s, the Reverend Ronald Selby Wright of Edinburgh's Canongate Kirk, established a holiday camp on the beach for youngsters and among those who spent summers here was a future British Prime Minister, the young Tony Blair, in his early Fettes College school days.[6]

The grain store barn at Skateraw was generously provided by local farmer Johnny Watson and it did not take long for Ricky to announce that it had officially become an outpost of the Edinburgh International Festival. On display, alongside his personal archive, were 10,000 works from fifty countries and a vast wall of black-and-white photographs recording his many exploits on the Road to Meikle Seggie.

Prophets are rarely honoured in their own land. While Professor Richard Demarco has a following which spans the generations, he has never been given the serious establishment recognition that his projects deserve. Perhaps it is fitting that his archive should momentarily come to rest on a windswept coastline – and all the more so if, as intended, it provides the catalyst for an even more ambitious development masterminded by Johnny Watson.

Johnny and his wife Sandra arrived at Skateraw several years after her father, Jack W. Taylor, had bought the farm from the Bowes family. The Taylors were from Falkirk, where their farming enterprise had been overrun and consumed by the massive British Petroleum development. So they moved on. At Skateraw, the climate is ideal for the growing of wheat, for distilling and bread- and biscuit-making, barley, for malting and soups, oilseed rape, for vegetable oil, Brussels sprouts, destined for supermarkets, and potatoes, to meet an ever-escalating demand for chips.

Jack's brother, Alec Taylor, already farmed Crawhill and Broomhoul, in East Lothian, so it made sense to relocate nearby. However, the march of so-called progress is unstoppable. Not long after he bought Skateraw, British Nuclear Fuels arrived on Jack's doorstep wanting to acquire land for the Torness Station. They were eventually persuaded to build further down the coast but having a cement plant on one side and a nuclear power station on the other is not an entirely desirable situation – albeit, some say, that it portends the future.

Johnny is the third generation of a family of West Linton-based seed merchants and, ten years ago, he bought over the farm from his father-in-law, allowing him to continue cultivating the land until his death in 2005. Meanwhile, the farmhouse became the headquarters of John Watson Seeds Ltd.

Like Demarco and the retinue of painters and creative human beings who have made a pilgrimage to Skateraw in his wake, Watson is deeply conscious of the spiritual quality of this pastoral and alluring landscape. With extremes of scenic coastal beauty and the rich abundance of wildlife caught between the two stark icons of the modern world, the imagery for the world of art is potent – 'Linking urban and rural living through the media of art and agriculture,' Johnny says.

To engage with this, therefore, the Skateraw Foundation was launched in 2008 to create an all-purpose arts and educational hub. A second barn will eventually provide facilities for artists in residence, exhibition spaces and auditorium facilities for lectures, educational seminars and performing theatre. Once again, an East Lothian farm is adapting to meet the challenges of the future.

Afterword

SINCE THE VICTORIAN era, photography, film and sound recording, followed by the Internet, have revolutionised historical research. When John Martine and his contemporaries composed their essays over a hundred years ago, they relied entirely upon the letters, public records, oral descriptions and drawings and paintings of their predecessors. Now, thanks to modern technology, we can stare directly into the eyes of the twentieth and twenty-first centuries and hear, first hand, the voices and sounds of the immediate past. To some extent this worries me. It makes everything too simple. I wonder if, in 100 years and more, there will be the same necessity to document in print that which has gone before or to employ the same degree of understanding that only the written word can expedite.

Film, sound and cyberspace may have taken over our world but it is the written word, encapsulated in faded manuscripts and often forgotten books, that reveals the truth, the physical manifestation of an author's mind. Books, with the wealth of information and analysis they contain, are the guardians against future misrepresentation and what impressed me most in my rediscovery of East Lothian is the proliferation of local history societies, all of them busy publishing their records and resurrecting forgotten memories – that and the very genuine interest in the subject shown not only by the old-timers but by those who might loosely be described as the 'incomers'.

I had long ago come to the conclusion that the majority of people take their immediate surroundings for granted. Not so in East Lothian, where you not only have the East Lothian Antiquarian and Field Naturalists' Society and the very excellent East Lothian Council's Libraries and Museums Service but also a proliferation of independently run groups at every turn. That is what makes the East Lothian community so special. There is a committed and very real fascination with the past.

But, in certain ways, I found this a trifle daunting. On a trip to America, I was asked by the customs official to explain my business. 'To give a talk to the American Scottish Foundation of New York,' I replied.

'What about?'

'Scotland,' I said.

'I wouldn't bother,' he sniffed, as he stamped my passport. 'They know far more about it than you ever will!'

He was most possibly right and the same logic probably applies to a book on the subject of East Lothian. Irrespective of ancestral voices, having spent virtually all of my life elsewhere, who am I to intrude upon local turf in such a way? Fortunately, I could not have been made more welcome. I was soon to discover that the mere mention of John Martine's name opened the doors but it was only as I progressed with my task that I realised the alarming scale of what I had undertaken – especially when I was asked what I was hoping to achieve. Was I writing a history of the county? Was it a contemporary lifestyle/travel book? Was it an autobiography? All three, in fact.

Then there was how to subdivide the book between the various interests – the towns, the villages, the farms, the landowners, the golf courses, the coastal resorts, the incoming enterprises and the ongoing heritage. It was at this juncture that I decided to latch on to John Martine's coat-tails – not with the intention of recycling his work but to edge it forward. So much has changed in the century between us; so much has been achieved that would have been beyond his grasp; so much has been lost in the name of progress.

Then there was the format to consider. The obvious approach would have been to divide up the territory as he did – parish-by-parish, twenty-four in all – but the very word 'parish' sounds so old-fashioned in this day and age so, instead, I decided to follow a logical stream of consciousness, moving from place to place through the centuries as the mood dictated. If, therefore, certain topics, historic events and destinations appear to come out of sequence, I apologise. Moreover, while Musselburgh, Tranent, Prestonpans, Cockenzie and Port Seton, Haddington, East Linton, North Berwick and Dunbar each have their very own distinct and vibrant personality, it is the surrounding farmland that provides the matrix. It was this that ultimately dictated my itinerary.

John Martine's understanding and loyalty to the land was intimate. I wonder if he could have possibly foreseen just how valuable a record he left behind him. I also suspect that he would have been amazed at the ongoing continuity of so many of the farms and families he wrote about.

We should never underestimate our arable birthright but, if there is one aspect of the relentless march of progress that needs constantly to be kept in mind, it is the encroachment of metropolitan life at the expense of old customs and skills. As more and more farm steadings are transmogrified into weekend escapes for townspeople, the fundamental utility value of our land

and the source of our food that it provides become increasingly vulnerable. Mercifully, East Lothian, in all of its diversity, has, so far, kept the faith.

To endorse such sentiments, I have to admit that having those serried ranks of ancestors looking over my shoulder was both a bonus and a liability. Some inevitably cast longer shadows than others but, ultimately, everything is what it is because of what it was. This is their story as much as it is ours.

Notes

CHAPTER ONE

1 Martine, John, *Reminiscences of the Royal Burgh of Haddington and Old East Lothian Agriculturists*, 1883; Martine, John, *Reminiscences and Notices of the Fourteen Parishes of the County of Haddington*, 1890; Martine, John, *Reminiscences and Notices of Ten Parishes of the County of Haddington*, 1894; Martine, John, *Reminiscences and Notices of the Parish of the County of Haddington*, 1999.

2 Author unknown, *From Threshold to Rooftree – Haddington Home of Jane Welsh Carlyle*, 1984.

3 Martine, T. C., *Long Ago People*, 1970.

4 Marshall, Rosalind K., *John Knox*, 2000.

5 The name of Knox in East Lothian can be traced back to 1441 when a William of Knox was witness to a charter (see Macleod, John (ed.), *Calendar of Writs 1166–1625*, Scottish Record Society, 1928, p. 51, which is preserved at Yester House). There are nine tombstones bearing the name of Knox in Morham churchyard but the earliest is dated 1660, near enough a century after the Reformer's death. Incidentally, around the same period, over at Stenton, a Bessie Knox and four other women were convicted of witchcraft by their own confession and were strangled and burnt.

6 Marshall, Rosalind K. *John Knox*, 2000.

7 Ibid.

8 Thomson, Thomas, 'Notices of the Kers of Samuelston', *Proceedings of the Society of Antiquaries of Scotland*, vol. I, pt 1.

9 Lockhart, J. G., *Curses, Lucks and Talismans* (1938). Lockart and the historian C. R. Beard concur that the Colstoun Pear only came into the Broun family as late as the late fifteenth century when George Broun married Jean Hay of Yester, whose forebear was Joanna (Jonet), the eldest of the four daughters and co-heiresses of the last Hugh Gifford. In which case, the assertion that it was a gift to the Brouns from the first Hugh Gifford is misplaced family mythology.

10 Martine, T. C., *Long Ago People*, 1970.

11 Thornbury, Walter, 'The Lord Mayors of London', *Old and New London*, vol. I, 1878.

12 Laurie, Peter G., *Sir Peter Laurie – a Family Memoir*, 1901. Sir Peter's mother had died when he was six and his father had married Isabella Carfrae, an aunt of Provost John Martine's wife. In Sir Peter's own words, his loathing of his stepmother 'changed his fate'. After a brief apprenticeship as a saddler, he migrated to London at the age of eighteen and joined a theatre company owned by the legendary actress Sarah Siddons. After becoming a saddler again, he made a strategic marriage to his wealthy employer's daughter and later achieved the then ultimate rags-to-riches dream by becoming Lord Mayor of London.

13 Martine, Peter, *Notes on Old Haddington*, 1830.

14 'Transactions of the East Lothian Antiquarian and Field Naturalists' Society', vol. II, pt. 2, 1930–31, in *Further Records of the Barony Court of Colstoun.*

15 Martine, T. C., *Long Ago People*, 1970.

CHAPTER TWO

1 Stewart, Lady Daphne, *Yester House, Gifford*, 1968.

2 Marshall, Rosalind K., *Ruin and Restoration: St Mary's Church, Haddington*, 2001.

3 Hamilton Palace, the largest and undoubtedly grandest private home in Scotland, was in the process of collapsing into the coal mining excavations of a century earlier. In the period before they moved to Lennoxlove, the Hamiltons had moved into nearby Dungavel House, their former hunting lodge, which today is a government-run immigration detention centre.

CHAPTER THREE

1 Martine, John, *Reminiscences of the Royal Burgh of Haddington and Old East Lothian Agriculturists*, 1883.

2 Ibid.

3 Ronay, Gabriel, *The Lost King of England: The East European Adventures of Edward the Exile*, 2002.

4 The legend began with his adult life as a soldier at Amiens, when he experienced a vision. At the gates of the city, so the story goes, he met a scantily dressed man whom he assumed to be a beggar. Impulsively, he swept off his cloak and cut it in half to share it with the man. That night he dreamed of Jesus wearing the half cloak and heard him say, 'Here is Martin, the Roman soldier who is not baptised; he has clad me.' (Sulpicius, *Life of St Martin*, Chapter 2.)

In the embellishment of a later century, he is said to have awoken the next morning to discover that his cloak had been returned to him whole, which prompted him to seek immediate baptism into the Christian faith. Inspired and reinvigorated, he afterwards travelled extensively throughout West Gaul (France) and many legends sprang up around him until he died at the age of eighty and was buried in a paupers' cemetery.

5 Gray, W. Forbes and Jamieson, James H., *A Short History of Haddington*, 1986.

6 Ibid.

7 Lawrie, Sir Archibald C., *Early Scottish Charters prior to AD 1153*, 1903.

8 Gray, W. Forbes assisted by Jamieson, James H., *East Lothian Biographies*, 1941 (Countess Ada).

> According to Dr Wallace-James, the St Martine family who appear to have come from Normandy via Sussex, owned considerable territory in East Lothian. Alexander St Martine had a daughter Ada who, Dr Wallace-James states was 'probably named after the Countess'. Among the Holyrood charters is one by William the Lyon confirming the gift of Ada St Martine of half a merk annually from the mill at Athelstaneford.

9 Miller, James, *History of Haddington*, 1844.

10 Black, George F., *The Surnames of Scotland*, New York Public Library, 1946.

11 East Linton Local History Society, *By the Linn Rocks*, 1999.

12 Letter from A. Montgomerie, Gimmersmill House, Haddington, 29 December 1954.

13 Miller, James, *History of Haddington*, 1844.

14 Ibid.

15 Black, George F., *The Surnames of Scotland*, New York Public Library, 1946.

16 Ibid.

17 Forrest, Catherine, *Living in St Andrews*, 1996, p. 131, and 'The Martines in St Andrews', *MacFarlane's Genealogical Collections*, vol. II, June 1900.

18 Black, George F., *The Surnames of Scotland*, New York Public Library, 1946.

19 Bannatyne Club, *Records of Ragman Rolls*, 1834.

20 John of Fordun, *Chronica gentis Scotorum*.

21 Bain, Joseph (ed.), *Calendar of Scottish Papers*, 1989.

22 Marshall, Rosalind K., *Ruin and Restoration: St Mary's Church, Haddington*, East Lothian Council Library Service, 2001, p. 21.

23 Urwin, Gerald, *Feat of Arms or the Siege of Haddington*, Calder Wood Press, 2006, p. 66.

CHAPTER FOUR

1 Martine, T. C., *Long Ago People*, 1970.
2 Ibid.
3 Ibid.
4 Martine, Peter, 'Old Haddington', *Transactions of the East Lothian Antiquarian and Field Naturalists' Society*, vol. X, 1966.
5 Horn, Barbara L. H., 'List of references to the pre-Reformation Altarages in the Parish Church of Haddington', *Transactions of the East Lothian Antiquarian and Field Naturalists' Society*, vol. X, 1966.
6 Ibid.
7 Montgomerie, A., 'A Note on an Altar in the Parish Church of Haddington', *Transactions of the East Lothian Antiquarian and Field Naturalists' Society*, vol. V, 1952.
8 'Sasine of the Altar of the Virgin and the Three Kings of Cologne, Haddington Parish Church, 20 October 1522', Scottish Record Office, GD1.39.
9 Forrest, Martin A., 'The Forrests of Haddington and the Reformation', *Transactions of the East Lothian Antiquarian and Field Naturalists Society*, 2002, pp. 13–24.
10 Ibid.
11 Martin A. Forrest is of the opinion that Gimmersmills was not only supplying grain to the licensed trade but was also involved with its production. The Forrests in Edinburgh from the early sixteenth century down to his great-grandfather in Dalkeith in the late nineteenth century were all involved in the licensed trade. In 1838, Sir James Forrest of Comiston, a descendant of the Reverend Alexander Forrest, became Lord Provost of Edinburgh.
12 Knox, John, *The Works of John Knox*, edited by David Laing, Edinburgh, 1846, vol. I, p.106.
13 T. C. Martine. *Long Ago People*, family paper, 1971.
14 Balfour Paul, Sir James (ed.), *Accounts of the Lord High Treasurer*, 1913, Appendix, pp. 694–5.
15 The assertion that John Knox was born in the village of Gifford does not hold true. The village of Gifford did not exist at the time of Knox's birth, nor for 100 years thereafter, being known previously as Bothans, on the Yester estate. This view is strongly confirmed by J. H. Jamieson in his excellent essay 'John Knox and East Lothian', published in *Transactions of East Lothian Antiquarian and Field Naturalists' Society*, vol. III, 1933, pp. 49–79.

Morham is a parish associated with John Knox (see Chapter 1) but although, his mother's family were certainly located there at the time of his birth and possibly other members of the Knox family, historians have, after considerable debate, concurred that his birthplace was most likely to have been in the Nungate of Haddington, where a house in the Giffordgate was long acknowledged as such.
16 Jamieson, J. H., 'John Knox and East Lothian', *Transactions of East Lothian Antiquarian and Field Naturalists' Society*, vol. III, 1933. The land was gifted to the town by Miss Barbara Watson, daughter of James Watson, the previous owner, who had died seven years earlier.
17 Martine, Peter, *Notes on Old Haddington*, 1830.
18 Jamieson, J. H., 'John Knox and East Lothian', *Transactions of East Lothian Antiquarian and Field Naturalists' Society*, vol. III, 1933.
19 Ibid.
20 Ibid.
21 Ibid.
22 Ibid.
23 Where the High Street meets the Sidegate stands the Haddington Goat Statue, two goats, their heads locked in combat. This was commissioned by the Norwegian Tandberg Electrical Company for display in its Haddington factory. When the business closed in 1979, the statue was gifted to the town.
24 Tindall, F. *Memoirs and Confessions of a County Planning Officer*, 1998.
25 In 2004, Michael Ancram succeeded his father to become 13th Marquis of Lothian.
26 Frank Tindall, County Planning Officer (1950–75), claims the credit for this information, which appears in his book *Memoirs and Confessions of a County Planning Officer*, 1998.

CHAPTER FIVE

1 Martine, T. C., *Long Ago People*, 1970.
2 Listed in SRS Court of the Lord Lyon 1318–1945. The Lord Lyon King of Arms at the time of the 1745 Jacobite Uprising was Alexander Brodie of Brodie, a staunch supporter of the Duke of Cumberland. In his 2001 essay, 'Ceremonial in Edinburgh: the Heralds and the Jacobite Risings', for the *Journal of the Heraldry Society of Scotland* (No 24), Sir Malcolm Innes of Edingight writes:

> Following the proclamation the vengeance of the government was swift. Eight days later on 25th September, by order of the Barons of Exchequer, the names of Roderick Chalmers, Alexander Martin(e), James Fordyce, heralds, and William Gray and James Clarkson, Pursuivants, were taken out of the list of Officers of Arms, and were not paid and not to be included in any future lists . . . four years later, through the good offices of Lord Lyon Brodie (who seems to have taken a lenient view of their misdemeanour), representations were made to the government which resulted in their reinstatement and payment of salaries.

3 Martine, T. C., *Long Ago People*, 1970.
4 *Memoirs of an Octogenarian*, East Lothian History Society Library.
5 James Miller, *History of Haddington*, Oliver & Boyd, 1844, p. 525.
6 Ibid.
7 Gray, W. Forbes assisted by Jamieson, James H., *A Short History of Haddington*, Spa Books, 1944, p. 98.
8 T. C. Martine, *Long Ago People*. Samuel Smiles Junior's book *Self-Help*, published in 1882, expounded a philosophy much favoured a century later by the British Prime Minister Margaret Thatcher.
9 *Journal of Edinburgh Head Post Office.*
10 Martine, T. C., *Long Ago People*, 1970.
11 Ibid.
12 Ibid.
13 Ibid.
14 Ibid.
15 Ibid.
16 Gillies, William, Exhibition Catalogue, 'Lamp of Lothian', 1970
17 Long, Philip, *William Gillies: Watercolours of Scotland*, 1994. Letter to Dr R. A. Lillie OBE on deposit at the National Library of Scotland, No. 316.41.

CHAPTER SIX

1 *Transactions of the East Lothian and Field Naturalists' Society*, vol. 14, 1974.
2 Tait, George, *The Parricide*, Bookseller, Haddington, 1838; Scott, W. R. (ed.), *Records of a Scottish Cloth Manufactory at New Milns, Haddingtonshire*, Scottish History Society, 1905; Simpson, Anthony E., 'Popular Perceptions of Rape as a Capital Crime', in *Law and History Review*, vol. 22:1, 2004.
3 Gow, Ian, *Scotland's Lost Houses*, Aurum Press Ltd, 2006.
4 Martine, John, *Reminiscences and Notices of the Parishes of the County of Haddington.*
5 Martine, John, *Reminiscences of the Royal Burgh of Haddington and Old East Lothian Agriculturists*, 1883.
6 There were three generations of Dr Robartses in a rival medical practice at Ennerdale, in Knox Place. Dr Henry Robarts came to Haddington in 1909. He was succeeded in the practice by his son James in 1944.

CHAPTER SEVEN

1 See McWilliam, Colin, *Lothian, except Edinburgh* (Pevsner *Buildings of Scotland*), 1978. In his picture research, George Angus has established the earlier date.
2 Family tree of the Maitlands of Lauderdale, courtesy of Viscount Maitland.
3 Ibid.
4 Martine, John, *Reminiscences and Notices of the Parishes of the County of Haddington*, 1899..

5 Tindall, Frank, *Memoirs and Confessions of a County Planning Officer*, 1998.
6 Gray, W. Forbes, assisted by Jamieson, James J., *A Short History of Haddington*, 1944.
7 Waterston, Robert, *Random Notes on Long Ago People*, printed for private circulation by George Waterston & Sons Ltd, 1964.

CHAPTER EIGHT

1 Martine, John, *Reminiscences and Notices of the Parishes of the County of Haddington*.
2 Sherry, Father Michael, *Nunraw Past and Present*, archive copy.
3 John of Fordun, *Scotichronicon*, c. 1400.
4 The price of £35,000 after deducting public burdens was at a rate of twenty-eight years' purchase on the present rental or twenty-seven years' purchase taking the temporary reductions into account – *Haddingtonshire Courier*, 1891.
5 McWilliam, Colin, and Wilson, Christopher, *Lothian, Except Edinburgh* (Pevsner *Buildings of Scotland*), 1979.
6 Martine, John, *Reminiscences of the Royal Burgh of Haddington* and *Old East Lothian Agriculturists*, 1883, p. 280.
7 Ibid., p. 279.
8 Thompson, David, *Reminiscences and Other Gems – The Darling Family* (privately published).
9 Bradley, A. G., *When Squires and Farmers Thrived*, 1927, pp. 165–73.
10 Thompson, David, *Reminiscences and Other Gems – The Darling Family* (privately published).
11 The Whiteadder River rises on the hillside of Clints Dod in the Lammermuirs and joins the Faseny Water three miles to the south-east. The Whiteadder Reservoir, which supplies water to East Lothian and Berwickshire, was created in 1968.

CHAPTER NINE

1 Brown, Robert, *A Treatise on Agricultural and Rural Affairs*, 1811.
2 *Agriculture of the West Riding of Yorkshire* surveyed by George Rennie, Robert Brown and John Shireff, 1793.
3 Martine, John, *Reminiscences of the Royal Burgh of Haddington and Old East Lothian Agriculturists*, 1883.
4 Ibid.
5 Ibid.
6 Ibid.
7 Lieutenant Sydney MacDonald of the 1st/4th Battalion Royal Scots (Lothian Regiment) was killed on 2 September 1918, aged thirty-one. He is buried at Buissy, Pas de Calais, in France. He left a wife, Mary, in Edinburgh.
8 Hope, Charlotte, *George Hope of Fenton Barns – A Sketch of his Life*, 1881.
9 Bradley, A. G., *When Squires and Farmers Thrived*, 1927.
10 Ibid.
11 Hope, Charlotte, *George Hope of Fenton Barns – A Sketch of his Life*, 1881. Napoleon IV, Prince Imperial, was the last surviving hope for the restoration of the Bonapartes to the throne of France. His death in Africa at the age of twenty-three in 1879 sent shock waves through Europe.
12 Ibid.
13 A Johannes de Dale witnessed a charter on the Yester estate in 1376 and his descendants appear have been around the county ever since – see *Calendar of Writs preserved at Yester House 1166–1503*, edited by Charles C. Harvey and John Macleod, 1916.
14 *Haddingtonshire Courier*, 1879.
15 Bradley, A. G., *When Squires and Farmers Thrived*, 1927.
16 The former Marillion rock singer Fish (Derek Dick) has a recording studio at Spitalrig.

CHAPTER TEN

1 Stewart, Lady Daphne, *Yester House, Gifford*, 1968.
2 Scott, Sir Walter, 'The Host's Tale', *Marmion*, vol. XIX, 1868.

3 This Gamel was apparently closely connected with the Church of St Andrews and therefore it could be assumed that Yestrith had previously been church land. Gamel, or Gamellus Hostiarius, witnessed charters in 1173 by Richard, Bishop of St Andrews (RPSA, *Liber cartarum prioratus Sancti Andree in Scotia*, 1841, pp. 134–9). Around 1189–1198, he witnessed a charter by Roger, bishop-elect of St Andrews, relating to the church of Haddington (RPSA, p. 153).

4 *The Statistical Account of the Parish of Garvald and Baro*, vol. XIII. Sir David Dalrymple took his authority from Fordun and comments that, 'Hugh de Gifford must either have been a very wise man or a great oppressor. Samuel Boyse (1702–49) was a Dublin-born poet who found patrons among the Scottish nobility.

5 Lady Daphne Stewart, *Yester House, Gifford*, 1968.

6 Father Richard Augustine Hay, *History of the Hays*, National Library of Scotland. In 1928, Marshall B. Lang wrote, 'The Handsome Hays, as was not unnatural, obtained by fortunate marriages the extensive estates of the Frasers in Peeblesshire, as also Lockerworth in Midlothian, Yester and Belton in East Lothian, Swed in Dumfriesshire, and Snowden, Carfrae and Danskine in Berwickshire. To that list we now add Whittingehame, as well as Stoneypath Tower, in our Parish.' (*The Seven Ages of an East Lothian Parish being the story of Whittingehame*).

7 National Library of Scotland, 14638/149. Information about Thomas Martine employed by Lord Tweeddale 1688: NLS 14665/140 employed on maintenance of church roof 1712–18.

8 Robert Waterston, *Random Notes on Long Ago People*, printed for private circulation, 1964. 'He [Walter Hay] was a queer bird who was accused of being a "maker of acquavitae" and who pretended to have a knowledge of medicine. His appearance was "offensive and unseemly, irreverent, disdainful, proud, boisterous," etc. He was deposed in 1606.'

9 *Signers of the Declaration: Historic Places Commemorating the Signing of the Declaration of Independence*, published by the United States Department of the Interior, National Park Service: Washington, DC (revised edition, 1975).

10 *East Lothian Courier.*

11 In 2007, Forbes Lodge was purchased by the Edinburgh-based accountant Andrew Hamilton and his wife Susan.

CHAPTER ELEVEN

1 Lang, Marshall B., *The Seven Ages of an East Lothian Parish being the Story of Whittingehame from Earliest Times*, 1929.

2 Ibid.

3 Rodger, D., Stokes, J., Ogilvie, J. and Miles, A., *Heritage Trees of Scotland, Forestry Commission Scotland*, 2006.

4 Harris, Paul, *Life in a Scottish Country House – the Story of A. J. Balfour and Whittingehame House*, 1989.

5 Ibid.

6 Ibid.

7 Harris, Paul, *Delightfully Imperfect: A Year in Sri Lanka at the Galle Face Hotel*, 2006.

CHAPTER TWELVE

1 Sayers, Doreen, *Doreen Sayers' Scrapbook – 100 years of Golf in North Berwick (1857–1962)*, 1996.

CHAPTER THIRTEEN

1 *East Lothian 1945–2000*, Fourth Statistical Account, vol. IV, p. 85.

2 Miller, James, *Lamp of Lothian: or the History of Haddington*, 1844.

3 Stewart, Lady Daphne, *Yester House, Gifford*, 1968.

4 Ibid.

5 Boswell, James, *The Journal of a Tour to The Hebrides with Samuel Johnson LLD*, 1785.

6 Gazetteer for Scotland: 'Newhailes' (available at www.geo.ed.ac.uk).

7 A reference to Prince Charles Edward Stuart's Jacobite army reaching Derby in December 1745 and the decision taken by his generals to retreat to Scotland.
8 It has been speculated that this was George Colt, a younger brother of the Reverend Oliver, who vanished around the time of Cromwell's invasion in 1650.
9 Burnet, Jane E. M., *A Reason for Inveresk – a Scrapbook of History*, 1999.

CHAPTER FOURTEEN

1 Ormiston's name derives from its original occupant, a Saxon settler called 'Orm', with the 'toun', meaning 'a settlement', being added on later.
2 Marshall, Rosalind M., *John Knox*, 2000.
3 Miller, James, *Lamp of Lothian: or the History of Haddington*, 1844.
4 Elphinstone Tower lay at a distance of one mile from Ormiston Castle. In the twentieth century subsidence, coupled with a huge crack in the western wall, made it dangerous and it was demolished in 1955. The north wall with one doorway can still be seen, while the south wall has completely disappeared.
5 Marshall, Rosalind M., *John Knox*, 2000.
6 Wallace was married to Beatrix Levington, who was brought up as the daughter of John Levington but she was, in fact, Lord Winton's natural daughter.
7 Knox, John, *Selected Writings of John Knox: Public Epistles, Treatises and Expositions to the Year 1559.*
8 BSW Timber plc centenary video, 'History of A. & R. Brownlie', with a commentary by Sandy Brownlie.
9 Mary was following in a Lammermuir tradition. In 1829, Marshall B. Lang noted in *The Seven Ages of an East Lothian Parish* that at Priestlaw, not far from Johnscleugh, Jean Punton had been doing the entire work of a shepherd for twenty-five years, being the only woman in Scotland at that time to do such work.

CHAPTER FIFTEEN

1 In the complex doctrinal cartwheels of the age, Gilbert Burnet moved on to become Professor of Divinity at Glasgow University, then Bishop of Salisbury. Through his writing, he too left a lasting legacy but will primarily be remembered for the guidance and influence that he exercised over his controversial disciple.
2 *The Coltness Collection*, p. 167.
3 This posthumous description of Andrew Fletcher of Saltoun by Thomas Rawlinson was published in 1732.
4 Burnet, Gilbert, *Memoirs of the Dukes of Hamilton, History of the Reformation of the Church of England and History of his Own Times.*
5 Gunn, Neil, 'Scottish Banking History', 2007.
6 'Subscribers to Darien Scheme', Catalogues of Advocates' Manuscripts, bookmark SCS.MC.58, National Library of Scotland.
7 Fletcher, Andrew, of Saltoun, 'Two Discourses concerning the Affairs of Scotland', 1698.
8 Mackenzie, W. C., *Andrew Fletcher of Saltoun: His Life and Times*, 1935.
9 *Statistical Account 1945–2000*, Saltoun.
10 Martine, Roddy, *The Secrets of Rosslyn*, 2006.
11 In 1782, Charles Sinclair had his claim to the dormant barony of Sinclair confirmed by the House of Lords. As Portcullis Pursuivant of Arms in Ordinary, his great-great-great-grandson Charles, 17th Lord Sinclair, served as an Extra Equerry to Her Majesty Queen Elizabeth, the Queen Mother. However, he died in 2004, having abandoned Herdmanston to make his home in Kircudbrightshire. The title is currently held by Matthew, 18th Lord Sinclair.
12 Martine, John, *Reminiscences and Notices of the Parishes of the County of Haddington*, 1899.
13 Wilson, John Mackay, *Wilson's Tales of the Borders*, 1890.

CHAPTER SIXTEEN

1 Martine, John, *Reminiscences.*
2 Keith, Edward, *History of the Trevelyan Family*, published privately in 1939.

3 Letters of Arthur Trevelyan, British Library.
4 Ibid.
5 'Elizabeth Trevelyan obituary', *Haddingtonshire Courier*, 15 May 1891.
6 Ibid.
7 The original bowling green was gifted to the village by Lady Ruthven, who died at Winton House in 1885.
8 Tattie Week was a school holiday in October when most of the youngsters went 'tattie howkin'' for pocket money.

CHAPTER SEVENTEEN

1 Miller, James, *The Lamp of Lothian, or The History of Haddington*, 1844.
2 The spelling of the Morison surname was obviously phonetic and an extra 'r' was added for the harbour.
3 Burnett, Allan, 'Industrial Ownership and Relations at Prestongrange', Prestoungrange Historical Series, 2000 (available at www.prestoungrange.org).
4 Baker, Sonia, 'Prestongrange House', Prestoungrange Historical Series, 2000 (available at www.prestoungrange.org).
5 Lawrence, W. R. C., *In Search of a Family: The Early History of the Burns Family of Dunedin, NZ*, 1988.

CHAPTER EIGHTEEN

1 Miller, James, *The Lamp of Lothian, or The History of Haddington*, 1844.
2 'Lord Adam Gordon wasted no time in writing to the Home Secretary firmly laying the responsibility with the civilian officials while they, in their published account of the riot, implied that the question "Why don't they fire?" had been asked in an almost rhetorical sense.' (Mullay, Sandy, *Scotland's Forgotten Massacre*, 1979, p. 33.)
3 Miller, James, *The Lamp of Lothian: or the History of Haddington*, 1844. On page 318, there is a partial list of those killed and wounded. Isabel Rodger was the sister of Archibald Rodger, who later published an account in the *Scots Chronicle* which led to a libel suit.
4 Martine, John, *Reminiscences.*
5 Ibid.

CHAPTER NINETEEN

1 Miller, James, *The Lamp of Lothian: or the History of Haddington*, 1844.
2 Cooper, Lady Diana, *The Rainbow Comes and Goes*, 1958.

CHAPTER TWENTY

1 Martine, John, *Reminiscences of the Port and Town of Leith*, 1888.
2 Martine, John, *Reminiscences and Notices of Ten Parishes of the County of Haddington*, 1894.
3 Ibid.
4 Letter from J. H. Jamieson to D. MacDougall, 26 March 1939, Haddington History Society, AK65-2583.
5 Martine, John, *Reminiscences and Notices of Ten Parishes of the County of Haddington*, 1894.
6 Christie's catalogue, 'Sale of contents of Huntington House', 1 November 1993.
7 Ibid.
8 BSW Timber plc centenary video, 'History of A. &. R. Brownlie', with a commentary by Sandy Brownlie.
9 Gilise was one of the witnesses to David I's charter for the Abbey of Holyrood c.1128. The name means 'Servant of Jesus', see Liber cartarum Sancte Crucis, 1840.
10 Black, George F., *The Surnames of Scotland*, New York Public Library, 1946.
11 Dryburgh, *Liber S. Marie de Dryburgh: Registrum cartarum Abbacie Premonstratensis de Dryburgh*, 1847, pp. 68–69. It appears that Adulf St Martine was not held responsible. As a gesture of atonement the land of Langlaw, nowadays a district of Mayfield in Edinburgh, was gifted to the Abbey of Dryburgh.

12 The de Morevilles accompanied William the Conqueror to Britain in 1066 from the commune of Morville in the canton on Bricquebec. Hugh de Moreville, who died in 1162, was among those who accompanied David I to Scotland.

13 Skirving, Archibald, 'Sir John Dalyrmple's Behaviour to me, Autobiographical note', see Basil Skinner, *Transactions of the East Lothian Antiquarian and Field Naturalists' Society*, vol. XII, 1970. Skirving is referring to Sir John Dalrymple, 4th Baronet of Cranston.

14 Carlyle, Thomas, from an unpublished note on the Skirvings, Adam and Archibald, Department of Manuscripts, National Library of Scotland.

CHAPTER TWENTY-ONE

1 Tully-Jackson, Jack and Brown, Ian, *East Lothian at War*, vols I and II, 1996, 2001.

2 Chalmers-Watson, Rupert, *The Fenton Barns Story*, 1978.

3 Ibid.

4 Lang, Marshall, *The Seven Ages of an East Lothian Parish being the Story of Whittingehame*, 1929.

5 Baker, Sonia (ed.), *East Lothian 1945–2000, Fourth Statistical Account, vol. IV, the Parishes of Aberlady, Athelstaneford, Dirleton (with Gullane), North Berwick, Whitekirk and Tyninghame*, p. 80.

6 Martine, John, *Reminiscences and Notes of the Parishes of the County of Haddington.*

CHAPTER TWENTY-TWO

1 Martine, John, *Reminiscences of the Royal Burgh of Haddington – Old East Lothian Agriculturists*, 1885.

2 The roles of Robert Stevenson and John Rennie in the building of the Bell Rock Lighthouse became the subject of controversy between their two families. Although the project was proposed by Stevenson and Rennie was appointed Chief Engineer on his recommendation, the latter's role in completing the project was subsequently largely played down by the Stevenson family – see Leslie, Jean and Roland Paxton, *Bright Lights – The Stevenson Engineers 1752–1971*, 1999, p. 35.

3 Martine, John, *Reminiscences of the Port and Town of Leith*, 1888, p. 23.

4 Strang, Charles A., *Borders and Berwick*, 1994.

5 *Haddingtonshire Courier*, 23 March 1919.

6 McNichols, Diane, Edwin Tweedie and Ellen Wyckoff, *The Tweedie Family – a genealogy*, 2005 (available at http://www.tweedie.com/TweedieBook.pdf).

7 A son, Thomas Martine Ronaldson (1881–1942) exhibited at the Paris Salon, winning a silver medal in 1926, and also at the Royal Academy, Royal Scottish Academy, Royal Institute of Oil Painters, Glasgow Institute of Fine Arts and the London Salon.

8 'Colonel Tweedie Obituary', *Haddingtonshire Courier*, 28 November 1941.

CHAPTER TWENTY-THREE

1 Leslie, Thomas, 'Smeaton – Famous "garden within a garden"', *Scottish Field*, November 1976.

2 Ibid.

3 Ibid.

4 'Family History – Hardie' (available at www.users.bigpond.net.au/hardiehistory).

5 From Tom Middlemass's notes.

6 Reece, R. H. W., *The Name of Brooke – The End of White Rajah Rule in Sarawak*, 1982.

7 *Country Life*, 1958.

CHAPTER TWENTY-FOUR

1 Tabraham, Chris, 'The Luffness Mystery Man', *Transactions of the East Lothian & Field Naturalists' Society*, vol. XXV1, 2006. In a later generation, Sir Robert de Pinkeney was a claimant to the Scottish throne on the basis that his grandfather, Sir Henry de Pinkeney, had married Lady Alice de Lindesay. Alice's grandfather, Sir William de Lindsay, had married Marjorie, daughter of Prince Henry, Earl of Huntingdon.

2 That same year (1552), Edward Seymour, Earl of Hertford, by then 1st Duke of Somerset, was executed at the Tower of London for treason.
3 Martine, John, *Reminiscences of the Royal Burgh of Haddington & Old East Lothian Agriculturists*, 1883.
4 Boswell, James, *The Journal of a Tour to the Hebrides with Samuel Johnson LLD*, 1868.
5 Martine, John, *Reminiscences of the Royal Burgh of Haddington & Old East Lothian Agriculturists*, 1883.
6 Anderson, Rev. John (ed.), *Calendar of the Laing Charters, AD 854–1837*, 1899.
7 'Who are the Yules?', Gullane & Dirleton History Society, 2003.
8 Ibid.
9 Weaver, Sir Laurence, *Houses and Gardens by E. L. Lutyens*, 1999.

CHAPTER TWENTY-FIVE

1 Martine, T. C., *Long Ago People*, 1970.
2 Statham, Craig, *Old Haddington*, 2007.
3 *Haddingtonshire Courier*, 1936. The rescuers were awarded medals for bravery.
4 Curr, W. S., *Transactions of the East Lothian Antiquarian and Field Naturalists' Society*, vol. II, part 2, 1930–31.

CHAPTER TWENTY-SIX

1 Robert Louis Stevenson's mother, Margaret Balfour (1829–97) was the aunt of Joanna Smith who married Thomas Dale of Scoughall.
2 Leslie, Jean, and Roland Paxton, *Bright Lights – the Stevenson Engineers 1752–1971*, 1999.
3 Martine, T. C., *Long Ago People*, 1970.
4 In 1918, Patrick Martine moved to Trinidad, Colorado, to join the famous Matador Land & Cattle Company, which was then headed up by a well-known Scottish character called Murdo Mackenzie. Patrick returned from America to visit his family in Haddington in 1927 but, shortly after his return to the USA that same year he was killed in a road accident.
5 Seaton, Douglas C., 'Royal Burgh of North Berwick' (available at www.northberwick.-org.uk/story_2.html).
6 Sayers, Doreen, *Doreen Sayers' Scrapbook – 100 years of Golf in North Berwick (1857–1962)*, 1996.
7 For a time, this painting was owned by a gentlemen's club in Glasgow. It was sold by Sotheby's to an American buyer for £750,000 in 2005.
8 Fragments of a letter from the Reverend Hector Macpherson, 7 Wardie Crescent, Edinburgh, to the Countess of Oxford and Asquith, dated 16 September 1933, were sold at auction by Shapes Auctioneers in 2006.
9 Williamson, A., *North Berwick and District*, 1907.
10 This replacement arch was gifted by John Dunlop, son of Councillor Dr J. C. Dunlop, 'by permission of Mr James Mitchell, farmer', *Haddington Courier*, 1935.
11 Aymer Vallance was an author and photographer, specialising in design and architecture. His books include *William Morris: His Art, his Writings, and his Public Life* (1897) and *Old Crosses and Lychgates* (1922).
12 'James Smith Richardson Obituary', *Proceedings of the Society of Antiquaries of Scotland*, vol. CII (1969–70).
13 *East Lothian Courier*, 1967.
14 *East Lothian Courier*, 1970.
15 Blaeu, Joan, *Atlas of Scotland*, 1654.

CHAPTER TWENTY-SEVEN

1 Marshall, Rosalind K., *John Knox*, 2000.
2 After the First World War, John E. Laidlay moved to Sunningdale in England, where he called his home Auldhame after the family farm at Seacliff.
3 Dale, Joanna, 'Scougall Jottings'.
4 Ibid.
5 Ibid.

6 Sir Walter Scott's historical novel *The Bride of Lammermoor* (published in 1819) is set in Scotland during the reign of Queen Anne. The story is fictional but was taken, according to Sir Walter, from a true story concerning an actual incident. The storyline concerns the tragic love affair between the Master of Ravenswood and Lucy Ashton, the daughter of Ravenswood's enemy, Sir William Ashton. The character of Ravenswood is allegedly based on that of Lord Rutherford, Sir William Ashton upon James Dalrymple, 1st Lord Stair, and that of Lucy upon his daughter Janet.
7 'Fletcher the Patriot', an account from Siol nan Gaidheal (available at www.siol-nan-gaidheal-usa.com/fletcher1.htm).
8 Rodger, D., Stokes, J., Ogilvie, J. and Miles, A., *Heritage Trees of Scotland*, 2006.

CHAPTER TWENTY-EIGHT

1 Isbicki, T., Christianson, G. and Kray, P., *Reject Aeneas, Accept Pius: Selected Letters of Aeneas Sylvius Piccolomini (Pope Pius II).*
2 In 2003, Tipu Sultan's 42-inch sword with a calligraphic hilt and encased in a velvet and silver scabbard was bought for £175,000 at a London auction by the Indian liquor millionaire Vijay Mallya.
3 Baker, Sonia, (ed.), *East Lothian 1945–2000, Fourth Statistical Account, vol. IV, The Parishes of Aberlady, Athelstaneford, Dirleton (with Gullane), North Berwick, Whitekirk and Tyninghame*, East Lothian Council Library Service for The East Lothian Fourth Statistical Account Society, 2006.

CHAPTER TWENTY-NINE

1 Martine, John, *Reminiscences and Notices of Ten Parishes of the County of Haddington.*
2 *East Lothian Courier*, 31 March 1967.
3 This Hope family farmed East Barnes at Dunbar, which Sir James (John) inherited along with the baronetcy from his father. Sir Harry Hope was MP for Forfar in Angus from 1924 to 1931. His brother Robert married Eleanor, daughter of the Reverend Marshal Lang of Whittingehame, and, in turn, inherited the baronetcy from his brother.
4 Martine, John, *Reminiscences and Notices of the Parishes of the County of Haddington.*
5 Ibid.
6 Martine, T. C., *Long Ago People*, 1970.
7 The first Battle of Dunbar between the English and Scots was fought in April 1296.
8 Muir, John, *The Story of My Boyhood and My Youth*, 1913.

CHAPTER THIRTY

1 Martine, John, *Reminiscences.*
2 John Broadwood & Sons, 'Company History' (available at www.uk-piano.org/broadwood/history.html).
3 Scotstarvet.
4 Gow, Ian, *Scotland's Lost Houses*, 2006.
5 Hope, Charlotte, *George Hope of Fenton Barns – A Sketch of his Life*, 1881, pp. 360–61. Here Charlotte Hope writes that her father had always had a great longing for the red land in the neighbourhood of Dunbar. He often talked of it as the 'Land of Goshen'. When Oxwell Mains was advertised for sale, he strongly advised his son to make an offer for it.
6 *Edinburgh Evening News*, Wednesday 18 May 1994.

Bibliography

Anderson, Irene, *Garvald – The Lairds, Tenants and Tradesmen*, Tantallon Press, 1995.

Baker, Sonia, (ed.), *East Lothian 1945–2000, Fourth Statistical Account, vol. IV, The Parishes of Aberlady, Athelstaneford, Dirleton (with Gullane), North Berwick, Whitekirk and Tyninghame*, East Lothian Council Library Service for The East Lothian Fourth Statistical Account Society, 2006.

Baker, Sonia (ed.), *East Lothian 1945–2000, Fourth Statistical Account, vol. IV, The Parishes of Inveresk (with Musselburgh), Prestonpans, Tranent (with Cockenzie and Port Seton)*, East Lothian Council Library Service for The East Lothian Fourth Statistical Account Society, 2007.

Barrow, Professor G. W. S., *The Anglo-Norman Era in Scottish History*, Oxford University Press, 1980.

Black, George F., *The Surnames of Scotland*, New York Public Library, 1946 and Birlinn Ltd, 1993.

Bradley, A. G., *When Squires and Farmers Thrived*, Methuen & Co., 1927.

Burnet, Jane E., *A Reason for Inveresk – A Scrapbook of History*, Courtyard Press, 1999.

Croal, A., *Sketches of East Lothian*, Grimsay Press, 2007. (Originally published by *Haddingtonshire Courier*, 1879.)

Dick, David, *A Millennium of Fame of East Lothian – 200 Lives of Achievement*, Clerkington Publishing Co. Ltd., 2000.

Ferrier, Walter M., *The North Berwick Story*, Royal Burgh of North Berwick Community Council, 1981.

Fletcher, Victoria, *Children of Yester*, Victoria Fletcher, 2000.

Gow, Ian, *Scotland's Lost Houses*, Aurum Press Ltd, 2006.

Gray, W. Forbes assisted by Jamieson, J. H., *A Short History of Haddington*, SPA Books, 1986. (Originally published in 1944 by the East Lothian Antiquarian and Field Naturalists' Society.)

Gray, W. Forbes assisted by Jamieson, J. H., *East Lothian Biographies*, East Lothian Antiquarian and Field Naturalists' Society, 1941.

Green, Charles, *East Lothian*, W. Green & Sons, 1907.

Haddington's History Society, *Haddington Royal Burgh – A History and a Guide*, Tuckwell Press, 1997.

Harris, Paul, *Life in a Scottish Country House – The Story of A. J. Balfour and Whittingehame House*, Whittingehame House Publishing, 1989.

Harris, Paul, *Delightfully Imperfect – A Year in Sri Lanka at the Galle Face Hotel*, Kennedy & Boyd, 2006.

Hay, Father Richard Augustine, *Genealogie of the Hays of Tweeddale*, T. G. Stevenson, 1835.

Herbert, David, *Second Son: An Autobiography*, Peter Owen Ltd, 1972.

Herbert, David, *Engaging Eccentrics: Recollections*, Peter Owen Ltd, 1990.

Hope, Charlotte, *George Hope of Fenton Barns – A Sketch of his Life Compiled by his Daughter*, David Douglas, 1881.

Hume Brown, P., *John Knox – A Biography*, Adam & Charles Black, 1893.

Jamieson, James H., 'John Knox and East Lothian', *Transactions of the East Lothian Antiquarian and Field Naturalists' Society*, Vol. III, 1941, pp. 49–79.

Kirby, Roger P., *The Trees of Haddington and District*, Roger Kirby, Millennium Forest for Scotland Trust, 2001.

Lang, Marshall B., *The Seven Ages of An East Lothian Parish being The Story of Whittingehame from Earliest Times*, Robert Grant & Son, 1929.

Leslie, Jean and Roland Paxton, *Bright Lights: The Stevenson Engineers*, published by the authors, 1999.

Long, Philip, *William Gillies: Watercolours of Scotland*, National Galleries of Scotland, 1994.

Louden, David, *The History of Morham*, William Sinclair, 1889.

Lyell, Annie, *Ye see it a' – The Ormiston Story*, East Lothian Council Library Service, 2001.

MacGregor, Geddes, *The Thundering Scot: a Portrait of John Knox*, Macmillan & Co., 1938.

Mackenzie, W. C., *Andrew Fletcher of Saltoun: His Life and Times*, The Porpoise Press, 1935.

McWilliam, Colin, and Christopher Wilson, *Lothian, except Edinburgh* (Pevsner *Buildings of Scotland)*, Penguin, 1979.

McNicoll, Diane D., *The Surnames of East Lothian: based on the Old Parish Registers of birth and baptisms of Haddingtonshire, Scottish Families Researched*, 1999.

Marshall, Bruce, *Father Malachy's Miracle*, William Heinemann, 1931.

Marshall, Rosalind K., *Ruin and Restoration – St Mary's Church, Haddington*, East Lothian County Library Service, 2001.

Marshall, Rosalind K., *John Knox*, Birlinn Ltd, 2000.

Martine, John, *Reminiscences of the Royal Burgh of Haddington and Old East Lothian Agriculturists*, John Menzies & Co., Edinburgh, 1883.

Martine, John, *Reminiscences and Notices of the Fourteen Parishes of the County of Haddington*, Turnbull & Spiers, 1890.

Martine, John, *Reminiscences and Notices of Ten Parishes of the County of Haddington*, William Sinclair, 1894.

Martine, John, *Reminiscences and Notices of the Parish of the County of Haddington*, East Lothian Library, 1999.

Miller, James, *Lamp of Lothian: or the History of Haddington*, James Allan, 1844.

Milne, John, *Gaelic Place Names of the Lothians*, McDougall's Educational Co., 1912.

Mullay, Sandy, *Scotland's Forgotten Massacre*, Moorfoot Publishing, 1979.

Pottinger, George, *Muirfield and the Honourable Company*, Scottish Academic Press, distributed by Chatto & Windus, 1972.

Ritchie, David. S., *By the Linn Rocks – The Story of East Linton and the Parish of Prestonkirk*, East Linton Local Historical Society, 1999.

Rodger, D., Stokes, J, Ogilvie, J. and Miles, A., *Heritage Trees of Scotland*, Forestry Commission of Scotland, 2006.

Sayers, Doreen, *Doreen Sayers' Scrapbook – 100 Years of Golf in North Berwick (1857–1962)*, Stephenson Press, 1996.
Statham, Craig, *Old Haddington*, Stenlake Publishing Ltd., 2007.
Stenhouse, Mary, *A History of Morham Parish*, Garvald & Morham Community Council, 1986.
Stewart, Lady Daphne, *Yester*, guidebook, Angus Sutherland Ltd, 1967.
Tindall, Frank, *Memoirs and Confessions of a County Planning Officer*, Pantile Press, 1998.
Tully-Jackson, Jack, and Ian Brown, *East Lothian at War*, vols I and II, East Lothian Council Library Service, 1996 and 2001.
Urwin, Gerald, *Feat of Arms: The Siege of Haddington*, Calder Wood Press, 2006.
Waterstone, Robert, *Random Notes on Long Ago People*, Geo. Waterstone & Sons Ltd, 1964.

Index